SACRED FEATHERS

The Reverend Peter Jones (Kahkewaquonaby) and the Mississauga Indians

Second Edition

Much of the ground on which Canada's largest metropolitan centre now stands was purchased by the British from the Mississauga Indians for a payment that in the end amounted to ten shillings. Sacred Feathers (1802–1856), or Peter Jones, as he became known in English, grew up hearing countless stories of the treachery in those negotiations, early lessons in the need for Indian vigilance in preserving their land and their rights. Donald B. Smith's biography of this remarkable Ojibwa leader shows how well those early lessons were learned and how Jones used them to advance the welfare of his people.

A groundbreaking book, *Sacred Feathers* was one of the first biographies of a Canadian Aboriginal to be based on his own writings – drawing on Jones's letters, diaries, sermons, and his history of the Ojibwas – and the first modern account of the Mississauga Indians. As summarized by M.T. Kelly in *Saturday Night* when the book was first published in 1988, "This biography achieves something remarkable. Peter Jones emerges from its pages alive. We don't merely understand him by the book's end: we know him."

DONALD B. SMITH is a professor emeritus of History at the University of Calgary.

Sacred Feathers

The Reverend Peter Jones

(Kahkewaquonaby)

and the Mississauga Indians

Second Edition

by Donald B. Smith

*And
there
are those
who receive
the seed in
good soil; they
hear the word, and
welcome it; and
they bear fruit
thirtyfold,
sixtyfold,
or a
hundred-
fold*

*Mark
4:20*

University of Toronto Press
Toronto Buffalo London

First edition published simultaneously by University of
Nebraska Press and University of Toronto Press in 1987.
Reprinted in 1995 and 1999.

Printed in the U.S.A.

ISBN 978-1-4426-1563-2

Printed on acid-free paper.

Library and Archives Canada Cataloguing in Publication

Smith, Donald B., 1946–
Sacred feathers : the Reverend Peter Jones (Kahkewaquonaby)
and the Mississauga Indians / Donald B. Smith.   2nd ed.

Includes bibliographical references and index.
ISBN 978-1-4426-1563-2

1. Jones, Peter, 1802–1856. 2. Mississauga Indians –
Biography. 3. Methodists – Ontario – Biography. I. Title.

E99.M68J65 2013   971.004'97333   C2013-901698-8

University of Toronto Press acknowledges the financial
assistance to its publishing program of the Canada Council for
the Arts and the Ontario Arts Council.

 Canada Council   Conseil des Arts
for the Arts   du Canada

University of Toronto Press acknowledges the financial
support of the Government of Canada through the Canada
Book Fund for its publishing activities.

To Dove, David, and Peter

Maps and Illustrations

Pahtahsega, "one who makes the world brighter," in English Peter Jacobs, the first Mississauga at the eastern end of Lake Ontario to attend school.

Kahgegagahbowh, "he who stands forever," in English George Copway, a Rice Lake Mississauga missionary, and later a writer and lecturer.

Shahwahnegezhik, known in English as Henry B. Steinhauer, a young Ojibwa boy from Lake Simcoe.

Peter Jones, an engraving probably made at the time of his second British tour, 1837–38.

Non-Christian Indian graves at Munceytown.

Following page 226

Maungwudaus, "a great hero," in English George Henry, with members of his dance troupe, 1851.

The poster advertising Maungwudaus and his dance troupe at Egyptian Hall, Piccadilly, London, 12 May 1845.

Two calotypes of Peter Jones in his native costume, taken in Edinburgh, 4 August 1845.

A calotype of Eliza Field Jones, taken in Edinburgh, 4 August 1845.

Peter Jones in Glasgow, Scotland, 30 October 1845.

Oominewahjeween, "the pleasant stream," in English William Herkimer, Peter Jones's leading opponent at the Credit Mission.

Several Six Nations chiefs at a reading of the wampum belts, 14 September 1871.

Echo Villa, Peter's and Eliza's home near Brantford, Canada West (Upper Canada).

The last drawing made of Peter Jones.

Dr. Peter E. Jones, the third son of Peter and Eliza Jones, wearing his father's tribal regalia, August 1898.

Introduction to the Second Edition

Peter Jones (1802–1856), known in Ojibwe as Kahkewaquon-aby ("Sacred Feathers"), worked for a full and equal partnership between the Mississauga, or Ojibwe, and the non-Aboriginal settlers. In the early and mid-nineteenth century the Ojibwe in what is now southern Ontario had lost much of their autonomy, and almost all of their traditional territory. Although the Mississauga had shared their land and resources with the newcomers the colonial government declined to recognize the Ojibwe's ownership of their remaining lands. Jones championed Mississauga land claims and their right to self-government.

When my biography of Peter Jones, *Sacred Feathers: The Reverend Peter Jones (Kahkewaquonaby) and the Mississauga Indians*, was first published in 1987, the University of Toronto Press hosted a most enjoyable reception to launch the book. It was held on the evening of Monday, 16 November 1987, in the Talking Room of the Native Canadian Centre of Toronto on Spadina Avenue. Harald Bohne, director of the University of Toronto Press, welcomed those present: academics, archivists and librarians, First Nation friends, my relatives, a number of friends from high school and university days, and marketing and editorial people from the University of Toronto Press. It was a career moment. About a hundred people attended.[1] Fred Wheatley said the opening prayer after which guests feasted on traditional First Nations foods: corn soup, bannock, wild rice salad, fish balls, and fruit salad. Members of the Anduhyaun (meaning "Our Home" in Ojibwe) Emergency Women's Shelter prepared the delicious light buffet.

Media visits that Monday in Toronto preceded the reception and book launch. On Tuesday evening I spoke in Port Credit to the Mississauga South Historical Society, then on Wednesday evening in Brantford at the Woodland Cultural Centre, and finally, on Thursday, to the Hastings County Historical Society in Belleville. A follow-up article by Julia Ashberry of the *Belleville Intelligencer*, "Sacred Feathers subject of book," appeared in the Saturday paper. In re-reading the piece I see that already I was thinking of a sequel to my biography of Peter Jones. She writes: "Within a few years, he plans to release *Mississauga Portraits*, a study of various prominent Mississaugas."

Mississauga Portraits: Ojibwe Portraits from Nineteenth-Century Canada, a collection of sketches of seven of Jones's leading Ojibwe contemporaries, now appears. The first chapter of *Mississauga Portraits* focuses on Kahkewaquonaby during the last months of his life in 1856. In particular it describes the month he and his English wife, Eliza, spent at the Toronto home of his best non-Aboriginal male friend, Egerton Ryerson, after whom today's Ryerson University is named. That chapter links *Sacred Feathers* with *Mississauga Portraits*. To celebrate the publication of *Mississauga Portraits* the University of Toronto Press has brought out a second edition of *Sacred Feathers*, accompanied by this new introduction.

How I do I explain an almost half-a-century long fascination with the history of the Mississauga First Nations on the north shore of Lake Ontario? To start, I will take a cue from the first line of Peter Jones's *Life and Journals*, which reads: "As persons who are about to take a journey together naturally desire to know something of each other, I shall commence by giving the reader a short sketch of my life."[2] Although I was born in Toronto in 1946 I grew up and attended school in Oakville, halfway between Hamilton and Toronto. Oakville was part of a Mississauga Indian reserve two centuries ago, but I cannot recall a single reference in school to the Ojibwe occupation of the area. In the 1950s Aboriginal Canada was not well known on the northwestern shore of Lake Ontario.

Mention of the First Nations surfaced at the two excellent summer camps I was fortunate to attend from age nine to sixteen. Camp Mazinaw in the Kawarthas was located very close to Bon Echo Rock, whose granite face rose one hundred meters above the waterline of Mazinaw Lake. In the mid-1950s we paddled many times by the mysterious pictographs or rock paintings just above the water's edge. North American Indians drew them in red ochre hundreds of years earlier. In 1959 this rock and the surrounding area became Bon Echo Provincial Park.[3] Shortly before then I had started attending Camp Kandalore in Haliburton. In the spirit of full disclosure I must report that I can still recite the words of the Omaha Tribal Prayer sang at the grand council at the camp term's end:

Wa-kon-da dhe dhu

Wapa dhin a-ton-he[4]

The leaders were respectful in their references to Aboriginal Canada,[5] although I do not recall meeting any Aboriginal workers at either camp. As historian Sharon Wall writes in *The Nurture of Nature: Childhood, Antimodernism, and Ontario Summer Camps, 1920–55,* contemporary Aboriginal people at southern Ontario summer camps in this period were "virtually invisible."[6]

My first working experience with Aboriginal people came in my second year at the University of Toronto. In January 1966 the college I attended sponsored the Trinity College Conference on the Canadian Indian. The Rev. John (Ian) MacKenzie, an Anglican minister, was the moving force behind the student group that organized the ambitious gathering. Ian MacKenzie later became the Archdeacon of Caledonia and was adopted by the Haida in 1975 and the Nisga'a people in 1979.[7] Great efforts were made to bring prominent Aboriginal political leaders and university students to the 1966 conference. Unlike today, when there are approximately 30,000 First Nation students enrolled in full-time university and college studies, in 1965–66 there were only approximately one hundred in all of Canada. First Nation leaders and university students came to Toronto from across the country, including Stan McKay from Winnipeg's United College, a future moderator of the United Church of Canada.[8] Fred Kelly, an Ojibwe from Northwestern Ontario who had been involved in the Aboriginal protest that fall against racial injustice in Kenora, Ontario, also attended. Forty years later Kelly was a member of the Assembly of First Nations team that negotiated the Indian Residential Schools Settlement Agreement.[9] Harold Cardinal, a Cree student from Alberta who was then studying at St. Patrick's College in Ottawa, was also one of the participants.[10] In panel discussions and seminars over a two-day period about 200 participants, non-Aboriginal and Aboriginal, exchanged views. The conference introduced me for the first time to Aboriginal issues.

The next summer I worked as a laborer with Aboriginal people on a railway extra gang in southern Manitoba and Saskatchewan. The majority of workers were Cree and Métis from around The Pas and from the Gillam, Manitoba, area, further to the north on the Hudson Bay railway line. The different culture and outlook of these Cree speakers fascinated me. While working at Expo 67 in Montreal the following summer, I made several visits to the Indians of Canada Pavilion. What a revelation that was. Financed by the federal government, but under First Nation control, the pavilion presented a North American Indian view of Canada through pictures and print. The gigantic 30-meter-tall teepee built out of steel and timber was one of the most popular pavilions at the world's fair.[11] Blunt and uncompromising, the exhibits contained statements such as: "The welfare of the Indian was regarded as proper work for retired soldiers, many of whom were kindly and well-intentioned, but treated their charges like amiable backward children"; "An Indian child begins school by learning a foreign tongue"; "Give us the right to manage our own affairs."[12]

After my obtaining my B.A. in History at the University of Toronto, I began my M.A. in Canadian History at the Université Laval in Quebec City in the fall of 1968. The early relationship of the French with the North American Indians in what is now Eastern Canada interested me. I decided to study the interpretations of this period by nineteenth- and twentieth-century French-Canadian historians. My M.A. supervisor, Pierre Savard, a young member of Laval's History Department, warmly welcomed the twenty-two-year-old anglophone from Ontario. I owe him so much for his encouragement and for his continued guidance through the nineteenth- and twentieth-century French-Canadian historical literature. I treasure the memory of his friendship, which continued right up to his untimely death at the age of sixty-two in 1998.[13]

My M.A. supervisor counted among his immediate ancestors his Huron grandmother,[14] but his graduate studies and subsequent research had been on the non-Aboriginal side of Quebec history, not the Aboriginal. My mentor realized his limitations in directing a thesis so connected with an aspect of Aboriginal history and consequently arranged for me to take a private seminar with Jacques Rousseau, the eminent Quebec botanist and ethnologist then teaching at Laval's Centre d'études nordiques.[15] For over a quarter of a century Dr Rousseau had travelled across northern Quebec studying the botany of the area, as well as the customs and behavior of the peoples living there. He was proud of the fact that his family tree included Étienne Pigarouich, a seventeenth-century Innu spiritual leader.[16] One quote from an article Dr Rousseau wrote in 1969 indicates his refreshing attitude towards the Aboriginal peoples. His views were remarkable for the late 1960s: "Let me say first of all that 'there is no Eskimo problem, nor any Native problem in Canada; but there is an acute White man problem in his behavior toward Natives.' Speaking as a White man—forgetting my small proportion of Indian blood—we came here two or three centuries ago, often unwelcomed; we took, usually without compensation or agreement, ground belonging to the Amerindian bands, and disturbed the Aboriginal population in its ways of living."[17] Thanks to the expert guidance of both Pierre Savard and Jacques Rousseau I successfully defended my thesis, "French Canadian Historians' Images of the Indian in the 'Heroic Period' of New France, 1534–1663," in the fall of 1969.

Research for what eventually became *Sacred Feathers*, and its sequel, *Mississauga Portraits*, began during my first year of doctoral studies in Canadian history at the University of Toronto. In early 1970 I wrote a research paper on Peter Jones and his fellow Mississauga writer and lecturer, George Copway, for Professor J.M.S. Careless's seminar on the history of nineteenth-century Ontario. At the time no thought surfaced that this preliminary study of the Mississauga First Nations might extend well over four decades. The incredibly rich manuscript sources in the Peter Jones Collection in the Victoria University Library convinced me to write my Ph.D. thesis on Peter Jones and the Mississauga on the north shore of Lake Ontario. I still have a summary of my proposed thesis, which was titled, "Methodist and Mississauga: The Methodist conversion of the Mississauga (Southern Ojibwa) in the first half of the nineteenth century." I wrote:

Indian sources materials do exist. For example, in nineteenth century Upper Canada, Kahkewaquonaby (Peter Jones), Kahge-gagahbowh (George Copway), Shahwudais (John Sunday), and a dozen other Ojibwa Methodist ministers wrote many published and unpublished accounts for Christian audiences. The native missionaries explained their ancient Ojibwa customs, the effect of Christianity, and the overwhelming impact of European settlement in their homeland. As the Ojibwa historian Basil Johnston has noted the Ojibwa Methodist writings reveal the 'dilemma and the problem of identity people face when they accept certain aspects of another culture but wish to retain their own' (in Read Canadian, *p. 169).*[18]

I was so fortunate that J.M.S. Careless agreed to be my supervisor. At the time Native history attracted little scholarly attention, although a breakthrough had been made in the mid-1960s with the publication of the first volume of the new *Dictionary of Canadian Biography/Dictionnaire Biographique du Canada (DCB/DBC)*. The debt of every Canadian is enormous to this incredible series of fifteen volumes, available in English and French, and now accessible online at www.biographi.ca. In 1966, the *DCB/DBC* brought forward the importance of Aboriginal Canada in its first volume, which covered the years 1000 to 1700. A striking passage in the essay by Jacques Rousseau and George W. Brown, "The Indians of Northeastern North America," reads: "THIS VOLUME of the Dictionary contains the biographies of 65 Indians. In many ways they are a group apart. For almost all of them the information is fragmentary. Like fireflies they glimmer for a moment before disappearing again into the dark forest of unrecorded history."[19]

Fortunately Professor Careless fully realized the importance of Native history. Just a few years earlier he had taken a revolutionary step for an Ontario historian writing on the period after the War of 1812. In his 1967 volume for the Canadian Centenary Series, *The Union of the Canadas, 1841–1857*, he provided a short summary of Aboriginal Ontario and Quebec in the 1840s and 1850s.[20] But this leading Canadian historian was the first to admit that he had made no special study of Aboriginal Canada. Consequently he approached Ed Rogers and asked if he would be willing to join in my doctoral supervision. I was delighted that the Ethnologist in Chief at the Royal Ontario Museum agreed to join my Ph.D. committee.

I owe so much to Ed Rogers who, like Jacques Rousseau, had extensive knowledge of North American Indians on the land from numerous visits to the communities and hunting and trapping grounds of Subarctic First Nation peoples. While a graduate student at the University of New Mexico, he did half a year of field work in 1957 in the American Southwest among the Mescalero Apache, although his primary research focused on the Mistassini Cree, on whom he wrote his Ph.D. thesis, which he obtained in 1958. He conducted ethnographical fieldwork with the Mistassini Cree in northern Quebec for over a year during 1953 and 1954, and returned on several other occasions. Upon becoming affiliated with the Royal Ontario Museum in Toronto he also began long-term fieldwork with the Ojibwe community of Weagamow (Round Lake) in Northwestern Ontario, spending a year there during 1958–59. He returned there many times for lengthy visits. For over thirty years Dr Rogers served as the Curator of Ethnology at the Royal Ontario Museum.[21] Basil Johnston, who worked with him at the Royal Ontario Museum in the late 1960s and 1970s, recalled how Ed valued consultation with Aboriginal people, saying that Ed believed "there were none better qualified to interpret their own cultures than Native people themselves."[22] Ed Rogers constantly encouraged me to continue with my Mississauga work. He did so right up to the time of our last visit in a Burlington hospital, shortly before his death in March 1988.[23]

My Ojibwe language teachers in the early 1970s, first Fred Wheatley and then Basil Johnston, provided invaluable insights. In the mid-1970s Basil began to write a series of bestselling books on the Ojibwe, one of the best known being his recollections of residential school, *Indian School Days* (1988). As the dust jacket states: "He creates marvelous portraits of the young Indian boys who struggled to adapt to strange ways and unthinking, unfeeling discipline." I liked very much his storytelling ability. As Native writer Thomas King has stated of *Indian School Days*, "It doesn't involve itself in making the Indians victims or victors." Instead, "you wind up seeing a very human side of Native life that you don't see in many books."[24] Basil has now written over fifteen books and has received many honors including the Order of Ontario, an honorary Doctor of Laws degree from the University of Toronto, and the 2004 Aboriginal Achievement Award for Heritage and Spirituality.

I entered a new world when I took Fred Wheatley's evening class at the old Native Canadian Centre of Toronto on Beverley Street. My notes from those classes are now deposited in the Trent University Archives in Peterborough. With the rigor of a young graduate student I marked each class's date on a notecard. Very interesting comments appear in my cards. On 26 October 1971 the Ojibwe Elder mentioned that in Ojibwe you do not use "please and thank you" all the time. "Thank yous" and "pleases" are not necessary among friends; "thank you" is used among strange company. And there is no goodbye, "that is too final." On another card, made

2 March 1973, I see a note that Fred mentioned that the Ojibwe believed that if you did not respect old people, if you did not respect animals, something bad would happen. The Ojibwe had all kinds of stories about punishment. Fred explained on 10 November 1970 that Ojibwe storytellers had "very rich descriptions, one is right in the story." The Ojibwe language has extraordinary depth. Fred told us on 13 October 1972 that the Ojibwe had an expression for a "woman who is pregnant and you can see it in her eyes" – although I missed writing down the actual word itself.

The Elder first taught us the "amenities," how to have a simple conversation. He provided the designations for family members, weather terms, the names of everyday objects and foods, and a great deal more. Probably on account of my summer camp experiences, I was most interested in the Ojibwe names for trees and animals, including bird, fish, and reptiles. We learned the names of many species of *kinebik*, or "snake."[25] Fred had great respect for the *mendehwed*, or "Massasauga rattler," a poisonous snake. The Ojibwe did not consider him an enemy because he warns you and common sense should tell you to be careful. Fred said the snake will always warn you at night with a buzz – "Real gentleman at night." Then there was the *mitigo sheeshee gweh*, or "hardwood rattlesnake." It looked like a rattler, but it did not bother humans. It would tackle a rat, the only snake that did so. Fred had found them dead together. If the *mussin duhmo*, or "water snake," bites, you should wash your hands because you bleed. A venomous snake's bite feels like the bite from a bass. There is no blood, although the bite leaves fine needle marks on the skin. Over the last forty years I have forgotten all the words for the species of snakes, apart from the word for "snake" itself, *kinebik*. In fact I have lost almost all my Ojibwe vocabulary, but not the word for "coffee." Fred constructed it himself. As he explained, Ojibwe is a picture language; when you talk you form pictures in your mind, when you stop the pictures end. What is "coffee" in Ojibwe? *Neebeeshabobetchebodegetchibooswagamig.* Translated literally this means a beverage that is ground, has an aroma, and when you drink it the sharpness is at the tip of your tongue.[26] Fred worked at the University of Toronto in the early 1970s. I recall several meetings at Hart House, where one of his jobs included the upkeep of rooms for distinguished scholars visiting the University of Toronto. At the time he was a custodian or caretaker or, in the University of Toronto language of the day, a "porter."[27] However, a new appreciation of Aboriginal Canada was just emerging. Although he had never attended university as a student himself, a faculty position opened up for him in 1974, when Fred received an appointment as an Ojibwe language professor at Trent University in Peterborough, Ontario. Fred taught in Trent's Native Studies Department until his retirement in the mid-1980s, when he became professor emeritus. As an Elder he was appointed with the same rank and status as any other professor. In 1983 he won the university's Symons Award for Excellence in Teaching.[28]

A new interest in everything relating to Aboriginal Canada grew at a rapid pace from 1969 onward. Trent University was a leader in the field. In 1969 it established the first Native Studies program in Canada.[29] Ironically, that same year the federal government awakened popular interest in Aboriginal Affairs when it introduced the "White Paper," a proposal to terminate Indian reserves and Indian status. This initiative led to tremendous resistance from the First Nations. The late 1969 publication of *The Unjust Society* by Harold Cardinal, now the President of the Indian Association of Alberta, informed the general public of the First Nations' grievances. The important book by the young Cree leader revealed the extent and the depth of Canada's mistreatment of North American Indians. Of the 25,000 copies in the first printing, 18,750 were advance orders.[30] It went on to sell nearly 80,000 copies.[31] A united front of First Nation political leaders succeeded in convincing the Liberal government of Pierre Elliot Trudeau to withdraw the White Paper in March 1971. The provincial and territorial First Nation political organizations worked next to secure the constitutional entrenchment of Aboriginal and treaty rights. The acceptance of the concept of Aboriginal rights by the Supreme Court of Canada in the Nisga'a (Nishga) case of 1973 led to a federal Native claims policy. The first comprehensive land claim signed was the James Bay and Northern Quebec Agreement in 1975.

The new interest in Aboriginal Canada was reinforced when an American book, *Bury My Heart at Wounded Knee*, was published in January 1971. The non-fiction bestseller by Dee Brown was reprinted thirteen times that year, and it sold five million copies.[32] Written from the viewpoint of the Plains people it narrated the history of the American West from 1860 to 1890, the thirty-year period in which the last resisting Native Americans were ruthlessly overpowered. In Canada an autobiography, *Halfbreed*, by Métis author Maria Campbell, awakened Canadians to injustices the Métis had endured. It came out in 1973 and sold well: 17,500 copies in hardcover and 8,000 in paperback.[33]

Despite these popular works, when Canadian historian James Walker reviewed the state of Canadian historical writing on Aboriginal Canada in 1971 and again in 1983,[34] he found only a modest interest in the Aboriginal peoples in the first two-thirds of the twentieth century. In spring 1944 Donald G. Creighton of the History Department at the University of Toronto published his *Dominion of the North: A History of Canada*, a popular work that went through numerous editions and re-printings in the decades to follow. Like so many other Canadian history books of the period the author avoided Aboriginal Canada in his opening pages and instead devoted his first chapter to "The Founding of New France, 1500-1663."[35]

A remarkable mid-twentieth-century exception to the omission of Aboriginal peoples in Canadian history books is volume one of Stanley Ryerson's people's history of Canada. *The Founding of Canada: Beginnings to 1815* appeared in 1960, with the second edition following in 1963. In the 1960s, Ryerson, a communist, was "a only marginal figure in the English-Canadian historical profession."[36] Yet, despite the low regard of academic historians, Ryerson was a perceptive critic who had done his homework on Aboriginal issues. In Chapter 27, "Indian and Negro Slavery, The Theft of Indian Lands," he reviewed the settlement frontier of Upper Canada. Ryerson described it as rife with "massive expropriation and eviction." Specifically he cited the example of the Mississauga, noting: "History, dead-pan, records that 'large portions of Upper Canada were thus relieved of the burden of the Indian title,' the lands being 'sold for their benefit'! The fact of the matter is that the Indians were disposed of their lands by a colossal operation of fraud, misrepresentation and legalized theft."[37]

Unequal Union: Roots of Crisis in the Canadas, 1815–1873, volume two of his history, came out in 1968. Within, Stanley Ryerson cited one of the works he used in its preparation, "Rev. Peter Jones: Life and Journals of Kah-ke-wa-que-na-by (1860)."[38] The short biographical note in the inside back cover of the 1975 printing of *Unequal Union* explained that Ryerson, then a Professor of History at l'Université du Québec à Montréal, was "a great-grandson of Egerton Ryerson." Stanley Ryerson would have known of his great-grandfather's close friendship with Peter Jones, as the Mississauga chief's *Life and Journals* are full of references to him. At the end of the book, for instance, Peter Jones's wife, Eliza, describes the last evening the two friends were together, 17 June 1856: "Dr. Ryerson prayed for the last time by the dying bed of his dear friend and brother."[39] Peter and Eliza left the next morning for their home at Brantford, where he died on 29 June.

In the 1970s, James Walker noted the seasoned gladiators of Canadian historical profession altered their brief references to Aboriginal peoples, observing that they dropped "the image of childishness and lack of civilization."[40] In *Canada: The Heroic Beginnings*, published in 1974, Donald Creighton, for example, adopted a gentler tone. Yet even so, Walker points out that in Creighton's book and those of many of his contemporaries, "the Indians are not even minor actors in the Canadian drama, simply stage-props against which others work out their roles."[41] They remained voiceless. In Donald Creighton's case his indifference and his ignorance of Aboriginal Canada are intriguing as his great-grandfather, Rev. Kennedy Creighton, a Methodist minister, knew and admired Peter Jones.[42] Apparently Donald Creighton knew nothing about his great-grandfather's close friendship with the most important Mississauga political and religious leader of the nineteenth century. When Peter's health sharply declined in March 1856, Rev. and Mrs. Creighton invited the Joneses to stay with them and try the healing waters at St. Catharines: "Mr. Stephenson, the proprietor of the springs keeps a first class hotel on the premises, where accommodations equal to any in Canada can be obtained, *but at a very high rate*. I know of no private boarding house that I could recommend as suitable for you. Mrs. C. & I have talked the matter over, and have concluded to offer you & Sister Jones the best accommodations the parsonage can offer."[43] Peter and Eliza took up the kind offer, and stayed with the Creightons in St. Catharines for a week at the end of April.[44] Unfortunately, the healing waters offered no respite. The journey to the Ryersons' house to consult medical specialists in Toronto followed, but the best educated physician in the city could not help. Peter Jones died two weeks later in Brantford, shortly after his return from staying with the Ryersons.

In the mid and late 1970s land claims negotiations contributed to a growing public interest in Aboriginal Canada. In the mid-1970s, the Mackenzie Valley Pipeline Inquiry, led by Justice Thomas Berger and also known as the Berger Commission, resulted in a new awareness of contemporary Northern Aboriginal issues in non-Aboriginal Canada. The recognition of the three Aboriginal peoples (Indian, Inuit, and Métis) in Canada in the new Constitution of 1982 constituted a new milestone. This new receptivity to the history and cultures of Aboriginal Canada led to university teaching opportunities, such as Fred Wheatley's appointment at Trent University.

My academic star rose the same year as Fred Wheatley's. I obtained a teaching post in Canadian history at the University of Calgary in 1974, the same year he was appointed to teach Ojibwe at Trent University. I successfully defended my Ph.D. thesis the following March. During the late 1970s to mid-1980s I recast my dissertation on the history of the Mississauga to the mid-nineteenth century into a biography of Peter Jones. In 1987 *Sacred Feathers* appeared in the United States in the University of Nebraska Press's American Indian Lives series, edited by LaVonne Brown Ruoff. It was co-published in Canada by the University of Toronto Press.

The early response to the book proved favorable. Several reviewers identified how Peter Jones energetically fought for the Mississauga. M.T. Kelly, for instance, in *Saturday Night* in May 1988, identified Jones' four main goals: "secure ownership of reserves, a transition to farming, access to education, and the same civil rights for Indians as for Englishmen." He saw an aspect of Peter Jones that I myself missed: "At various times in his life Jones was described as kind, grave, natural, gentle, and unassuming. In spite of being an effective preacher and leader Jones seems to have retained that kind of stillness, almost withdrawal, that many Indians think of as a proper public presentation of self."

Most reviewers recognized and commented on the research behind the biography, one of the first biographies of a nineteenth-century North American Indian to be based on their own writings. Jones's writings and those of his wife, Eliza, as well as references to him in Methodist and Indian Affairs records, allowed his life to be fully recreated. Donald C. MacDonald wrote positively in the *Toronto Star*, on 30 January 1988: "The result is an outstanding scholarly work, of more than normal interest to general readers in southern Ontario. The Reverend Peter Jones emerges as a major figure in Canadian Indian history, worthy company for Tecumseh and Joseph Brant."

On 29 November 1987 in her *Toronto Sunday Star* column, Book World, Beverley Slopen captured the freshness of one of my most important research moments. She recorded my description of the moment Patricia Appavoo of the Victoria University Library at the University of Toronto showed me an 1832 portrait of Peter Jones. Thirteen years later it would grace the cover of *Sacred Feathers*. I told her: "I just stared at it. I must have gazed at it for half an hour. He was 30 years old, on the brink of his career, and he was courting Eliza. I saw a very approachable, dedicated person. There is a softness in his eyes and a sense of humor." The Victoria University Library also had a portrait of Eliza by the same artist. I described to

Ms Slopen the effect of seeing both portraits together: "I had been studying them for so long it was like meeting someone. They just sort of stepped out of the portrait frame." My motivation in writing *Sacred Feathers* was to tell the story of a remarkable relationship, as well as the life of an important North American Indian.

The academic reviews also proved positive. In my opinion, the one that carried the most weight was written by the distinguished religious historian John Webster Grant in *Studies in Religion/Sciences Religieuses*. He generously termed the biography as "worthy," one in which Peter Jones emerged "so vibrantly alive." Without knowing my intention to do so he then suggested that I continue on with the history of the nineteenth-century Mississauga. Grant perceptively identified in *Sacred Feathers* a number of ambiguities in my presentation of this important Ojibwe leader:

Jones defended traditional Indian ways against white calumny even while he was doing his best to eradicate them. He argued vigorously for the inalienability of Indian reserves, but appealed to the legislature to validate his private claim to a portion of reserve land his father had negotiated for him. He sought to raise his sons as Indians in a near-mansion that might have been transplanted from England. Living in two worlds, did he succeed in reconciling them even in himself? More detailed attention to such contradictions would have slowed the pace of the narrative, but one hopes that Smith will return to them in a future study.[45]

The idea already planted in my brain, John Webster Grant's comments provided the necessary additional incentive to write *Mississauga Portraits*. Ed Rogers also strongly encouraged me when I visited him in the hospital when he was suffering from cancer, which eventually took his life in 1988. In a companion study, he assured me, I could place Jones's life in a wider context, beside the life stories of seven other contemporary Ojibwe.

From the late 1980s onward contemporary Aboriginal issues became ever more pressing. The failure of the federal government to settle the complex, two-century-old land claim of the Mohawks at Kanesatake (Oka) contributed to violence and a 78-day armed stand-off in the summer of 1990 between the Mohawks and the federal and Quebec governments. The Oka Crisis proved the catalyst for Ottawa's creation of the Royal Commission on Aboriginal Peoples. The report tabled in the House of Commons in 1996 and the accompanying research papers constitute the most in-depth analysis ever undertaken on the First Nations, Inuit, and Métis in Canada.

So much has happened in the treatment of the Aboriginal peoples in Canadian historical writing since the late 1980s. Suddenly the Aboriginal peoples – who had never disappeared, except in Canadian history books – re-emerged. It is unfair to single out special workers in the vineyard of Canadian historical writing, but in my opinion one stands above all the rest: the late Olive Dickason. She was a giant. The Métis historian, who came to historical work after a successful career in Canadian journalism, set the bar in the 1990s. Her *Canada's First Nations: A History of Founding Peoples from Earliest Times*, published in 1992[46] is an extraordinary accomplishment. This essential study concisely summarizes the latest historical research on Aboriginal Canada. Throughout she emphasizes the importance of the Aboriginal peoples in Canada's history, placing them fully in the center. She notes Aboriginal Canada's links before European contact to the great North America Indian metropolises to the south, in present-day Mexico. Her research rests on the widest possible search of the available documentary and published sources. She placed great emphasis on the First Nations' antiquity in the Americas, their active participation after European contact in the fur trade, their spirit of resistance to outside control in the eighteenth and nineteenth centuries, and their refusal to abandon their North American Indian identity in the twentieth.

J.R. Miller, another distinguished Canadian historian, has written a number of books to describe and explain the relationship between the Aboriginals and newcomers.[47] In 1994 he contributed a useful literature review on "Native History" in *Canadian History: A Reader's Guide: Volume 2: Confederation to the Present* (1994).

He noted in his essay his amazement at the "explosion of historical writing since 1982." What a contrast, he added, for "when an
earlier edition of this Guide was published a decade ago, it was not
considered essential to include a section of works on these themes.
However, if it was possible to overlook Native subjects in 1982, it is
not now."[48] The "explosion" of historical work on Aboriginal Canada continued throughout the late 1990s. As Keith Thor Carlson,
Melinda Marie Jetté, and Kenihi Matsui noted in their 2001 article, "An Annotated Bibliography of Major Writings in Aboriginal
History, 1990–99," in the *Canadian Historical Review*, "The current vigour of Canadian Aboriginal history is remarkable, given the
field's relative obscurity a generation ago."[49] In the early twenty-
first century historical interest in Aboriginal Canada continued to
grow. The recent controversy about Indian residential school education has generated a great deal of interest in the history of Indian
affairs in Canada. The federal government's apology to the Aboriginals for residential schools on 11 June 2008 is part of the new context in which *Mississauga Portraits* was completed.

In *Mississauga Portraits* Peter Jones reappears, but now with
seven other multi-dimensional individuals. All research notes
for both books will be donated to the Victoria University Library,
at the University of Toronto, which already holds the invaluable
Peter Jones Collection. Following the normal access procedures,
interested scholars, and creative writers, can gain access at the Victoria University Library to my collection of Mississauga research
material.

The text of *Sacred Feathers* remains as it first appeared in 1987.
Two corrections to picture captions, however, must be pointed out.
Subsequent research has revealed that image 17 is a photograph
of Rev. Peter Jacobs, Jr., who became an ordained Anglican minister, rather than a portrait of Pahtahsega, or in English, Rev. Peter
Jacobs, the Methodist missionary and father of Peter Jacobs, Jr. Similarly, image 15 is most likely Catherine Sutton, the daughter of
Nahnebahwequay, Mrs Catherine (also written Catharine) Sutton,
rather than Mrs Sutton herself. One tiny error that I can now correct appears on page 22, where I state that a fit Mississauga warrior

could run "eighty kilometers in a day, the distance from Toronto to Niagara." It should read "eighty miles [130 kilometers]."[50]

Historical interpretations can be multiple and conflicting. Our own biases, faith, nationality, gender, as well as life experiences, color any interpretation of events. No historical interpretation is final in any respect. In these two companion volumes I record my interpretation of the history of the Mississauga First Nations in the nineteenth century. I encourage others to examine this same material from their different vantage points and cultural backgrounds. The discovery of new sources, the probing of the records with new questions and perspectives, the application of new research knowledge, as well as a complete familiarity with the Ojibwe language, will all contribute to a deeper understanding. Future scholars will have their own emphasis and will make their own selection of details from the rich surviving documentation. Additional sources will come to light, particularly through the digitalization of nineteenth-century Canadian newspapers, an initiative that has barely begun.

All royalties from the second edition of *Sacred Feathers* and from *Mississauga Portraits* will be donated to the Sacred Feathers (Kahkewaquonaby) Scholarship in Native Studies, awarded to a student at the University of Toronto with an interest in the study of North American Aboriginal peoples. The award is presented on the basis of financial need, with preference given to students in the Aboriginal Studies Program. Warmly I thank Len Husband of the University of Toronto Press for his successful recommendation that *Sacred Feathers* be reprinted with a new introduction, to accompany the publication of its sequel, *Mississauga Portraits*. My thanks to Lisa Jemison for her copyediting of the new introduction, and to my friend Kristin Gleeson for her comments on an early draft.

Don Smith, Calgary, 17 March 2013

NOTES

1 "New Book Release," *Boozhoo: Newsmagazine of the Native Canadian Centre of Toronto* 1, no. 4 (December/January 1988), p. 7.

2 Peter Jones, *Life and Journals of Kah-ke-wa-quo-na-by (Rev. Peter Jones), Wesleyan Missionary* (Toronto: Published by Anson Green, at the Wesleyan Printing Establishment, 1860), p. 1.

3 Robert Stacey and Stan McMullin, *Massanoga: The Art of Bon Echo* (n.p.: Penumbra Press, 1998), pp. 24–5, 99.

4 Ernest Thompson Seton and Julia M. Seton, compilers, *The Gospel of the Redman: A Way of Life* (Santa Fe, New Mexico: Seton Village, 1966), p. 21. The Setons state the English translation means: " Father, a needy one stands before Thee. I that sing am he."

5 Kandalore's owner and director was Kirk Wipper, an extraordinary individual. See Nora Ryell, "Kirk Wipper founded the Canadian Canoe Museum," *Globe and Mail*, 8 May 2011.

6 Sharon Wall, *The Nurture of Nature: Childhood, Antimodernism, and Ontario Summer Camps, 1920–55* (Vancouver: UBC Press, 2009), p. 229.

7 John Perry, "A Life Ministering to First Nations," *Tidings: The University of King's College Alumni Magazine*, Winter 2004, p. 22.

8 For background on Rev. Stan McKay, see Joyce Carlson, *Journey from Fisher River: A Celebration of the Spirituality of a People through the Life of Stan McKay* (Toronto: The United Church Publishing House, 1994).

9 Marlene Brant Castellano, Linda Archibald, Mike DeGagné, "Fred Kelly," in *From Truth to Reconciliation: Transforming the Legacy of Residential Schools* (Ottawa: Aboriginal Healing Foundation, 2008), p. 11.

10 Donald B. Smith, "From 'Indians' to 'First Nations': Changing Anglo-Canadian Perceptions of the North American Indian in the Twentieth Century," *Constitutional Forum* 13, no. 3 and 14, no. 1 (2005): p. 84.

11 Pierre Berton, *1967. The Last Good Year* (Toronto: Doubleday Canada Limited, 1997), p. 145.

12 The exhibit quotations appear in John Lownsbrough, *The Best Place to Be Expo 67 and Its Time* (Toronto: Allen Lane, 2012), p. 204.

13 Cornelius Jaenen, "In Memoriam, Pierre Savard," *Canadian Historical Association, Bulletin* 25, no. 1 (1999): p. 6.

14 Conversation with Pierre Savard, 12 June 1994.

15 A full scholarly biography of Jacques Rousseau remains badly needed. For the moment the best source is probably Camille Laverdière and Nicole Carette, *Jacques Rousseau, 1905–1970: Curriculum, Anthologie, Témoignages, Bibliographie* (Sainte-Foy: Les Presses de l'Université Laval, 1999).

16 Jacques Rousseau, *L'Hérédite et l'Homme* (Montréal: Les Editions de l'Arbre, 1945), p. 74.

17 Jacques Rousseau, "The Northern Québec Eskimo Problem and the

Ottawa-Quebec Struggle," *Anthropological Journal of Canada* 7, no. 2 (1969): p. 2.

18 Basil Johnston's essay, "Indians, Métis and Eskimos," appeared in Robert Fulford, David Godfrey, and Abraham Rotstein, *Read Canadian: A Book about Canadian Books* (Toronto: James Lewis & Samuel, 1972), pp. 168–74.

19 Jacques Rousseau and George W. Brown, "The Indians of Northeastern North America," *DCB*, vol. 1, 1000 to 1700 (1966): p. 5.

20 J.M.S. Careless, *The Union of the Canadas: The Growth of Canadian Institutions, 1841–1857* (Toronto: McClelland and Stewart, 1967), pp. 153–5.

21 I am very grateful to Mary Black Rogers for biographical notes on her husband, written in December 1987.

22 Basil Johnston, "Dr. Ed Roger, My Friend," in *Aboriginal Ontario: Historical Perspectives on the First Nations*, ed. Edward S. Rogers and Donald B. Smith (Toronto: Dundurn Press, 1994), p. xvi.

23 His ashes were buried that August in the Weagamow Lake cemetery, 200 kilometers north of Sioux Lookout, a very great privilege accorded by his longtime Ojibwe friends. Shaun Herron, "ROM curator to be buried among Ojibwa, Rogers loved the northland," *Burlington Spectator*, 25 August 1988.

24 Thomas King, 2 May 1990, quoted in Hartmut Lutz, *Contemporary Challenges: Conversations with Canadian Native Authors* (Saskatoon, Sask.: Fifth House Publishers, 1991), p. 111.

25 I warmly thank Cecil King, the recipient of the 2009 Aboriginal Award for Education, and Cathy Littlejohn. In the fall of 2008, they put my notes in computer files and into two vocabulary lists, one from Ojibwe to English and the other English to Ojibwe. There is no standard form for writing Ojibwe in English. I have simply followed the spellings in Ojibwe that Fred wrote on the blackboard in class.

26 "Teaching Ojibway: A Conversation with Fred Wheatley," *Boozhoo: News Magazine of the Native Canadian Centre of Toronto* 1, no. 4 (Special 25th anniversary issue): p. 40.

27 My thanks to Harold Averill of the University of Toronto Archives for help with this terminology.

28 "Obituary. Fred Wheatley," *The Globe and Mail* (Toronto), 13 August 1990.

29 Shona Taner, "The Evolution of Native Studies in Canada: Descending from the Ivory Tower," *The Canadian Journal of Native Studies* 19, no. 2 (1999): p. 293.

30 "The Unjust Society," *Quill & Quire*, 12 December 1969, p. 2. Clip-

pings in B.Y. Card Fonds, 91-129 item 110, Box 5, University of Alberta Archives.

31 Mel Hurtig, *At Twilight in the Country: Memoirs of a Canadian Nationalist* (Toronto: Stoddart, 1996), p. 156.

32 Donald L. Fixico, "Bury My Heart at Wounded Knee and the Indian Voice in Native Studies," *Journal of the West* 39, no. 1 (2000): p. 7.

33 Judy Steed, "Maria Campbell's Second Spring," *The Canadian* in the *Calgary Herald*, 13 January 1979, p. 6.

34 James W. St. G. Walker, "The Indian in Canadian Historical Writing," Canadian Historical Association, *Historical Papers* (1971): pp. 21–51. James W. St. G. Walker, "The Indian in Canadian Historical Writing, 1972–1982," in *As Long as the Sun Shines and Water Flows: A Reader in Canadian Native Studies*, ed. Ian A.L. Getty and Antoine S. Lussier (Vancouver: University of British Columbia Press, 1983), pp. 340–57.

35 Donald G. Creighton, *Dominion of the North: A History of Canada* (Cambridge, Mass.: Houghton Mifflin Company, 1944), pp. 1–50.

36 Donald Wright, *The Professionalization of History in English Canada* (Toronto: University of Toronto Press, 2005), p. 125.

37 Stanley B. Ryerson, *The Founding of Canada: Beginnings to 1815*, new edition (Toronto: Progress Books, 1963), p. 241.

38 Stanley B. Ryerson, *Unequal Union: Roots of Crisis in the Canadas, 1815-1873*, second edition (Toronto: Progress Books, 1973), p. 451. The first edition appeared in 1968, the second in 1973.

39 Eliza Jones in Jones, *Life*, p. 415.

40 Walker, "Canadian Historical Writing, 1972–1982," p. 346.

41 Ibid.

42 Kennedy Creighton was Donald Creighton's great-grandfather on his mother's side, and a great-uncle on his father's. I thank Donald Wright for this information. Rev. Creighton liked the Ojibwe, and later served as the Methodist missionary at Rama from 1879 to 1884. Generally his Sunday service filled the church "when the Indians are at home." It could accommodate about 300 people. Miss. Soc. Report 1881/1882, pp. xxiv-xxv. This meant he was attracting almost the entire community. The total Rama population was about 250 in 1880, and no doubt some neighboring non-Aboriginal Methodists attended as well. Gabrielle Lotimer, "Rama Reserve," *Reflections of the Past: The Story of Rama Township* (Washago, Ontario: Township of Rama, 1989), p. 388. Rev. Creighton's concern for the Rama school, which lacked proper school supplies, is raised in the article, "Indian Mission-School, Rama," *CG*, 19 May 1880. The unnamed author includes this reference to Rev. Creighton, "close by [the school] is a pretty stone church, with a

crowded attendance, a good organ, an excellent choir, and an indefatigable pastor."

43 Kennedy Creighton to "My dear Brother [Peter Jones]," dated St. Catharines, 21 March 1856, PJC VUL.

44 Eliza Field, 1856 Diary, entries for 24 to 30 April 1856, PJC VUL.

45 John Webster Grant, "Review of *Sacred Feathers*," *Studies in Religion/ Sciences Religieuses* 18, no.1 (1989), p. 97.

46 Olive Patricia Dickason, *Canada's First Nations: A History of Founding Peoples from Earliest Times* (Toronto: McClelland and Stewart, 1992).

47 J.R. Miller, *Skyscrapers Hide the Heavens: A History of Indian-White Relations in Canada* (Toronto: University of Toronto Press, 1989); J.R. Miller, *Shingwauk's Vision: A History of Native Residential Schools* (Toronto: University of Toronto Press, 1996); J.R. Miller, *Lethal Legacy: Current Native Controversies in Canada* (Toronto: McClelland and Stewart, 2004); J.R. Miller, *Compact, Contract, Covenant: Aboriginal Treaty-Making in Canada* (Toronto: University of Toronto Press, 2009).

48 J.R. Miller, "Native History," in *Canadian History: A Reader's Guide: Volume 2: Confederation to the Present,* ed. Doug Owram (Toronto: University of Toronto Press, 1994), p. 179.

49 The reference appears on page 123 in the March 2001 issue.

50 My thanks to Patrick Mackenzie for this correction, in a graduate reading course, 26 November 1990. Peter Jones wrote in his *History of the Ojebway Indians* (p. 75): "The Indian men are swift travellers on foot. I have known them to walk with ease fifty and sixty miles a day, and some have accomplished the journey from Niagara to Toronto, a distance of eighty miles, in one day, and that too when there was only a narrow Indian footpath."

Preface

At three o'clock on the afternoon of 14 September 1838, three men left the private apartments of Lord Glenelg, Her Majesty's colonial secretary. As they passed through the east wing of Windsor Castle, the servants immediately recognized His Lordship, who had served four prime ministers. What a strange trio it was: the elegantly attired Scottish lord; a well-fed clergyman tightly bundled in his black clothes; and a mysterious third man, exotically dressed in fringed and beaded buckskin and wearing moccasins ornamented with porcupine quills.[1]

As they walked through the myriad candlelit rooms, halls, and long corridors—past hundreds of portraits, busts, and gilt clocks—the foreign dignitary rehearsed his greeting. The tall, dark-skinned man carried an unusual message from the Ojibwas (or Chippewas, as the white settlers pronounced the word) to their sovereign. The petition bore the roughly sketched totems, or coats of arms, of Sloping Sky, The Approaching Roaring Thunder, The God of the North, Sky Man, and eighteen other warriors living at the Credit River, twenty kilometers west of Toronto.

The petition contained a message of vital importance for all the Ojibwas, or Mississaugas (as the white settlers termed the Ojibwas living on the north shore of Lake Ontario), for to the south, the Americans had begun to remove fifty thousand Indians from their ancestral lands in the eastern United States, sending them west of the Mississippi.[2] In Upper Canada Sir Francis Bond Head, the previous lieutenant governor, had attempted in 1836–37 to relocate

Canadian Indian bands from the fertile south to rocky and barren Manitoulin Island on the north shore of Lake Huron. The Indian visitor believed his people retained the right to "the undisturbed possession of those small tracts of land reserved for their use at the time they surrendered their immense territories to the Crown of England."[3] The petition's exact words now came back to him as he rehearsed one final time what he would tell the queen: "Our people have been civilized and educated, and the Gospel of Jesus Christ has been preached to us. We have also learned the ways of the white people; they have taught the children of the forest to plough and to sow. . . . Will your Majesty be pleased to assure us that our lands shall not be taken away from us, or our people. . . . "[4]

When the trio reached the antechamber to the White Drawing Room, Glenelg disappeared to inform Queen Victoria of her Indian petitioner. Moments later a court official opened the black doors. Before them stood an attractive young woman about twenty years of age, near the center of the reception room below the crystal chandelier.[5] To Her Majesty and the half-dozen lords and ladies in attendance Lord Glenelg announced, "Kahkewaquonaby, or Sacred Feathers, a chief of the Chippewa Indians of Upper Canada."

Sacred Feathers approached, bowing several times. The queen returned his bows, then walked toward him, extending her hand for him to kiss. The Indian knew the exact etiquette to follow. When they met, he immediately knelt on his right knee and held up his right arm. As Victoria placed her hand on his he lifted and kissed it, then rose to present the petition. What a physical contrast they presented: the tall, muscular Indian and his delicate queen, just under five feet tall.

The Indian began by explaining the Christian Indians' prayer that "her most Gracious Majesty's Government may be pleased to secure to them and their posterity for ever all their lands on which they have located themselves."[6] Lord Glenelg, he added, had already accepted the Indians' request for title deeds to their reserves, documents that would prevent their removal.

Glenelg immediately bowed to the queen, who bowed in return, acknowledging her minister's wise judgment. Thinking she might wish to keep it as a curiosity, Sacred Feathers then offered her the document, to which he had attached white and black wampum. Victoria smiled and replied; "I thank you, sir, I am much obliged to you."

From a firsthand witness of North American Indians the young queen already knew a little about their customs. Sir Charles Augustus Murray, the new master of the queen's household, had spent several months in 1835 with a Pawnee Indian band on the American plains. (In 1839 he published an account of his American journey, dedicating it to Her Majesty.)[7] Long interested by Murray's tales of the character and society of the North American Indians, the monarch asked Sacred Feathers to explain the meaning of the wampum strings attached to his petition.

The Indian chief informed the queen that the white beads represented peace and prosperity but that the black wampum at the end of the long white strings symbolized danger, suspicion, and fear. Yet when the lieutenant governor of Upper Canada carried out Lord Glenelg's instructions and granted title deeds it would sweep the path clean, removing all obstacles to friendship. Then the Indians would take out the black beads.

Some discussion followed of Sacred Feathers' year-long visit to Britain to raise money for the mission work in Canada, then the interview drew to a close. The queen was engaged to join Lord Melbourne, her prime minister, Lord John Russell, and Lord and Lady Portman on a riding party. The queen bowed, indicating that the interview had ended. The Indian did the same, stepping backward until the queen turned her back. Lord Glenelg and the lords-in-waiting then escorted the Indian chief and the Reverend Robert Alder to an adjoining room, where the two guests were served a substantial meal before they left for London.

The visit impressed the queen greatly, for that evening she recorded in her diary: "Soon after the Council I went into the White drawing room, attended by Lady Portman, and my Lord, Groom and Equerry, etc., and Lord Glenelg introduced an Indian Chippewa Chief—who is a Xtian [Christian] and came with a Petition. He is a tall, youngish man, with a yellowish complexion and black hair; he was in his National dress, which is entirely of leather; leather leggins, etc. He kissed my hand; he speaks English very well, and expressed himself very well."[8]

By 1838 Sacred Feathers, or Peter Jones to use his English name, had spent nearly half his life working for the moment when the Ojibwas could "walk side by side with their white neighbours, and partake in all the blessings and privileges enjoyed by the white subjects of her most gracious Majesty, the Queen."[9] He felt that the Indians could advance only if given solid legal guarantees on their few remaining lands. Once the Indians had the boundaries of their reserves protected forever and the legal right (based on their land-ownership) to vote for members of Parliament and to serve on juries, the two races would be on an equal footing.

Peter Jones, a unique man of extraordinary vision, lived well in advance of his times. A century and a half ago very few Indians had his knowledge of the white people's customs and habits. The son of a white surveyor and an Ojibwa (or Mississauga) woman, he symbolized the fusion of two cultures in early Upper Canada. Reared to the age of fourteen among the Mississaugas, the Ojibwa-speaking Indians on the north shore of Lake Ontario, he knew his mother's people's language and customs. His seven years with his father, from age fourteen to twenty-one, had taught him the language and habits of the Europeans. From 1823 to his death in 1856, he acted as a bridge between the two cultures, going back and forth between them and helping them understand each other. The story of his life in itself provides a history of early white-Indian relations in Upper Canada, years in which the central issues were land and education.

It is now nearly twenty years since I first discovered Peter Jones. My introduction came in 1969, when I read his autobiography and his history of his tribe. Subsequent research unearthed letters, his wife's diaries, and much unpublished material.

Many authorities have said that the problem of researching Indian history lies in the absence of Indian-produced source materials—and yet a wealth of written material has survived on the life of this remarkable man. Since I grew up in Oakville, Ontario, near the banks of Sixteen Mile Creek—a Mississauga Indian reserve as late as 1820—the idea of writing a modern biography of this prominent Mississauga Indian greatly appealed to me. In 1975 I completed my Ph.D. thesis on the history of the Mississaugas, and for the next ten years I researched my study of Sacred Feathers.

After nearly two decades of work on the life of Sacred Feathers, one hope remains to be fulfilled. Samuel Johnson once wrote that it is impossible to understand a man if you do not understand any of his language.[10] I hope that one day a native Ojibwa speaker will examine Sacred Feather's numerous translations of the Bible and of Wesleyan hymns.[11] His choice of Ojibwa words, and his manner of expressing concepts, would—I know from my little knowledge of the language—reveal much about him. Let this biography be only the first book-length study of Sacred Feathers!

Many people helped with this biography. I would like to thank my Ph.D. thesis advisers, J. M. S. Careless of the University of Toronto and E. S. Rogers of the Royal Ontario Museum; my Ojibwa language instructors, Fred Wheatley of Trent University and Basil Johnston of the Royal Ontario Museum; Lloyd King of the New Credit Reserve; and my parents. My wife, Nancy Townshend, later gave me constant encouragement during the recasting of the thesis from a dissertation on the Mississaugas into a biography of Sacred Feathers. I am also grateful to Helen Burgess, former editor of *The Beaver* magazine, for her encouragement. I am particularly indebted to LaVonne Brown Ruoff, and to my readers, Olive Dickason of the University of Alberta and Helen Hornbeck Tanner, for their comments on the entire manuscript. E. S. Rogers kindly read the three opening chapters.

I am grateful to *The Beaver* and to *Ontario History* for permission to use sections from my published articles:

"The Transatlantic Courtship of the Reverend Peter Jones," *Beaver* 308, no. 1 (Summer 1977): 4–13.

"Eliza and the Reverend Peter Jones," *Beaver* 308, no. 2 (Autumn 1977): 40–46.

"Peter and Eliza Jones: Their Last Years," *Beaver* 308, no. 3 (Winter 1977): 16–23.

"Historic Peace-Pipe," *Beaver*, 315, no. 1 (Summer 1984): 4–7.

"The Dispossession of the Mississauga Indians: A Missing Chapter in the Early History of Upper Canada," *Ontario History* 73, no. 2 (June 1981): 67–87.

Most of the manuscripts relating to Peter and Eliza Jones are in the Toronto area. I am most grateful to the staff of the United Church Archives, the Victoria University Library, the Ontario Archives, and the Baldwin Room of the Metropolitan Toronto Library for their invaluable assistance since 1969—my thanks to Glenn Lucas, Tony Rees, Mary Ann Tyler, Brian Ross, Ernie Nix, and Neil Semple at the United Church Archives; to Lorna Fraser, Patricia Appavoo, Len Dutton, and Anne Schultz at Victoria; to Leon Warmski at the Ontario Archives; and to Edith Firth, Christine Mosser, Sandra Alston, Christopher Clapp, John Crosthwait, and William Parker at the Baldwin Room, Metropolitan Toronto Library.

That this book could be written is due to several persons: first to Sacred Feathers's English wife, Eliza Field Jones. During her lifetime Eliza carefully safeguarded all of her husband's, and her own, precious manuscripts—diaries, letters, notebooks, and books—and his Indian artifacts. She gave her husband's artifacts and much of his written material to her third son, Dr. Peter Edmund Jones, shortly before her death in 1890. Dr. Jones presented a number of his father's Indian objects to the Smithsonian Institution in Washington in 1898 (where they are today) but kept the other items. Apparently, in support of the band's land claims at the turn of the century, he sent the Credit River band's Letterbook, 1825–42, Entry Book, 1831–48, and Council Minutes, 1835–48, to the Department of Indian Affairs. These invaluable sources are now in the Public Archives of Canada ("The Paudash Papers," RG 10, vol. 1011). Upon Dr. Jones's death in 1909 his widow, Charlotte Jones, inherited the collection, and at some point before her death in British Columbia in 1921 she donated much of it to the Archives of Victoria University. Eliza gave all her own manuscripts to her son Charles's widow Hannah Eleda Jones, who died in 1903. The Archives of the Victoria University Library obtained Eliza's diaries and letters in the mid-1950s, as well as two portraits, one of Eliza Field and one of Peter Jones, completed in 1832 by the London artist Matilda Jones. Peter Jones's library, originally donated to the Vernon Public Library in Vernon, British Columbia, was given by that institution to the United Church Archives in the late 1970s.

I am indebted to the following descendants of Augustus Jones for valuable genealogical information: Florence (Mrs. J. C.) Hill of Oshweken, Ontario; Wilma (Mrs. Andrew) Jamieson of Oshweken, Ontario; Harold Senn of Victoria, British Columbia; Effie (Mrs. Robert) Montour of Oakville, Ontario; and Thelma McIntee of Gibson, British Columbia. Madeline Baker of Jordan Station, Ontario; G. G. Phillips of Ottawa, Ontario; and Donald Jones of Dundas, Ontario also assisted with genealogical information on the Jones family. Mr. and Mrs. Hagglund of Paris, Ontario, allowed me to visit Augustus Jones's old farm on the Governor's Road, now the Dundas Highway. Phil Monture, the Six Nations Land Researcher, helped me locate Augustus's land grants from Joseph Brant.

Several of the descendants of Eliza Field Jones's brothers and sisters helped with the presentation of the Fields' family history: Basil Anderson of Bideford, Devon, England; Cecil Field of Eastbourne, Sussex, England; Bernard ffield of Lymington, Hampshire, England; Paul ffield of Cohasset, Massachusetts; Paul ffield of Orchard Park, New York; Jane Hollins of Littlehampton, Sussex, England; Thomas Layburn of Putney Hill, London, England; and Edna Peacock of London, England. John Baker of Slough, England; and Densmore Walker of Fleet, Hampshire, England; gave me information on the J. C. and C. Field Company.

Over the past fifteen years many others have helped me to find valuable letters written by and about the Reverend Peter Jones. My thanks to all who assisted, and in particular to the following. Arvilla Louise Thorp of Aldergrove, British Columbia, kindly showed me several letters and autographed books of Peter and Eliza Jones now in her possession, which came to her through her grandfather, the stepson of Dr. Peter Edmund Jones. David Hume of the Public Archives of Canada helped innumerable times over a fifteen-year period John Landen introduced me to the Catherine Sutton Collection in the Owen Sound–Grey County Museum, Owen Sound,

Ontario. Al Hiebert of Vernon, British Columbia, showed me Peter Jones's library (which the Vernon Museum and Archives has since donated to the United Church Archives in Toronto). Kathleen Cann, the archivist of the Bible Society, Swindon, Wiltshire, England, furnished photocopies of several of Peter Jones's letters. Bob Gibney of Althouse College, University of Western Ontario, pointed out a valuable letter about Peter Jones written by Egerton Ryerson. Michael Wilson of Leeds, England, furnished me with several photocopies of letters from the Methodist Archives, John Rylands Library, Manchester, England.

I would also like to thank for their assistance with my research on Peter Jones: Andrew Bethell of London, England; Donna Bloomfield of Red Deer, Alberta; David L. Braddell of Reston, Manitoba; Cynthia Bunnell of Brantford, Ontario; Reg Campion of Pipestone, Manitoba; Betty Clarkson of Mississauga, Ontario; James A. Clifton of the University of Wisconsin at Green Bay; Glenn Crain, then director of the Woodland Indian Cultural Educational Centre in Brantford, Ontario, and Lillian Monture, then librarian of the Centre; Stan Cuthand of Saskatoon, Saskatchewan; Conrad Graham of the McCord Museum, Montreal; John Webster Grant of Toronto; Valerie Grant of the Royal Ontario Museum; Macdonald Holmes of Edmonton, Alberta; John Honderich of Toronto; Dean Jacobs and his family of Walpole Island, Ontario; Amalie Kass of Cambridge, Massachusetts; Arthur Kewley of Peterborough, Ontario; Franz Koennecke, Morriston, Ontario; Bryan La Forme of the New Credit Reserve, Hagersville; William Lamb of Islington, Ontario; John Leslie of the Treaties and Historical Research Centre, Department of Indian and Northern Affairs, Ottawa; Heather Lysons of Edmonton, Alberta; Sir Robin Mackworth-Young, librarian of Windsor Castle, Berkshire, England; Mel, Myra, and John Macleod of Port Credit, Ontario; Craig Macdonald of Dorset, Ontario; David McNab of the Office of Indian Resource Policy, Ontario Ministry of Natural Resources; Mrs. N. F. J. Marshall of Wellington, New Zealand; Enos Montour of Beamsville, Ontario; Barbara Nair of Toronto; Mary Pattison of Toronto; Michael Quealey of Toronto; David Roberts of the *Dictionary of Canadian Biography* in Toronto; Margaret Sault, researcher for the New Credit Research Department, Hagersville, Ontario; Sara Stevenson of the Scottish National Portrait Gallery in Edinburgh; Darryl Stonefish of the Moravian Delaware Reserve, Thamesville, Ontario; John Sturm of Ann Arbor, Michigan; Gladys Taylor of the Curve Lake Mississauga Reserve, Curve Lake, Ontario; Carleton Wells of London, Ontario; Don Whiteside of Ottawa, Ontario; and Mr. and Mrs. S. E. Wyatt of Brantford, Ontario. Bennett McCardle of Ottawa, Ontario, and Jim Morrison of Haileybury, Ontario, assisted with a number of research items.

Several other individuals greatly assisted. My sincere thanks to the staff of the University of Calgary Inter-Library Loan Office for bringing in hundreds of microfilms for my research. I thank David Ohasi and Graham Storms of Toronto, and the Photography Department of Communications Media, University of Calgary, for the reproduction of many of the illustrations. Marta Styk of the Department of Geography, University of Calgary, drew up the three maps; and Barbara Nair of Toronto prepared the index.

I received financial support for my Ph.D. work through the Ontario Graduate Fellowship Plan in 1969–70 and 1973–74 and from the Canada Council in 1971–73. I am very grateful for a special grant in 1976 from the Canada Council (now the Social Sciences and Humanities Research Council) that allowed me to visit the Minnesota Historical Society in St. Paul, the Wisconsin Historical Society in Madison, and the Smithsonian Institution in Washington, D.C., and as well as the Guildhall Library and the British Museum in London. The granting of a special Killam Resident Fellowship in the fall of 1982 allowed me to complete much of an early draft of the book. My thanks to my typists Ancit Dourado, Barbara Redmond, Jodi Steeves, and Joyce Woods, all of Calgary.

To all who helped, my sincerest thanks. Any errors and omissions, of course, are my responsibility.

An Indian Boyhood

Tuhbenahneequay's wigwam stood on what the whites called Burlington Heights, a promontory rising thirty meters above Lake Ontario. Facing east one had a magnificent vista of Burlington Bay, with the Beach, a white sandbar eight-kilometers long, separating the bay from the lake. The young woman knew this area intimately, for she had been born and brought up here.[1] The hunting territory of Chief Wahbanosay, her father, lay at what the French traders had called Fond du Lac—in English, the Head of the Lake.

Outside the air was still and cold. The birth of Tuhbenahneequay's second child had come in the midst of *peboon* (winter).[2] Apart from a midwife she was alone, for the Indians believed that at all times the woman's power to give birth and the man's power to hunt must be kept separate. The warriors feared they would become paralyzed or lose their hunting ability if they broke the taboo and entered the wigwam of an expectant mother.[3]

Wrapping herself in warm rabbit skins, Tuhbenahneequay held her baby to her breast. She resembled the other young Ojibwa women, with reddish brown complexion, jet black hair parted neatly in the middle, high cheekbones, and even, white teeth. In height Mississauga women averaged only five feet, a good eight inches shorter than the men.[4]

Twenty-one in January 1802, Tuhbenahneequay had been born at the time of the great war between the English and the Long Knives, as the Mississaugas called the Americans. During the struggle the

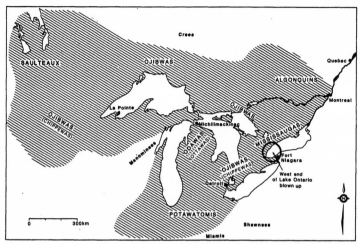

Map 1. The Lands of the Anishinabeg and Related Peoples, about 1800

English had, as the Mississaugas said, given them "very sharp hatchets." The Indians had indeed killed many Americans, but not enough, for Britain had lost the American Revolutionary War.

The first white settlers, the Loyalists, came north as political refugees after England's defeat. Generously, Wahbanosay and the Mississaugas welcomed them and, when asked, made extensive lands available to them. For twenty years afterward the Indians hunted and fished for the white newcomers and furnished them with venison, salmon, ducks, maple sugar, and wild rice. In return the English proved, in the Mississaugas' eyes, an ungrateful people. After having fenced off all the land they needed for growing their crops and enough pastureland for their cattle, they demanded more. The Mississaugas now realized that their English allies wanted the whole north shore of Lake Ontario.

Luckily for Wahbanosay's band, their territory lay in an area the white man initially regarded as undesirable. The swarms of mosquitoes in the summer deterred the Loyalists, as did the hundreds of rattlesnakes and the bears and wolves. Most of the early white settlers, in fact, had bypassed Burlington Bay and continued farther inland to higher, drier, and more easily worked land.[5]

Twenty years after the Loyalists' arrival the Mississaugas kept largely to themselves, but Tuhbenahneequay did know three of the newcomers. The band traded regularly with Richard Beasley, at whose store on Burlington Heights they bought axes, guns, knives, pots, kettles, and other useful articles. They had become dependent on these durable trade goods, though in the not-so-distant past their ancestors had made their own stone axes, bone knives and arrow points, and clay pots. The Ojibwa bands living between Lakes Superior and Huron and Hudson Bay, the inland Indians, still did so.[6]

Tyenteneged, as the Mississaugas pronounced his name—the Mohawk the whites called Joseph Brant—was the second stranger known to Wahbanosay's people. The Mississaugas called his people (several thousand had come north after the defeat of the British in the Revolutionary War) Nahdooways, or "snakes." Much animosity remained between the two Indian groups. Three generations earlier, about 1700, the Ojibwas had defeated the Iroquois in a series of skirmishes on the north shores of Lake Erie and Lake Ontario.[7] But they regarded Brant differently from the rest, for the Mohawk war chief had helped the Mississaugas conduct their affairs with the Indian Department. Having great trust in his honesty and fairness, the Mississaugas elected him one of their chiefs.[8] Brant lived in a large white house at the north end of the Beach, where Burlington Bay emptied into Lake Ontario. To Tuhbenahneequay's firstborn son he had given his own name, Tyenteneged.[9]

A number of Mississaugas had worked with the third newcomer, the surveyor Augustus Jones, who had a farm at "the small stone or gravely place" at the south end of the Beach, the spot the whites called Stoney Creek. From 1787 to 1800 he had surveyed many townships along Lake Ontario's northern shore, as well as Dundas Street, which led westward from York to London, and Yonge Street, which extended from York north to Lake Simcoe. Wahbanosay himself had guided the young American on a number of his journeys into the interior.[10] From his Indian crews, and from Tuhbenahneequay herself, the surveyor had learned to speak Ojibwa.

For fifteen years Augustus Jones had worked with Indians, and he enjoyed their company. He learned Mohawk as well as Ojibwa. Over the years Joseph Brant had become so close a friend that, to be near each other, the two men had built their houses at each end of Burlington Beach.[11] No doubt Brant himself first introduced the surveyor to Sarah Tekarihogen, the young daughter of Henry Tekarihogen, the head chief of the Mohawks. Sarah, then eighteen—less than half Augustus's age—became his wife in an English ceremony in April 1798.

The Mississaugas liked and trusted the surveyor, who involved himself in their world and adapted to their ways. The surveyor's wilderness skills also earned their respect. Unlike most of the "people with hats," as the Ojibwas called whites,[12] Jones had a robust constitution and managed well in the bush—on snowshoes in winter and by canoe in summer. Yet regardless of his abilities Wahbanosay knew that to survive a man needed a partner on the trail—someone to set up and break camp, to repair his moccasins, to make his snowshoes in winter. When his daughter came of age in the mid-1790s Wahbanosay invited the American to take her on his journeys.[13]

When Augustus first lived with Tuhbenahneequay he tried to persuade her to become a Christian and to adopt a settled way of life. The young Mississauga woman refused, arguing that Augustus should live in the Indian way. Unable to change her mind, the white surveyor then married Sarah Tekarihogen, a Christian convert,[14] but his marriage did not solve his emotional dilemma—he still loved Tuhbenahneequay.

For several years Augustus had two wives, living with Sarah when on his farm and with Tuhbenahneequay when in the forest. Tyenteneged, Augustus's first son, later known in English as John Jones, arrived in 1798,[15] the very year of his father's marriage to Sarah Tekarihogen. Tuhbenahneequay's and Augustus's second son, to be known as Peter Jones in English, was born on 1 January 1802, two years after Augustus had given up full-time surveying for farming.

Wahbanosay saw nothing wrong in Augustus's having two wives, for among his people a man could have as many as he could support.

Tuhbenahneequay herself did not object, but she did insist that she keep the two children and raise them as Indians. With their father's approval they, as Peter Jones later wrote, "were left entirely to the care and management of our mother, who, preferring the customs and habits of her nation, taught us the superstitions of her fathers—how to gain the approbation of the Munedoos (or gods), and how to become successful hunters."[16]

Augustus, of course, knew the Bible's injunction against more than one wife. His father, a Welsh emigrant who had settled on the Hudson River in New York, had certainly made it clear to his son that polygyny was not recognized in English law. But Augustus, while away on the frontier, had paid no more attention to Christian practice than had thousands of French or English fur traders before him. Many had simultaneously maintained two relationships—one in a distant settlement and one in the forest. But with the arrival of white women in Upper Canada in the 1780s and 1790s and the beginning of an established settler society along the north shore of Lake Ontario, such freedom vanished.

For all his originality and disregard of white conventions, Augustus valued his social status. The ambitious surveyor, of modest origins in New York, wanted to become a large landholder. Having spent several years of his youth on the vast Colden family estates near Newburgh on the Hudson River, Augustus knew the power and influence land brought. Cadwallader Colden (1688–1776) had served as lieutenant governor of New York, and his sons and grandsons had obtained important posts in New York in the last years of English rule. A letter from Cadwallader Colden II, a Loyalist, had helped Augustus obtain his position as a crown surveyor in Canada in 1787.[17] During his early years in Upper Canada Augustus secured extensive lands at the Head of the Lake, and later he obtained grants from Joseph Brant of lands totaling nearly ten square miles on the Grand River to the west.[18] He also acquired town lots in Newark (Niagara) and York.

Augustus Jones wanted the respect of his fellow white settlers. In his own county of Lincoln the surveyor-farmer served as a militia captain.[19] He also made a great personal sacrifice. Wishing to keep his social position in the white community, Augustus severed his emotional ties with Tuhbenahneequay after their second son's birth.

For the next fourteen years Augustus lived permanently with his Iroquois wife and saw his Mississauga sons only on his trips through Wahbanosay's hunting territory or whenever the band camped on his farm at Stoney Creek. But he did remain interested in their welfare. In September 1805 he requested that Wahbanosay and seven other Mississaugas grant his sons a tract four miles square on the east bank of the Credit River. Joseph Brant and two white friends of Augustus's witnessed the signing of the document.[20] Just in case the Mississaugas ever sold all their lands, he wanted his sons to have their share of their mother's birthright.

Augustus's two sons grew to manhood as members of Wahbanosay's small band of fifty or sixty. Within the band almost everyone was related by blood or by marriage. Among his own people Peter Jones was known as Kahkewaquonaby or Sacred Feathers, the name his grandfather gave him at the naming feast held a few days after birth. For the ceremony Wahbanosay had invited all the members of his winter encampment to his large birchbark wigwam, shaped like a walnut shell with the entrance at one end. When the guests stepped in from the January cold, two fires blazed in the center, the smoke rising through a smoke hole above.[21] As the shadows danced on the ceiling, the men, their wives, and the children took their seats on the fresh pine boughs that covered the frozen ground. At the feast Wahbanosay sang and beat his drum but did not eat. Only at the end of the meal (part of which was offered as a sacrifice) did the chief say his prayer to the thunders, one of the greatest forces in the universe.

In Mississauga society everyone belonged to a clan or totem as well as to a hunting group like Wahbanosay's. The clans took their names from natural objects such as trees, birds, animals, or fishes. The totems among the Mississaugas included Eagle, Reindeer, Otter, Bear, Buffalo, Beaver, Catfish, Pike, Birchbark, White Oak Tree, and Bear's Liver. Each Mississauga child inherited the clan designation of his or her father. The members of a totem group treated each other as relatives, and the Mississaugas considered it unlawful for those with the same totem to marry, even if one of them belonged to a distant band.[22]

The individual clans owned a number of names. Since Wahbanosay belonged to the Eagle totem, for instance, his family possessed several designations of the thunders or thunderbirds, which took the form of gigantic eagles that fed on monster snakes. Everyone had heard the flapping of its wings and tail, which caused great rumbling or thunder in the skies, and had seen his fire arrows, the lightning, which killed the serpents and carried them to the skies. The name Wahbanosay chose for his grandson had a special meaning, since it had been borne by one of his sons who had died at the age of seven.[23]

Wahbanosay took his grandson, wrapped in soft moss and skins, on his lap and slowly pronounced his name, "Kah-ke-wa-quo-na-by." Placing several eagle feathers in his tiny hands, he dedicated the child to the thunderbird. The chief also presented the baby with several sacred objects—a wooden war club symbolizing the thunders' power and a miniature birchbark canoe, which would bring him success in crossing the waters—an appropriate gift for Sacred Feathers, who as an adult crossed the North Atlantic six times.

Sacred Feathers, at first strapped to a cradle board and carried on Tuhbenahneequay's back or securely fastened in a birchbark canoe, followed his people's annual cycle.

The Mississaugas divided the year into four seasons and twelve moons.[24] The hardest period was winter or *peboon*, the season of freezing weather. The winter hunting and trapping season extended from November to March. When the days once again became longer and brighter, relatives and friends reunited at the sugar bush to tap the maple trees and boil the sap. They termed spring *seegwun*, the sap season. After their sugar making many of the families visited the trading post and then traveled to the Credit River for the spring salmon run. About the first of May[25] they held their religious festivals, dances, and games, after which the community broke up into smaller bands and Wahbanosay's group returned to their camp on Burlington Bay. When, as the Iroquois said, the white oak leaves had reached the size of a red squirrel's foot,[26] the women planted corn. During summer, or *neebin*, the abundant season, they collected many types of berries. Toward the end of summer the women harvested their corn at the Head of the Lake, and families gathered the large quantities of wild rice growing in the shallow lakes and slow streams. With the beginning of fall or *tuhgwuhgin*, the fading season, many of the Mississaugas at the western end of Lake Ontario went by canoe to the Credit River for the fall salmon run. The Credit River encampment again numbered in the hundreds. In the late autumn the Mississaugas again traveled into the interior to their family hunting grounds.

On the forest trails Wahbanosay and the warriors walked first, always on the lookout for game and for hostile Indians. The women came next, carrying the birchbark covering for the wigwam and the skins used to close the entrance. In the winter they carried everything on their backs. Individual families, or perhaps a group of two or three families, hunted and trapped together. Close together they set up their warm wigwams, snugly chinked with moss and banked outside with cedar boughs. With the arrival of spring the families again returned to the sugar bush and then brought in their furs to trader Beasley's store on their way to the Credit River.

Shortly before Sacred Feathers's birth Augustus had begun farming full time at the Head of the Lake, and Tuhbenahneequay saw him only when the band camped in the woods on his farm in the summer. Their relationship having ended, she had married by tribal custom Mesquacosy, a Mississauga warrior. She had a baby girl, Wechekewe-kapawiqua, in 1807; another boy, Pemikishigon, followed about 1811; another daughter, Sakagiwequa, in 1814; and another son, Wahbunoo, in 1817.[27]

Tuhbenahneequay spent much time instructing her children on how they must behave. She never struck them, patiently teaching them, that they must exercise self-control and never become upset or lose their tempers. When frightened they must keep still, for the enemy could learn their location from just one cry.[28] Like all Ojibwa parents, Tuhbenahneequay gave her children great freedom to romp, to investigate things, to ask for whatever they wanted. Punishment hardly ever occurred. Hardihood, self-reliance, and an absence of fear were cultivated.

As soon as the children understood the spoken word, they heard about the lives and deeds of their forefathers. The elders told their tales during the long winter evenings, for once snow fell the spirits slept and would not be upset when people spoke about them.[29] Nearly every winter evening grandparents and older relatives entertained them, telling them how the Ojibwas originated, how the totems came about, and how the world was made.

Nanahbozhoo, the superbeing, the spirit who gave the earth its present form, created the world. In the beginning, Wahbanosay or one of his wives would begin, there was an enormous flood. With great difficulty Nanahbozhoo managed to save many of the birds and animals, which he placed on a raft he had hastily constructed.[30]

What could he do now? Nanahbozhoo thought deeply for a long time. To form a new world he must obtain a small amount of earth from which to make new land. Finally he spoke to the birds and the animals. The loon caught its food by diving, and it could stay underwater for a long time. Nanahbozhoo asked the bird to swim to the bottom and grab a handful of earth. It vanished for what seemed an eternity. Surely if any of the diving birds could reach the bottom the loon, the strongest, would succeed. But it finally surfaced dead. Next he sent the otter, known for diving to great depths, but it too failed. The beaver also drowned. It seemed a hopeless task, for the water was so deep that no living creature could reach the bottom. After restoring the loon, the otter, and the beaver to life, Nanahbozhoo, in desperation, called upon an animal who lacked the strength of the others, the lowly muskrat. It was gone the longest of all, and its lifeless body eventually floated to the surface.

Nanahbozhoo pulled the body onto the raft. Despondently he examined the muskrat, then danced with joy, for he found soil tightly clutched in each of its paws and its mouth. With the mud the muskrat brought Nanahbozhoo fashioned his new world. He first rubbed the soil with his hands until it because fine dust. Strewing the dust on the waters, he blew upon it until it grew. Very quickly the new ground reached beyond the horizon, and a huge island sat in the middle of the water. The Earth Maker restored the muskrat to life, and in gratitude he promised that his best diver would never become extinct but would multiply and grow, which explains why muskrats are so plentiful today.

To conclude his work Nanahbozhoo then made a journey across the great island he had made. As he traveled, the superbeing created the various tribes of Indians and placed them in different parts of the earth, giving them various religions, customs, and manners. He taught them to hunt, to use medicinal plants, and to grow the sacred plant tobacco, through whose smoke the Indians could communicate with the spirits. Nanahbozhoo then withdrew to sit at the North Pole overlooking all the activities of the human beings he had placed on earth. Almost every fall one sees his signal. Just before he dozes off for his winter sleep, the Earth Maker fills his great pipe and smokes for several days. The smoke arising from his pipe produces Indian summer.

As soon as children could understand such things, parents, grandparents, and elders taught them about the Great Spirit, who had sent Nanahbozhoo as his agent to teach his laws about how one must live on the great island. Responsible for the origin of all life, the Creator was essential for the Indians' survival. Over campfires, in wigwams, on forest trails, the children learned of the Supreme Being and his law: to share with fellow human beings all kinds of food and any game killed; to respect the long dwellers on the Great Island, the elderly men and women, especially the great teachers who had fasted and received dreams and visions; never to interrupt when the aged were talking; never to quarrel or fight among themselves or steal from one another.

The elders also spoke of the Great Spirit's antithesis, the Evil Spirit, who had the power to injure anyone who offended him. To avoid his wrath, the wise offered sacrifices to protect their health and their good luck in hunting. For example, before drinking the Indians always offered the Evil Spirit whiskey. After all had received their small draughts the men poured some alcohol on the ground, giving the devil his share. If it soaked in quickly, they knew the Evil Spirit had accepted their offering.[31]

The Indians could not rely for direct protection on the Great Spirit, because his responsibilities were already too all-encompassing. The Creator, as Sacred Feathers later wrote, could not "concern Himself with the follies of poor earthly beings, whose existence lasts only as it were for a day." They could, however, address their problems to the Great Spirit's intermediaries, the lesser spirits.[32]

Because the Ojibwas lived close to nature, they did not envisage any great chasm separating them from the rest of creation. Everything around them was alive and had power.[33] Humans had to stay on good terms with all objects, for they had the supernatural power to punish anyone who wasted them. The Mississauga elders, for instance, avoided cutting down living trees to save them from pain. When green trees were cut, the elders told Sacred Feathers, you could hear them wailing from the ax's blows.[34]

The Mississaugas believed that any remarkable physical feature on the landscape contained particularly powerful spirits. An unusual rock by a riverside, a strangely twisted tree, a waterfall, or an unusually fast river possessed spirit power. The Indians approached waterfalls in particular timidly, leaving sacred tobacco on a rock nearby as an offering. Before the great falls of Niagara the Mississaugas walked the most respectfully of all, for the master of all the other waterfalls lived there.[35]

Evidence of powerful spirits surrounded the Mississaugas. At the Head of the Lake the Indians frequently heard sounds like explosions or the shooting of a great gun. The elders told Sacred Feathers that the spirits living in the escarpment's caverns immediately west of Burlington Bay caused the volleys by blowing and breathing. The deep, awful sound of the spirit of the falls of Niagara could be heard at times for sixty kilometers, shaking the air and the earth itself. At the Credit River the Indians often heard the water god (who lived at the foot of a high hill in a deep hole, three kilometers from the river's mouth) singing and beating his drum.[36]

Naturally Wahbanosay's people most revered those forces believed to have the greatest power, such as the sun and the moon. Every evening at sunset the old men thanked the sun for the blessing of heat and light during the day. Every morning at the sun's rising they chanted hymns of praise to welcome its return. Visible eclipses of the sun caused panic. Believing that the sun was dying, the Mississaugas stuck embers upon the points of their arrows and shot them upward hoping to rekindle it, shooting until it reappeared. Similarly, they held in high esteem the moon—or "night sun"[37]— and the stars that guided them in darkness. Wahbanosay and the elders warned Sacred Feathers never to point at the moon, for the moon would consider it a great insult and instantly bite off his finger.[38]

The Mississaugas knew that spirits surrounded them. The Mamagwasewug or elves were small friendly beings who might play tricks on humans but never harmed them. Although invisible, the little creatures could show themselves. Many elders had talked to these strange beings, who stood about a meter high. Walking erect, they had human form but their faces were covered with short hair. The elves loved shooting off guns they had stolen from the Indians or taken from graves. Often the Indians heard them in a large pond near Burlington Bay. Here some elders had once seen them paddling a stone canoe, but when they gave chase they quickly crossed over to a high bank and disappeared. After they vanished nothing could be heard but a distant rumbling. Another tribe of Mamagwasewug lived, the old people said, on the east bank of the Credit River, nearly two kilometers from the lake. The little people loved scarlet cloth and bright prints, and if an Indian could give them these they promised a long life or success in hunting.[39]

Unlike the friendly Mamagwasewug, the Indians feared the Waindegoos, the most dreaded of all the supernatural beings. As a boy Sacred Feathers learned of these monsters, tall as pine trees and as powerful as the spirits themselves. The terrifying giants in their travels pulled down and pushed aside dense forests as a man would part tall grass. Invulnerable to arrows or bullets, in winter the monsters devoured Indians. Persons known to have eaten human flesh were also called Waindegoos.[40]

Underwater monsters were an ever-present menace. These giant serpents had an awful power, particularly in the Great Lakes. Once Sacred Feathers witnessed the sacrifice of a black dog to the water serpent, the dog being the greatest sacrifice of all.[41] Before leaving for York (present-day Toronto) by canoe the Mississaugas tied a large stone around the dog's neck and threw it into Lake Ontario, with the prayer that the water monster would grant the Indians smooth water and fair winds.[42]

The world was full of perils for the unwary. The Indians believed that the animals they killed for food and skins had given up their lives to permit people to live. To show their respect for this exchange of lives, the Ojibwas had a large number of rituals for butchering game and for disposing of bones and uneaten portions. An unsuccessful hunter, believing he had neglected some duty and thus raised the wrath of the master animal that ruled the deer, the bear, or the beaver, devoted the first game he took to hosting a religious feast, to which he invited friends and relatives. Before he prepared his feast, he often sang and beat his drum all night to make amends for neglecting his duty to the spirit.[43]

The Mississaugas considered all dreams important, for during sleep the soul was freed from the body and could communicate with the spirits. Dreams were remembered and interpreted. While Sacred Feathers was still very young the band elders encouraged him to go without food or water for days at a time. The Mississaugas fasted, one of them once explained, so that "the Great Spirit and his agents may reveal themselves to us while suffering with hunger and thirst. It is also done to enable us to travel many days without food and water in time of trouble or war."[44]

The elders told Sacred Feathers many stories of those who had persevered and had communicated with the spirit world. Some had gained immortality, like the group of young people who fasted so long they became skeletons. Through their perseverence in their vision quest, they had won the blessings and aid of the spirits, who whisked them into the air, giving them the magic power to go wherever they wished. The Indians called them the Pahgak or flying skeletons.[45] Once while out hunting, Old Peter told Sacred Feathers that he heard in the distance the shouts of a Pahgak. The boy shivered at the thought of being so near such a powerful spirit.[46]

The elders constantly reminded Sacred Feathers of the need to make a vision quest—to obtain, through fasting, a guardian spirit to guide and protect them through life. Animals, birds, and fish could speak with them and, in a dream or vision, give their power. To stress its importance the elders told stories like the following: Years ago, hostile Indians had detected a Mississauga war party. Although the Mississaugas paddled with all their might, their enemies still gained on them. At this point each warrior called on his guardian spirit. The protector of one man, a sturgeon, gave the canoe its own speed, leaving the enemies' canoes far behind. But the short-winded fish soon tired, allowing the enemy to advance rapidly. The other Mississauga warriors—with the exception of one young man, who from his unkempt and ragged appearance they considered a complete fool—called upon their protectors. For a time these appeals kept them ahead, but at length they had exhausted the strength of all their guardian spirits.

At this critical moment the foolish-looking young man asked for his medicine bag, which in their flight he had taken off his hip and misplaced in the canoe. "Where is my medicine bag?" The others could not understand him. "Keep paddling. Be quiet. Don't trouble us." But he persisted. "Where is my medicine bag?" One of the warriors, seeing it on the floor of the canoe, picked it up and roughly threw it at him. Grabbing the bag, the young man hastily put in his hand and pulled out an old pouch made of the skin of a duck. When he touched the water with the pouch, the canoe instantly outdistanced the enemy canoes. The young man then took up his pouch, wrung out the water, and replaced it in his bag. He told the others, now suddenly attentive, that in a fast he had dreamed of this bird, and true to his vision, it had delivered him. The elders concluded: "The old warriors were astonished at the power of the young man, whom they had looked upon as almost an idiot, and were taught by him a lesson, never to form a mean opinion of any person from their outward appearance."[47]

At about the age of ten, Sacred Feathers went on his first vision quest. Rising before dawn, he pounded a piece of charcoal into powder and blackened his face to indicate his purpose. During the fast he did not drink or eat, and only toward sunset did he wash his face and eat a little of the broth prepared for him. The young boy stayed in the forest alone for several days hoping to have a vision, the elders having instructed him to notice every remarkable dream, event, or sound. To have a vision of a gray-headed old man promised a long life; seeing a pretty woman meant he would be blessed with more than one wife. To dream of sharp-pointed weapons or anything that protected against the arrow, tomahawk, or bullet gave invincibility in battle. If he were blessed, an animal, bird, or fish might talk to him, becoming his spiritual helper for the rest of his life. Songs which came to men and women in dreams made the power granted much stronger and could be used in healing the sick and in any serious undertaking.[48] Yet, though he went on many vision quests, Sacred Feathers never had any vision or dream.[49]

The boy learned from his elders how to hunt and fish. He was apprenticed to men like Old Peter, accompanying them on their traplines and in the hunt. The hunters taught him what terrain certain animals frequented, the times of day they fed, and when and where they slept. The young boy listened and observed until he could read the smallest sign on the ground or in the bushes—a trace of mud on a stone, a leaf turned back, a broken blade of grass. He knew by the thickness on the breasts of ducks and by the fur of his beaver skins whether the coming winter would be severe or mild. By noting when the beavers repaired their dams and if the muskrats build their houses earlier than usual, he could predict whether the cold would set in early.[50] On the trail Sacred Feathers became familiar with the edible berries, mushrooms, roots, and even bark. During the summer he learned many survival skills. Sacred Feathers paddled a canoe almost as soon as he could walk. The young Indian also became expert at spearing fish and frequently brought home a large supply. Like other boys his age, he was taught to swim and thought nothing of crossing a river or lake two kilometers wide.[51]

Sacred Feathers, a bright, gifted boy, mastered his lessons quickly. He began his training for the hunt by using a bow and arrow. He and his playmates shot at marks or at birds and squirrels, and they soon become good marksmen. When he brought home the first game he had killed, Tuhbenahneequay and the elders made a feast in his honor, giving thanks to the Great Spirit for his success.[52]

Once he had satisfied his elders that he could stalk and kill large game, they gave him his first gun.[53] The warriors also invited him to join a large hunting party that traveled over 150 kilometers into the Genesee River country near present-day Rochester, New York. Their medicine was good, for they shot a number of bears. In honor of the master spirit that ruled the bear, the party held a bear-oil feast—each man drank a quarter of a liter of the oil.[54]

Sacred Feathers had an enjoyable childhood growing up at the Head of the Lake in the decade before the War of 1812. Years later he wrote: "Perhaps I may be partial in my judgement, as it was on the romantic Burlington Heights I first drew my breath, and, in my youthful days, was accustomed to traverse the shores of its clear waters in the light birchbark canoe; here I ranged the forest, and shot many a partridge, squirrel, and pigeon, where now may be seen the fine brick or stone house, and the productive farm of white man."[55] He grew up in the last decade of freedom for the Indians at the head of Lake Ontario, a brave and self-reliant Indian boy, shaped by the teachings of his mother and her people. On the eve of the War of 1812 Sacred Feathers, a proud Mississauga, identified only with them. And yet in two respects he differed from the others. First, unlike many of the other teenage boys, he had never had a vision in his fasts and had no guardian spirit. Second, though he belonged to the Eagle totem, his membership in the clan came through his mother, not his father as was the ancient custom. At least one band member would remember him three-quarters of a century later as "a half white man."[56]

The Mississauga Indians

In their language, Wahbanosay and his band called themselves "Anishinabe," in its plural form "Anishinabeg"—"human beings" or, to adapt a second meaning of the word, "men par excellence." The Anishinabeg belonged to the Algonquian linguistic family, which extended far beyond the Great Lakes—eastward to the Atlantic Seaboard and westward to the Rocky Mountains. Around the Great Lakes the Europeans designated four groups among the Anishinabegs in the nineteenth century: Ojibwas or Chippewas; Ottawas or Odawas; Algonquins or Algonkins; and Potawatomis. Each could understand the others without much difficulty, though there were minor differences in pronunciation and grammar from place to place.[1] In the early nineteenth century the Ojibwas lived around Lake Superior, on the north shore of Lake Huron, and throughout southern Upper Canada; the Ottawas lived in present-day northern Michigan, near Detroit, in the Maumee valley of northwestern Ohio, and on Manitoulin Island; the Algonquins lived in the Ottawa valley; and the Potawatomis inhabited the eastern shore of Lake Michigan.

The Great Lakes Algonquians in present-day Ontario relied almost exclusively on hunting and fishing and planted very little. To the southeast of these Algonquian tribes in the early seventeenth century lived members of the area's other major language group, the Iroquoians, which included the Huron Confederacy, the Hurons' trading partners the Petuns, and the Five Nations or Iroquois Con-

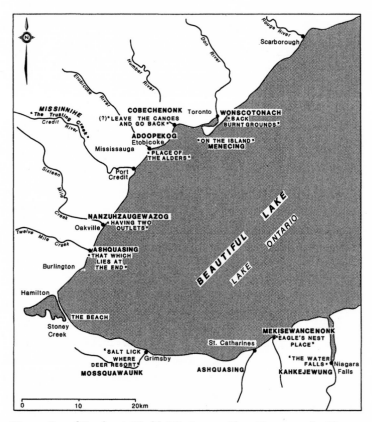

Map 2. Sacred Feathers's World: Mississauga Place-Names at the Western
End of Lake Ontario

federacy. Immediately west of the Five Nations, below Lake Erie,
lived the Eries. The group of allied tribes, called the Neutrals by the
French, lived between the Hurons and the Iroquois. The Iroquoians'
territories in the early seventeenth century corresponded with the
good agricultural land, the Hurons and Petuns dwelling on the
southern shore of the Georgian Bay and the Five Nations—Mohawks, Oneidas, Onondagas, Cayugas, and Senecas—across Lake
Ontario in what is now northern New York State.[2] A semisedentary

people, the Iroquoians relied heavily on horticulture for their survival as well as on hunting and fishing.

Although the tribes shared the same culture and spoke similar tongues, the Europeans on their arrival found the Hurons and Iroquois at war with each other. Eventually the Five Nations or Iroquois dispersed the Huron Confederacy in 1649–50 and then attacked the Petuns, the Neutrals, the Eries, and the Hurons' allies the Great Lakes Algonquians.[3] For the next forty years the Five Nations used present-day southern Ontario to secure furs to trade with the Dutch, then with the English. They also traded for furs with the northern Algonquians. To serve as bases for their own trapping and for the northern trade, they established a series of settlements along the north shore of Lake Ontario.

In the mid-1690s their fortunes changed. Weakened by disease and by mounting casualties from their skirmishes with the French, the Iroquois were no longer the formidable foes of half a century before. The Anishinabeg saw their opportunity and took the offensive, migrating southward from Lake Superior and the north shore of Lake Huron. About 1700 they pushed the Iroquois out of present-day southern Ontario.[4] The warfare was so bloody that even in Sacred Feathers's boyhood a smoldering hatred still existed between the two Indian groups. Many of his band believed that the Iroquois "were lurking about for the purpose of killing some of the Ojebways." The warriors cautiously kept up a strict evening watch to fend off any surprise attack.[5]

By coming south the Algonquians acquired rich new hunting and fishing grounds, and many obtained European names. Most frequently, in English, all the newcomers in the area bounded by Lakes Ontario, Erie, and Huron were termed Chippewas or Ojibwas. The whites also used another name for the Ojibwas on the north shore of Lake Ontario: Mississaugas. In 1640 the Jesuit fathers had first recorded the term *oumisagai*, or Mississaugas, as the name of an Algonquian band near the Mississagi River on the northwestern shore of Lake Huron.[6] The French and later the English, for unknown reasons, applied this name to all the Algonquians settling on the north shore of Lake Ontario. Only a tiny fraction of these Indians could have been members of the actual Mississauga band, but once recorded in the Europeans' documents, the name became the dominant one.

The term Mississauga perplexed the Algonquians, or Ojibwas, on the north shore of Lake Ontario, who knew themselves as Anishinabeg. The Ojibwas at the eastern end of Lake Ontario near the Bay of Quinte and present-day Kingston believed the name came from the many rivers, the Moira, Trent, and Gananoque, that flowed through their hunting territories into Lake Ontario. *Minzazahgeeg,* after all, meant people living where there are many mouths of rivers.[7] But at the western end of the lake a different theory prevailed. About one-quarter of the western Mississaugas belonged to the Eagle clan or totem, pronounced in their dialect (which differed slightly from the Ojibwa spoken among the Mississaugas to the east)[8] Ma-se-sau-gee. Wahbanosay's band felt that the Europeans derived their name from their dominant totem.[9]

Sacred Feathers grew up fully aware of the previous occupants of the northwestern shore of Lake Ontario, since several Iroquoian place-names remained. Niagara, in Mohawk Oh-nya-ka-ra ("on or at the neck"—the neck joining the head, Lake Erie, to the body, Lake Ontario), was one. The great lake on whose shores the Ojibwas had settled also retained its Iroquoian name, Ontario, "beautiful great lake." The area for some kilometers around the foot of the important portage remained Toronto, an Iroquoian word the Mississaugas took to mean "looming of trees."[10] The Mississaugas had their own name for the long peninsula extending out from Toronto's shoreline—Menecing, "on the island."

The Mississaugas, who traveled a great deal by water, named rivers and lakes for their physical appearance. To the west lay the Askahneseebe, "horn river," known to the whites as the Thames, whose shape resembled the antlers of a deer. Lake Erie became Wahbeshkegoo Kechegahme, "the white water lake," from its color contrast with the green and blue waters of the upper Great Lakes. Into Lake Erie flowed the Pesshinneguning, "the one that washes the timber down and drives away the grass weeds," or Grand River. As the annual flooding cleared away the swamp grass, the Indians planted spring corn here on the river flats. Thirty kilometers east of Burlington Bay flowed the Missinnihe, "trusting creek," where the white traders came annually and gave them "credit" for the following year.[11] Because they held the Credit River "in reverential estimation as the favorite resort of their ancestors,"[12] the Mississauga bands at the western end of the lake became known collectively as the Credit River Indians.

Beyond the Credit lay the Adoopekog, "place of the black alder," a word still recognizable in Etobicoke. Just past the Adoopekog, and the river the English would call the Humber, one came to Menecing, the long peninsula, now the Toronto Islands, which formed a deep harbor. On a clear day, at Menecing you could see spray rising like a cloud from Kahkejewung, "the water falls," or Niagara Falls, over sixty kilometers directly across the lake. The Mississaugas brought their sick to the peninsula to recover in its healthful atmosphere.[13]

The boundary of the Credit River Indians' tribal hunting territory extended eastward from Long Point on Lake Erie along the shore of the lake to the Niagara River, down the river to Lake Ontario, and then northward along the lakeshore to the Rouge River just beyond Menecing. It extended in the interior to the ridges dividing Lake Ontario from Lake Simcoe, then along the dividing ridges to the headwaters of the Thames, then southward to Long Point, the place of beginning.[14]

The Mississaugas became known for their ability to transmit information. Living as they did at the foot of the ancient Toronto Carrying Place, the portage between Lake Ontario and Lake Simcoe, they received many Indian and French visitors. This shortcut between Lake Ontario and the Georgian Bay led in the early eighteenth century to Michilimackinac, the center of the rich northern fur trade of the upper Great Lakes. On one wampum belt the symbol for the Mississauga band at the western end of Lake Ontario is an eagle perched on a pine tree at the Credit River. The symbol represented the band's "*watching* and *swiftness* in carrying messages."[15]

During Sacred Feathers's youth messengers kept the Credit River Indians in contact with the neighboring Anishinabeg bands. The runners followed the ridges, where the forest was not so thick. These men, trim and fit, hardened by life in the outdoors, easily covered eighty kilometers in a day, the distance from Toronto to Niagara. They could travel between Toronto and Georgian Bay in four days in winter and three in summer. The Indians reached Detroit from Niagara in eight days and considered this a short trip.[16] Nearly a century earlier adventuresome Anishinabeg warriors had journeyed fifteen hundred kilometers from the north shore of Lake Ontario to join raiding parties against the Cherokees living in the southern Alleghenies.[17]

The Mississaugas traded furs with the French at the mouths of the Humber, the Credit, and Niagara in the early eighteenth century. A few French words entered the Ojibwa vocabulary, such as an expression that Sacred Feathers himself used, *boozhoo, boozhoo,* the Ojibwa version of *bonjour,* "good day."[18] In the 1720s French posts on Lake Ontario offered the Mississaugas everything from buttons, shirts, and ribbons to combs, knives, looking glasses, and axes.[19] The Mississaugas, living so near to French posts, became close allies. They fought in Montcalm's army in the late 1750s during the final struggle between France and England for North America.[20]

With the withdrawal of the French in 1760 the Mississaugas made a new alliance with the English. Half a century later the elders explained to Sacred Feathers what they had done: "when the French came, they [the Mississaugas and the French] bound their hands together with an *iron chain;* but when the English came, they broke asunder that chain, which had already become rusty, and then their great Father, the King of England, bound their hands together with a silver *chain,* which he promised should never rust and never be broken."[21]

During Sacred Feathers's boyhood the elders remembered most vividly the American Revolutionary War. Faithful to the British cause, men of his grandfather's generation had joined the Ojibwas of

Lake Superior, the Odawas or Ottawas around Detroit and Michilimackinac, and the Algonquins of the Ottawa valley in British raiding parties. Wabakinine, the head chief of the Credit River Mississaugas, had himself traveled to Niagara, to Detroit, and to Michilimackinac to convince other Anishinabeg chiefs to ally with the
British, and he had joined war parties against the Americans.[22] From
the Delawares (Lenni Lenapes), Shawnees, and other southern Algonquian tribes the Mississaugas knew of the American settlers'
constant encroachments on Indian lands. They too had always respected Sir William Johnson, the northern superintendent of Indian
affairs, and after his death in 1774 they attended the councils of his
successors: his nephew Guy Johnson (to 1782) and then Sir William's son Sir John Johnson. At Fort Oswego on the south shore of
Lake Ontario, the English officers had promised them that the king's
"rum was as plenty as the water in Lake Ontario: that his men were
as numerous as the sands upon the lakeshore:—and that the Indians, if they would assist in the war, and persevere in their friendship to the king, till it were closed, should never want for money or
goods."[23]

Wahbanosay and the other Mississauga warriors had appreciated
the constant supply of iron axes with fine cutting edges, the durable
iron kettles, the wool clothing (which, unlike leather, did not shrink
when wet), and most important of all, guns—weapons that could
shoot farther and with greater power than bows.[24] During the American Revolution the Mississaugas' reliance on European trade goods
increased dramatically. This same dependency had contributed to
their decision to allow their British allies to settle among them.

After the Crown's defeat, Britain desperately needed land to give
to the Loyalists, those Americans and Iroquois who had fought on its
side and could no longer stay in the new independent republic. To
obtain land on the north shore of Lake Ontario they had to strike a
deal with the Mississaugas. Twenty years earlier, in 1763, the British
government (then involved in suppressing Chief Pontiac's rebellion
around Detroit) had officially recognized the Great Lakes Indians'
title to their hunting grounds. The Royal Proclamation of 1763 had

become the Magna Carta of Indian rights in British North America, immediately prohibiting the purchase of Indian lands by private individuals. Before any further settlement could legally proceed, Indian land must first be surrendered to the Crown. Britain, anxious to keep her Indian alliances intact in the event of another North American war, continued to apply the royal proclamation north of the Great Lakes.[25] When approached, the Mississaugas agreed to the land purchases, mainly because they wanted the flow of gifts from the British to continue.

Another reason for the Indian's openness lay in their misunderstanding of the surrender's meaning. There was nothing in the Mississaugas' traditions or experience that enabled them even to imagine the private ownership of land and water by one person. Although a family could use a certain area as its hunting and trapping ground, that land still belonged to every other band member, as much as to the supernatural beings and the natural world (plants, birds, animals). The Mississaugas had always regarded the presents the French supplied as a form of rent for the use of the land where the French posts stood and as a fee for the right to travel over their country. The Indians' behavior after making the agreements demonstrates that they continued to believe they had granted the English only tenant status, the right to use the land during good behavior.[26] The Mississaugas understood that they had retained the right to "encamp and fish where we pleased"[27] throughout their territory.

A third reason helps explain the Indians' willingness to allow their allies to use much of their hunting grounds. Weakly organized, the bands on the north shore of Lake Ontario had a small population, numbering in the 1780s only about two hundred warriors. Scattered among a dozen or so small bands, their population was spread out along roughly five hundred kilometers of lakefront. Although the one thousand Mississaugas[28] retained contact with their Anishinabe kinspeople on Lake Huron and to the immediate west on the Thames River, they did not hold regular councils with them. Unlike the Iroquois Confederacy or Six Nations (the Five had become the Six Nations when the Tuscaroras, a southern Iroquois group from the Carolinas, joined about 1722), they lacked a league council of chiefs. Weakly organized, dependent on European trade goods, and seeking an advantage for themselves, the Mississaugas agreed to the land purchases—whose wording the elders soon learned they had not understood.

The first purchase with the Mississaugas occurred during the American Revolution, shortly after the first white Loyalist refugees arrived at Niagara early in 1781. Guy Johnson invited Wabakinine and the leading Mississauga chiefs and warriors to Fort Niagara. In return for "three hundred suits of Clothing" the Crown gained a corridor of land approximately six kilometers (four miles) wide on the west bank of the Niagara River. Johnson reported to Governor Haldimand that the Mississaugas were "well satisfied," as indeed they were—game had been very scarce the previous winter and they needed help.[29]

The next surrender took place two years later at the eastern end of the Lake. Captain William Crawford, a Loyalist officer who had accompanied the Mississaugas on several raiding parties during the Revolutionary War, obtained all the lands from the Toniata River, a tributary of the St. Lawrence below Gananoque, to a river in the Bay of Quinte "within Eight Leagues of the Bottom of Said Bay." The purchase, for which no deed survives, apparently extended back from Lake Ontario "as far as a man can Travel in a Day." For this vast tract, with its loosely described northern boundary, the Indian leaders asked for and obtained clothing for all members of their bands, guns for those without them, powder and ammunition for their winter's hunting, and "as much coarse Red Cloth as will make about a Dozen Coats and as many Laced Hats."[30]

More purchases followed, each of which confirms that the Mississaugas believed they were granting only the use of the land. Once the British promised presents "as long as the sun shall shine, the waters flow, and grass grows,"[31] the Indians allowed them the use of as much land as they needed. Apparently at some point during the summer of 1784—again no deed or indenture survives—the Mississaugas at the eastern end of the lake made a second agreement with

Captain Crawford. The government understood that it was obtaining all the land on and above the Bay of Quinte, to run "northerly as far as it may please Government to assign."[32] It could set whatever boundary it desired.

Initially both the Mississaugas and the British felt they had gained from the agreements. The Mississaugas believed they had made a series of useful and profitable rental agreements for the use of their land, in return for gifts and presents in perpetuity. The British, in contrast, understood that they had extinguished the native title to the land and that the Crown had obtained full proprietary rights.

More agreements followed in the mid-1780s. In 1784 Wabakinine and the Credit River Mississaugas yielded the Niagara peninsula— roughly all the land from Burlington Bay to the headwaters of the Grand River and then south to Long Point on Lake Erie.[33] The British in 1787 and 1788 purchased all of the central portion of the Mississaugas' remaining lands along Lake Ontario's shoreline, from the Etobicoke Creek, just west of Toronto, to the head of the Bay of Quinte.[34] These agreements in 1787 and 1788 were as vague as ever, opening up the land behind the lake, in the words of one white witness, "as far back as a man could walk or go on foot in a day"; or in the Indians' understanding, as far back as a gunshot fired on the lakeshore could be heard in the interior.[35]

In the 1790s the Mississaugas realized their British allies' interpretations of the agreements. The Indians believed the British had misled them. Initially they had imagined that, at most, the British would establish a few settlements along the lake. In reality, however, roughly five thousand had reached the north shore of Lake Ontario in 1783–84, and more continued to arrive. By 1791 the whites numbered nearly 20,000. In the year of Sacred Feathers's birth, 1802, settlement extended for nearly twenty kilometers around the Bay of Quinte. It formed a narrow strip along the Lake Ontario shoreline from the Bay of Quinte to York, where farms extended twenty-five kilometers up Yonge Street. The white settlers now occupied all the narrow strip of good land below the escarpment around the Niagara peninsula, and even partway up the Lake Erie shore, where settlement had begun in the early 1790s.[36]

The Indians had expected the white settlers to treat them as their benefactors, but instead the newcomers erected fences and denied the Indians the right to cross their farms. Moreover, the Indian Department did little to protect the Indians on the lands they had strictly reserved for themselves: namely, their camping spots along the lake, their burial grounds, and their fisheries between the Head of the Lake and Toronto.[37] In 1805 Chief Golden Eagle, speaking for Wahbanosay and the other Mississauga chiefs of the Credit River band, scolded the officers of the Indian Department:

while Colonel Butler was our Father we were told our Father the King wanted some Land for his people it was some time before we sold it, but when we found it was wanted by the King to settle his people on it, whom we were told would be of great use to us, we granted it accordingly. Father—we have not found this so, as the inhabitants drive us away instead of helping us, and we want to know why we are served in that manner. . . . Colonel Butler told us the Farmers would help us, but instead of doing so when we encamp on the shore they drive us off & shoot our Dogs and never give us any assistance as was promised to our old Chiefs.[38]

A generation after the initial surrenders the Mississaugas resented the loss of their lands. During Sacred Feathers's youth he learned from the tribal elders that when the English came:

Our fathers held out to them the hand of friendship. The strangers then asked for a small piece of land on which they might pitch their tents; the request was cheerfully granted. By and by they begged for more, and more was given them. In this way they had continued to ask, or have obtained by force or fraud, the fairest portions of our territory.[39]

Friction had reached its peak during the 1790s, the most serious racial incident occurring just six years before Sacred Feathers's birth—the murder of Wabakinine, the head chief of all the Mississaugas at the western end of Lake Ontario, and of his wife.[40] In mid-August 1796 Wabakinine had left the Credit River to sell salmon. The chief, his sister, and his wife camped at York, as the English now called Toronto, on the waterfront opposite Berry's tavern. The rest of the band had camped on the peninsula.[41] Early in the evening a queen's ranger had offered Wabakinine's sister a dollar and some rum to sleep with him. Just before midnight the soldier, accompanied by two white settlers, came for her. Seeing the white men pull the chief's sister out from her resting spot under a canoe, Wabakinine's wife shook her husband to awaken him. Half asleep and half drunk, the big, muscular Indian staggered from under his canoe and in the darkness lunged awkwardly at the white men. The soldier grabbed a rock and repeatedly struck the Indian. Not yet finished, he kicked him in the chest and left him lying senseless on the ground. The men now seized Wabakinine's wife and viciously beat her. When the other Indians heard the wailing they rushed over from the peninsula, but the white men had left. Hurriedly they took the women and the chief to their campground, and early the next morning they left by canoe, returning to the Credit. The chief died that same day from his injuries, and his widow followed a day or so later.

The death of Wabakinine and his wife almost caused an Indian uprising in Upper Canada.[42] When the administrator, Peter Russell, wrote Governor Simcoe on 31 December 1796 about the trial of the murderer and his acquittal for "want of evidence" (the Indians, though invited, had not attended the trial to give evidence—yet another example of their lack of understanding of British law), he ominously added that the tribes in the rear of York must be appeased before they began to "harass the back settlements."[43]

Only 240 white settlers lived at York, and only 435 lived in the neighboring townships of York, Scarborough, and Etobicoke. True, large white settlements existed in the Bay of Quinte and Niagara regions, but York remained cut off from them in winter. The threat was real. York's garrison consisted of only 135 men, with another 25 or so at Newark.[44]

The rebellion never occurred, thanks largely to Joseph Brant of the Six Nations. Almost half of the Six Nations had come north as refugees, and two Iroquois Loyalist settlements now existed in Upper Canada. From the land secured from the Mississaugas in the east, the Crown had assigned Captain John Deserontyon and his approximately one hundred Mohawk followers a reserve later termed Tyendinaga, on the Bay of Quinte.[45] They had given Joseph Brant and his two thousand followers a larger tract in the west: ten kilometers wide on each side of the Grand River, or the "Six Nations River" as the Mississaugas now called it.[46] When the Mississaugas approached Joseph Brant to send his four hundred warriors to join them in avenging Wabakinine's murder, the Iroquois war chief, who had twice visited England and had an intimate knowledge of Britain's military strength, cautioned them against an uprising. Reluctantly Wahbanosay and the other chiefs followed his advice and kept their Mississauga warriors in the camps.

Russell and his council, fully realizing the potential threat of a pan-Indian alliance in Upper Canada, secretly followed the age-old British colonial policy of divide and rule. They notified the officers in the Indian Department, William Claus at Niagara and James Givins at York, "to do everything in [their] power (without exposing the object of this Policy to Suspicion) to foment any existing Jealousy between the Chippewas and the Six Nations; and to prevent as far as possible any Junction or good understanding between those two Tribes."[47] Then the government sat back and waited for the link with the Six Nations to weaken as their traditional hostility with the Ojibwas, dating back to the seventeenth century, resurfaced.

By 1805—when Sacred Feathers was just three years old—the Mississaugas' close bond with the Six Nations broke. In that year, without consulting Joseph Brant, the Mississaugas sold nearly one hundred thousand acres along the shoreline of Lake Ontario between the Head of the Lake and York. Wahbanosay himself was one of the signatories. Animosity between the two tribal groups, notwithstanding all the public protestations of goodwill, had never been far beneath the surface. The Iroquois regarded the Ojibwas with contempt[48] and scorned them as "stinking of fish," since they greased their bodies with fish oil.[49] In turn the Mississaugas detested the Iroquois. Only in moments of extreme crisis could the Confederacy and the Mississaugas unite, and then apparently only for short periods.

Another explanation of the Mississaugas' enfeebled response to

Wabakinine's murder arises from their sharp decline in population. Sacred Feathers himself had survived the epidemics, but the highly contagious diseases of smallpox and measles had carried off many children and adults. The Credit band in 1798 had numbered 330 persons, with three additional families at the Credit River. Only a decade earlier the population had been over 500. In the 1790s the epidemics killed off one-third of the Credit band,[50] greatly weakening the community. The traditional ways of controlling disease had proved powerless.[51]

The lack of Indian allies also weakened the Mississaugas. To the south of the Great Lakes lived thousands of fellow Algonquians— Shawnees, Miamis, and Delawares (Lenni Lenapes)—who in the early 1790s had defeated large American armies. Yet by 1796 these Ohio tribes no longer constituted a military threat. After the Americans' victory at the Battle of Fallen Timbers in August 1794 they had burned the Indians' cornfields and villages. The next summer the hungry and ragged Indian delegations had ceded most of the present state of Ohio at the Treaty of Greenville.[52]

Alcohol abuse also explains the lack of a Mississauga response to the murders. The Indians, who themselves had no fermented beverages, may have first accepted the traders' alcohol for religious reasons. Ordinarily fasting sometimes led to dreams and visions, but now rum could produce instantaneous results.[53] At first, as long as they spent only several weeks a year at the coastal posts, the Mississaugas did not come to rely on alcohol, but when game declined and the Indians began living much longer each year near the settlements, alcohol abuse became a serious problem.[54] By the mid-1790s the new habit of constant drinking contributed to serious malnutrition, resulting in apathy and depression.[55]

Finally, the Mississaugas could not launch an effective uprising without the help of another European power. By the late 1790s they had become dependent on manufactured goods and on the services of European blacksmiths to repair their guns. With Britain and America at peace in the late 1790s, the Mississaugas' only possible allies were the Spaniards and the French agents in Louisiana.[56] But the distant Spaniards—despite Russell's fears—never constituted a serious threat. Without substantial numbers of Indian allies, dependent upon the British for manufactured goods, weakened by disease and alcoholism, cautioned against rebellion by Brant, then separated from the Iroquois, the Mississaugas could do little, and in the end they accepted their fate. Active and passive resistance continued, but the opportunity for a native rebellion quickly passed. It had vanished by the time of Sacred Feathers's birth in January 1802.

Other hardships beset the Mississaugas at this time. In late December 1797 the looting of Indian burial sites had reached such proportions that the authorities—to their credit—issued a proclamation protecting them.[57] Around the garrisons British soldiers continued to molest native women. In 1801, for example, four soldiers descended on a small Mississauga encampment near Kingston. When the Indian men tried to protect their women the whites beat and severely injured them.[58] Even the annual presents given by the government became a mixed blessing as the rum merchants plied the Mississaugas with liquor to get hold of the goods they had just received.[59]

The settler population brought with them from the Thirteen Colonies, or quickly acquired, a negative opinion of Indians. They saw nothing to admire in the natives. The white farmers never traveled out on the traplines with native families and discovered how demanding a life it was. The vast majority of whites had contempt for the Mississaugas, whom they viewed as indigents who needed an entire township or two to support one Indian family. They spoke of the Indians' land as a "wilderness," empty and unused. Many early settlers shared Mrs. John Graves Simcoe's opinion that they were an "idle, drunken, dirty tribe."[60]

The Mississaugas quickly learned the farmers' sentiments. In the winter of 1793 David Ramsay, an eccentric white trader who spoke Ojibwa, wrote down their complaints in a memorial to Lieutenant Governor Simcoe. Ramsay, a strange character who, twenty years earlier, had killed eight Ojibwas now became their champion, recording in his primitive English all their grievances. The white man intruded "on our hunting ground which is our farm." At the Indians' fisheries, and in the settlements, "when white people sees anything that they like they never quit us untill they have it. . . . The taking or stealing from us is nothing, for we are only Massessagoes."[61]

The negotiations of 1805 for the Mississauga Tract between York and the Head of the Lake marked the end of the Mississaugas' blind trust in the British. In early agreements the Indians had allowed the British to set their own boundaries, but no longer. When approached to surrender all of the tract, they declined. As Golden Eagle, who again spoke for Wahbanosay and the other chiefs, explained:

Now Father when Sir John Johnson came up to purchase the Toronto Lands [1787], we gave them without hesitation and we were told we should always be taken care of, and we made no bargain for the Land but left it to himself. Now Father you want another piece of Land—we cannot say no; but we will explain ourselves before we say any more. . . . I speak for all the Chiefs & they wish to be under your protections as formerly, But it is hard for us to give away more Land: The young men and women have found fault with so much having been sold before; it is true we are poor, & the women say we will be worse, if we part with any more; but we will tell you what we mean to do.[62]

Golden Eagle added that they would sell only the coastal portion of the tract, retaining for themselves the interior section as well as small reserves and the fisheries at the mouths of Twelve Mile (Bronte) and Sixteen Mile (Oakville) creeks and along the Credit River. The government accepted these conditions.

Shortly after its agreement with the Mississaugas the government of Upper Canada established two new townships on the lakefront: Nelson, named in honor of England's most famous admiral, and Trafalgar, named for his great naval victory over Napoleon in 1805. When they named the two townships immediately north of Trafalgar and Nelson, however, they retained the Mississaugas' titles for Twelve Mile and Sixteen Mile creeks. But through ignorance they reversed the names. The township north of Trafalgar, in which

Sixteen Mile Creek flowed, received the name Twelve Mile Creek (Ash-qua-sing, contracted to Esquesing) and the government gave the township north of Nelson, through which Twelve Mile Creek ran, the Indians' designation (Nan-zuh-zau-ge-wa-zog, reduced to Nassagaweya) for Sixteen Mile Creek.[63]

Neither side, Indian or white, understood the other. The names Nelson and Trafalgar were as foreign to the Mississaugas as Esquesing and Nassagaweya were to the settlers. Some years later the Upper Canada *Gazette* at York wrote: "We have known little of what may be denominated the interior character of the Indians—that is their peculiar customs, habits, superstitions, and traditionary legends."[64] In many ways the gulf separating the two societies was infinitely deeper than that dividing the British and the Americans. Those two nations, however, began their second North American war in less than thirty years, in 1812, the year Sacred Feathers reached the age of ten.

Sacred Feathers Becomes Peter Jones

Chapter 3

The War of 1812 reached Burlington Heights in the spring and summer of 1813. In May the Americans raided Fort York and burned it to the ground. Only a spirited British attack in June at Stoney Creek had checked the American advance, preventing the capture of the Heights. If the Heights had fallen, Upper Canada all the way to Kingston would have been lost as well.[1] Aware of the strong and defensible position of the Heights, the British army had made it their headquarters, cutting the trees down in swaths, mounting guns, digging trenches, and requisitioning Richard Beasley's house as their command post for the campaign.

Although he was too young to take up arms himself, Sacred Feathers immediately felt the war's impact. During the attack on York he had lost his grandmother Puhgashkish, a cripple who had to be left behind as the Indians fled into the forest. She was never seen again.[2] Other Credit Indians, like his uncle Sloping Sky, or Joseph Sawyer as he was known in English, fought for the British at Detroit and at Queenston Heights and had been among the defenders at York during the American attack.[3] Two Mississauga chiefs were wounded, and at least one warrior, White John, had died fighting for the Crown.[4]

Sacred Feathers had seen with his own eyes the war's carnage and destruction. The day after the battle at Stoney Creek, he and his brother had visited the battlefield, thick with dead men, horses, guns, swords, tents, and baggage. He never forgot the scene of devastation,[5] the bodies of the dead strewed over the ground like freshly caught salmon.

An American naval invasion at the Head of the Lake followed the engagement at Stoney Creek. In late July an American force landed at the Beach, just south of Joseph Brant's house, then occupied by his son John (Joseph Brant had died in 1807). The Americans had planned to attack the British encampment on Burlington Heights, but once their scouts learned how well the British had fortified their position, they withdrew.

At the Head of the Lake, much of the Mississaugas' hunting territory lay devastated. More serious, however, was the human invasion. What had up to then been a fairly isolated area, trapped and hunted by no more than fifty to sixty Indians, suddenly became open ground. Well over a thousand British soldiers and militiamen, with hundreds of their Indian allies, gathered on the Heights. Then came the British defeat at Moraviantown to the west, leaving southwestern Upper Canada in American hands. Ta-kuh-mo-sah "he who walks over water", or Tecumseh as the British called the great Shawnee chief, leader of the Indian confederacy fighting with Britain against the Americans, died in the battle. Suddenly in late October 1813 two thousand Indian refugees arrived at Burlington Heights pleading for food.[6]

During these troubled times Sacred Feathers went on his first vision quests. The arrival of white settlers, then this incredible war, had rendered the Mississaugas' universe unrecognizable. Although the spirit world was real to him, Sacred Feathers never experienced a vision.[7] The Indians believed that after the arrival of the white settlers many of the spirits had left. The water creature living on the Credit River had taken his leave in a tremendous flood, retreating into Lake Ontario when the white people began taking salmon from the river. Similarly, the supernatural beings in the caves at the Head of the Lake, who made noises like the volley of gunfire, had left for the interior when the alien presence approached.[8]

The trauma the Mississaugas experienced around 1800 cannot

be overemphasized: the entry of thousands of foreigners, the introduction of frightening new diseases like smallpox, measles, and
tuberculosis, the decline in the game population. Had their old
religious guardians forsaken them? At least one important Mississauga chief in the early nineteenth century believed so, and began
publicly to deny the values of his culture. Possessor of Day, or John
Cameron as he was called in English, a man in his middle forties at
the time of the War of 1812, prepared to become a white man.[9] The
trader David Ramsay had talked to the Credit River chief many
times and had taught him to read some English. Ramsay had even
convinced him that the world was not an island but a sphere.

To argue that the world was a sphere denied an essential tenet of
the Indians' religion. The Mississaugas, Sacred Feathers later
wrote, believed that whenever a person died the soul traveled toward the setting sun, to the dividing river that separated this world
and the blessed country where one enjoyed good hunting, feasts,
and dances. At the river souls found a serpent in the shape of a pole,
the only means of crossing the swollen river. Once on the serpent's
back, the souls of the good hunters and good persons easily crossed
over, but the souls of the cowardly, and the wicked turned giddy
and fell into the river to be carried away into unknown regions.
John Cameron now told his fellow Indians that he accepted the
whites' interpretation of a heaven above the earth and a hell, or bad
spirit's house, below.[10]

Cameron went further. He began living year-round in the log
house he built on the flats of the Credit River. Shortly afterward he
started raising Indian corn and potatoes. Finally, Possessor of Day
stopped wearing his breechclout and buckskin leggings and donned
a pair of store-bought trousers.[11]

Throughout Sacred Feathers's boyhood two Mississauga leaders
opposed each other. On the one hand stood John Cameron, dressed
like a white man and denying the truth of his people's traditions,
and on the other stood Golden Eagle, the band's spokesman, a chief
and religious leader. By the outbreak of the War of 1812 Golden
Eagle had led his people for nearly two decades, encouraging the

young men to be good hunters, warriors, and holy men.-[12] Now the respected elder sought the assistance of those supernatural forces that gave him power. Alone in a secluded spot he prayed, fasted, and drew closer to the sources of his spiritual energy. At last in a dream a spearhead appeared, a sign confirming his invincibility against arrow, tomahawk, or bullet. Upon his return to the encampment he summoned his followers.

Golden Eagle gathered the band to tell them of his special powers. He would prove the power of the old way. According to Sacred Feathers, who either was a witness or heard about the incident immediately afterward, the old man first explained his gift of invincibility. After instructing a warrior to fire when given the signal, the holy man picked up a tin kettle and walked a short distance away, then turned and held the kettle before his face to catch the bullet.

His followers knew the power of his dreams. Had he not cured the sick? Predicted the weather? Indicated where game might be found in times of scarcity? As instructed, the marksman fired. Golden Eagle fell. To the band's horror when they examined his lifeless body, they found that the bullet had killed him on the spot.[13]

Without any doubt this incident, which occurred at some point during the War of 1812, led Sacred Feathers to question the power of dreams and spirit helpers. He never forgot the chief's violent death. Years later he could describe it as graphically as if it had happened the day before.

After 1813 no further military clashes occurred at the Head of the Lake, though the British did execute eight of their own men at their military camp on Burlington Heights. Perhaps Sacred Feathers, a boy of twelve, saw the prisoners, all convicted of treason, arrive on 20 July 1814. On the deforested Heights the British that day cut down from the rude gallows the eight dangling forms, then chopped of their heads and publicly exhibited them.[14]

Peace came to Upper Canada in 1815. A census at the Head of the Lake the following year recorded a population of nearly seven hundred,[15] which meant that the whites outnumbered the Mississaugas more than ten to one, perhaps even fifteen to one. Faced with the war's devastation of the area's wildlife and the increased white settlement after it, many of Wahbanosay's people left for the more isolated Thames and Grand River areas to the west or moved eastward to join their fellow Credit River Indians at the Twelve Mile and Sixteen Mile creeks and at the Credit River itself.[16] Over a twenty-year period they had lost their head chief Wabakinine, their spokesperson Golden Eagle, and Wahbanosay himself, whose name has disappeared from the documentary record by the War of 1812.

After the war the Mississaugas' society rapidly disintegrated. Many proud warriors, now unable to provide for their families, lost their self-esteem. In despair a number gave up, and alcohol abuse grew. Sacred Feathers knew of relatives and friends who had perished in the winter from exposure while intoxicated or in the summer from drowning. Others had died from wounds and internal injuries received in brawls. He had seen drunken husbands fiercely beat their wives or drag them by the hair while the children screamed with fright, "the older ones running off with guns, tomahawks, spears, knives, and other deadly weapons, which they concealed in the woods to prevent the commission of murder by their enraged parents." Once while drunk his uncle, Joseph Sawyer, sold his son and another Indian boy to a white man for nine liters of whiskey, though both the boys later escaped. All his life Sacred Feathers remained haunted by the "drunken frolics" he had witnessed as a boy. He never touched alcohol as an adult.[17]

What could the Indians do to rebuild their communities? Scattered in tiny groups along the lakeshore, they could no longer support themselves by hunting and fishing. To survive the women had to make baskets, brooms, wooden bowls, and ladles and sell them to the whites. Many Indians now wanted to adopt new ways,[18] but who would teach them how to farm and adjust to a settled way of life? John Cameron himself did not really know, for Ramsay, his fur-trader friend, had died. Verbally the Indian Department encouraged the Mississaugas to become a farming people, but the department lacked the necessary funds and personnel to help. The native people in the years immediately after 1815 needed a go-between, an individual versed in the practices of both the Indians and the Europeans, someone who could articulate their needs to the government officials. Lacking such a leader, the band's situation became more desperate.

The government believed that the Credit River band faced extinction. Two years after the War of 1812 Francis Gore, lieutenant governor of Upper Canada, noted that the Indians at the western end of the lake had "now dwindled to a very inconsiderable number."[19] Malcolm MacGregor, a retired army officer, reported after a visit to the Credit River that the natives' control was "merely nominal, as the River has been constantly and at pleasure, encroached upon and plundered of its Fish by the Whites."[20] Finally the Indian Department's response came in 1818. Its representatives arrived, not to help the survivors, but rather to purchase the Mississaugas' remaining lands between the Head of the Lake and York.

With no apparent opposition the Credit Indians, their spirit broken, acquiesced. They requested only that they be allowed to hold back the three small reserves at the mouths of the Credit River, Twelve Mile Creek, and Sixteen Mile Creek. Pessimistically they believed that their community might soon be extinct, and to their request that they be allowed to keep "the little ground at the Mouths of Rivers" they added: "we will not have it long."[21] In just one generation their numbers had declined by nearly two-thirds, from over five hundred to barely two hundred.[22]

William Claus, deputy superintendent general of Indian affairs, came again two years later. On 28 February 1820 he promised the Indians help if they allowed the sale of all but two hundred acres of their remaining lands. The entire proceeds from the sale of the nine thousand acres (two thousand additional acres would go to the Crown as an allowance for the Governor's Road)[23] would "be applied towards educating your Children & instructing yourselves in the principles of the Christian religion—and that a certain part of the said Tract [two hundred acres] never surrendered will be set apart for your accommodation & that of your families, on which Huts will be erected as soon as possible."[24] The written indenture clearly specifies that all but two hundred acres of the Credit River Indians' lands will be sold, but none of the Mississaugas could read English or even vaguely understood the whites' legal system.

The Mississaugas had a totally different idea of the meaning of Claus's proposals. The Indians, they recalled in 1829, nine years later, had agreed because they believed Claus had told them: "The white people are getting thick around you and we are afraid they, or the yankees will cheat you out of your land, you had better put it into the hands of your very Great father the king to keep for you till you want to settle, and he will appropriate it for your good and he will take good care of it; and will take you under his wing, and keep you under his arm, & give you schools, and build houses for you when you want to settle."[25] Then Claus had provided them with a fat ox, some flour, and a keg of rum, which they guzzled in a drunken frolic.[26] The Indians left believing that the Crown would protect their land, for the band wanted "to keep it for our children for ever."[27]

During these final transactions in 1818 and 1820 Sacred Feath- ers and his older brother Tyenteneged no longer lived among the Mississaugas. The settlers now called them Peter and John Jones. The transformation of Sacred Feathers into Peter Jones and Tyen- teneged into John Jones had begun in 1816, a most unusual year.

The summer of 1816 was much colder all over the Northern Hemisphere than in any year since the last ice age. An immense volcanic eruption the previous year in the Dutch East Indies (now Indonesia) had thrown an immense amount of fine dust into the atmosphere. For several years the dust circled the earth in the high stratosphere, reflecting the sunlight back into space and thereby reducing the amount of light reaching the ground. In May and June of 1816 the dust shadowed the higher latitudes. Late frosts hit Quebec in mid-May, then snow fell for three days in early June, covering the ground more than a foot deep in some places. In Upper

Canada snow fell in June and July, and killer frosts came throughout northeastern North America through to August.[28]

At some point in this extraordinary year Augustus Jones, now nearly sixty, traveled into the interior to find his two young Mississauga sons. The retired surveyor now believed that the Credit River Indians would disappear as a community. When he found his sons they listened, then in the year without summer they made their choice. Their decision says a great deal about their understanding of their special identity. True, their mother had raised them as Anishinabeg, "men par excellence," but the two young men, one fourteen and the other eighteen, also knew their father, from their band's visits to his farm. Perhaps they should go with him and learn the customs of the white people, then return. They belonged to their father as well as their mother. As John himself later wrote, he and Peter were "not purely Indians."[29] The two resolved to try living in the settler's world. Dressed Ojibwa style in breechclouts, moccasins, leggings, and blankets tossed over their shoulders, they followed Augustus on the narrow forest path back to Stoney Creek.

Since Peter could speak only a few words of English, Augustus immediately enrolled him in the neighboring log-cabin school. George Hughes, an intemperate Irishman, was his first teacher. Occasionally Hughes came to school drunk, but when sober he proved an excellent teacher. He took great pains to drill the Ojibwa-speaking boy in English.[30] It took Peter some time to catch on, for English sounded very different when spoken by his American father and his Irish teacher. Learning English proved a tremendous challenge for the young Indian. In Ojibwa almost four-fifths of all words are verbs, whereas in English nouns, adjectives, and adverbs predominate. The better Ojibwa orators put the verb first in a sentence, before the noun, so in English the Anishinabeg had, in effect, to talk backward, placing the noun first. Cultural differences between the European and Anishinabeg worlds magnified the difficulties—for example though occasionally the Indians used the French word *boozhoo* (*bonjour*), no word existed in Ojibwa for good-bye. They regarded the expression as too final and instead would say something like "I'll return your visit."[31] The languages reflected the fact that the English settlers and the Anishinabeg had different cultures and different preoccupations.

Peter must have found English an impoverished tongue, especially in its vocabulary for describing nature. So specific is Ojibwa, for example, that a person could not say "tree" without including internal and external vowel shifts specifying which tree—alone or grouped, what kind of tree, and whether it grew on a hill or was coming into leaf.[32] George Copway, an Ojibwa contemporary of Peter's, once wrote that many Indian words contained more meaning than entire English sentences: "It would require an almost infinitude of English words to describe a thunder-storm, and after all you would have but a feeble idea of it. In the Ojibway language, we say 'Be-wah-sam-moog.' In this we convey the idea of a continual glare of lightning, noise, confusion—an awful whirl of clouds, and much more."[33]

Peter gave all his energy to his studies. He must have come home each night from school with new stories to tell his father in Ojibwa. How strange that the English, for example, used two words to designate the color *zhawishkwa:* green and blue.[34] Augustus might well have laughed, for the Welsh also did not distinguish between blue and green. They used the word *glas,* which covered English blue and part of the ranges of green and gray as well.[35] Colors, he would explain to his son, were regarded differently in many languages.

Sitting all day on a school bench seriously tested Peter's powers of endurance, but he had self-discipline and applied himself. In class he recited the Church of England catechism and read from the New Testament. During the nine months Peter attended George Hughes's school, he also learned to "cipher," to add and subtract small sums.[36] His father, his stepmother, and his Iroquois half-brothers and half-sisters all spoke English at home, which gave him constant practice. His older sisters Catherine, Rachel, and Polly also went to the school,[37] and they helped him with his lessons.

At home Peter came to know his older sisters best. His half-brother Henry was only eight, and Joseph and Sally were still babies. Of his three half-brothers (Augustus, Jr., arrived in 1818) and four half-sisters, Polly, then eleven, became the closest to him.[38]

It was a bewildering year. His stepmother Sarah—though she dressed in her Mohawk costume—ran the household as if it were a European home. All at once Peter struggled with a foreign language, a new family, and a completely new set of customs. He was asked to eat with a fork, not with his fingers, and to use a plate instead of a wooden bowl.[39] No longer did he live on fresh game and fish. He regularly ate the white people's beef. At night he slept in a bed with sheets instead of a blanket on the bare earth near the fire. He must not wear a breechclout and leggings but had to dress like a white man in shirt and pants. He must cut his long hair. At home the Mississauga hunter had to feed the pigs and take care of the cows.

With great perseverance Peter and his brother remained at Stoney Creek and did not slip away into the forest to rejoin their mother and her band. Slowly their grammar improved, and the number of Ojibwa words and phrases they mixed with their English declined. Deciding in 1817 that Peter had acquired a good working knowledge of English, Augustus ended his schooling and began preparing him to run his own farm. Augustus drove into him the values of the whites—the need to work hard, to save money, to plan for the future, and above all else to acquire land.

One might think Augustus Jones would have enjoyed a position of respect in Upper Canada. To a certain extent the militia captain and large landowner did, initially, but with the increased settlement before the War of 1812 the moral and then the racial climate was altered. By 1815 or so Augustus was looked down upon by many of the recently arrived white settlers for having an Iroquois wife who dressed in her native costume.[40] Among the white farming population, many of whom came from the United States, memories of the Indian Wars remained too fresh for intermarriage to be accepted.

No doubt because of this new racial climate, Augustus left the Head of the Lake in 1817. He wanted his Iroquois and Mississauga children to have a fresh start, among Indians. But he also had another reason for leaving. From conversations with the oldest settlers in the area and the visits of Mississaugas to his farm, his new neighbors learned that once he had had two Indian wives simultaneously.[41]

Augustus had done his best, from the moment of his second son's birth in 1802, to adapt to Upper Canada's new moral climate. In 1802 he and his Iroquois wife had become Methodists and were regarded by the local Methodist preachers as "truly christian people."[42] But he did not hide his past. Although he had finally ended his relationship with Tuhbenahneequay, he had still tried to be fair to his Mississauga family, always welcoming his former wife and her band to camp on his land.[43] For some time Joseph Sawyer, Tuhbenahneequay's younger brother, had even lived at the farm with Augustus and his Iroquois family.[44] Moreover, when the band seemed on the verge of dispersal Augustus had taken his two Mississauga sons onto his farm.

To spare his children from the rumors about him and their two Indian mothers, Augustus left with his Iroquois wife and Indian children. He settled along the major roadway he had originally surveyed: Dundas Street or the Governor's Road, where Joseph Brant had granted him a strip of twelve hundred acres extending about ten kilometers eastward from the Grand River.[45]

On the plains bordering the Grand River, just east of present-day Paris, Peter learned to farm. For five years, Peter worked side by side with him. It was hardening experience, toughening both body and soul. In the settlers' world land existed to be exploited, and they took much from the earth and gave back little in thanks and respect. By the time he reached twenty the young Mississauga had mastered most farming skills. He had also learned an important new concept foreign to the Mississaugas, that land and water, the resources by which men lived, could be privately owned and controlled.

In his free time Peter visited his Mohawk friends. Together they swam, wrestled, had footraces, played lacrosse, and in the winter threw the snow snake, a hard, smooth stick about two meters long, with eyes and a mouth like a snake. The players took the snake by the tail and threw it along the snow or ice with all their might. Whoever sent his snake the greatest distance a certain number of times won the contest.[46] Peter also loved to listen to their fiddling and to dance. As he later wrote, "Being young and volatile, I was soon led to join with them, and became very fond of dancing after the manner of the white people."[47] The Mohawks liked him, adopting Peter into the tribe as De sagondensta, "he stands people on their feet," one who literally picks people up and stands them upright.[48]

Peter lived happily in his first years on the Grand River. The 1,800 Iroquois outnumbered the area's 430 whites[49] roughly four to one. While Upper Canada, with its population of 100,000 whites[50] had become a settlers' colony, the valley of the Grand still remained Indian territory.

On his father's farm Peter lived amid an Indian community that had given up some aspects of its old way of life. Back in the Mohawk valley in New York the Mohawks, as the most easterly Iroquois nation, had lived beside white settlers for decades. A number of Mohawks had become Christians. Some families, in fact, could boast of having belonged to the Church of England for nearly a century. Some Mohawk Christians, particularly his father's friends, lived very much like whites. For over a generation Mohawks had built the same type of log houses as the white frontier settlers. In the Mohawk valley in the 1760s and early 1770s a few well-to-do Indian farmers had begun to construct their own frame houses. Much else had changed in their old way of life. On the Grand River some Mohawk women still cultivated Indian corn and potatoes with a hoe, but on the larger farms men grew wheat, oats, timothy, and peas, preparing the land with plows pulled by oxen. A small number of Grand River Mohawks had even built barns to house their hogs, cows, and oxen and to store their grain and hay.[51]

Despite his early fears of living among the "Nahdooways," Peter now felt quite at ease. Some of the Mohawks shared his mixed racial background. In the Mohawk valley in the eighteenth century a number of whites had settled among the Six Nations. Some were taken prisoner of war as children; others were runaway servants and army deserters or, most important, traders, who had married Mohawks and lived as they did.[52] Descendants of these whites had come north after the American Revolution. Several of Joseph Brant's Loyalist friends, some with Indian wives and mixed-blood children, had also settled on the Grand.[53] In his father's neighborhood Peter never had to learn Mohawk, since a good number of young Mohawks spoke English.[54]

His father's close Iroquois friends included bilingual and bicultural individuals like Henry Aaron Hill, a son-in-law of Joseph Brant. The well-educated Henry, a devout member of the Anglican church, read the Sabbath prayers at the Mohawk chapel.[55] Oneida Joseph, a veteran of the American Revolutionary War and the War of 1812, also a staunch Anglican, was a good friend of Augustus Jones. He later made Peter a full Iroquois costume.[56]

Peter also knew the two most powerful Mohawk leaders in the community. Henry Tekarihogen, his stepmother's father, then quite elderly, had served as the head chief of the Mohawks since the mid-1780s. An agreeable man, quiet, steady, and religious, he read the prayers at the Mohawk chapel for many years until blindness stopped him. After Joseph Brant's death in 1807, Catherine Brant supported Henry in his attempt to carry out the deceased Joseph's policies of helping the Mohawks adjust to the white settler society around them.[57]

From his early childhood Peter had known Catherine Brant. The Mississaugas had adopted her to replace the deceased head chief Wabakinine's wife and had given her Wabakinine's favorite sugar bush just east of Burlington Bay. Catherine loved to go to the sugar camp when the sap rose and help her family's black slaves make sugar. (Since the 1780s Joseph had had a retinue of black slaves whom he had captured or who had run away to join him in the American Revolution.)[58]

The intricacies of Iroquois culture fascinated Peter. In Iroquois society all titles and rights were transmitted in the female line. Catherine, as the Turtle clan matron, had the right to choose her clan's chiefs, foremost of whom was the tekarihogen. Relatives helped her make her decision, but she had the final word, and the Mohawk council would ratify her choice. After the death of the last tekarihogen this powerful woman had named her half-brother Henry to the post. She named her son John Brant to the office after Henry's death in 1830. When Catherine died in 1837 the right of nomination passed to one of her daughters and then to one of their descendants.[59]

Catherine's background would have greatly interested Peter, since they had, in one sense, a common bond. Peter knew that Catherine's father, like his, was white.[60] Yet in Mohawk society this mattered not at all. The European origins of Catherine's father, George Croghan, a white trader, made no difference, for among the Six Nations descent is reckoned through the female line. Only persons with Mohawk mothers are considered Mohawks.[61] Among the Mississaugas, however, the fact that Peter's father was white had, strictly speaking, left him without a clan identification.

In 1820 Peter reached the age of eighteen and had spent four years with his father and his Iroquois family. Augustus and his wife, remaining true to their Methodist principles, had tried to teach their children a strong Christian morality. The retired surveyor ordered his children not to work or hunt on the Sabbath, but in the summer and fall, when the deer were plump and tempting, Peter often stole a gun, slipped out the window, and went hunting for the day without his father's knowledge.[62]

While among the Mississaugas, Peter had first learned of Christianity. One day some women had gone to sell baskets and brooms to a white woman. Using the few English words the Indian women understood and the few Ojibwa words she knew, the white settler had told them about the son of the Great Spirit. On returning, the Indian women explained what they thought the white woman had said: "A long time ago the Great Spirit sent his son into this world to make the white people good and happy, but the wicked people hated him and after he had been here a little while they took and killed Him."[63]

Peter had heard much more about Christianity at George

Hughes's school and from his father and stepmother. By his own admission it attracted him, particularly after he read passages from the Bible and heard sermons at the Mohawk chapel. "But when I looked at the conduct of the whites who were called Christians, and saw them drunk, quarreling, fighting and cheating the poor Indians, and acting as if there was no God, I was led to think there could be no truth in the white man's religion, and felt inclined to fall back again to my old superstitions." Nor did Peter believe that Christianity had improved the conduct of all the Mohawk Christians.[64]

In 1820, however, Peter changed his mind. Later he stated that he had accepted Christian baptism as a duty to his father and to the Great Spirit. Self-interest also contributed. He hoped his conversion would entitle him, he later wrote, "to all the privileges of the white inhabitants." At the Mohawk chapel the Reverend Ralph Leeming, the Anglican clergyman at Ancaster, baptized him into the Church of England, with Henry Aaron Hill, the Mohawk catechist, standing as his godfather. But the ceremony really meant very little to him: "I continued the same wild Indian youth as before."[65]

In the early 1820s the Jones family grew again as Peter's oldest half-sisters married. Polly, his favorite, united in 1821 with Jacob Brant, a grandson of Joseph Brant, and Rachel and Catherine both married white settlers. The partners chosen by Rachel and Catherine showed the ease with which they crossed between Indian and white worlds. Augustus's children were truly the products of two cultures. Of Peter's three half-brothers the eldest, Henry, married first an Indian woman and after her death a white woman. Joseph's choice was a Mississauga Indian, and Augustus, Jr., married an Englishwoman.[66] Joseph Brant himself had always favored racial intermarriage as a means of teaching the Iroquois the ways of the Europeans.[67]

Henry Tekarihogen, Catherine Brant, and men like Oneida Joseph and Henry Aaron Hill all believed that the Iroquois must transform their economy from hunting and horticulture to herding and agriculture. They had kept up Joseph Brant's struggle after his death, encouraging whites like Augustus Jones to join them on the reserve. They leased or sold them extensive portions of the reserve. The progressives, as the faction later became known, argued that with the money raised Iroquois farmers could buy seed and new equipment. They also believed that the white farmers would introduce new farming equipment and agricultural techniques to the reserve.[68]

Among the six tribes, the Mohawks and the Oneidas had always been closest to the Europeans, since they had adopted Christianity in their ancestral homeland before the other tribes. On the Grand River the Tuscaroras and a number of Cayugas also drew ever closer to the whites. In contrast, the conservative Senecas, Onondagas, and Lower Cayugas on the southern section of the Grand had resisted change, the introduction of commercial agriculture, and the settling of whites on the Grand River.[69] The teachings of Handsome Lake (1750?–1815) had greatly influenced these Six Nations people. The Seneca prophet from western New York had argued that the Indians should simply reform their traditional religious customs and ceremonies and should not become "whitemanized."[70] This new religious tradition, known as the longhouse religion, had spread to the Grand River by 1804, gaining adherents especially among the non-Christian Iroquois.[71]

Growing up among the Christian Mohawks and not being an Iroquois himself, Peter remained uneffected by the longhouse religion. He went in a different direction. Encouraged by their father, both Peter and his brother John wanted to achieve success and advancement by the whites' terms. Now that their younger half-brothers could replace them on the family farm, they could return to school. John left to study surveying at the small village of Hamilton,[72] a cluster of buildings around the first courthouse and jail built at the Head of the Lake. (The tiny hamlet had received its name just before Augustus Jones and his family left for the Grand River in 1817.) Peter himself enrolled at a school at neighboring Fairchild's Creek.

To pay his school fees and board, Peter approached his sister

Catherine and her husband, a stonemason. All summer long he worked for Archibald Russell making bricks, spending almost all his time in the mud. He had a goal, one that sustained him all summer, "that if I had a better education, I might get employment in an Indian trading establishment."[73]

While attending school for three months that winter, Peter boarded with Enos Bunnell, a farmer in his middle forties, and his wife and five young children. Bunnell, originally from Connecticut, had come north to Upper Canada in 1802. Members of the Church of England, Enos and his family regularly attended services, when offered, at His Majesty's Chapel of the Mohawks.[74] At church they came to know Augustus Jones and the newly baptized Peter. Probably the Bunnells first told the Joneses about the school and welcomed their friend's son to board with them.

Since the building stood so near Enos Bunnell's farmhouse, the students called it Bunnell's schoolhouse. Joseph Thomas, then in his late teens, attended immediately after the War of 1812. From his recollections one has a picture of this one-room log cabin school in the era when Peter Jones knew it. The teacher, an American named Forsyth, used American (not British) books: Mavor's Spelling Book, the English Reader, Morse's Geography, and Daboll's Arithmetic. These, no doubt, also served as Peter's texts:

The spelling-book opened up with the alphabet and gradually advanced; a few illustrations of the commonest of our domestic animals were given, with a brief descriptive article of each. These were interspersed nearly to the end, where were found columns of words of five or more syllables, the first being "abominableness." The so-called English Reader was almost entirely made up of extracts from the best English authors, but it also contained extracts from speeches made by Ben. Franklin, Patrick Henry, etc. The geography seemed to be made up especially to extol and enlarge the U.S. at the expense of Canada. To give an instance: the little State of Rhode Island was allotted more space in that work than could be spared for Canada, although the latter consisted of two

Provinces. The Arithmetic proved to be the best of the books, and was a work of decided merit.[75]

The Bunnell family enjoyed their lodger's company. Years later they still recalled how they had come to love him as a son. One can imagine their Indian guest at suppertime telling the children in his slightly accented English about the exploits of Nanahbozhoo, of the Pahgaks or flying skeletons, of the friendly little people, and of the deadly Waindegoos. Then at night on his slate—by candlelight—he reviewed his exercises. He so wanted to make something of himself. Yet he was always good-humored and considerate. Enos Bunnell and his wife kindly reduced his board one shilling a week "because he had given them so little trouble and so much pleasure."[76]

By the spring of 1823 Peter believed he had learned enough to qualify for a clerk's position at a fur trading post on Lake Simcoe, or Georgian Bay, or perhaps faraway Sault Ste. Marie and the distant North West. Over the past seven years he had separated himself from the old way of life of his mother's people. If they had initially considered returning, neither he nor John now thought of doing so. His contact with his father and his Iroquois stepmother, his half-brothers and sisters, his Mohawk friends, and white settlers like George Hughes, the Bunnells, and his schoolmaster at Bunnell's schoolhouse had all altered Peter's outlook. Unlike the followers of the code of Handsome Lake, he had become convinced that the Indian must follow the way of life that the whites called "progress."

Born Again

By mid-March 1823, signs of spring were multiplying. The days became longer and warmer. Patches of bare earth appeared as the snow thawed. Overhead the first geese honked on their flight north-ward. The arrival of the new season marked the end of Peter's school term, for by mid-April he had to return to his father's farm. May was the busiest time of all, when the work of two months—plowing, sowing, and planting—was crowded into one.[1]

Once at home the young man appeared to have readjusted to the farm, but inwardly he had not. Among the Christian Mohawks and the whites, he had come to reject many of his Mississauga religious beliefs. In effect he had abandoned his original faith without accepting another in its place. His spiritual crisis arose that summer.

The previous fall Thomas Davis, a cousin of Joseph Brant who lived only two kilometers or so west of Augustus Jones, had began reading portions of the Scriptures and morning prayers to his neighbors in Mohawk. Davis, then in his middle sixties, felt that only true Christianity could save the Mohawks. Baptized years before as a member of the Church of England, the tall, dignified war chief, a veteran of both the American Revolution and the War of 1812, enjoyed considerable respect among the tribe.[2]

Shortly before Peter's return from school, the revival at Davis-ville—as the Mohawks named the area around the chief's farm—had begun. At Chief Davis's request Edmund Stoney, a Methodist lay preacher, commenced his Sabbath calls. Every Sunday the short, rotund Irish shoemaker came to Davisville to hold a short service. Stoney enthusiastically taught the sacred Bible stories to the hardened warrior, twice his age, and to his Indian neighbors. He was effective. Those Sunday meetings led Chief Davis to say, before "my religion was in my head and I only prayed with my mouth. The missionary came and spoke *to my heart.*"[3] One Sabbath Peter heard Edmund Stoney give a "good warm talk" on the theme "Marvel not that I said unto thee, Ye must be born again." Peter listened with great attention[4] to the preacher's explanation of personal sin and the need to renounce it by accepting Christ Jesus and being born again.

One can easily understand why the young Mississauga felt drawn to these Mohawk Christians. Like them, Peter detested drunkenness for the "evil it had done to my poor countrymen, many thousands of whom have had their days shortened by it, and been hurried to destruction."[5] Everywhere the whites promoted the vice, selling liquor to the Indians. The tiny village of Brantford, eight kilometers to the south, already had two taverns or "liquor holes," nicknamed by the Methodists Sodom and Gomorrah.[6]

Peter and the Davisville Christians had more in common than an abhorrence of alcohol. They shared the same outlook toward non-Indian society—the Indians must adjust to it. Chief Davis said: "I have told our people that they must set a good example for their children, and learn them to read, pray, and work, for it is a great sin to bring up their children in idleness."[7]

The Christian community at Davisville attracted Peter. To his satisfaction, these Mohawk Christians appeared to have bridged the division between Christianity and their old Indian faith, drawing out the similarities between the two religions. Among the Six Nations even some of the non-Christians confessed that "essentially" the two religions were "the same, as they both lead us to reverence and obey the Creator and to live like brethern [with] our fellow creatures."[8]

The young Mississauga's contact with Chief Davis and Edmund Stoney led him to look favorably on Christianity and in particular on Methodism. The arrival of Seth Crawford, a young American from

Saratoga, New York, further strengthened Peter's regard for the Methodists. Peter met Seth that spring, and in his words "the piety of this young man, together with his compassion for the poor Indians, made a deep impression on my mind."[9]

Awakened by a dream summoning him to lay aside all worldly concerns and devote his life to bringing the Christian gospel to the Indians, Crawford had left Saratoga in a one-horse wagon, carrying all his possessions with him. Once he learned of the work of Chief Davis and Edmund Stoney, he went immediately to Davisville. Determined to learn Mohawk, he boarded with an Iroquois family near Chief Davis's home. Using the chief as his interpreter, the American gospel worker spoke constantly to the Mohawks of Almighty God our creator and his son Jesus Christ.

From his conversations in May with Chief Davis, Edmund Stoney, and Seth Crawford, Peter realized more than ever before that the Christians worshiped the same Supreme Being as the Mississaugas. But unlike the Indians the Christians believed that God remained very close to the world and cared directly about people's future and well-being. The Creator himself, in fact, so loved human beings that he himself had descended to earth and lived there as a man for thirty years.[10] Peter now understood that he could do away with all spirit intermediaries and reach God directly, through Jesus.

William James, the famous American philosopher and psychologist, identified the traditional pattern followed by the convert to the Christian faith: uneasiness of soul, a desire to be saved, the sudden perception of the depravity of mankind, the instantaneous realization that salvation can come only through God's grace and not one's own efforts, and finally the contentment of realizing one is "saved."[11] By the late spring of 1823, Peter Jones had passed through the first stage of the conversion experience—uneasiness of soul—and entered the second—a desire to be saved.

The young man asked himself many questions in the late spring of 1823. The happenings at Davisville also intrigued his half-sister Polly, to whom he was very close. One of their white neighbors, Mrs. Thomas, who had belonged to the Methodist society in her native

Ireland, invited Peter and Polly to join her at a Methodist camp meeting in Ancaster Township, just west of Hamilton. In late May the three religious seekers walked the thirty kilometers east toward Ancaster.[12]

The American-based Methodist Episcopal church, a denomination that had first entered Upper Canada in the 1790s, sponsored the camp meeting. For fifty years the Reverend John Wesley, an ordained Anglican minister in England, had kindled and nurtured what became one of the greatest revivals of faith in the history of the English-speaking world. Wesley's totally disciplined, hence methodical, approach to Christianity earned the minister and his followers the name Methodists. Nearly a century after he had founded the Methodist movement, it emerged as one of the most dynamic Protestant churches on the North American frontier.

The theology behind Wesleyan Methodism, like that of a number of Protestant evangelical denominations, rested on the concept of original sin, which began with Eve's eating the forbidden fruit. For Wesley every man and woman since Adam and Eve carried inherited sin. Yet at the same time the English clergyman recognized the power of God's love, mercy, and forgiveness. He endorsed the doctrine of atonement, that since Christ died for each of us as an individual, it is within the power of God that all be rescued from hell's fires. To save humanity God had sent his son Jesus Christ to suffer and die on the cross as an atonement for the original sin. Salvation can be achieved by any seeker through God's grace, freely given to all those who have faith in Jesus. After repenting the sinner can chase the devil out and be "born again."[13]

Repentance was only the first step and had to be followed by an earnest struggle to achieve Christian perfection, the overcoming of the will to sin. To keep his followers on the road to Christian faultlessness, John Wesley laid down a series of rules of behavior that became a guide strictly adhered to by his followers on both sides of the Atlantic. Methodists must observe the Sabbath, avoid alcohol, spurn "costly apparel," and never sing "those songs" or read "those books which do not tend to knowledge or love of God."[14] They must find time for private and public devotions, and most important of all, they must participate in the weekly class meeting in which each member gave personal testimony. Man's constant, all-consuming struggle should be to reach out to God, to prepare his soul for eternity.

John Wesley aimed to provide preaching and fellowship—a new religion of the heart—within the Church of England, not to establish a separate church. Many Anglican clergymen, though, opposed him, disapproving of his evangelistic methods. Barred from church pulpits, Wesley preached in houses, barns, fields, wherever he could find an audience. Methodism attracted great support among the common people and the poor, and later across the Atlantic in North America.

The American Revolution had led to the formation of the independent Methodist Episcopal church and a break with the Anglican establishment in the United States. After the Revolution only an independent church could appeal to Americans. Discredited by its royalism, the Anglican church had almost ceased to operate, leading Wesley, on his own authority, to consecrate a bishop for the United States. In 1784 the Methodist Episcopal church was formed as a separate denomination. (After John Wesley's death in 1791 the British Methodists themselves organized as a denomination along Presbyterian lines, to be named the Wesleyan Methodist church.)

In its American form Methodism expanded quickly as a denomination marked by easy-to-understand and highly emotional services. The Methodist Episcopal church imposed no educational requirements for its circuit riders. The candidate for ordination simply proved before a committee that he had read and understood a set of prescribed books. In the absence of colleges and theological schools, the early laborers taught each other Wesley's teachings from his *Sermons*, which they carried in their saddlebags.[15] The preachers lived on a pittance, determined as they were to save the souls of others.

John Wesley had a genius for organization. Wherever he preached he organized the newly converted into classes grouped in local societies. Wesley demanded that conversion must be confirmed by changed habits of life. In his *General Rules* (1743), he outlined the class leader's responsibility to visit each member weekly "to enquire how his soul prosper" and "to advise, reprove, comfort, or exhort."[16] Above the class leader he placed the exhorter and the local preacher, both licensed converts under the discipline of a senior preacher. This organizational structure had been transfered to North America. Each of the societies formed part of a circuit, an area served by one or more itinerant preachers and governed by a quarterly official board that included the local or lay preachers (men like Edmund Stoney, who had received the call to preach but had not left their secular occupations). Over the circuits stood the conference, composed of all the itinerant preachers. The annual conference controlled the appointments of the preachers to their circuits and all matters of discipline.

Itinerancy was the basic principle of the Methodist system. British circuits were large, but those in North America were immense— two hundred kilometers and more. The minister had to keep constantly on the move, fulfilling a monthly preaching plan that allowed him to meet as many appointments as possible, often more than one each day. He had to set up classes, appoint their leaders, counsel class leaders and local preachers, perform marriages and funerals, advise in family matters, bring news, and spread the gospel. In his work the circuit rider used all the techniques of the experienced revivalist, including hymn singing. Charles Wesley, John's brother, wrote over six thousand verses, including some of the finest hymns in the English language (including "Hark the Herald Angels Sing"). Firmly based on Scripture, the hymns conveyed every aspect of the Christian's life.

The circuit rider preached every day of the week, except perhaps Monday. The preaching itself related to the people's daily life, sermons delivered without abstractions, in John Wesley's words, "plain truth for plain people." A North American innovation became one of the leading methods of reaching frontier audiences, the camp meeting. Prompted by curiosity to see how the Methodists worshiped, in the early summer of 1823 Peter Jones and his sister Polly had set out to observe one.[17]

So many Methodists lived in the Ancaster area that the local population called it Methodist Mountain.[18] Men and women dressed in homespun converged on the two-acre campground from all directions—on foot, on horseback, in wagons—some from one-room shacks and log cabins as far as eighty kilometers away. As he approached the camp-meeting circle, Peter heard hymns sung and people reciting prayers.

A brush fence surrounded the carefully selected encampment, a site with ample drinking water, shade trees, and pasture for the horses as well as timber for tent poles and firewood.[19] Tents made of coarse linen formed an inner circle enclosing the worship area. That night the camp-meeting organizers lit fire stands, the blazing torches adding an eerie touch to the colorful services.[20]

For the next five days and nights the worshipers focused on the preachers' stand. A large platform accommodated the Reverend William Case and his fellow preachers a meter or so above the milling crowd, where they could better be seen and heard. In accordance with John Wesley's wish, the women sat on the right, the men on the left.[21]

William Case, presiding elder of the district, had general oversight of the encampment. A short, slender man, he dressed in parson gray. As a veteran of nearly twenty years' work in Upper Canada, the American-born minister had known Augustus Jones before the War of 1812; in fact in 1809 he had baptized his eldest Mississauga son, Tyenteneged, as John Jones.[22]

Once Peter stepped onto the grounds he felt among the true believers of the Great Spirit. But after he heard the first sermons and witnessed the prayer meeting, he began "to feel very sick in my heart."[23] By the Sabbath, the third day, the Mississauga heard the powerfully awakened all around him crying out for mercy. It affected him as well: "I thought the black-coats knew all that was in my heart and that I was the person addressed." Tears streamed down his cheeks.

Peter's anxiety intensified on the fourth day. He felt very low. Throughout the morning sermons he wept but tried to hide his head behind the people in front of him so no one would see him "weeping like an old woman, as all my countrymen consider this to be beneath the dignity of an Indian Brave." That afternoon, amid the shouting, prayers, and preaching, he feared that he "should sink down to hell for my sins, which I now saw to be very great, and exceedingly offensive to the Great Spirit."

By the evening of the fourth day Peter had accepted the ministers' concept of original sin. As they explained, God had first made man holy, upright, and in his own image; but man had fallen from this state by disobedience to his creator. Man's heart, in consequence, had become wicked and depraved, held firmly by Satan. To bring man to him, God in his mercy had sent his son into the world to do good, teaching man about his depravity. Only through acceptance of Jesus Christ could all of mankind escape Satan's grasp.[24]

Peter went out alone in the forest and prayed on his knees: "Oh! thou great and good Spirit, have mercy upon me, a poor Indian, for the Sake of Jesus Christ thy Son."[25] He returned to the meeting and knelt down among the white worshipers. The preachers prayed fervently for his soul. "When I first began to pray my heart was soft and tender, and I shed many tears, but strange to say, sometime after my heart got as hard as a stone. I tried to look up, but the heavens seemed like brass. I then began to say to myself there is no mercy for poor Indian." At midnight Peter, tired and discouraged and emotionally exhausted, returned to his tent and immediately fell asleep.

Still Peter subconsciously believed that the Great Spirit had created the white and Indian races separately, giving the white man his religion in a book and the Indian his religion in his heart.[26] His Methodist friends had to tell him once again that "our Lord Jesus Christ had died for Indians as well as for white people."

Having noticed his absence from the all-night meeting, Edmund Stoney and another preacher came to Peter's tent to awaken him. Polly had just surrendered herself to Jesus! Once again Peter had hope.

At the prayer meeting Peter again fell upon his knees and begged God for mercy. In the background Edmund Stoney and Polly prayed with all their hearts for his conversion. Then it happened. He had his vision. With the first light, Peter surrendered completely and claimed "the atoning blood of Jesus, and He, as my all sufficient Saviour, who had borne all my sins in His own body on the cross." Old things passed away and everything became new:

That very instant my burden was removed, joy unspeakable filled my heart, and I could say "Abba, Father." The love of God being now shed abroad in my heart, I loved Him intensely, and praised Him in the midst of the people. Every thing now appeared in a new light, and all the works of God seemed to unite with me in uttering the praises of the Lord. The people, the trees of the woods, the gentle winds, the warbling notes of the birds, and the approaching sun, all declared the power and goodness of the Great Spirit.

On the final morning of the meeting William Case gathered the hundreds of worshipers for a fellowship meeting. Among the numbers who rose up to acknowledge their conversion stood Methodism's first Mississauga convert. Peter never forgot the presiding elder's exact words when he recognized him: "Glory to God, there stands a son of Augustus Jones, of the Grand River, amongst the converts; now is the door opened for the work of conversion amongst his nation!"

That afternoon Peter, Polly, and their Irish friend Mrs. Thomas walked home toward Paris along the Governor's Road. Others on foot or in wagons most likely sang old Methodist hymns with verses like this one:

> *When I set out for glory,*
> *I left the world behind;*
> *Determined for a city*
> *That's out of sight and mind.*
> *And to glory I will go.*

Then they repeated the hymn's refrain:

Ho! every one that thirsts,
Come ye to the waters;
Freely drink and quench your thirst,
With Zion's sons and daughters.[27]

Upon returning to the farm Peter began to search the Scriptures and to pray a great deal. In his own words, he renounced "the world, the flesh, and the devil."[28]

Only two years before Peter's and Polly's conversions, William Case and four other Methodist preachers from the church's Genesee Conference, to which Upper Canada then belonged as a district, had formed the Committee on Indian Affairs. Alvin Torry, the first Methodist missionary on the Grand River, later recalled that in 1821 "I doubt if there was a man in the Genesee Conference, excepting Br. Case, that believed that the Indians in their pagan state, as we now found them, could be Christianized."[29] But Case, aware of the Jesuits' work among the Hurons in the seventeenth century and that of the Anglicans among the Mohawks in the eighteenth, persisted despite his colleagues' skepticism. In 1822—as the presiding elder of the district in which Torry served—he selected the twenty-four-year-old preacher to take the gospel to the settlers and Indians living along the Grand River.

Alvin Torry, accepted the call. During his first months on the Grand River, though, the stern-faced young American failed to make any Iroquois converts. The Cayugas and Onondagas, adherents to the code of Handsome Lake, showed no interest. "We not like your Bible-religion; it says, Drink whiskey! Look at the Mohawks! They have Bible-religion and they all get drunk! We not want it!" Nor did the Mohawks themselves want anything to do with "Methodist religion."[30]

Only when Torry met Chief Davis, Seth Crawford, and the newly converted Peter and Polly Jones, did his work begin. Just one week after the Ancaster camp meeting, twenty Indians crowded into Chief Davis's house to hear the visiting missionary's first sermon, while many others peered in through the doors and windows. The house soon rocked with sobs and the cry: "Oh, my sorry, wicked heart! Oh, my sorry wicked heart! I shall go to the bad place." Around the room shuffled twenty Indian men and women wringing their hands and crying. Having found a congregation, Torry now formed his first Methodist Indian society—making Seth Crawford the class leader.[31]

The Anglican Mohawks around Davisville took note of the religious revival on the reserve. They soon developed a saying that the Methodist preachers used wolf's brains as a medicine to make the people cry and shout aloud. At their meetings they threw the powder into the air, and when the congregation inhaled it they caught the spirit of the wolf, causing them to cry and howl.[32]

During Torry's absences Seth Crawford led the weekly service. Within two months about a dozen Indians had joined the Methodist society. The number doubled again by October, making the room in the chief's house too small for the congregation and the growing day school. To make space the old Iroquois chief turned over his entire house and retired to a log cabin in the woods. Seth and Peter and the Indian converts rushed to finish a new log building; when completed early in 1824, it became both church and schoolhouse.

Peter's conversion gave him a new source of energy and a new clarity of vision. Now he realized he must tell his people that Jesus had come to die for all of the peoples of the world. In 1824 he returned to the Credit River to tell of his conversion and to attract the Mississaugas to the Grand River.[33]

Tuhbenahneequay became one of the first Mississauga converts. She returned with her son to Davisville, where the Methodists baptized her as Sarah Henry. In turn she brought her young nephew David Sawyer to the settlement to hear the missionaries and attend the school. Upon his own conversion David, then twelve years old, walked fifty kilometers to tell his parents, who were living along the north shore of Lake Ontario. Soon after their arrival the Methodists converted Peter's uncle, Joseph Sawyer, and his wife.[34] Peter's Mississauga brother John Jones (who had been nominally baptized in 1809) also joined the church with his Mohawk wife Christiana Brant, a granddaughter of Chief Joseph Brant.

At first Peter had some difficulty speaking Ojibwa correctly, for he had hardly used it on the Grand River. He said things in a mixed-up unfamiliar way that the Mississaugas found hard to follow, but after some practice his Ojibwa did return. As he himself said, "I felt it my duty to warn my Indian brethren to flee from the wrath to come. I found no difficulty in addressing them."[35] He soon made the new Christian concepts comprehensible to his Indian audience as no white minister could. That first autumn and winter more of Peters' Mississauga relatives, then wandering around the shores of Lake Ontario, arrived at Davisville, and many joined the Christian community.

All summer, as Peter worked a second season at his brother-in-law's brickyard, he thought of further assisting his church. His vision of Jesus, his own guardian spirit, had grown in intensity until he could think of "nothing else but trying to proclaim the Gospel of Christ to my poor benighted brethren." He must tell as many Indians as possible that they could approach the Great Spirit through his son. They needed no other intermediary.

During the winter of 1823–24 Peter opened a small day school at his father's house, where he taught Indian orphans about religion and how to read and write. He prayed night and day for his mother's people: "When I walked in the woods, I was praying for them; when I sat down by the way, I was praying for them; and when I awoke in the night, I was praying for them."[36] Each Sabbath afternoon he helped Seth Crawford with the Sunday school at Davisville. Peter also taught that spring at the new school.[37] His young Mohawk friends, with whom he had once fiddled and danced, could not recognize this totally changed man.

The Methodists noted with great pleasure their Mississauga convert's commitment. In a letter to William Case, Seth Crawford reported in March 1824: "We are not a little encouraged that one of the Indian youth, a Chippaway, begins to exercise his gifts profitably. PETER (for that is his name) lately opened the meeting by a few words, and then prayed. His words were with trembling, but the blessing of the Lord attended."[38]

Case knew how badly his church could use the bilingual son of

Augustus Jones. The Methodists needed someone to preach in
Ojibwa, to interpret for their preachers, and to translate hymns and
Bible passages and establish Ojibwa-language equivalents for key
Christian terms. They needed a go-between, a bicultural, bilingual
individual able to present Christian doctrine to the Indians in intel-
ligible terms.[39] The young Mississauga soon proved his worth.

In 1824 Peter Jones made a very important convert at the Credit
River, Chief John Cameron, long known for his openness to the
Europeans' ways. Shortly before his death in 1828, the old chief told
Peter how long he had waited for the new faith: "For many years past
I have again and again wished that the good white christians might
come and plant the christian religion amongst us, and teach us the
right way we should go; but no one cared for our souls, until the Lord
himself raised up one of our own people to tell us what we must do to
be saved."[40]

Upon his arrival at Davisville, the chief pitched his tent at the
mission house and sent his young wife, Peter's half-sister, to school.
Influenced by his example, Indians came in from the forest to attend
church services and learn the new ways. Nor did Cameron's contribution end there. In the early spring of 1825 he himself returned to
the Credit River, and as a direct result of that visit the Mississauga
converts soon sighted more Credit Indians, walking in a long file,
winding in and out among the tall oaks of the plains on their way to
Davisville.[41]

Peter formally joined the Methodist church as an "exhorter" on 1
March 1825. The circuit riders often rewarded men like him who
had shown speaking ability in the class meetings by licensing them
to "exhort." An exhorter spoke after the local preacher gave a sermon
or assisted a traveling preacher on his circuit rounds.[42] Peter did all
of these and also, in the presiding elder's words, began traversing
"the forest in search of the wild men of his nation" to talk to them of
Jesus and the Great Spirit.[43] His father supported him in his work,
and on 28 June 1825 he gave his son his copy of *A View of the
Evidences of Christianity* by the English theologian William Paley.[44]

Peter's dedication to helping the Mississaugas came from his intense belief in Jesus.[45] He must share the good news with his people. Second, he reached out to his people, convinced as he was that Christianity was essential for a settled people's success. As he told a white audience in the summer of 1826:

If it had not been for the benevolent, who sent the gospel to you, you would, perhaps, now be as we poor Indians are. For we are told that your fathers, the inhabitants of Britain, once lived in tents, wore leggins, and were strangers to the religion of Jesus Christ. Now you are clothed, have houses, and the bible to read. But these people, the former proprietors of your lands, are poor and without houses; and what is more, they are without the knowledge of God and the way of salvation.[46]

When Seth Crawford left to return to New York State in early April 1825, the weight of the mission fell on Peter's shoulders. He was ready. Beginning that spring, the Methodists' most promising Indian convert introduced European farming to the Mississaugas at Davisville. He selected and cleared land, bought seed potatoes and oxen, and taught his people to plow.[47] He wanted these Indian Christians to become the equals of the whites, free and self-supporting—independent. His faith in a living God, ever-present, ever-seeing, wonderful to love, terrible to offend, gave him enormous personal strength. By mid-June 1825 fifty Mississaugas[48] had followed his lessons.

A definite pattern existed to life at Davisville that summer. About sunrise a long tin trumpet sounded, summoning the faithful to the chapel for morning devotions, where all joined in the singing and two or three prayed in Mohawk or Ojibwa. The children stayed for school, learning to read from the New Testament. While the children prepared lessons their parents went to the fields, where Peter instructed them in farming. Each Sunday Alvin Torry held two church services and a Sunday school for the Indian children.[49] A cultural revolution had begun.

The Mississaugas' Cultural Revolution

Chapter 5

The letter signed in a loose, scrawling hand "Peter Jones alias Kahke-waquonaby" astonished James Givins. In thirty years no warrior had ever sent him a note in English written in his own hand. Hurriedly the Indian agent at York read the message:

> *By the request of Capt. John [Cameron] and others of the Mis-sessagues in those parts, I take the liberty to write a few lines to you wishing you to send an information respecting their presents to what times you will be ready to issue them, or to what time you would wish them to come down, there are about fifty of the Nation who have planted corn and potatoes, and who have embraced Christianity, and are attending to the means of education; they do not wish to come down till they get a sure word from you, for they are at present busy hoeing their corn.*[1]

"Hoeing their corn"? "Embraced Christianity"? The puzzled Indian agent had dealt for over three decades with the Mississaugas[2] and never had any of them, apart from the eccentric John Cameron, expressed any interest in farming or in Christianity. Givins sent the Indian runner back with the message that he would distribute the annual presents in the second week of July.

Peter and his party of about fifty set off on their two-day trek from the Grand River to the Credit on 7 July. We know the exact day, for on the advice of William Case Peter had begun to keep a diary. In single file the men proceeded, followed by the women, a number with babies in cradle boards strapped on their backs, then came the children.[3] They camped that first evening on the farm of Ebenezer Jones, Peter's uncle, at Stoney Creek. Starting early the next morning the Indians quickly traveled the last fifty kilometers, arriving at the Credit River flats before sunset.[4] The Indian Christians' hymns, all translated by their young leader, became stronger as they approached the encampment, hymns with verses such as:

> *Jesus Ish pe ming ka e shódt,*
> *Me sah oúh a pa ne mooh yáhn;*
> *Ne wâh pah tahn kah ne e shódt*
> *Ki ya neen ka ne e shah yáhn.*

> *Jesus my all to heaven is gone,*
> *He whom I fix my hopes upon:*
> *His track I see, and I'll pursue*
> *The narrow way till him I view.*[5]

Chief James Ajetance, or Captain Jim as the whites termed him, watched carefully the arrival of the Christian caravan. They went immediately to the clearing around John Cameron's log cabin, where the Methodist converts pitched their wigwams well apart from those of their non-Christian relatives. Sacred Feathers's success troubled Captain Jim. He knew the young man well, for just before the outbreak of the War of 1812 he had adopted him. Having just lost his own son, also named Sacred Feathers, Captain Jim had asked Tuhbenahneequay to let him take her boy as his own. Accepting the honor of having her son raised at the Credit by a leading chief, Tuhbenahneequay had agreed.[6]

That evening memories of Peter's horrible months with Captain Jim no doubt returned to him. Just after he had joined the chief and his family, Captain Jim and the adult band members had begun a long drunken spree, leaving the young boy outside in the intense cold for several days without food. For the rest of the winter he could not walk. In the spring, when Tuhbenahneequay learned of her son's lameness, she and a female relative immediately left for the Credit.

Taking turns, they carried the crippled boy on their backs fifty kilometers to Stoney Creek, where proper care and the warm summer weather restored his injured limbs.[7] Nearly fifteen years later, the Christian converts' leader blamed whiskey and not Captain Jim for his ill treatment. Peter knew that when anyone became "keushquabee" (meaning "the head turns round and the man is crazy"), "this leads to other acts of wickedness."[8]

Peter had his first opportunity to meet the entire band and their immediate white neighbors two days later on the Credit River flats. He faced about three hundred people, white and Indian, first speaking in Ojibwa, then exhorting the audience in English. No copy of his sermon has survived, but we do have a full summary of the remarks he made on a similar occasion but one year later. In July 1826 Egerton Ryerson, the future founder of the modern Ontario public school system, then a young Methodist preacher of twenty-three, heard Peter Jones speak twice near Newmarket to non-Christian Ojibwas from Lake Simcoe. After giving his sermons in Ojibwa Peter summarized them in English for his friend. Using Ryerson's notes we can re-create what the Mississauga missionary must have said to the Indians on the Credit River flats, 10 July 1825.[9]

Having himself accepted the difficult concept of sin, Peter used it extensively in his preaching. He first explained that originally the Great Spirit had made man a holy being.

Keehe Kesha Muneto (the Great Good Spirit) made all things: He made man good and happy; gave him a command, saying, if you keep this you will always live, have plenty, and be happy; but if you disobey, you will be sickly, and miserable, and die. Man disobeyed the good law, and thereby lost the favour of his Maker, as also the purity and happiness in which he was made. This disobedience, brothers, is the cause of all the sufferings of men—of all the miseries you feel.

But hope existed, for the Great Good Spirit, Peter continued;

so pitied the world that he sent his only beloved Son to teach men how they might become good and happy again. After his beloved

Son had taught men what they must do, he then himself died for our sins, that we might be saved from them in this world, and from misery in the next. Brothers! the beloved Son did die for us; but he now lives again. After three days he was raised up from death: He talked with his brethren many times, and then in their sight he ascended up to Ishpeming (Heaven) to ask mercy for us: He is now praying for us, saying, O Father! show mercy to miserable sinners, for I have died for them.

Peter sternly warned the wicked. All people, Indian and white alike, could escape hellfire only by making true repentance toward God, and giving their hearts fully to Jesus Christ. One day God would destroy the world with fire; "When this destruction should take place, the Great Spirit would first take the good people out of it." Only two places existed after death—one for the good, the other for the wicked, who would be "driven away to a place of fire, where (Muchemoneto) the evil spirit was."

How did Peter's Indian audience respond to his message? That some of the non-Christian Anishinabeg in the early nineteenth century had already acquired a conception of a place of torment— possibly from Roman Catholic missionaries in the French period— considerably helped his and the Methodists' joint cause. In the early 1820s, for instance, an elderly non-Christian Ojibwa from Lake Simcoe related to his grandson Shahwahnegezhik, later named Henry B. Steinhauer, a story of what would happen when the world ended: "In vain will any one turn to the rocks, for every thing shall be burned, and water shall also be burned. Those that have been good in this life, and the brave warriors, shall possess a flourishing country where there is plenty of game, and every other thing; but the murderer, the indolent, and all sorts of wicked men shall be excluded from that happy country."[10] But if the concept of sin was not entirely new in the 1820s, the ideas of a Son of God, and the existence of a Holy Spirit uniting man to God were.

From their myths the Algonquians understood the concept of a messenger from the Great Spirit. This prepared the Mississaugas for Peter's introduction of Jesus Christ, the Son of God. The Great

Spirit, Peter explained, so loved human beings, white, red, and black, that he sent his son into the world to teach them the proper way to live, and how they could earn a place in heaven. The Holy Spirit, or clean soul, converted and regenerated the sinner. As David Sawyer, Peter Jones's first cousin, later summarized the lesson, "the *love* of God in heaven made the golden chain—Jesus Christ brought it down to us in the pit, and the Holy Spirit helps us to lay hold of it by faith and the Grace of God & promises in Christ pulls us up towards heaven."[11]

Peter's sermons made a deep impression. His words went like arrows to their targets. Mississaugas fell to the ground as if dead; some wildly rejoiced, and others cried aloud for mercy. As the young native missionary wrote William Case in the late fall of 1825: "I have indeed, for my part, experienced the greatest blessings since I have been labouring here among my nation; frequently in our meetings, the Lord pours out his Holy Spirit upon us, like as in the ancient days, so that the noise of praise to God is heard afar off."[12]

It says much for Peter's powers of persuasion that he made two important converts that summer day on the Credit River flats: Bluejay, the most inveterate drunkard in the tribe, and Ebitonge, later baptized as Benjamin Crane, a well-spoken young man of twenty-five. Both men knelt with the Indian Christians, indicating their acceptance of the gospel.[13]

Two days after the Credit River meeting the converts traveled the twenty kilometers east to the council fire on the Humber. Arriving in the late afternoon, they first set up their wigwams and later in the evening assembled for prayers, repeating the most important Peter had taught them:

> *Noo-se-non ish-pe-ming-a-yah-yan;*
> *tuh-ge-che-e-nain-dah-gwud*
> *ke-de-zhe-ne-kah-ze-win.*

> *Our Father in heaven who art;*
> *supremely adored be thy name.*[14]

While the widow Wahbanosay—Peter's late grandfather's second wife—and others taunted and ridiculed them, the converts stood their ground, praying and shouting back "praises to our Lord and King."[15] At ten o'clock the next morning the government boat arrived from York loaded with the Indians' annual presents.

What a contrast the two groups presented. The non-Christians waited in holiday dress. Some warriors wore their hair sticking up in a tuft, the rest of the skull being closely shaved—with chests, arms, and faces all daubed with red paint or with green, black, white, and yellow. On their arms shone metal bands. Rings dangled from their ears. Opposite them stood the Christian converts, very plain looking, with their hair neatly tied and hanging down their backs. While some of the women retained their old costumes, the men dressed almost like Europeans in plain shirts, trousers, and hats. Peter Jones even carried a watch.[16]

Colonel Givins and some officers arrived first, then the Reverend John Strachan and his wife, with several gentlemen from York. Strachan, the leading Anglican cleric in the colony, also served as chief adviser of the lieutenant governor, Sir Peregrine Maitland. When the short, stocky minister, all dressed in black, asked Peter to assemble the Christian children to sing hymns, the Indian quickly did so.[17]

What a sight it must have been: the Christian and non-Christian men seated separately in circular rows, then the women and the children in adjacent rows. The more than two hundred Indians sat with legs crossed while their chiefs, one Christian and one non-Christian, distributed the presents piled in a large heap: red and gray cloth, chintz, blankets, rifles, powder, and lead.[18] While the chiefs cut up the cloth for division and handed out the presents, the Christian children from Davisville sang two favorite Methodist hymns.

During the singing the most powerful cleric in the colony hid his true feelings. Only ten days earlier the Reverend John Strachan had made a particularly vicious attack on those, whom he termed in his sermon "uneducated itinerant preachers," men who preach the gospel "without any preparation to teach what they do not know, and which . . . they disdain to learn."[19] But Strachan's sharp mind worked quickly. Now was not the time to contest the Methodists' control, for something must be done immediately for the Indians. Methodism would be fine for now, but as soon as possible, once he had Anglican clergymen available, he would send ministers of the Church of England to the Mississaugas.

Aware of the Crown's agreement in 1820 to build a village on the Credit River and introduce Christianity among the Indians, Strachan now made a very useful proposal. For lack of a Mississauga leader who understood English and European society, the government had done nothing since 1820. But now such a man existed. Peter Jones could become the necessary link to the Mississaugas, the bicultural and bilingual agent needed to convert his people to Christianity. And perhaps—the Reverend Mr. Strachan now took the long view—he could later be persuaded to join the Church of England. After the giving out of presents the archdeacon suggested that the Christian Indians settle permanently at the Credit River, where the government would help them build a village. The Indian converts met immediately after Strachan's departure and unanimously agreed to accept his advice.

Peter Jones's performance at the present-giving ceremony led to more conversions. The promise of government help to construct a settlement proved he could obtain results. When the fifty original converts returned to Davisville, forty-five more Credit River Indians accompanied them. By early August Peter could report to Agent Givins that about half the Credit River band had become Christians. Among that number stood the widow Wahbanosay, only a few weeks before one of Methodism's most vocal opponents but now as steadfast in her faith as Peter Jones's own mother.[20]

Tuhbenahneequay's example had already encouraged others in their faith. One day when she was returning from York in a canoe in company with other Indian women, a group of white men overtook them. Pulling their boat alongside the canoe, the whites invited the Indians to drink. The converts refused, but the rowdies persisted:

"Surely a little will do you no harm." To silence them Tuhbenahnee-quay asked for the bottle. The men smiled on handing her the whiskey—but not for long. Peter's mother simply reached over the far side of the canoe, poured the whiskey into the lake, then returned the empty bottle.[21]

During the winter of 1825–26 at Davisville, and later at the Credit, the converts entrusted Peter Jones with all their affairs. He and his brother John alone knew the meaning of the settlers' laws and edicts. The very fact that he, a young man in his early twenties, had become the leader of the community indicates the cultural revolution then in progress. John Cameron and James Ajetance had been almost forty—twice Peter's age—when the Credit River Indians elected them chiefs before the War of 1812.[22] They had won their community's respect for their leadership, observed over several decades. Peter, though, had obtained his position in only a year or two, based solely on his knowledge of the Europeans and their customs. The native Christians realized that only the Jones brothers could deal effectively on their behalf with the white missionaries, the Indian Department, and the white settlers.

Early in April 1826 Peter and John led the Davisville Christians back to the Credit. Colonel Givins had promised that the government would have twenty-five acres of land plowed on the river flats, three kilometers from the river mouth, and that their houses would be ready by fall. The Indians immediately put up a bark shelter to serve as their chapel and school. On the crest of the western embankment above the flats they also cleared village lots.[23] By the end of the summer of 1826 the remainder of the band, including some of the last holdouts, Captain Jim and his family, joined the Methodist church.

Several factors had led to Peter Jones's speedy conversion of so many of his own relatives and their friends. First, Christianity meant assistance—with the depletion of their hunting grounds the Indians desperately needed aid. If they became Christians the government, the white Methodists, and the Jones brothers would help them become farmers, ensuring their survival. Second, to many

Christianity appeared as a necessary aspect of a settled way of life. Amid the cleared fields and in their permanent villages, the Son of the Great Spirit protected the white farmers from freezing, disease, and starvation just as the Indians' guardian spirits once did for the Mississaugas. Third, the discipline of the new religion appealed to some. In Methodism's ironclad rules against "ardent spirits" a number of Mississaugas saw a way out of their dilemma, a release from the new drug. The desire for assistance, the apparent suitability of Christianity for a settled way of life, and the need for new social controls all brought the Credit Indians to Methodism. But there was another factor that proved even more important in securing converts.

Above all else Peter Jones's intercultural skills made Christianity familiar and accessible to his native audiences. The young Mississauga could draw out, for example, the similarities between the ancient Hebrews and the Anishinabeg. William Warren, a mixed-blood contemporary of Peter Jones in Minnesota, noted several common practices in his *History of the Ojibway Nation:* "their faith in dreams, their knowledge and veneration of the unseen God, and the customs of fasting and sacrifice." Warren also underlined the similarities "between the oral traditions and lodge stories of the Ojibways with the tales of the Hebrew patriarchs in the Old Testament. . . . The tradition of the deluge, and traditions of wars between the different Totemic clans, all bear an analogy with tales of the Bible." No doubt Peter emphasized the same common Ojibwa and biblical stories and beliefs, helping to make the Bible culturally relevant to his listeners. Would not the Mississaugas see in David's vanquishing of Goliath evidence of his spirit power? A description of Saint Paul's conversion might recall the experiences of the Anishinabeg who were strong in spiritual power. Did not Jesus' forty days and forty nights in the wilderness constitute a vision quest?[24]

The talented interpreter also introduced hymns to bring out the similarities between Christianity and the Indian's old religious beliefs. The Wesleyan hymns he translated, for example, taught the same values of right dealing, honesty, and general uprightness that the Mississaugas had learned from childhood. In addition Peter used the Ten Commandments. Although the first two did indeed conflict with the Mississaugas' former teachings:

> *1. Thou shalt not have more Gods but me.*
> *2. Before no idol bow thy knee.*

The others could readily be accepted:

> *3. Take not the name of God in vain:*
> *4. Nor dare the sabbath day profane.*
> *5. Give both thy parents honour due.*
> *6. Take heed that thou no murder do.*
> *7. Abstain from words and deeds unclean:*
> *8. Nor steal, though thou art poor and mean.*
> *9. Nor make a wilful lie, nor love it:*
> *10. What is thy neighbour's, dare not covet.*[25]

Peter always began his Christian instruction with the Lord's Prayer, the Ten Commandments, and the Apostles' Creed.[26]

The Mississauga converts incorporated the new concept of the Son of God into their religious outlook. For some Jesus apparently replaced their protective guardian spirits. He appeared in dreams and in daily life. Just two months before the issuing of presents at the Humber, for instance, Pedwawayahsenooqua related to Peter Jones a remarkable event: "She dreamed that the heavens and the earth passed away with a great noise, and the Son of God made his appearance, and called her to himself."[27] Often out walking by herself the widow Wahbanosay could be overheard talking to Jesus, since "he makes me very happy in my heart."[28] While desperately ill Polly Ryckman, a Credit River convert in her mid-forties, told Peter Jones, "the presence of Jesus is all the time around about my bed."[29]

The converts—to understand fully the Savior's message—wanted to learn to read "the Book of God."[30] Keshishawasike, baptized as John Crane, was unusually tall for a Mississauga, six feet four inches "with a lofty carriage that would do credit to a guardsman."[31] Crane wanted to read so badly that he constantly carried a

New Testament with him. He asked every boy or girl he met to name particular words he pointed out and then learned the words by their shapes.[32] In the Methodist Sunday school at Davisville, and later at the Credit, the Jones brothers and the white minister taught the adult Indians their ABC's. Even old Peggy Tunewah, in her mid-sixties, would attend, hoping to learn to read Peter's Ojibwa translations of the Indian hymns and of the Scriptures.[33]

Eagerly the Christian converts embraced Christianity's rules. The social revolution penetrated deeply into Indian society. No Christian Indian hunted or fished on the Sabbath or even cut firewood on that day.[34] Mayarwaseke, or John Muskrat, a man in his mid-forties, followed the regulation so strictly that he always cut his pipe tobacco on Saturday for use on the Sabbath.[35]

Perhaps the greatest transformation came in drinking habits. Peter considered alcohol the greatest evil introduced by the whites,[36] and he waged war against it. Before her conversion Peggy Tunewah had scrubbed and washed floors for innkeepers, who paid her in whiskey. After she joined the Methodist church the aged woman became a total abstainer.[37] Similarly John Keshegoo, a man in his late twenties who had frequently been seen drunk on the streets of York, renounced alcohol after his conversion in June 1826.[38] John Tobeco, about fifty years old, typified the new Indian attitude. Hired by a trader to hunt deer, he and his son James once came back laden with skins worth nearly one hundred dollars. The trader asked them, "Well, what will you have from my store?" To which John replied, "We want one yoke of oxen and a chain, and the rest in flour and pork, and no whiskey at this time. I want the oxen to plough up my field." He and his son returned home to the Credit driving their own oxen, loaded with provisions for their family.[39]

Many changes came in 1825 and 1826 in the way the Indians lived, worked, and thought. Those who already had acquired European or Europeanized names from the settlers, such as James Adjutants (Ajetance), John Crane, John Secord, and Sam Waupanep (Wahbeneeb), retained them. Frequently the missionaries—perhaps following a precedent established by the colonists—selected the name of the individual's father, whether living or not, as the new family name. Manoonooding, "the pleasant wind," son of Chechalk, became James Chechalk. Similarly Myawekapawy, Quinipeno's or Golden Eagle's son, received the name John Quinibina (Quinipeno). As for the Herkimers, since they were of mixed ancestry, they retained the name of their father Lawrence Herkimer, the Rice Lake fur trader, a son of the Colonel Johan Jost Herkimer, United Empire Loyalist.

Whenever Methodist missionaries found Indian names difficult to write or pronounce, they replaced them with English ones. Pahoombwawindung, "the approaching roaring thunder," became Thomas Smith. Naningahseya, "the sparkling light," a son of the ancient warrior called Old Jack by the whites, became William Jackson. Apparently Ashowoniquodweby, "the cloud that rolls beyond," obtained his new name, Peter Olds, by the simple inversion of his English nickname, Old Peter.

Occasionally the Indians received the names of great Methodist leaders. Alvin Torry, for instance, baptized Enimokosy, the son of Pipiquon and his wife Notinoqua, as John Wesley. If a missionary body paid for a young person's education it often reserved the right to select his name. The Young Ladies Society of John Street Chapel in New York City, for example, specified that an Indian boy's English name be that of a popular Irish evangelist, the late John Summerfield. Indeed, when the society paid for the education of Sahgahgewagahbaweh, the son of the deceased White John, he entered the Cazenovia Seminary in New York State as John Summerfield.[40]

The Indians' conversion to Christianity introduced much more than just European names. They moved from wigwams scattered over a wide area to log homes set close together in a straight line. This adjustment began the moment the Christian families took possession of their twenty new houses in the fall of 1826. By leaving their wigwams on the river flats in the winter of 1826–27, the converts abandoned communal living. Formerly three families had resided side by side, and sometimes as many as six to eight lived in the longer wigwams, large enough for two fires. Now two families shared each small dressed-log cottage, with a wall dividing each from the other's room.[41]

Changes followed rapidly for the converts: a new faith, European names, a fixed residence, and the adoption of a new economic base— agriculture. This led to new economic and social roles for both men and women. Formerly the men had hunted and fished, leaving the women to build the wigwams. The women dressed the skins, cooked, made clothing, took care of the children, gathered firewood, prepared the fires, and planted Indian corn. If a warrior performed any of these tasks the other men laughed at him.[42] But now the men kept up the log cabins, planted the fields, brought in the fuel, and supplied provisions. The women remained at home sewing, making garments for themselves and their family, and washing clothing and dishes. The women ate with the men at a table.

Daily conduct changed. The Indians washed off the fish oil they had daubed on their faces, hair, and arms to protect themselves from mosquitoes and blackflies.[43] With the oil went their acrid odor on hot days—as well as their relief from insect bites. Like good Methodists they dressed plainly and constantly were clothed. No longer did the women go bare from the waist up in summer. The male converts in summer wore more than moccasins and deerskin breechclouts.[44]

Important social customs changed with conversion. Husbands with more than one wife had to send away all but one. They had to support the other women and their children by them, but they could live only with the first woman they had married. Second, women now gained the right to choose their own husbands as the practice of parents' arranging marriages declined.[45]

Throughout late 1825 and 1826, Peter Jones constantly encouraged the Credit Indians to become "a new race of people,"[46] the equals of the whites around them. He also sought to protect their economic interests, to do whatever was in his power to establish a firm financial base for the settlement. To do so he acted first on the Indians' fishery and then on the question of their annuities from the government.

For other thirty-five years white fishermen had raided the Credit

Indians' fishery during the spring and fall salmon runs.[47] The Indians, in petitions drafted by their young leader, protested the appearance of "the lowest and most immoral class" of settlers, who often scattered "the offals of the fish" at the river mouth to prevent the salmon's passage upstream, allowing the white adventurers to catch them with nets along the lakeshore. To protect themselves the Indians requested that the governor secure the fishery to them. To help conserve the resource, the Mississaugas promised to fish only five nights a week and not to catch salmon for sale after 10 November. Once the Indians at last secured the privilege from the Upper Canadian legislature in 1829, they could charge a respectable price for their fish.[48]

Fearlessly Peter challenged Colonel Givins at the annual present-giving ceremony in July 1826. The government paid only £472 10s. in its annual land payment, not, as Peter pointed out, the £522 10s. specified in the purchase of 1818. Totally unprepared for the inquiry, Agent Givins replied that "he was not at liberty to explain" why the £50 had been withheld.[49]

At the Credit, John Jones proved Peter's greatest ally. Although he suffered from very poor health, he assisted as much as possible with the band's affairs and aided Peter in his struggle with James Givins. In 1829 John asked the agent to furnish the band, as part of their annual presents, "twine, Ropes and lead sufficient to make a couple of Large Nets which would supply them with herrings and white fish which abound in Lake Ontario." The Credit Indians no longer wanted "trinkets and gaudy coloured clothes."[50] Having received a good education among the whites, John taught at the village school during the first years of the settlement. The Reverend John West, fresh from several years in the Red River settlement in the North West, visited the Credit in the summer of 1826. The Anglican clergyman noted of John Jones: "He appeared every way qualified as a schoolmaster, and under the lively influence of Christian principles was devoted to his work. Many of his scholars had made considerable progress in reading, and they sang delightfully some of Doctor Watts' hymns for children."[51]

Christiana, John Jones's nineteen-year-old Mohawk wife, a granddaughter of Joseph Brant, also helped enormously. The young woman, who wore braids though she dressed in the European fashion, taught the Indian women Methodist hymns. Christiana's father Jacob Brant had attended the charity school affiliated with Dartmouth College in New Hampshire for two years.[52] To the Credit women she became a role model, giving them advice and instruction in housekeeping.

Peter could also count heavily on Polly Jones Brant, his closest sister, and her husband Jacob Brant, Jr., Christiana's brother.[53] Like Christiana, Jacob had acquired a thorough knowledge of farming and of white customs. Lucy Brant, Christiana's and Jacob, Jr.'s, mother, a fine Mohawk Christian, had come to join her son and daughter at the Credit.[54] The John Joneses and the Brants proved useful allies.

Among the Mississaugas themselves a half-dozen men also knew how to farm. The trader Ramsay had taught Chief John Cameron a little about agriculture, and Joseph Sawyer had learned firsthand on the farm of his brother-in-law Augustus Jones at Stoney Creek. The three Herkimer brothers, Lawrence (Negahnub), Jacob (Keweyob), and William (Minowagiwan, "the pleasant stream"), had all previously helped white farmers, as had Metwechings, or Samuel Wahbeneeb. The John Joneses, the Brants, the Sawyers, the Camerons, the Herkimers, and the Wahbeneebs formed Peter's core group of helpers.

In the fall of 1826 Peter also received the support of a gifted white minister, the Reverend Egerton Ryerson who became the first permanent Methodist missionary to the Ojibwas. Ryerson, a second-generation Loyalist, belonged to a family with six sons, five of whom became Methodist preachers. Brought up on a farm, he was resourceful and self-sufficient. The Indians would also appreciate that he was an avid hunter.[55] Young, dynamic, and intelligent, Egerton entered his new post with great enthusiasm, working side by side with the Indians, eating native food, and living in their homes. He also learned their language, since only one-eighth of the band really spoke English.[56]

Three years previously Egerton had been present at the Ancaster camp meeting when Peter Jones had accepted Christianity. Approximately the same age, the two men got along extremely well. Of all the Methodist missionaries Peter knew, Egerton Ryerson became his closest and most loyal friend. Years later Egerton would describe his Indian brother as "a man of athletic frame as well as of masculine intellect;—a man of clear perceptions, good judgement, great decision of character."[57]

During his very first week among the Credit River Indians Egerton learned how well Peter had organized the community. The young Methodist preacher had called for a subscription to pay for the construction of a permanent joint church and school building. Peter explained the request in Ojibwa; then, in Ryerson's words, "never did the Israelites, when assembled and called upon by King David ... to subscribe for the erection of the Temple, respond with more cordiality and liberality, in proportion to their means, than did these converted children of the forest."[58] The women came forward with their proceeds from selling baskets, mats, and moccasins; the men brought their earnings from selling salmon. In less than an hour the Indians had given forty dollars and promised sixty. Aided by contributions Egerton had raised himself and by the funds the Jones brothers collected from many Methodists on the York, Yonge Street, Hamilton, and Niagara circuits, the Credit River Indians finished their combined frame church and school in two months.[59]

Having once worked for half a year with a carpenter, Egerton proved a very practical helper at the Credit. He showed the congregation how to undertake basic carpentry: to plane boards, shingle roofs, and make window frames and log floors. In the fields he also took off his coat, rolled up his sleeves, and showed the Indians how to do things with their own hands. Peter Jones was thinking of missionaries like Egerton when he later wrote:

Such men, and such only, are really calculated to do lasting good among Indians; men who are not afraid to blacken their hands by logging the timber, and burning the wood in the field; men who are not ashamed to work in their shirt sleeves; men who do not say to the Indians, *"Go and do this or that"; but who say to them, "Come on brethren": such men only can convince the Indians that they are their friends and wish to do them good. . . . The Indian is a free man and will not be driven. Gain his confidence and esteem, and then you can do anything with him.*[60]

Egerton found the Indian Christians "teachable, willing and apt to learn." He loved his year at the Credit River. He boarded at John and Christiana Jones's, sleeping with a single blanket or two on a bare wooden plank. Years later he wrote, "I was never more comfortable and happy."[61] Egerton's presence had another benefit for the mission: it allowed Peter to undertake lengthy missionary tours throughout Upper Canada.

The Credit Indians became very attached to their young white minister. Captain Jim, once a staunch opponent but now a leading champion of the new faith, approached Egerton in mid-December 1826. The chief, speaking on behalf of the band, began: "Brother, as we are brothers, we will give you a name. My departed brother was named Cheehock; thou shalt be called Cheehock." The name Cheehock meant "a bird on the wing," an appropriate title for the energetic Egerton.[62]

Thanks to their young Mississauga leader, to their first white minister, and to the Credit River Indians themselves, much had been accomplished in the band's first year of village life. The white Methodists through financial aid, and the Indian Department by constructing the village, had also admirably supported them. Basil Hall, an English traveler, commented in July 1827 on the transformation of a group that only a few years earlier had seemed doomed to a "total and speedy extinction." When he called at the Credit Mission Hall he discovered: "They had all neat houses, made use of beds, tables, and chairs, and were perfectly clean in their persons. . . . Most of the children, and a few of the older Indians, could read English; facts which we ascertained by visiting their school. . . . The whole tribe profess Christianity, attend divine service regularly. . . . They now cultivate the ground. . . . The number of Indians at the Credit village is only 215; but the great point gained, is the fact of reformation being possible."[63]

The southern Anishinabeg's cultural revolution had begun. Peter Jones and other native helpers, with the support of the Reverend William Case and the Methodist Episcopal church, had already by 1827 carried the news of the Credit experiment to the west, the east, and the north. Already in the east and the north it had strongly taken hold, and there too Christian Mississauga communities had taken form. To keep the native workers in the field, the new Indian converts generously donated their silver brooches, earbobs, armbands, and nose jewels, which the missionaries then sold to jewelers. The Indian women also made baskets and brooms for sale to raise money for the "blessed work of God."[64] Instead of aspiring to become warriors, the young Mississaugas at the Credit River now wanted to become Methodist preachers, interpreters, and teachers.

"Go Ye into All the World"

Chapter 6

The tall, muscular Mississauga faced the large white and Indian audience. That Sabbath day in late January 1827 he took his sermon from the Gospel of Mark, chapter 16, verses 15–20: "Go ye into all the world, and preach the gospel to every creature. He that believeth and is baptized shall be saved, but he that believeth not shall be damned."[1] Over the past two years the native preacher had traveled from Indian communities along the Thames to the St. Lawrence River, from the north shore of Lake Ontario to Lake Simcoe and Rice Lake.

The crowd had assembled at Moses Blackstock's home in Cavan Township, just west of Rice Lake. It was a cold winter day, no doubt with an icy northwest wind piling the snow against the log house. No windbreak existed, for the white man—regarding trees as obnoxious enemies—cut them down around his dwelling.[2] By the door stood the Mississaugas' rifles, since the Indians, out of politeness, always left their firearms outside the white man's cabin.[3]

Inside a blazing log fire made the large, crowded room delightfully warm. The settlers had put their outer clothing on the few pieces of crude furniture or on the uneven wooden floor. The heat of the fire on the buckskin, and the wood smoke, gave the cabin a pungent, agreeable wilderness smell. Whites and Indians stood tightly packed. About a hundred Indians had hastily left their trapping grounds[4] to meet Sacred Feathers.

Before the sermon an original mixture of sounds issued from the farmhouse. In their rich, soft voices the Anishinabeg sang the grand old Methodist hymns as translated by the visiting native missionary, while the white settlers sang the same melodies with English words. Until the previous fall the two groups had lived totally isolated from each other, never joining socially, let alone in prayer.

The first settlers had entered Cavan Township just ten years earlier, attracted by the good soil and the relatively easy access to Cobourg on "the front"—the lakefront of Lake Ontario. Most of these Protestant families came from northern Ireland, the remainder from England and southern Ireland. Within a decade they had cleared much of their new home, named after county Cavan in Ireland, and had put up their first log homes and barns. Although Presbyterians predominated,[5] a number of Methodists lived in the township, among the most energetic being Moses Blackstock,[6] the host of the prayer meeting.

Almost overnight an amazing transformation had occurred in the white farmers' perceptions of Indians. A race that one Rice Lake settler had once described as "poor, drunken, dissipated" became in his eyes "sober, religious, and generally speaking, more moral and virtuous than their white brethern."[7] Many settlers wanted to meet the Indian Methodists' leading native preacher.[8]

The Rice Lake Anishinabeg already knew much about Sacred Feathers, and they respected him as one of them. He could run down a wounded deer and find his own food on a missionary journey. If deer proved scarce and fish were not available, he peeled off the bark of the hickory tree, cut out chips, and boiled them to extract the sweet juice. If starvation threatened in winter, he boiled and ate the moss called *wauquog*, taken from the pine trees. Like his people, he had disciplined himself from childhood to survive in the wilderness.[9] But as the reports had said, he knew the whites ways as well. He could farm, build a log cabin, even make his own shoes.[10]

What drove him on? Years later Peter stated his life's philosophy in one sentence: "I cannot suppose for a moment that the Supreme Disposer has decreed that the doom of the red man is to fall and gradually disappear, like the mighty wilderness, before the axe of the

European settler."[11] The Christian gospel would save them. He felt an obligation to go and preach to his fellow Indians everywhere. His campaign to save his people had begun two years earlier, 150 kilometers to the west.

Often Peter must have thought back to that first missionary journey. May had been a pleasant month to make the trip, with its bright skies and sunshine. Needing an Ojibwa interpreter, the Reverend Alvin Torry had asked Peter to join him. The Canadian Methodists' first missionary tour would be to the Indians along the Thames River: to the Munsees, closely related to the Delawares, and to the Ojibwas.[12]

The two men, their Bibles carefully packed in their saddlebags, had ridden west from Davisville. At first they passed large clearings with farmhouses, recently enlarged, and sizable barns, signs of the new prosperity of what only a decade earlier had been wilderness farms. Slowly the land to the west became more heavily wooded, and the number of farms declined. The clearings ended on the third day, after Westminster. Unable to proceed farther on horseback, the two men walked by an Indian footpath to Munceytown on the Thames, thirty kilometers away, led by a white guide named Kilburn and by John Carey, the young schoolteacher at Westminster.[13]

The Munsees, Algonquian-speaking Indians who called themselves Lenni Lenapes, "original people,"[14] had come north to Upper Canada toward the end of the American Revolution. At the moment of European contact the Lenni Lenapes had occupied most of present-day New Jersey, Delaware, eastern Pennsylvania, and southern New York.[15] The English had given them a new name, one derived from Sir Thomas West, the third Lord De La Warr. The English had named a magnificent bay along the mid-Atlantic coast after Sir Thomas, the first governor of their colony at Jamestown, Virginia; and as time went by the Lenape people living near "De La Warr Bay" and along the banks of the river that emptied into it became known as the Delaware Indians.[16]

The Munsee-speaking bands in the Hudson River valley had first come in contact with the Dutch in the early seventeenth century.[17]

After the English took over the Dutch colony in 1664 they had forced the Lenni Lenapes westward, a number migrating to join the Minisink band on the headwaters of the Delaware River. They became incorporated with the Minisinks, and in time Munsee replaced Minisink as the name of this new grouping.[18] Later the Munsees drifted farther west to the upper Susquehanna and upper Allegheny rivers, and by the late eighteenth century they moved into Ohio, while a smaller number went into Upper Canada.

The three white men and the Mississaugas stopped at Chief George Turkey's wigwam. The elderly Munsee chief lived five kilometers from Munceytown, a settlement of about two hundred. When Peter met him he called him grandfather,[19] for the Algonquians honored the Lenni Lenapes as "the grandfather tribe," the original inhabitants of the land nearest the rising sun.[20]

George Turkey and his family listened with attention to his visitors and also prayed and sang with them. How fortunate that George, now seventy years old, knew English. He had learned it from the settlers in his younger days and from the British and Loyalist soldiers he fought beside in the War of 1812.[21] The Munsee chief's ancestors were among those Indians who had left the Hudson River valley and the western part of present-day Connecticut, settling on the upper Delaware River. Raised at Chenango in present-day western New York, George had come north with his people to Upper Canada during the American Revolution. They had settled a few years later on the Thames River.[22] Of the Munsee chiefs, Turkey and Westbrook were among the few who spoke English.[23]

That evening the chief invited his four guests to stay in one of his wigwams and gave them blankets and boards to sleep on. Not accustomed to such hard beds, the three white men spent a terrible night, but Peter slept well.[24]

A prerequisite to the evangelization of Indians was a knowledge of native languages, as the Reverend Alvin Torry discovered at the Munsees' village. About fifty Munsees attended the Methodist meeting, but when the tall, bulky white man got up and spoke in English the warriors could not understand him. They walked away until Peter addressed them in Ojibwa, a tongue many had learned as a second language.[25]

The Munsees listened, but not all agreed with their guest's message. For over a century the whites had dispossessed them, harassed them, and driven them westward. The American's atrocities had been legion. In March 1782 the Long Knives had beat to death with mallets and hatchets, and then scalped, ninety Christian Lenni Lenape and Mahican Indians at the Moravian mission of Gnadenhütten, "tents of grace," in Ohio. Then the Americans had burned the buildings, including those holding the corpses (sixty of the victims were women and children).[26] The Munsees had not forgotten. Some of the relatives of those murdered Indians now lived only fifty kilometers down the Thames River, at Moraviantown, established as a place of refuge in the early 1790s.

As a result of the Gnadenhütten massacre, many Munsees hated the whites and their religion. Through their interpreters, two Munsee chiefs told Peter during his second visit several months later: "The Indians had been murdered after they had embraced Christianity. Many years ago the Moravians preached to the Indians on the other side of the lake, and when they had got a good many to join them, they so contrived it as to have their own brethren confined to a house, where they were all murdered and burned up." The young Mississauga immediately replied that a wicked band of whites had executed the deed, not the Moravian preachers.[27]

Once again Peter explained the true nature of Christianity, telling how its teachings had been given to all men in the good book that told of the Great Spirit's son Jesus the savior of mankind: "Now the Great Spirit has not given you any such good book; but he has given it to us, and has told us to hand it to our red brother. . . . Now brothers, we come to hand you this book, and to learn your children to read it, that they may be wise and good."[28]

From the evidence of the Reverend Abraham Luckenbach, the Moravian missionary at neighboring Moraviantown, we know how effectively Peter Jones could speak to the Lenni Lenapes in Ojibwa. The minister noted in his diary on 5 April 1828, on Peter's second visit to Moraviantown: "In closing he brought greetings from the Chippewa brethern and gave a prayer in Chippewa language and made a deep impression. Many could understand the language." Three years earlier his address in Ojibwa to the Munsees of Muncey-town also went well.[29]

Peter's final appeal led his Munsee opponents to concede one point. Though they wanted to hold to their old ways, they would not oppose those Munsees who wished otherwise. John Carey, the white teacher, could live among them. The pro-Christian chiefs Turkey and Westbrook welcomed him, and within three months the young American, aged twenty-four, had eighteen Munsee children in his school. Since the Methodists had so little money, John Carey's parents in Schoharie, New York, provided their son with all his clothing, books, and school supplies as well as nearly a hundred dollars' worth of clothing for his pupils. He stayed at Munceytown in the years to follow, despite a death threat.[30]

While in the Thames River area Peter also made a visit to the neighboring Ojibwa band of Chief Tomiko, whose encampment lay about ten kilometers downriver from Munceytown. Unlike the Munsees, this isolated group had no previous knowledge of Christianity. Peter Jones had no success whatever on this visit or on a second in August. Tomiko politely received him, but he and the other chiefs wanted nothing to do with the Christian message. They told him: "The whites are Christians, and it makes them no better. They have done us much injury. By various pretences they have cheated us out of our lands. We will first retire to the western Indians. We will have nothing to do with the whites or their religion."[31]

Over the next five years Peter returned several times to the Thames River Ojibwas. His conversion in 1827 of Peter Beaver, Chief Tomiko's nephew, eventually led to the entry of the neighboring Sable River band into the Methodist church.[32] In 1829 the native preacher also converted John Tomiko, Chief Tomiko's son.[33] Yet the old chief and the great majority of the Ojibwas of the Thames still refused Christianity as late as that year.[34]

The traditionalists remained strong in the Thames River country. Chief Kanootong of the Bear River band explained to Peter that the Indians must honor their own religion. If the Creator had wished the Indians to worship like the whites, He would have made them white. Instead, He presented to the white people across the great waters a religion written in a book. To the Indian He "gave His way of worship written in his heart."[35] Emphatically the hardened warrior, who had fought beside Tecumseh in the War of 1812,[36] told his young visitor that he would hold to his old ways.

The missionary campaign among the Mississaugas at the eastern end of Lake Ontario had proved much more successful. One year of hard work had led up to the meeting at Moses Blackstock's in January 1827. Unlike the Thames River area, the Bay of Quinte had experienced large-scale white settlement since the 1780s and the arrival of several thousand white Loyalists. A hundred Loyalist Mohawks had also settled on the Bay of Quinte at the Tyendinaga (Deseronto) reserve given them after the American Revolution.[37] The establishment of farms and additional settlements in the decades to follow disrupted the Mississaugas' fishing and hunting. As among the Credit River Indians to the west, a breakdown of the Indians' social structure began after the War of 1812. Many Indians were hungry for new religious guidance, since their old religion seemed incapable of protecting them. Even before Peter Jones arrived at the Bay of Quinte in early 1826, one Mississauga had already begun to consider Christianity.

At approximately the same time that Alvin Torry and Peter Jones set out for Munceytown in May 1825, a Mississauga boy of sixteen had entered the village of Belleville and asked to be educated. Upon meeting the intelligent boy, several pious people offered to provide his board while he attended school.[38] They called him Peter Jacobs, a very rough duplication of the sound of his flowing name in Ojibwa—Pahtahsega—"he who comes shining" or "one who makes the world brighter."[39]

Peter Jacobs's parents had both died from drinking to excess, and two brothers, a sister, and a brother-in-law had followed from the

Chechalk

Quenepenon

Wabukanyne

Okemapenesse

Wabenose

Kenebonecence

Osenego

Acheton

1. The totems or clan symbols of the leading Mississaugas at the western end of Lake Ontario. Wabenose was Peter Jones's grandfather and like all the others except Quenepenon, or Golden Eagle, who was a member of the Otter totem, he belonged to the Eagle totem. The chiefs made their marks on the document acknowledging the transfer to the crown of the area they called Toronto on 1 August 1805. From the map between 1:58 and 59 in *Canada, Indian Treaties and Surrenders: From 1680 to 1890*, 2 vols (Ottawa: Brown Chamberlin, Printer to the Queen's Most Excellent Majesty, 1891; facsimile edition reprinted Toronto: Coles, 1971).

2. Paul Kane's painting in 1846 of Menominee Indians spearing fish by
   torchlight on the Fox River in present-day Wisconsin could easily
   have been painted half a century
   earlier—about 1800, during the
   spring or fall salmon runs on the
   Credit River. The Mississaugas
   used the same fishing techniques
   as their fellow Algonquians on the
   Upper Great Lakes. Courtesy of the
   Royal Ontario Museum, Toronto,
   Canada.

3. Paul Kane's painting of an Ojibwa
   village near Sault Ste. Marie, Upper
   Canada, in the mid-1840s. It repre-
   sents very well what Chief Wahbanosay's encampment might have
   looked like at the head of Lake Ontario during Sacred Feathers's early
   boyhood. Courtesy of the Royal
   Ontario Museum, Toronto, Canada.

4. The camp meeting was the red-letter week of the Methodists' year, given up entirely to prayer and singing. The sketch, the earliest extant of any Methodist camp meeting in Upper Canada, was made in 1859 at the spot the Mississaugas termed Mossquawaunk, the "salt lick where deer resort," or as the white settlers termed the area, Grimsby. United Church Archives, Victoria University, Toronto, Ontario.

5. The Reverend William Case and his second wife, Eliza Barnes Case, also a mission worker. The American-born preacher was the father of the early Methodist Indian mission work in Upper Canada. When Case saw Peter Jones stand up among the converted at the Ancaster camp meeting of 1823 he exclaimed, "Glory to God, there stands a son of Augustus Jones, of the Grand River, amongst the converts; now is the door opened for the work of conversion amongst his nation!" United Church Archives, Victoria University, Toronto, Ontario.

6. Egerton Ryerson, Peter Jones's best lifelong friend—in effect his blood brother. Still renowned as the founder of the modern Ontario school system, Ryerson served as the first ordained Methodist missionary to the Credit River Indians in 1826–27. He later became superintendent of education for Canada West (Upper Canada) in 1844, serving in that office until his retirement in 1876. From the July 1838 issue of the *Wesleyan-Methodist Magazine,* published in London, England.

7. The Indian village on the Credit River during the winter of 1826–27. The houses, just completed, were dressed log cottages with two rooms, of the type erected as a second house by settlers who had been on their farms five to ten years. Two families occupied these houses, each family having its own room. Originally twenty of these two-family houses were built. From Egerton Ryerson, *"The Story of My Life,"* ed. J. George Hodgins (Toronto: William Briggs, 1883), p. 59.

8. Eliza Field Jones sketched her "first Canadian home" shortly after her arrival at the Credit Mission in the fall of 1833. Here we see, from left to right, the school and council house, the church, and Peter's tiny study—which was Peter's and Eliza's first home until they constructed their own house. On the top of the flagpole in the center of the drawing is a small house for martins to nest in—their presence being considered a good omen. From Ryerson's *"The Story of My Life,"* opposite p. 72.

9. Titus Hibbert Ware completed this watercolor of Anishinabeg in the Lake Simcoe area (at Coldwater) in 1844. The Indian men adjusted to European dress more easily than did the women, but they still wore moccasins and colorful sashes around their waists. Metropolitan Toronto Library, T 14386.

10. The Mississaugas obtained new names, homes, occupations, and a new language, all in the space of a few years. Here a number of Mississaugas have written their English and Indian names and drawn their totems in an album kept by Eliza Field Jones. Arvilla Louise Thorp, Aldergrove, B.C.

same cause.[40] Without any close relatives, he had grown up poor, hungry, and often very cold. When he walked into Belleville he owned only a knife, a blanket, and a coat.[41]

The Belleville Methodists took a great interest in the clever, good-looking Indian, who called himself a "wild partridge."[42] He had presence even at sixteen. From a surviving photograph taken some thirty years later one can see his handsome features and powerful frame. The young Mississauga could carry 180 pounds on a portage.[43]

At Belleville a white minister told Peter Jacobs, who knew a little English, of "a beautiful heaven, where nothing but joy was to be experienced, and of the awful flames of hell, where the wicked shall be cast if they do not believe in the Christ Jesus." The idea troubled him. He asked the minister if the same God the white man worshiped concerned himself with Indians. When told that he did, Peter prayed in English, thinking that God could understand only that tongue. Throughout January 1826 he prayed, but without achieving peace of mind. Years later he recalled the agony of this period: "I felt just like the wounded deer. You know we North American Indians are great deer-hunters; and when we shoot the deer in the heart with bow and arrow, he runs away as if he was not hurt, but when he gets to a hill he feels the pain, and he lays down on that side, and turns over; and so he wanders about till he perishes. I felt pained in this way. I felt pain in my heart, but could not get better."[44] Then he met Peter Jones.

In early February the Reverend William Case invited Peter Jones and Chief John Crane to the Bay of Quinte. They reached Belleville on 9 February. On that date Peter noted in his diary: "Here I met with an Indian lad named Peter Jacobs, who was learning to read, and appeared very anxious to be instructed in the Christian religion and reading."[45] At the noonday lunch the Mississauga missionary gave thanks to the Creator in Ojibwa: "O Father! I thank thee for giving bread to our bodies." Peter Jacobs needed to hear no more: "If God understands your Ojibwa, he will understand mine." He began to pray in his own language. Shortly afterward God heard his prayers and the Holy Spirit entered his heart.[46] He later enrolled at the Credit Mission school when it was established.

Over the next two weeks Chief John Crane and Peter traveled on horseback, then by sleigh and on foot through snow almost knee-deep, to the isolated Indian camps. News of their arrival attracted Mississaugas to Belleville from as far as fifty kilometers away.[47] Before his Indian audiences Peter always explained what the Reverend William Case had told him: that all people, Indian and white, were "brothers by creation, that God was our Father, that he made one man at the first, and that all nations spring from him." He stressed that whites and Indians belonged to the same race. The differences in skin color between whites and Indians arose "from circumstances, such as the climate and our mode of living."[48]

Among those attracted to hear Peter Jones stood a warrior named Shawundais, whose name meant "sultry heat" such as the sun gives out in summer just before a refreshing rain. Strongly built and tall, he had once commanded the respect of his community but had lost it through his heavy drinking. Apart from the words "pint," "quart," and "whiskey" he knew no English. This veteran of the Battle of Chrysler's Farm in the War of 1812 covered his face with red paint, wore feathers in his hair, a blanket and leggings, and silver ornaments on his chest. He carried a rifle on his shoulder and a tomahawk and scalping knife in his belt.[49] Yet appearances can be deceiving. Shawundais, or John Sunday as the settlers called him, wanted to learn more about Christianity.

Peter Jones's greatest problem in converting the Anishinabeg to Christianity lay in convincing them that whites and Indians could share the same religion. As William Case had recommended, the Mississauga preacher first reviewed the story of Adam and Eve and emphasized that the Indians and whites had not been created separately. Then Peter reached the only important distinction that did exist. All men, he explained, travel down one of two roads: "the broad road that leads to destruction, and the narrow road that leads to heaven." When John heard that all drunkards walked the wide path to everlasting fire, he trembled. The hardened warrior could not sleep for four nights, convinced he belonged to the devil.[50]

Only several months later did John Sunday find peace. On Peter Jones's second missionary tour to the Bay of Quinte, he asked John to pray in Ojibwa. He did so, saying only, "O Keshamunedo, shahnane-meshin," O Lord have mercy on me poor sinner. It happened. Those few Ojibwa words led John to shout and shake with joy. "I feel something in my heart," he told Peter, who replied, "The Lord blesses you now."[51]

By the end of Peter's second tour on 31 May the Reverend William Case had baptized twenty-one adults. The energetic preaching of Sunday, Jacobs, and William Beaver, another native convert, led the Christian community to double to forty-three by mid-June.[52] William Beaver summarized his approach in these words: "I tell 'em they must all turn away from sin, that the Great Spirit will give 'em new eyes to see, new ears to hear good things; new heart to understand, and sing pray: all new! I tell 'em women, they must wash 'em blanket clean—must cook 'em victuals clean like white woman— They must all live in peace, worship God, and love one another."[53]

Peter Jones and his evangelistic team kept to their winning formula. Over several days they concentrated on teaching would-be converts to memorize the Ten Commandments, the Lord's Prayer, and those portions of the Scripture translated into Ojibwa. The interpreter would pronounce a sentence, which everyone repeated after him. They also taught them hymns. Thirty years later William Case still remembered the "impressive answer" of the first converts to the preachers' final question: "Dost thou renounce the devil and all his works?" "They then all repeated with full voice, Aah; at the same time lifting their feet, they brought them down on the floor with a force that made the timbers of the old chapel to tremble again."[54]

At his missionary superintendent's invitation, Peter Jones returned several times to the Bay of Quinte in 1826. Almost all the 130 Mississaugas in the Belleville area and fifteen families around Kingston, roughly ninety people, accepted Christianity. Only three or four Mississauga families in the Kingston area refused the new faith.[55]

The gospel spread elsewhere through the Anishinabeg country in

1826. Whenever a convert met a non-Christian, conversations began. Over campfires tales of the new faith spread rapidly. With the help of John Sunday and his friend John Moses, Peter Jones also carried the gospel to the Lake Simcoe Indians in July 1826. Forcefully Sunday and Moses warned their Indian audiences that if they refused to hear, "eternal fire" would be their reward forevermore.[56] One of the three Lake Simcoe chiefs, the sixty-year-old William Snake, decided to convert.[57] In the following two summers Peter and his native workers expanded the work around Lake Simcoe.

Peter Jones continually stressed the concept of sin. In 1827 the Reverend Thaddeus Osgood, the organizer of several charitable schemes to help the poor and the North American Indians, heard one of his sermons to the Lake Simcoe Ojibwas. Peter had begun with the Ten Commandments:

At a certain time, a cloud descended upon Mount Sinai, one of the mountains in the eastern part of the world—It thundered—it lightened—the earth trembled and shook—and the Almighty God, the Great Spirit, spoke with an audible voice these words, and afterwards wrote them on tables of stone.

The native missionary paused. As requested, the Indians then stood up, repeating in turn each of the commandments. Then the speaker's tone suddenly changed:

Now you have all broken these commands, for they were as much designed for you, as for those to whom they were first given. And the Great Spirit is offended with you for having done the things you ought not, and having left undone things which you ought to have done. But he is willing to pardon your sins, and forgive all your transgressions, if you do sincerely repent.

To assure you of his good will and kindness to the human race, he has sent his Son from heaven, to seek and save that which is lost. You are all in a lost and miserable condition, and unless you repent, you must perish; that is, be miserable for ever.[58]

By the fall of 1827 a hundred Lake Simcoe Indians had accepted Methodism. A year later the figure had risen to nearly 400 out of the total population of 515, including Yellowhead, the head chief, who only a decade earlier had been the first signatory of the agreement surrendering 2,500 square miles of land immediately south of Georgian Bay to the British Crown.[59]

The Rice Lake Mississaugas first received Christianity in August 1826. As elsewhere along the north shore of Lake Ontario, the fur trade had greatly disturbed the stability of their communities. Charles Fothergill, who lived at Rice Lake for eighteen months before becoming Upper Canada's king's printer in 1821, described the Rice Lake whiskey traders as "the most unprincipled miscreants it is possible to conceive." Within the short space of a few months, he added, four suicides and two murders occurred among the small tribe, "entirely owing to the unrestricted use of ardent spirits."[60]

Since the War of 1812 settlement had advanced further northward from York to Newmarket and Holland Landing, the northern terminus of the old Toronto portage and of the new road, Yonge Street. Similarly, settlement extended to the northeast toward Rice Lake, where in 1825 over two thousand Irish immigrants settled.[61] Every year the European farmers took more and more of the Indians' trapping territories.

The Rice Lake Indians first witnessed a Methodist meeting in late August 1826. About a hundred Mississaugas from the Credit River and the Bay of Quinte had gathered to attend the annual conference of the church at Hamilton, near Cobourg. William Beaver translated the white ministers' sermons, and Peter Jones and John Sunday preached in Ojibwa. In the enthusiasm of the moment Joseph Sawyer, Big Jacob (John Sunday's brother), and Peter Wasson set off to invite the Rice Lake Mississaugas to join them.

On their arrival at Rice Lake the messengers shook hands all around, then one of them began to speak of "Jesus Christ, Ke-sha-mon-e-doo O-gwe-sin" (the Benevolent Spirit's son), who had come down to the world to save people. The Indian Christians explained that Jesus had left a book containing all his commands and sayings, which the black coats had at the camp meeting. The messengers then sang a hymn, knelt down, and prayed to the Great Spirit that the Rice Lake people would join them. About thirty agreed. All night the Indians traveled over a rough road through the forest, wading deep creeks. At the campground they found the Credit and Grape Island Indians, in the words of one young witness, "singing, some praying, and others lying about the ground as if dead."[62]

Peter Jones, his Indian helpers, and the Methodist ministers in one day converted all the newcomers, including the head chief, George Paudash. In squads they then taught the Rice Lake Indians the Lord's Prayer and the important hymns. The new converts clapped their hands, and these lovers of music rhythmically shouted, "Jesus nin ge shah wa ne mig," Jesus has blessed me. The gospel next spread to the country between Lake Simcoe and Rice Lake—to Lake Scugog and Mud (Chemong or Curve) Lake.[63] At the time of Peter's visit to Moses Blackstock's cabin in Cavan, January 1827, about one-third of the three hundred Rice, Mud, and Scugog Lake Indians had already accepted Christianity.[64]

The converts' enthusiasm astonished the Methodists' Indian workers. At Lake Simcoe Peter Jacobs found the Indians wanted him to continue preaching at eleven P.M. They told him: "When we were Heathen we never gave up drinking the fire-water the whole night, and why should we now go to bed? Why should we not go on singing and praising God till daylight?" Jacobs, young and energetic, agreed and preached through most of the night.[65]

By the summer of 1828, twelve hundred of the five thousand Indians near settlements in southern Upper Canada received religious instruction from the Methodist preachers and their native helpers.[66] The center of the great Anishinabe missionary effort was the Credit Mission. John Carroll, a prominent Methodist preacher in the mid-nineteenth century, later recalled this period. "A more lively, lovely, happy and holy community than that Indian society at the Credit was for many years, I do not believe ever existed."[67]

Peter Jones had only two fears. He recorded the first in his diary in the summer of 1828: "I see only one difficulty in the way of the Gospel taking the wings of the morning and flying to the Western or Pacific Ocean, and making the wilderness vocal with the high praises of God, and that is the opposition it will meet from the

Roman Catholics."[68] A second threat also existed, that posed by the Reverend John Strachan and the Church of England, supported by the lieutenant governor of Upper Canada.

For Peter the danger posed by both the Roman Catholics and the Anglicans was real. Well taught by his first Methodist advisers, he saw them as advocates of inferior, dangerous versions of Christianity. He wrote in 1828 of the Roman Catholics, for example, "they neglect to teach them [the Indians] the depravity of the human heart, and the necessity of coming to Christ alone for pardon and mercy: in this way they make the Indians ten times more the children of the devil than they were before."[69] Similarly, he had little respect for the Church of England, whose clergy among the Mohawks, he wrote in 1830, "have for a century past been in the habit of administering that holy ordinance to notorious drunkards, Sabbath breakers, and whoremongers."[70]

Opposition

The council on Indian land rights began at the York garrison, three kilometers west of the town site.[1] Fifteen years earlier Britain and the United States had fought one of the major battles of the War of 1812 there. Over sixty British regulars and five civilians had died unsuccessfully defending Upper Canada's tiny capital. The American success proved costly, though, with 320 killed or wounded. Brigadier General Zebulon Pike, second-in-command of the expedition, remembered as an explorer of the American Southwest—Pikes Peak is named for him—lay among the dead.[2]

From 1813 to 1828 York's population had doubled—nearly tripled—to over two thousand.[3] The town on 30 January 1828 extended along the lakefront from the garrison in the west to the mouth of the Don River in the east. York still lacked paved streets. All the houses were small wooden structures, one story high, except for a few three-story brick buildings in the main business area. Behind the town rose the dense forest, with only one major gap apparent along the ridge, the route followed by Yonge Street, reaching northward to the farms on the way to Newmarket and Holland Landing.[4]

The Indians walked to the fort from the west, the east, and the northeast. Chief James Ajetance, Peter Jones, and several warriors approached from Credit Mission, twenty kilometers to the west. Their band, numbering about 225, had settled into their new log houses and had begun to clear land for farming. From the east also came John Sunday and four Mississauga warriors from the Bay of

Quinte. William Case, using funds supplied by the American Methodists, had just built a mission for them on tiny Grape Island, roughly ten acres in size, ten kilometers east of Belleville. The first houses had recently been completed on the island for the 130 Mississaugas around Belleville and about 40 converts from the Kingston area. Finally, Chief George Paudash arrived from Rice Lake in the northwest. Still without a village, he and his people at Rice Lake and Mud Lake, numbering about 300, lived in wigwams winter and summer.[5]

At the fort commander's quarters the man the Mississaugas called "the Wolf" stood before them.[6] Fifteen years earlier—during the defense of York—James Givins had commanded about fifty Indian warriors, including Joseph Sawyer and William Yellowhead of Lake Simcoe. The several hundred Indian and British sharpshooters had briefly held up the American invasion army of 1,700.[7]

James Givins remembered the week-long occupation of York. The Americans captured, sacked, and partly burned the fort, then the would-be liberators of Upper Canada put to the torch almost every public building in York, including the Parliament buildings. They also opened the jail and released all the criminals. Quite justly in the Wolf's opinion, the British had retaliated. The following year they attacked Washington, burning the American Capitol and the president's house (which when rebuilt became known as the White House because the walls were whitewashed to hide the fire marks).[8]

John Sunday, broad shouldered and powerful, addressed the Indian agent. According to Indian etiquette, he first shook hands with everyone in the room,[9] including each of the British officers. As requested, Peter Jones interpreted from Ojibwa into English the chief's concerns about his people's land rights. "We have but lately had our eyes opened,"[10] the chief began. His people desperately needed more land. Grape Island lacked sufficient wood and pasture. Could they cut logs for their buildings on the king's neighboring islands? Did they still own any of the neighboring islands in the Bay of Quinte near their new village? The elders said they had reserved them at the land surrenders.

Following Chief Sunday a younger man, majestic in appearance and with a fine, commanding voice, stepped forward. For a year Chief Paudash had exhorted on the Methodists' behalf.[11] He came not about land but about housing. Speaking in Ojibwa—since he knew no English—he explained how his brethren on his right hand now lived comfortably in houses, as did those on his left. Would the government do the same for the Rice Lake Indians as it had done for the Credit Indians, and as the missionaries had done at Grape Island? Would His Majesty build his people a village using the Rice Lake Indians' own annuity money?[12]

At the end Chief James Ajetance, the oldest of the three chiefs, addressed the council. Captain Jim, then a man of sixty, had been a boy during the American Revolution, a young man at the time of the first land purchases, a seasoned warrior by the outbreak of the War of 1812. Of the three chiefs he had the most reason to be nervous in a British garrison: he had known the murdered Chief Wabakinine and his wife. Outside the council room he heard the harsh commands and the marching of the British soldiers at their drill.

Chief Ajetance began his remarks with a compliment, thanking the Indian agent for supplying the Credit Indians with comfortable homes. Then indirectly he raised his major concern: "Having heard some bad birds crying that we did not own any lands on the Credit, we wish to know from our great father how much land we really possess." In 1820, had the Credit Indians not merely placed their lands in the safekeeping of the government? They had said nothing about their sale. Givins first listened, then dropped his bombshell. The Wolf informed the Credit chief in Ojibwa that they had surrendered all of their lands outright.[13] After the council Givins told Peter and John Jones to go immediately to see Major Hillier, the lieutenant governor's secretary, at Government House. The campaign to weaken the Methodists' hold on the Indians had begun.

The two brothers set off for town across the bridge over Garrison Creek, down the frozen path along the lakeshore. When they reached the big house, which loomed off the road, they soon knew they were held in official disfavor—Hillier let them wait. An hour later he appeared, but only to tell them to return the next morning at eleven.[14]

Agent James Givins helped plan this anti-Methodist campaign. He had spent three years during the Revolutionary War as an American prisoner in Williamsburg, Virginia.[15] Thirty years later, in 1813, these same rebels had attacked York, causing great damage and loss of life. On the floor of his dining room bloodstains still remained from the wounded men his wife had cared for immediately after the battle.[16] The Americans later looted his house, stealing two carpets, curtains, cutlery, clothes, and an English saddle, even running off with "the glass and gilt frame encompassing a picture of the Battle of Trafalgar."[17] The Indian agent hated Americans, and by association that meant Methodists as well.

For thirty years James Givins had administered the Mississaugas' affairs. Now these Methodist Indians contested him, claiming tracts that the Indian Department considered long surrendered. Who was to blame? The Wolf held the American Methodists responsible. After the council at the garrison he reminded Major Hillier of "the too great influence already exercised over them [the Credit Indians] by those designing white persons . . . Methodists, and the greater part of them from the United States of America."[18]

The Reverend John Strachan strongly supported any attempt to undermine the Methodists' Indian influence, as did Sir Peregrine Maitland, the lieutenant governor of Upper Canada. They regarded the Methodists as subversive plotters determined to bring Upper Canada into the American union. In fairness to Strachan and Maitland, the Methodists in 1828 were vulnerable to the charge of being American controlled. The American Methodist Episcopal church had indeed founded the Upper Canadian church. Although Upper Canada had become a separate conference in 1824, only in 1828 did it gain its full independence.

To understand Sir Peregrine's strict, uncompromising approach to the Methodists one must know something of his social and military background. He came from the same privileged social world that Jane Austen (one of Sir Peregrine's aunts married Jane Austen's older brother) described in her novels. His father was a country squire, his maternal grandfather a general, and his maternal great-grandfather a duke.[19] At the age of fourteen Peregrine had entered the foot guards, a division of the future Grenadier Guards, rising to the rank of major general. Throughout the Napoleonic Wars he had served in Wellington's army in Spain and later commanded the First Foot Guards at the Battle of Waterloo in 1815. His elite group of two thousand shock troops had broken the famous last charge of Napoleon's Imperial Guard.[20]

As an administrator the handsome, now white haired governor[21] had a career soldier's idea of discipline. Hypersensitive to any attack on order and stability, he tolerated no open dissent. He had only three close advisers in his inner circle, the first being Major George Hillier, his civil secretary, a close friend who had served with him throughout the Peninsular and the Waterloo campaigns. His second adviser was John Beverley Robinson, the articulate and self-assured attorney general, a second-generation Loyalist and a former student at the Reverend John Strachan's school, years before at Cornwall, Upper Canada. So close in fact was Robinson to Strachan that the Anglican clergyman called him his adopted son. Finally, Mr. Strachan himself advised the lieutenant governor; in fact during the early years of Maitland's administration he had been his chief adviser, in effect his prime minister.[22] On Indian matters James Givins, whose daughter Caroline had married Major Hillier, also belonged to the small governing clique.[23]

Maitland regarded the Indians' affiliation with the Church of England as a prerequisite for government support. Speaking through Agent Givins, he had told the Credit Indians as much on 8 August 1826. The Wolf had warned the Indians that the governor would "cast them off" if they attended any more Methodist camp meetings. For a short time the Credit Indians stayed away, but they did not renounce Methodism.[24] Peter Jones had kept the Indians loyal to to their church.

When the Jones brothers called at Government House on the morning of 31 January 1828, Major Hillier again kept them waiting. A full two hours passed before he finally summoned them into the presence of the Reverend John Strachan, Attorney General Robinson, and Indian Agent Givins. The Anglican clergyman made the official announcement that the governor "did not feel disposed to assist the Indians so long as they remained under the instruction of their present teachers, who were not responsible to the Government for any of their proceedings and instructions." Only if the Credit Indians—and the Jones brothers—joined the Church of England would the government continue to assist the band. If Peter and John consented to join the Church of England their salaries would be increased, and they could gain entrance to the future college then contemplated at York. They could study to enter the ministry of the Church of England.[25]

The governor's inner circle had miscalculated once again. They applied pressure to the wrong men. After the caution against attending camp meetings in 1826, Peter—who normally kept such emotion out of his diary entries—exploded. Was man not a free agent with "a right to worship God according to the dictates of his own conscience"? Did not the king's laws grant all his subjects the liberty "to worship God as they felt it their duty . . . if a man thought it right to retire to the woods to pray, who had a right to prevent him?"[26] Sir Peregrine's pressures and enticements had not convinced Peter in 1826 that he should join the Church of England, nor did they in 1828. When Sir Peregrine left Upper Canada in late 1828 to become the new lieutenant governor of Nova Scotia, Peter and John remained staunch Methodists.

As Maitland's replacement the Colonial Office selected Major General Sir John Colborne, a second distinguished veteran of the Battle of Waterloo.[27] The new appointee at first publicly pursued a more conciliatory policy toward the Methodists than had his predecessor. Impressed by the Methodists' model village at the Credit, Sir John suggested in early May 1829 that the "order and regularity which has been established among them . . . be extended to other tribes." But in the same note to Sir James Kempt, governor general of Canada, Colborne indicated, his public declarations to the contrary, that he wished to check the "Methodist Preachers from the United States . . . by employing religious teachers from England."[28]

The governor's long-range plan included an eventual invitation to the British Wesleyans to enter Upper Canada in force. Thanks to their own financial success the group had emerged by the 1820s as middle-class conservatives, obsessed by authority—which made them quite acceptable to Sir John Colborne. Had not Jabez Bunting, the leading British Wesleyan Methodist, been reported in 1827 to have said that Methodism was as opposed to democracy as it was to sin?[29]

Aware of the new governor's dislike of the "American" Methodists, James Givins tried himself to dislodge them from the Credit Mission. Since the defeat of the French the British had installed each new Ojibwa chief by presenting him with a silver medal from the sovereign. The chiefs, who called the medals their "hearts," accepted them as their sign of office, usually at the present-giving ceremonies in the summer. Because John Cameron had died in October 1828 and James Ajetance had followed shortly afterward, the Credit Indians had appointed two new chiefs. They selected Peter Jones as Chief Cameron's successor and Joseph Sawyer as head chief succeeding James Ajetance. That summer, however, the Wolf refused to accept the Indians' choices, sternly telling them that "they had done wrong" in electing them. He ordered them to go back and hold another council.[30]

The men withdrew, then returned. They held firm. Metwechings, or Samuel Wahbehneeb, acted as spokesman: "*Father*, we have grown up from childhood to manhood before your eyes. You have seen how poor, wretched, and miserable we have been." Then Wahbehneeb pointed to Peter Jones: "This young man was the first to open our eyes by telling us the words of the Great Spirit. He has laboured for our good, and we owe much to him for what we now are."[31] Unanimously they refused to back down. Without any alternative, James Givins accepted the two, presenting each with a medal and a Union Jack.[32]

Unlike Sir Peregrine Maitland, who had directly opposed the Methodists' Indian mission work, Sir John Colborne played a double game. On the one hand he told Peter Jones in late June 1829 that it made no difference who educated them, "the main object is to benefit the Indians,"[33] while on the other hand he privately worked to promote the interests of the Church of England.

Sir John's first intervention came at Lake Simcoe and at Matchedash Bay on the Georgian Bay. Impressed by Peter Jones's and the Methodists' outstanding success at the Credit River, the lieutenant governor now believed that the government of Upper Canada could duplicate it. Early in 1830 he announced the new "civilization policy." The imperial government would build settlements on the Credit model throughout the province, two of the first being at the Narrows at the northern end of Lake Simcoe and at neighboring Coldwater near Matchedash Bay. Yet notwithstanding his promises to Peter Jones to leave alone the Indians already evangelized by the Methodists, Sir John sent an Anglican minister and a white teacher to the Matchedash people.[34] Without native assistants, though, the government school failed to attract any students.[35] In contrast, the Methodists' school at Matchedash, taught by James Currie, a Scot, and David Sawyer, Peter Jones's first cousin, continued to prosper, as did their classroom near the Narrows under William Law, an Englishman, and Benjamin Crane, one of the first Credit River converts.[36]

Faced with failure, the government became more aggressive. T. G. Anderson, the Coldwater Indian agent, led the attack. For years he had been a fur trader on the Mississippi River and during the War of 1812 had commanded the British attack on the American-held Fort Prairie du Chien on the Mississippi in 1814. As a result of his seizure of the fort, he gained a post in the Upper Canadian Indian Department.[37] In the fall of 1830 Anderson allowed Gerald Alley, an agricultural instructor appointed by the government, to disrupt the Methodists' school at Yellowhead's island near the Narrows. According to a Methodist account, as soon as he arrived on the island Alley presented himself at the schoolhouse and then—without any formalities—ordered, in the words of teacher William Law, "that he should take out of my school, the first class, in order to teach the most forward boys."[38] Law refused. The next summer, when the Methodist instructors attempted to move into the new school at the

Narrows, they claimed that Alley had boarded it up.[39] Repeatedly the government attempted to curb the Methodists' advances among the Anishinabeg of Coldwater and the Narrows.

The government's campaign to advance the Church of England no doubt confused the Indians. As Egerton Ryerson later recalled, the first Mississauga converts "supposed that there was but one kind or denomination of Christians."[40] Now the Indian agents spoke in praise of the "king's religion."[41] They also heard from the Metis and a group of Anishinabeg from Lake Michigan of the "French religion,"[42] as they called the Roman Catholic faith, and this soon constituted an even greater threat to Peter Jones and his evangelistic team.

During the French regime the Jesuit fathers had operated active missions among the Algonquian-speaking Indians of the Great Lakes. The missions had ended, though, shortly after the British conquest, leaving among the Upper Lake Algonquians only a distant memory of the "Blackrobes."[43] In the early nineteenth century only one mission station, Lac des Deux Montagnes (Lake of Two Mountains), fifty kilometers west of Montreal on the Ottawa River, welcomed the Anishinabeg of the Great Lakes.[44] The Roman Catholic mission, run by the Sulpicians of Montreal, baptized those visiting Algonquian Indians who expressed an interest in Christianity. In 1831, for example, John Sunday met a group of Indians on Georgian Bay who told him they had become Christians in Montreal, "a great while ago."[45] One of the Sulpicians' early converts at their mission, Jean-Baptiste Assiginack, or Blackbird, became the catalyst of a Roman Catholic revival in the Upper Lakes.

Blackbird, an Odawa or Ottawa Indian, had attended the Sulpicians' school at Lake of Two Mountains as a boy.[46] Originally from L'Arbre Croche (Crooked Tree), an Odawa settlement near Lake Michigan on the Lower Michigan peninsula, Blackbird had fought for Britain in the War of 1812. After the war he had served as an Ojibwa interpreter for the English garrison on Drummond Island, seventy-five kilometers southeast of Sault Ste. Marie. But once the chief heard that a Roman Catholic mission would be established at

L'Arbre Croche, he returned to his people, leaving his post at Drummond Island. His immediate supervisor T. G. Anderson, later appointed Indian agent at Coldwater and the Narrows, commented after receiving Blackbird's resignation: "A man of equal capacity with Assekinnick, to fill the situation, cannot be found in this part of the Country."[47]

At L'Arbre Croche Blackbird had been preceded by an Indian named Andowish, who had also lived for some time at Lake of Two Mountains. There he too had adopted the Roman Catholic faith. On his return Andowish had interested his own relatives, who in turn had approached their Metis kin at neighboring Michilimackinac, the great fur trading center.[48] The Metis invited a visiting clergyman to include the Indians at L'Arbre Croche in his journey. At L'Arbre Croche the priest empowered Blackbird to act as the missionary in his absence. Every Sunday thereafter Blackbird, in his nephew's words, "preached to his people and taught them how to pray to God and to the Virgin Mary and all the saints and angels in heaven."[49]

Peter Jones fully realized the consequences of the Roman Catholic revival in late 1828. After the British closed their fort at Drummond Island and moved the garrison to Penetang, seventy-five voyageur families of mixed European and Indian descent, speaking French as well as Ojibwa, moved into the northern periphery of the Methodists' territory.[50] Overnight the nucleus of a strong bicultural Roman Catholic community, with close ties to the resident Indian population, had been established immediately west of Matchedash and Lake Simcoe.

As soon as the British completed their new garrison they began to distribute the annual presents to the Indians of the Upper Great Lakes at Penetanguishene. Eager to obtain presents and the goods the traders offered for a quarter to a sixth of the price charged in distant Indian country,[51] native groups came from as far as the western end of Lake Superior. Blackbird, who had himself once helped distribute the gifts at Drummond Island, traveled with his people to Penetang, and there in June 1830 Peter Jones first heard him speak.

Blackbird, then in his late sixties, posed the native Methodists' greatest challenge. The renowned orator spoke, in Peter's words, "with great animation and was very conclusive in his remarks."[52] Among the Odawas and the Ojibwas of the Upper Great Lakes (the two tribes' languages are essentially the same tongue) he enjoyed "great influence."[53] Blackbird's decision to settle permanently at Coldwater in 1832[54] placed a serious obstacle in the way of any future Methodist advances in the area. Some months previously the Roman Catholics had already approached John Assance, the Matchedash chief, trying to attract him into their church.

Peter Jones had long considered the chief "a man of considerable thought and understanding."[55] They were related by blood, the chief's mother having come from the Credit River; Peter's grandmother was her eldest sister.[56] At John Assance's request Peter had interpreted for him in August 1828 before William Benjamin Robinson, the attorney general's brother, who served as a justice of the peace in Newmarket.[57] The Matchedash chief had complained about a white man who had severely beaten one of the members of his band, but Robinson refused to issue a warrant to arrest the man because the chief could not cite the day of the month when the beating occurred.[58] Would the presence of a large and dynamic Roman Catholic community at neighboring Penetang lead Chief John Assance to consider Roman Catholicism? The thought must have crossed Peter's mind.

In addition to their Anglican and Roman Catholic opponents the Methodists also confronted the Indian traditionalists, who remained formidable. In the late summer of 1829 Peter did interest many of the Saugeen Indians on the southeastern shore of Lake Huron in Christianity,[59] but he made little impression on the Walpole Island Indians around Lake St. Clair. Head Chief Pazhekezhik-quashkum, "he who makes footsteps in the sky,"[60] a respected holy man, guided the several hundred Ojibwas on the large island, roughly fifteen kilometers long and over five kilometers wide.[61]

Born on the Maumee River in Ohio approximately a hundred kilometers south of Detroit, probably well before the outbreak of the

American Revolution, Pazhekezhikquashkum had later lived on the west shore of Lake St. Clair. In the late 1820s the elderly chief had moved with his three sons across the border to Walpole Island.[62] Although he was an Odawa Indian, he became the political and spiritual leader of the Walpole Island Ojibwas as well as the island's Odawas.

Pazhekezhikquashkum was distinctly antiwhite. He believed that both his "father," the king of England, and his "stepfather," the president of the United States,[63] had hurt his people. To him the analogy drawn by a number of Great Lakes Indians comparing the English and American nations to a pair of scissors aptly summarized the Indians' condition. As the Reverend John Heckewelder, a Moravian minister in Ohio, reported the story:

By the construction of this instrument, they said, it would appear as if in shutting, these two sharp knives would strike together and destroy each other's edges; but no such thing: they only cut what comes between them. And thus the English and Americans do when they go to war against one another. It is not each other that they want to destroy, but us, poor Indians, that are between them. By this means they get our land, and, when that is obtained, the scissors are closed again, and laid aside for further use.[64]

After their long journey around the Georgian Bay then down the eastern shore of Lake Huron to Lake St. Clair, Peter and his native Christian helpers had reached Walpole Island in early August 1829. They found the elderly chief at his village. Magic poles stood erect at the door of every wigwam. One pole held a sacrificed dog near its top, others carried tobacco, skins, and feathers. When Pazhekezhikquashkum called his principal men together the next day, thirty warriors appeared and sat cross-legged in a ring behind their head chief.[65]

The head chief welcomed the Credit Indians as brothers and allowed Peter to present his message. At the end of his guest's remarks he replied. No, he and his people would not change their religion. Why should they? Was the whites' religion better? While the chief agreed with his Mississauga guest that strong drink had destroyed the Indian societies, he asked his visitors: Who makes the firewater? Who sells it to the Indian? Who lies and cheats the Indian? "Now the white man's religion is no better. I will hold fast to the religion of my forefathers, and follow them to the far west."[66] Peter and his followers made two further journeys to Walpole Island but they never convinced the old man to change his opinion.[67]

Similarly, the Ojibwas on the St. Clair River opposed Christianity. Wawanosh, an important chief on the Canadian side of the border, also refused to join the Methodists. The stoutly built man who had fought with the British in the War of 1812 at Michilimackinac, Detroit, Queenston Heights, and Lundy's Lane, saw no need in 1829 or the early 1830s to abandon the old religion.[68] Nor did his wife, when she saw how plainly the Christian Indian women attired themselves. "Do all the women dress like these when they become Christians?"[69]

Other traditionalists in the Lake St. Clair area also resisted the Methodists. Believing that the white and Indian missionaries had "Great Spirit Medicine," they avoided everything they had touched: a piece of bread, a cake, any kind of food. If they ate such food, the traditionalists believed, the Christians would gain an irresistible power over their spirits, and they could no longer refuse the new religion.[70]

Among the Ojibwas of the Thames Peter Beaver, converted by Peter Jones in 1827, had a very difficult time. The traditionalists opposed him with a vengeance. Once a woman had almost tomahawked him while he prayed, grabbing his hair and twisting his head around.[71] Under the strain of the constant taunts of his people, the young Indian's spirit broke. He went berserk, threatening to kill everyone around him. Finally early in 1831 he took his own life.[72]

The loss of Chief Kegedoons also proved a great blow. The leader of the Saugeen Indians had welcomed Peter Jones during Peter's visit to Lake Huron in late July 1829.[73] That December Kegedoons and twenty of his people had traveled overland to the Credit to see for themselves the Christian settlement. Greatly impressed by what he found, Kegedoons rose at a prayer meeting and told his hosts: "My brothers and sisters whilst in my own country I heard what the Great Spirit had done for you, so I came to see for myself what all this meant. I have opened my ears to the words spoken by your ministers & what I had heard by the hearing of the ear I now see with mine own eyes. Brothers & Sisters, the Great Spirit has planted a *tree* at this place whose top reaches the skies—you have found this tree and are climbing up towards the abode of the Great Spirit."[74] Most of the Saugeens in Kegedoons's group converted to Christianity at the Credit. By the spring of 1831 nearly half of the two hundred Saugeens, including Kegedoons himself, had joined the Methodists.[75] But that fall the chief disappeared. Near the new settlement of Goderich the Indians found his lifeless body, "bruised and mangled in such a way as to make it evident that he had been murdered." In Chief John Assance's words, "we do not believe the whites would do this but fear some unknown people of our own colour—lurk about to shed our blood." A century later Kegedoons's great-grandson still believed he had been murdered.[76]

In the face of all of this opposition—Pazhekezhikquashkum's objections, Peter Beaver's suicide, and the death of Kegedoons— Peter Jones saw the hand of the devil. He later wrote, "if witchcraft still exists in the world, it is to be found among the aborigines of America."[77] With all his powers Peter worked to demolish "the empire of Satan" and erect the "standard of the cross . . . throughout our western wilderness."[78] But to defeat what Peter called Indian witchcraft and to combat the Anglicans and the Roman Catholics, the Methodists required help. The expense of maintaining nearly a dozen missions had taken a great toll on the church's finances, as the Reverend William Case knew only too well. To hold their gains, to expand them, to fight the opposition, the white and native Methodists needed money.

Fund-Raising

Chapter 8

The tenth anniversary of the Missionary Society at the John Street Chapel in New York City featured Kahkewaquonaby and the Indian children's choir. Methodists from farms as far north as mid-Manhattan traveled by foot or by hackney coach down Broadway to the rapidly expanding city of 200,000. Over the hilly terrain they passed orchards and gardens with fruit trees in blossom, the peach and cherry trees finishing, the plum and apple just beginning. The Christians soon reached the outskirts of the great metropolis, its skyline dominated by the spires of its one hundred churches and the cupola of City Hall completed just before the War of 1812.[1]

The anniversary began at 7 P.M., 4 May, and the small but growing crowd continued southward. Halfway between City Hall and Wall Street, the original boundary of the old Dutch settlement of New Amsterdam in the 1650s, they reached John Street and its famous chapel, the mother church of American Methodism. The granite building, completed in 1818, stood on the original site of the first Methodist preaching house in America, erected in 1768.[2]

Thanks to its magnificent harbor and to the Erie Canal, which linked the Hudson River with the Great Lakes, by 1829 New York had become the leading city west of the Atlantic. Only a decade or so earlier it had replaced Philadelphia as the largest urban center in the United States, and in the late 1820s it superseded Mexico City as the greatest metropolitan center of the Americas.[3] Approximately as many people lived in New York City in 1829 as in all of Upper Canada.[4]

The completion of the Erie Canal four years earlier had led to an abundance of jobs and brought great prosperity to the city. Back and forth went the barges, carrying grain, meat, metals, furs, lumber, and manufactured goods. New York had attracted an increasing amount of trade because of the canal, which in turn led merchants to build additional storehouses for the goods and more boats to carry them. As a result more vessels called at New York for cargoes, and the port's prosperity multiplied.[5]

It seemed that people from all over the world lived in and visited New York except the area's original inhabitants. The descendants of the Munsee-speaking tribes of the Hudson and Delaware river valleys now had their homes hundreds of kilometers away—some in Upper Canada and others in western New York, Wisconsin, Missouri, and soon Kansas.[6] Only a few Munsee place-names remained in New York, the only reminder of their former presence, the most prominent being Manhattan itself, or Manahah tank, "the place where they gather the wood to make bows," as the Munsees in Upper Canada translated the word.[7] Only the Munsees knew other important Lenni Lenape place-names such as Koo-ek-wen-aw-doo, "the grove of the long pine trees," the site of Philadelphia.[8] New York and the Eastern Seaboard had become the whites' country.

Prominently seated amid the Missionary Society's officials in the foremost pew was the wealthy Francis Hall, forty-four years old. The society's secretary knew firsthand about the rapid growth of his city and his adopted country. As editor of the weekly New York *Spectator* and coeditor of the influential daily the New York *Commercial Advertiser*, he kept abreast of all developments in his city and in the Union itself. Exactly thirty years earlier Francis, at age fourteen, had left his native England.[9]

The nearly two hundred pews filled quickly. Methodists had come from the city itself and from the farms to the north, and others had crossed over by steamer from Brooklyn, population ten thousand, on neighboring Long Island. Much had already been said about the fine melodious voices of the Canadian Indian converts,[10] who now neared the end of their three-month fund-raising tour. Again New York's Methodist community came forward to give both their moral and their financial support to the Indian missions and to hear the young native converts sing.

The service began. Bishop Elijah Hedding presided, giving the opening prayer. Until the previous fall the American bishop had headed the Methodist Episcopal church in Upper Canada as well as that of the United States, but now the Canadian church had become completely independent of its American parent. Beside the bishop stood the Reverend Nathan Bangs, the Missionary Society's treasurer, six feet three with ample locks falling down upon his shoulders. In his youth Bangs had served in Upper Canada, where he had met and married his Canadian wife. While on the Niagara circuit the young American missionary had known Augustus Jones and his Iroquois wife, who had both become devout Methodists.[11] Carefully, in his pronounced New England accent, Bangs read the society's tenth annual report.

The Missionary Society had achieved remarkable results in just ten years' time. The Methodist Episcopal church now claimed approximately 2,500 Indian members, 1,000, or two-fifths of them, within the newly independent Upper Canadian church, to which, even after the separation, the American Methodist Episcopal church continued to give seven hundred dollars a year for its Indian mission work. In the United States itself great progress had been made with two southern groups, the Choctaws in Mississippi and the Cherokees in Alabama, Tennessee, Georgia, and North Carolina. Among the Choctaws the Methodists had made 600 converts, and there were 800 among the Cherokees.[12] Peter Jones had followed the progress of the Cherokees closely.

The Cherokees, about 15,000 strong, still held a huge tribal territory, 400 kilometers long by 150–200 kilometers wide. By every test the tribe constituted a distinct nation, with its own political constitution modeled on that of the United States, its own public schools, and its own newspaper. Sequoya, an Indian genius, had devised a Cherokee alphabet. Most of the Cherokees' leaders were well educated. A number had acquired the whites' concepts of property and become owners of plantations, mills, and stores, and some even owned slaves. Many had become Christians. There had been considerable intermarriage between Indians and whites, so much so that by the mid-1820s an estimated one-quarter of the Cherokee population had some white ancestry. Just a year before in 1828 the Cherokees had elected as their principal chief John Ross, a mixed-blood Cherokee who in October 1829 became a member of the Methodist church.[13]

The young Canadian Indian missionary knew of the tribe's advances, being most impressed of all by the invention of "an alphabet for that language, which has been adopted by the nation."[14] His own niece, Catherine Brown Sunegoo, was named after Catherine Brown, an exemplary Cherokee Christian who had died at the age of twenty-three.[15] For Peter the Cherokees epitomized what the Upper Canadian Indians could become: self-supporting Christian farmers.

After Nathan Bangs finished reading the lengthy report, he turned the anniversary service over to the Reverend William Case. With great pride, the Canadian missionary superintendent introduced Peter Jones, who in turn presented the five Indian boys, from eight to twelve years old, and two girls aged thirteen and fourteen. For the audience the young students sang:

> *Jesus shall reign where'er the sun*
> *Does his successive journeys run . . .* [16]

Then Peter Jones quizzed them to show how well they could spell and speak English.

A young boy of twelve, Shahwahnegezhik from Lake Simcoe, attracted attention for his remarkably musical voice.[17] Only weeks before a friend of the missions in Philadelphia had offered to pay for his education. In return Shahwahnegezhik took his sponsor's name, Henry Steinhauer.[18] While in Philadelphia John Neagle, a well-known American artist, had painted the new Henry Steinhauer's portrait.[19]

Peter's short talk followed the students' presentation. He showed the audience some of the religious objects that convert Peter Beaver of the Sable River had given him. As the native missionary wrote in his diary: "The object in showing these cast-off gods was to set forth the power of the Gospel in pulling down the strong holds of Indian superstition and idolatry."[20]

The tour had proved enormously successful, with crowds of a thousand at a chapel in Troy, New York, two thousand at the John Street Chapel in New York City, and three thousand at a Baltimore gathering.[21] Since February Peter and the Indian children, with William Case and two female teachers, Hetty Hubbard and Eliza Barnes, had journeyed throughout the most densely populated sections of the northeastern United States. Peter had never before seen such audiences. As he wrote in his diary when he had first reached New York on 19 March: "An Indian preacher is a new thing in this city, and therefore hundreds came to see and hear."

From his father Peter had heard what New York and the Hudson River valley had looked like during his youth, when he had studied surveying there during the American Revolution. Now, half a century later, much had changed. The population of the United States immediately after the Revolution had not yet reached four million. In 1829 it was about to pass thirteen million. The original union of thirteen states had now expanded to twenty-four.[22]

America's technological advances, in particular, astonished the young Indian missionary. In 1829 the Americans prepared to introduce English steam locomotives in the United States. One of George Stephenson's celebrated locomotives, in fact, was exhibited in New York early in 1829.[23] Peter saw much on the tour that was new to him, including a microscope in Newark, New Jersey, "which magnified a flea as large as a coon, and a spider as large as a bear."[24]

The American Methodists contributed generously to the cause of the Upper Canadian missions. To maintain their nine stations the Canadian Methodists needed annually two thousand pounds, or eight thousand American dollars, to pay the missionaries, interpreters, and teachers, purchase school supplies, and build and maintain the mission buildings. Out of this sum the Canadian Methodists also financed the lengthy missionary tours to Lake Huron and, in the early 1830s Lake Superior. Thanks to the large donations of the Americans in 1829, William Case and Peter Jones collected, after all expenses had been paid, approximately $2,400, or £600,[25] roughly 30 percent of the funds needed for one year's operation of the missions.

Peter's initial hesitation and fear in addressing white audiences had subsided. Three years earlier he had mentioned in his diary that he entered a white people's chapel "in fear and trembling, feeling my weakness and unworthiness to speak to so large an assembly of polished people."[26] On the tour, however, the shortcomings of the white Christians became much more apparent. Peter was astounded by the behavior of the white Methodists at a church meeting at Utica, New York. He recorded in his diary on 10 May: "At 2 P.M., dinner was announced, when all rushed to the table like a herd of hungry swine around a trough of swill. I thought that these gentlemen were more greedy and hoggish than the wild Indians in the woods; for they would not allow their hunger to impel them to use such impetuosity to get to the eatables."[27] No longer did the white Methodists intimidate him.

In New York, Baltimore, Philadelphia, and Boston, Peter appeared at ease in the pulpit and on the podium. In the spirit of the moment, though, he did occasionally become carried away. On his visit to Philadelphia, for example, he told a large audience:

My white friends, there was a time when all this country belonged to our Indian fathers. Our fathers used to fish in these rivers and hunt through these woods; and where your houses now stand, there stood their wigwams. But the white men came across the great waters,—and the Indians drank the fire waters and they died. And now we are almost all gone,—there are a few in the west, and a handful of us in the north. And what do the Indians ask of you? do we want our land back again? No: we do not want our land back again! Do we want your fine houses, or your fine farms? No: we do not! All we say is, Send us the gospel—send us missionaries, and we are satisfied.[28]

At the age of twenty-seven Peter remained largely under the sway of his mentor the Reverend William Case. The missionary superintendent had taken great interest in him, guiding him and trying to mold him into the perfect church worker. He had directed him away from political questions, such as the Indians' land rights, to spiritual problems. To Peter he was "a kind father, the guide of my youth, the director of my early labors amongst my Indian brethren, the ever faithful counsellor and warm friend."[29]

William Case always advised young preachers like Peter to devote their lives totally to the church. Constantly he recommended: "Converse sparingly, and conduct yourself prudently with women."[30] Certainly he himself had done so, remaining a bachelor into his late forties. But on the evening of 4 May 1829 the Elder Case surprised everyone.

Immediately after the Missionary Society anniversary service the Reverend Nathan Bangs and the Indian visitors from Upper Canada walked over to Francis Hall's home, next to the church. There the Reverend Mr. Bangs united in marriage the tall, slender, round-faced missionary, now nearly fifty, and Hetty Hubbard, described by a fellow Methodist in very un-Methodist terms as a woman of "perhaps thirty-four, possessing a very fine figure."[31] Eliza Barnes, a fellow teacher, also "passionately fond"[32] of William Case, had lost out. During the ceremony she acted as Hetty's bridesmaid.

Once back in Upper Canada the missionary superintendent, now with many domestic responsibilities, had to delegate more of his work to others. The annual Upper Canadian conference in the fall of 1829, on Case's recommendation, named Peter Jones "A Missionary to the Indian Tribes,"[33] charged with visiting the existing missions and reaching out to still unconverted groups. His circuit now had a circumference of nearly fifteen hundred kilometers.[34]

The new appointment came at a difficult moment for the young native preacher, for it appears that Peter also wanted a life's partner. A very poignant note, really the first clue to his personal discontent, appears in his diary in mid-March 1829. Peter records at Poughkeepsie, New York, that he preached to a very attentive congregation in the local Methodist church. The "holy fire of the Lord prevailed," causing many to shed tears during his sermon. At the end of the address "a beautiful girl of about 18" approached him. What she said made an impression, for he recorded her words in full in his diary: "Indeed I should like to go with you to your people. I could teach them to sew, knit, and read, for I was taught to knit and sew when I was eight years old. I would love you as well as anybody; indeed I would." Without elaboration Peter adds, "the distance was great, and we had no means of conveying her to the Missions."[35] The silence is revealing.

Six months later on 13 September Peter began a spiritual diary, which contains the second clue about his desire to have a wife. He began by setting up an elaborate discipline for the following one-month period: to rise at 5:00 A.M. and pray; to read a portion of the Scripture while on his knees at 6:00 A.M.; to pray again at noon, at 4:00 P.M., and at sunset. Just before retiring at 9:00 P.M. he would read the Scripture once again and praise God "for the mercies of the past day." He followed this regime, but even this rigorous schedule of prayers failed to purify him. Two weeks later he wrote, "my mind is depraved, and that my heart is desperately wicked." On 3 October he complained of his "carnal mind." The entry for 1 November reads: "the more I look into my heart the more I see that depravity of my nature."[36]

The years 1829 and 1830 proved incredibly active, a period when Peter immersed himself in his work. In the summer of 1829 he led a group of native exhorters to Lake Huron and Lake St. Clair. He next visited Lake Simcoe, Rice Lake, and Grape Island in the Bay of Quinte. Often he left with his pack wrapped in a blanket, held by a tumpline slung across his chest, with gun in hand and carrying a small store of powder and shot. In the spring of 1830 he went again to Munceytown, then Lake St. Clair, and in the summer to Lake Simcoe, Penetang on the Georgian Bay, and then in August to Grape Island, home of the missionary superintendent.[37]

The Reverend William Case's missionary showpiece occupied much of the ten-acre island. From the water the twenty-three log cabins and the public buildings—chapel, schoolhouse, hospital, general store, blacksmith's shop, and mechanic's shop—all neatly whitewashed, looked large and impressive. The buildings, paid for by funds raised in the United States, stood on each side of a long street with the superintendent's residence at the center.[38]

The ten-kilometer canoe journey from Belleville took Peter roughly two hours. Upon his arrival the two hundred Grape Islanders gathered to welcome him, among them the Reverend William Case and a very large Mrs. Hetty Case, then in the final days of her pregnancy. Wisely Peter postponed discussing his personal business until after Hetty had given birth. For the next week the visitor simply followed the rigorous daily schedule that Case had instituted on the island. At 4:00 A.M. the superintendent blew a cow's horn to wake the entire village. He sounded the time for breakfast at 6:30 A.M., for the noonday meal at 12:30, and for supper at 5:00 P.M. During the day the villagers said their prayers immediately after their meals in the morning, at noon, and at night. The final blowing of the horn announced the hour for rest at 9 P.M.[39]

With all the biblical questions he received from the young schoolchildren, Peter's days passed quickly. "When Moses was found in the water, who then took care of him and brought him up?" "Why did they make Joseph a coat of many colors?" "What became of the mother of Jesus when he was crucified?" He loved the young Grape Islanders' interest in the Bible.[40]

Unfortunately, Peter's good friend John Sunday had left the island a few weeks earlier on a missionary tour to Lake St. Clair and Lake Huron. In fact, the very day that Peter had arrived on Grape Island, 6 August, John had addressed a group of Indians five hundred kilometers to the west. At Amherstburg on the Detroit River Chief Sunday told the Indians of the war then being fiercely waged to the east, the struggle that Peter Jones and the Methodists had begun:

Brothers, I desire to tell you, that where I have come from, the Indians are at war—many of the Indians and the white people have already rose up and flew to their arms. The evil spirit, the devil, who lives under the earth, is the one with whom the Indians, and the white people are at war—they are fighting for the Great Spirit who is in heaven, and are marching forward. We are now travelling and

*visiting our Indian brethren, to call for volunteers, that we may
become strong to kill the devil.*[41]

While on the island Peter must have thought constantly about
John Sunday's remarks at the Fort York Council of 1828. The inade-
quacy of the reserve was so obvious. Roughly two hundred Anishinabeg still lived crammed together on the island,[42] so small they could
not even keep a cow there. Daily the Indians had to paddle to an
island a kilometer away to tend their crops, while others had to cross
to a second island to look after their cattle and then visit another
island to collect firewood.[43] It was absurd. At the Credit Mission
Peter's band had the use of nearly four thousand acres adjacent to
their settlement.

On 10 August[44] Keche makahdawekoonahya, "the big black-coat
man,"[45] emerged triumphant from the mission house. Proudly he
told the villagers that Hetty had given birth to a healthy girl, Eliza
Jane, named after her bridesmaid. Two and a half weeks before his
fiftieth birthday, the Elder Case had become a father.

Shortly after the happy announcement Peter now approached the
superintendent with his surprise—his own marriage plans. He had a
friend at the Credit River whom he would like to marry. Could he do
so? As Peter reported to his brother John on 13 August:

*Since I have been here, I have ascertained the mind and wish of
Brother Case, about changing my mode of life. He thinks, that
according to the situation of things, and my standing in the Church,
that it will not do for me to think about getting burdened with a
wife at present. . . . You can communicate this intelligence to sister
Anna in such a way as your wisdom may direct. . . . If our Friends
have any regard for me, and for our family, I am sure they will
readily agree in opinion with those that have experience and are at
the head of the Church.*[46]

William Case considered the question entirely from the Indian
missions' standpoint. Clearly the trusted native missionary, bilingual and bicultural, constituted the essential link between the

Indians and the whites. The Reverend John Strachan had recognized this and, several years earlier, had tried to win him over to the Church of England. Just a few months before, John Colborne himself had attempted to entice Peter away by proposing that he become an Indian agent.[47] At all costs William Case wanted Peter totally free to work directly with the Anishinabeg. Peter obeyed. Poor Anna's name never surfaced again in his correspondence. Apart from her first name, nothing more is known about her. Was she an Indian convert? A white mission worker? A white farmer's daughter from the Credit River area? No record survives.

The missionary superintendent's rejection of Anna greatly upset Peter, and in the weeks to follow he worked out his sorrow by applying his Methodist standards just as William Case did, in the strictest manner. When he made a surprise inspection of the Grape Islanders' homes on 3 September, for example, he recorded the most minute and inconsequential details, including a misplaced teakettle, a home with unmade beds, and several with dirty floors:

WM BEAVER'S—*Women absent—table, floor, cupboard, good but dusty. . . . JOHN SIMPSON'S—Floor neat—table and chairs good—cupboard good—beds good but not made. BRO. HURLBURT'S [Thomas Hurlburt and his wife were white mission helpers]—All neat like a white squaw's house, except the tea kettle, which was out of place. . . . JOHN SALT'S—Floor poor and dirty—corn husks etc., lying all about the floor—cupboard very dirty—beds poor—table poor and dirty. JOHN SNAKE'S—No one at home—all looked well in the house.*[48]

Frustrated and unhappy, Peter Jones needed a challenge worthy of him—and just months later he received it.

The Methodists' financial crisis in 1830 helps explain Case's decision about Peter's marriage. Since there existed no permanent fund to support the missions in Upper Canada, they survived only through donations. Financially the situation had become so desperate that by the summer of 1830 Eliza Barnes had to make an urgent fund-raising tour to New York, Philadelphia, Baltimore, and Boston.

The gifted fund-raiser collected $1,300 or roughly £300,[49] but the Upper Canadian Methodists urgently needed more. They were so poor that they had to approach the New England Company, a wealthy English missionary body, to construct the mission buildings at Rice Lake and Mud Lake. Fortunately the New England Company agreed to do so.[50] Although the Methodist mission workers were paid very small salaries—Case himself received less than half what a mechanic or urban tradesman earned—by the spring of 1831 some salaries could not be paid.[51]

For over seven years William Case's fixed goal had been to convert the Indians of Upper Canada to Methodism. He needed additional sources of capital, since "the most promising Boys should be put to higher Schools. . . . The work requires translators, teachers of Schools, Interpreters, and Ministry."[52] But where would the money come from? The Upper Canadian Methodists knew that the well-established Wesleyan Methodists in Britain annually collected nearly fifteen times[53] as much as the American Methodists. The Methodists now played their trump card and approached Upper Canada's leading Indian preacher to make a fund-raising tour of Britain. Peter accepted. He would travel there with the Reverend George Ryerson, Egerton's brother.

One short missionary tour in February preceded Peter's departure for Britain the next month. He traveled to Lake Simcoe to see William Yellowhead, head chief of the approximately six hundred Anishinabeg who lived in the area, and to explain his English mission. Of all the Ojibwa chiefs Egerton Ryerson considered Yellowhead "the most interesting, intelligent,"[54] but even Yellowhead had no idea of the immensity of the British Empire. On learning of the journey the head chief said to Peter: "I shake hands with our Great Father over the great waters; when you see him tell him my name; he will know who I am, as he has often heard of me through our fathers the governors and Indian agents, who have sent my messages to him. Tell him I am still alive."[55]

On their way to Britain George Ryerson and Peter Jones traveled to New York, stayed at Francis Hall's, then boarded their ship on 24

March.[56] Bad news awaited them in New York. Early in 1829 a new American president had been inaugurated—the old Indian fighter Andrew Jackson. The tall, gaunt general had included in his platform relocation of all the Indians living east of the Mississippi. Within little more than a year the Congress had passed his Indian removal bill, which the president signed into law on 28 May 1830. By spring of 1831 the Choctaws, a southern tribe with a strong Methodist community, prepared for removal.[57] Now pressures began building up for the relocation of the Cherokees.

For months Peter had been aware of the American pressures to expel Indians from their homelands. He termed the advocates of such policies wicked. In a letter written on Grape Island on 23 August 1830, he summarized what he considered to be their philosophy: "Come let us make a *law*, and let us drive them away from their little reserves, and from the graves of their fathers, and send them away to the northern regions, or beyond the Rocky mountains, and let them there perish by their own countrymen in bloody Indian wars, or let them starve to death. Then we shall have their fine rivers and their rich flats, so we shall eat, drink, and be merry."[58] The Americans had made the War Department the agency in charge of relations with the Indians.[59]

Francis Hall brought Peter up to date during the week the Indian missionary and George Ryerson spent at his house before sailing. The editor, a determined opponent of the forced removal of the churchgoing Choctaw and Cherokee farmers, argued against the injustice in both the *Commercial Advertiser* and the *Spectator*.[60] On the long—five-week—voyage to Britain Peter spent much of his time correcting his translations, an English dictionary by his side. He also prayed for the safety of the Indian Christian communities in the eastern United States. The ship reached Liverpool on 30 April.

Liverpool's great docks, tall ships, and elegant buildings impressed him. Peter and George Ryerson had come to the world's foremost industrialized country. England and Wales alone contained as many people as all of the United States and British North America combined, roughly fifteen million. Next to London, Liverpool was the greatest port in the British Empire. It had nearly as many people as New York City itself.[61]

On the stage to London the next day Peter saw new wonders. The intense cultivation of the countryside, and the roads "as smooth as a floor," astonished him. To save money Peter and George Ryerson rode the three hundred kilometers to London on top of the coach, traveling all day and through an unusually frosty night. They arrived in London just in time to be present at the Wesleyan Methodist missionary meeting on 2 May.[62]

The coach forced its way through the narrow, crowded streets of London. The population of the greatest metropolis in the British Empire now reached over 1,500,000. Within fifty years London had doubled in size, to become by far the largest and richest city in the world, making New York look like a village. As Peter noted in a letter to his brother John, here the people "are as thick as musquitoes."[63]

After presenting themselves at the Wesleyan Methodist mission house, the two men left immediately for a meeting at Exeter Hall. Though he had not slept at all the previous night,[64] Peter accepted the invitation to speak to the huge assembly. He liked the challenge and performed well, in turn attracting other invitations. Over the next ten days he spoke at the British and Foreign Bible Society on the fourth, the British and Foreign School Society on the fifth, the Naval and Military Bible Society on the tenth, the anniversary of the London Missionary Society (before four or five thousand people) on the twelfth, and a London Religious Tract Society meeting on the thirteenth.[65]

After the Religious Tract Society gathering, Peter noted in his diary how "desperately fond of new things" the English were. The announcement of a North American Indian's address at a public meeting drew crowds of people: "I am gazed upon as if I were some strange animal,"[66] he wrote to his brother John on 30 May. In turn the Indian was himself very curious and visited, in addition to the Protestant churches and chapels, a Jewish synagogue and a Roman Catholic church.[67]

Peter liked the English, "a noble, generous-minded people . . . very open and friendly," though he did find their excessive curiosity annoying.[68] Looking beyond to the financial rewards the tour could bring the Upper Canadian missions, he ignored the inquisitive looks and patiently answered the countless questions. Cheerfully, for almost a year, he regularly dressed up in his Indian costume, wearing the embroidered buckskin coat made by the Credit Indian women, his colorful sash wrapped around his waist, the beautifully decorated deerskin leggings and moccasins, and his silver medal around his neck.[69] He put everything he had into his work, though as the weeks passed he increasingly disliked the ordeal. In all he obtained over £1,000. For his participation at a number of their missionary meetings throughout England the Wesleyan Methodists donated £300 to the Upper Canadian work, and Peter collected £732 from his own appearances. In total he gave over sixty sermons and made one hundred speeches on the history and way of life of his fellow Indians.[70]

A skillful public speaker, Peter always tried to include interesting anecdotes in his talks; in fact, early in his career he had begun to keep an "Anecdote Book." Like adding raisins to dough, he used his stories to enliven his Christian message. A favorite account concerned the Saugeen Indians, who, when they first arrived at the Credit Mission, had asked for guns "to shoot our enemies, as we are engaged in war." Taken aback, Peter asked what they meant. The Indians replied, "Translations of His Holy Scriptures," which they called their "spiritual guns."

While on his lecture tours Peter wrote down others' stories, such as this description of hell: "so intensely hot, if one was taken out of hell fire and put into a hot furnace he would there freeze to death." He also recorded for future use the comparison of prayer to an arrow shot by an archer: "The person who prays without faith is like the Archer who only gives a slight pull upon his bow so that the arrow does not rise—But the person who prays in faith is like the man who pulls upon the strength of his bow with all his might, and sends his arrow up so that it penetrates the skies, and opens a window for the blessing of God to drop down upon him who shot the arrow of faith."[71]

While in England Peter spoke in London, Bristol, Birmingham, Liverpool, Manchester, Leeds, Hull, York, and many smaller centers. He wrote back to his brother John on 3 October, "The meetings that I have attended have been very large, and often hundreds have been obliged to go away, as there would be no room for them in the Chapels." The only pause in his schedule had come in late May and June in Bristol, where a very serious illness, probably pneumonia, almost carried him off. The disease kept him confined to his bed for seven weeks.[72]

By a strange coincidence James Cowles Prichard, an English physician who became a doctor mainly for the opportunities it gave him to undertake ethnological research, was one of the two physicians who saved his life. He and Dr. Brady came every day until Peter showed signs of recovering. Already Dr. Prichard had begun to publish his multivolume studies on the races of the world. How appropriate that Peter Jones, the future author of a history of the Ojibwa Indians, would be treated by a man who, with justice, has been called the founder of English anthropology.

In the early nineteenth century a great debate was being fought over the origins of the races of the world. Prichard, as the leading advocate of the unity or monogenist school, argued against the polygenists, who claimed that the races were not all one species. The advocates of the polygenist theory claimed that the races of mankind did not share common ancestors but were created separately. They frequently extended this to deny that the nonwhite races were people at all and maintained that missionary efforts among them were a waste of time and money. Prichard's whole scientific life was spent demonstrating the essential unity of all human races. A quarter of a century later Charles Darwin would prove that all the world's races belong to a single species, but in the early 1830s the controversy still raged.[73]

The young native preacher met a number of prominent religious thinkers in England. He visited, for example, Dr. Adam Clarke, the celebrated biblical commentator, who knew at least twenty languages and dialects. Dr. Clarke liked the native missionary so much that he invited Peter to spend several days at his home. Before they parted he presented Peter with George Stanley Faber's weighty three-volume *Origin of Pagan Idolatry Ascertained from Historical Testimony and Circumstantial Evidence.* The Indian preacher also met Richard Watson, an eminent Methodist theologian, and Samuel Drew, author of a well-known essay on the immortality of the soul. Through Methodist friends in Bristol, Peter called upon Hannah More, one of the most popular religious writers of the day—the shrewd, perceptive woman who in her youth had so greatly impressed the already legendary Dr. Samuel Johnson, author, poet, playwright, and compiler of his famous English dictionary in 1755. Miss More, then in her early eighties, commented after hearing the visiting Indian pray, "a Bishop could not pray any better."[74]

Peter enjoyed excellent conversation and hospitality during his travels. As a boy he had participated in one of the Mississaugas' most enjoyable feasts, the *kahgahgeshee* or crow feast. Meat or fish was spread in great abundance on bark trays before the guests, who arranged themselves around them "like a flock of crows round a dead carcass." The Indians often said that the whites' overflowing table was in itself a complete crow feast.[75] In England Peter daily partook of the several *kahgahgeshees* eaten by his hosts. Breakfast began at eight or nine in the morning with coffee or tea, bread and butter, and sometimes fried bacon, fish, or eggs. A large dinner arrived at 2:00 P.M., completed with fruit, nuts, and a few glasses of wine. At 6:00 P.M. came tea, with bread and butter and sometimes sweet cakes. Supper, consisting of the leftovers from dinner, was served at about nine or ten.[76]

Amid his fund-raising Peter carried on his work of translating and also revised and proofread the parts of the New Testament that were being published by the British and Foreign Bible Society. While in the city he corrected his brother John's translation of the Gospel of John, making all the revisions requested. With the translations' publication in late 1831 it became the second Gospel to be translated by the Jones brothers. They had already completed the Gospel of Matthew, which was published in York during Peter's absence.[77]

Peter's long months in London made the city's contrasts much more apparent to him. At private homes he met the economically privileged, the wealthy English Methodists "who live on roasted beef, plum-pudding, and turtle soup," and "get very fat and round as a toad."[78] Then, just outside on the narrow cobblestone streets, "you may see the poor man who knows not where he may get his next meal."[79] The inequities puzzled him. Similarly, he visited the most beautiful churches he had ever seen and listened to the most eloquent sermons he had heard, yet in this same Christian land he heard people curse and saw men and women drunk in the streets.[80] Even more serious, "atrocious barbarities" still occurred in this civilized country. In the city he learned that men called Burkites killed innocent people and sold their bodies to surgeons for dissection.[81]

Besides wishing to complete further translations of the Gospels for the Bible Society, Peter had a more personal reason for wanting to be near London. Toward the end of his recovery from his serious illness, an interesting young woman, then visiting her sister in neighboring Gloucester, had called upon Peter's hosts in Bristol. Peter's diary entry for 24 June 1831 reads simply: "We had several visitors at Mr. Wood's this evening, among whom was Miss E. Fields, of London, who gave me an invitation to visit her mother at Norwood."[82] After Peter had completed his fund-raising tour of northern England, they met again in London. Before Peter left England in late April—Anna now long forgotten—he had fallen in love with Eliza and proposed to her. This time he acted on his own, without asking anyone else's opinion, even that of the Reverend William Case.

Eliza

Chapter 9

Before Eliza Field left England her fiancé warned her that the white settlers opposed interracial marriages: "The fact is my beloved Eliza, it is that *feeling of prejudice* which is so prevalent among the *old American settlers* (not Indians in this country). They think it is not right for the whites to intermarry with Indians."[1] Would she now refuse to marry him? He need not have worried. In her reply Eliza simply announced she was leaving for Liverpool to board a packet boat to New York. There, on 8 September 1833, she married Kahkewaquonaby.

Racial intermarriage had occurred in North America from the arrival of the first Europeans. In what is now western Canada, by the 1830s the number of mixed-bloods, or métis, numbered in the thousands. But in the highly settled areas of British North America and the United States interracial unions hardly ever occurred by this date. Ten years after his own marriage Peter Jones estimated that in the settled areas of Upper Canada only three or four Indian men were married to white women, and only three or four Indian women to white men.[2] Without fully realizing the implications, Eliza prepared to enter a colonial world rife with racial prejudice as the white wife of a North American Indian.

Eliza had grown up in Lambeth on the south bank of the Thames, a district crowded with boat yards, wharves, and potteries. She spent her childhood in the area once known as "Lambeth Marsh" immediately behind the riverside, not far from where Royal Festival Hall stands today. Eliza's parents raised her to be proudly British. At age eleven she saved, and kept all her life, the 22 June 1815 issue of the London *Times*. It contained the Duke of Wellington's dispatch sent after his victory over Napoleon at Waterloo.[3]

In the year of Eliza's birth, 1804, and for a good decade thereafter, Lambeth still remained a relatively small town with considerable uninhabited marshland. The completion of the Waterloo and Vauxhall bridges in 1816 and 1817, though, and the draining of more and more land, had transformed the community. From 1801 to 1831 Lambeth's population trebled to nearly 100,000. The sudden boom brought new social problems to the town. In 1831 the figures for charges of drunkenness rose higher in Lambeth than in any other part of the London area.[4]

As a local factory owner and property owner Eliza's father, Charles Field, worried about Lambeth's rapid decline. He belonged to a family of candlemakers who had lived in Lambeth for over two centuries. A devoted Christian, Charles Field belonged to the Surrey Chapel, founded and led by the Reverend Rowland Hill, a graduate of Eton and Cambridge—a baronet's son who had become one of the leaders of the Anglican revival of the late eighteenth century. In revolt against the religious indifference of the age, Hill, the last of the great evangelicals, had struggled for nearly half a century to build up Surrey Chapel, until its congregation had become London's largest. His chapel undertook charity work throughout Lambeth and the immediate area, aiding the sick and impoverished. Eliza taught Sunday school and helped in her parents' church until her marriage.[5]

Human beings are full of contradictions, and Charles Field conformed to the general pattern. He did indeed have a social conscience, being genuinely concerned about the sick, the maimed, and the "honest" poor, but that did not preclude his owning two comfortable houses. The first stood in Lambeth Marsh near the factory and the second ten kilometers to the south in Norwood, which on account of its elevation above the valley rose clear of London's smoke. Until the 1850s the hamlet remained delightfully rural, with surrounding meadows and cornfields, sparkling trout streams, and great tracts of woodland. As late as 1802 a hermit known only as Matthews the hairyman lived there undisturbed in a cave in the wood. Gypsies still frequented the great North Wood or Norwood.[6]

Charles built Holly Cottage on the Norwood street now known as Gipsy Road when Eliza was a young girl. Here the Fields came to escape Lambeth's dirt and growing decay. At Norwood Eliza kept her pony, riding freely over the neighboring countryside. She loved the village and its inhabitants, fresh and unsophisticated. What a joy, she recorded in her diary in 1829, "to turn . . . the eye from countenances wan with care, flushed with intemperance, or ghastly with famine, to cheeks brown with wholesome exercise, or ruddy with health and contentment."[7]

As a child Eliza benefited from all the comforts and luxuries affluence provides. She attended a fashionable boarding school in neighboring Peckham for eight years, studied landscape painting under Monsieur E. Bouquet, a French drawing master then living in London, went on riding trips through Gloucestershire near the Welsh border, and spent vacations at Brighton on the English Channel,[8] where King George IV had just built his fantasy out of the Arabian Nights, the Royal Pavilion. While in Lambeth and Norwood the young woman spent many hours helping her stepmother: directing, as the eldest child, the activities of her twelve brothers and sisters and instructing the family servants in their daily tasks. Most important of all, she participated actively in the Surrey Chapel, teaching Sunday school and visiting her church's sick or destitute members.[9]

To understand Eliza one must know more about the person who exercised the greatest influence on her moral and religious principles: Rowland Hill. Fortunately Robert Southey, the poet and historian, described him well after a meeting in 1823, the very year that Eliza, aged eighteen, joined his chapel:[10] "Rowland, a fine tall old man, with strong features, very like his portrait. . . . His manner was animated and striking, sometimes impressive and dignified, always remarkable; and so powerful a voice I have rarely or never heard. . . .

The manner, that of a performer, as great in his line as Kean or Kemble; and the manner it is which has attracted so large a congregation about him, all of the better order of persons in business."[11]

At Surrey Chapel Rowland Hill preached a social Christianity, emphasizing the need to work for the improvement of life on earth as well as to prepare for the world to come. He supported a number of reform groups, from the Anti-Slavery movement and the Book Society for Propagating Religious Knowledge among the Poor to a Benevolent Society for the "relief and instruction of the sick poor in their own homes." During harsh winters he sponsored soup kitchens for the poor. At the turn of the century the energetic minister had also helped found the London Missionary Society as well as the British and Foreign Bible Society.[12] The year that Eliza joined Surrey Chapel she copied out in a notebook five rules of daily use, her code of living:

1. Begin with GOD. *Never neglect to make prayer first. Should any thing unforeseen occur to shorten, yet upon no account, and for no pretence, omit the duty. Though short, be devout, earnest, serious. Be this your motto, "Begin with God." Ps. v. 3.*
2. Expect trials, and to have your will often thwarted. Seek strength for the day of trial, and grace for the duty of that day. Deut. xxxiii.25.
3. Watch occasions of good, to improve, and of evil to shun them. Rom. xii.9.
4. Make the best of that which looks ill, and let not the sins of others provoke you to sin.
5. Be not weary of well doing. Gal. xi.9. Nor cease from "striving against sin," Heb. xii.4.[13]

At Surrey Chapel Eliza had another close clerical friend, the Reverend Theophilus Jones, a bachelor then in his late thirties. The Welshman served as Hill's assistant. Theophilus and Eliza walked and rode together several times during Eliza's visit to see friends in Brighton, in the fall of 1829. In her diary on 16 October Eliza noted, "I lament my slowness to learn and improve from the conversations and advise of good ministers." No doubt talks with the likes of the serious Welsh preacher led Eliza to write in her diary that same year: "Plays, balls, public concerts, cards, private dances, serious, consistent Christians must resist these things, because the dangerous spirit of the world & the flesh is in them all."[14]

The Reverend Theophilus Jones's marital intentions toward Eliza remain unknown. He had traveled to Brighton to be with her on at least one occasion. But if he wanted Eliza's hand he moved too slowly, for a year and half later—at the moment of her call on her Bristol friends James and Martha Woods—Eliza remained unattached. In her diary Martha Woods had already recorded her first impressions of her extraordinary guest, the converted Indian chief:

June 12th. . . . What I wish to record of him is that he is an exemplary Christian, a man of deep piety, great humility and Christian simplicity, walking closely with God—in short he is a Bible Christian—The above traits of character have all been eminently exhibited under our roof during a season of affliction which put to the test all his graces. . . . The Physician and Surgeon who attended him had very considerable doubt of his recovery for some time . . . he has so won the hearts of all our family by his temper and affability of manners together with his gratitude for all that has been done for him.[15]

Unfortunately, Eliza's diary for 1831 has not survived, and her initial response to the Indian preacher remains unknown. Probably the twenty-seven-year-old woman reacted much as the English press did that fall when he resumed his speaking and fund-raising tour. In Sheffield, for example, the *Courant* wrote, "Kahkewaquonaby is a very fine looking man, apparently about 30 years of age." His ability to speak English "with tolerable fluency and considerable correctness" and his "gentle and unassuming" manners impressed the Liverpool *Courier*. When the chief spoke in Halifax the *Express* noted his "great modesty and unaffected simplicity" and added that "the subject of religion and the great objects of his mission . . . seem to engage his constant attention."[16]

We know that they met again only a week later, for Eliza's autograph album contains Peter's entry signed, in his best script, "Kahkewaquonaby alias Peter Jones Indn. Missionary from U. Canada. Bristol July 1st 1831: I am glad to see the general spread of the Light of the Gospel of Christ, our blessed Saviour, both in Europe and America, and also among the Islands of the seas, Keshamunedoo the Great Spirit is making bare his great arm and is gathering the poor pagan nations into his blessed fold. . . . O that all the Heathen could see the King in his beauty and worship him in spirit and in truth."[17]

Peter's devotion to God, his kind manner, and his exciting strangeness attracted her. She invited him to visit her family. He accepted. Once he arrived in London from his northern tour he became a welcome guest at both the Norwood and Lambeth residences of Charles Field.[18] On those visits he learned how well the English loved their roast beef, "as sweet as bear's meat is to an old Indian hunter," and found they relished their plum pudding as much the Indians did a beaver's tail.[19]

Eliza's father and stepmother and her numerous brothers and sisters enjoyed their visitor's company. Two years after Eliza's mother Elizabeth Field had died in childbirth in 1820, Charles Field had remarried and at age forty-four had begun a second family. Within ten years the energetic Charles had increased his progeny from seven to thirteen, his second wife, Mary, giving birth to the last, Edmund, on 10 January 1832.[20] At Norwood and at Lambeth Peter delighted in telling the younger Fields Indian tales and explaining Indian customs.[21] He loved children. One can picture him sitting cross-legged on the floor, regaling the little ones with the same tales he had told the Bunnell family's children ten years earlier: about the flying skeletons, the friendly little people, the giant monster, and the fearsome Waindegoos.

England proved as marvelous and strange to Peter as his Indian tales did to Eliza's family. The Englishwomen's dress, for example, greatly puzzled him. Their bonnets, he wrote home on 30 December 1831, "look something like a farmer's scoop-shovel," and their sleeves were as "big as bushel bags, which make them appear as if they had three bodies with one head." But he then added, "with all their big bonnets and sleeves, the English ladies, I think, are the best of women."[22] Well might he have added that line, for already he was falling in love with one. With Eliza he could talk freely about every issue that concerned him, he was so at ease with this gifted, creative woman. In Eliza's diary for 1832 she wrote under the date 4 January the Ojibwa he had taught her: "Chippeway words: Geneshee kiss me, Kiminwanemin I love you."

Eliza guided her friend through Lambeth and London. On many of their walks around Lambeth, Peter and Eliza passed the site of her father's old school, Carlisle House, on Carlisle Lane, just a block from Eliza's birthplace on Royal Row. While walking by, Eliza must have told him of the neighborhood's scandal, the grisly murders of 1531. In that year the cook of the first Carlisle House, then the London residence of the bishops of Rochester, poisoned seventeen members of the household as well as two of the neighboring poor by adding poison to some yeast. As punishment, the authorities boiled the cook in oil.[23]

Peter and Eliza visited the Fields' candle and soap factory, which was near their home. Throughout the neighborhood one could smell the spermaceti, wax derived from the oil in the head of the sperm whale, which was used in candlemaking. One also caught the strong odors of the fats and oils used to make soap. As progressive business-men, Charles and his brother John had recently introduced the first machines into the factory. Proudly Charles explained to Peter their functions as well as the general routine of the business. The factory made candles in the winter, demand being greatest when days were short; in summer the emphasis switched to soap, since people washed more often in the warm months.[24]

Together Peter and Eliza saw "tourist" London. Though he does not mention his companion by name, Peter did visit Westminster Abbey, possibly with Eliza—the abbey was only a short walk over Westminster Bridge from the Fields' home in Lambeth Marsh. There they saw "the place where the Kings of England are crowned, and the royal chairs that they sit on when they are crowned." No barriers then cordoned off the thrones from the public, and as they went by Peter could not resist: "I took the liberty to squat myself down upon them as we passed by, so that I can now say that I, a poor Indian from the woods of Canada, sat in the king's and queen's great crowning chairs."[25] Eliza loved his naturalness.

Their relationship developed quickly. Peter respected Eliza's commitment to her church and to the poor and underprivileged. She truly believed, as he did, that education and environment alone explained character. By 1 February Eliza already gave thought to the contribution she could make to the Canadian mission work. "Oh," she wrote, "that my God would deem me worthy to be employed in such a glorious work." On the afternoon of the second she read William Cowper's poems to her friend at Norwood, and that evening she confided in her diary, "I feel as tho' I could lay open all my heart to the friend I love." Since his work in England would soon be over, Peter had to act quickly. In mid-February he proposed. Eliza's joy was complete—but not her father's.[26]

The wealthy factory owner had always been protective toward his firstborn daughter. When Eliza went off on her riding trips, for example, he advised her to be careful, not "too bold" on a new horse.[27] He wanted her to be happy and comfortable. Charles's concern about Peter, a man whose religious zeal and spirit of sacrifice he admired, arose in part from his anxiety about the Indian's income. Could the missionary who earned in a year what the rich industrialist did in a day properly support his daughter? Then, too, Peter was a Methodist and the Fields were Anglicans. It took Peter and Eliza a month to win her father over to their side. Finally on 15 March Eliza recorded the welcome news: "Determined last evening that my dear friend return to C[anada], as early as possible, consult his relations & friends on this important affair, try and make as many desirable arrangements as his situation will allow, if these matters are settled to Papa's satisfaction he has promised not to withhold his consent & in this case my dear friend will return if all be well early next year."

Throughout the spring of 1832 Eliza had doubts about her ability to aid her future husband. The talents in demand at an Indian mission were domestic, and Eliza since childhood had been surrounded by servants, so she had few of these.[28] But eagerly she set out to learn, visiting a close friend in the country "to gain a little information in household concerns." There Eliza watched her friend make pies and puddings and observed closely when the servant made bread. Later that week her friend taught her to knit socks and stitch a shawl.[29]

To prepare herself for her new life at an Indian mission in Canada Eliza read widely, recording the titles in her diary. She found "very interesting" the recently published novel *The Last of the Mohicans*, by the American James Fenimore Cooper. She also consulted church histories, John Bunyan's *Pilgrim's Progress*, and travel accounts of North America. For a few days in July 1833 the future Mrs. Jones struggled with a history of Canada but found it "tamely written—with little incident and little information."[30] Basil Hall's *Travels in North America* proved much more useful and entertaining, for in it Eliza found "my dear loves name mentioned."[31] She must have read to her family the reference to the Credit Indians and the "missionary of the name of Jones, whose mother was a Mississauga, and his father a white man," who through his "own virtuous efforts" had "reclaimed his Indian brethren from the degradation into which they had fallen."[32]

During his last months in England in the spring of 1832 Peter attended missionary society meetings in London and gave sermons in various London churches on Sundays. He preached twice for the Reverend Mr. Hill at Surrey Chapel.[33] In April an unexpected letter had arrived requesting his presence at Windsor Castle on 5 April to meet King William IV and Queen Adelaide.

When Peter reported everything to the Fields the day after his visit, old Charles must have been impressed. The soap- and candle-maker had visited Windsor, but never at the king's invitation. Peter had brought back a ring with the king's likeness, William's gift to his Indian visitor.[34] The king and queen had talked with Charles Field's future son-in-law for half an hour, and after the interview Peter and several of the king's lords had dined in a banquet hall on roast chicken, beef, potatoes, and tarts, served in silver dishes. Charles Field's connection with Windsor Castle came through the tradesmen's entrance. In the London directory for 1832 his firm "J. C. and J. Field" advertised that they were "Wax-chandlers and Bleachers to his Majesty"[35]—they supplied the king with candles.

One other surprise awaited Peter before he left England. The London artist Matilda Jones finished his portrait and that of his fiancée. The minaturist, daughter of a prominent Methodist family in Bristol, had painted two portraits of Peter. Probably Eliza encouraged Peter to select the one he did: the second portrait, which gave him the more European appearance. Miss Jones kept the first and submitted it to the Royal Academy, where it was hung in 1832.[36]

Despite her father's acceptance there was much opposition to Eliza's wedding plans among her family and friends. Two days before Peter left England on 27 April Eliza noted in her diary: "I feel such a weight of anxiety, many friends raise various objections and from every quarter they say—How can you think of giving up all." Within the family the Reverend John Dowling of Gloucester, her brother-in-law, violently opposed the union. The earnest cleric, one of whose great concerns in life was the suppression of novels because of the "power they possess of raising the passions, and producing an excitement which is very far from salutary to the moral being,"[37] looked on the affair, in Eliza's words, "with horror."[38] Possibly the well-read cleric subscribed to the polygenists' argument that the North American Indians were a separate and, as many of them claimed, inferior creation. Even Eliza's father was still not truly reconciled to the union. Half a year after Peter's departure he told his eldest daughter, on the eve of All Saints' Day, "You do not mean to go, if you go you will break my heart." Then a week later he reversed his decision and forbade the match.

No doubt at this point Charles Field had just learned more about Peter's father. This proved quite a shock, for though Peter had never disguised the fact that his father was a surveyor of Welsh descent, he had failed to mention that his white father had once been married simultaneously to two Indian women. When the wealthy factory owner learned of Augustus Jones's two wives, he wanted to call off the engagement. The Reverend Robert Alder, the Wesleyan Methodist missionary superintendent, immediately assured Charles that the son was not necessarily like his father, who in any case had long repented his sin. Finally Charles relented, and Eliza recorded on 2 December, "altho' he cannot recommend it as a prudent step, he will no longer oppose."

Another problem arose. By the end of the year it became apparent that Peter could not, as planned, return to England in 1833. He suggested instead that Eliza take a packet to New York, where they would be married. His close friend, the Reverend Egerton Ryerson, then in England, could accompany her on the passage—a suggestion that Charles Field, almost at the end of his tether, did not like at all. Only the lengthy arguments of Robert Alder and Egerton Ryerson, testifying yet again to Peter's character, and his daughter's insistence that she marry the Indian missionary convinced Charles once again to change his mind.

All summer long Eliza prepared for her departure. After a reunion of the entire family at Norwood, Eliza left for Liverpool on 5 August. On the following day she and Egerton Ryerson boarded the *United States*, bound for New York. The wind being fair, they sailed that day. Her father, hoping to ease her transition to Peter's tiny log cabin, sent his daughter off with English bone china and Turkish rugs.[39]

A very quick crossing brought Eliza to New York four days ahead of her fiancé, which gave her a chance to view the city. The sophisticated Englishwoman found America's great metropolis "fine," but rather primitive, "so different to any thing English it would [take] years to make me think it worthy to have a comparison."[40]

Eliza found New York as backward in its racial attitudes as in its architecture. The very month that she left Britain, August 1833, marked the abolition of slavery in Britain and throughout the British Empire, an action she applauded.[41] But the United States had retained slavery and had imposed new tyranny on the Indians. Reelected in 1832, Andrew Jackson continued to remove thousands upon thousands of Indians from the eastern United States to lands west of the Mississippi River. She found racial prejudices openly expressed and opinions voiced that the Indians constituted a substandard, inferior race. Many felt that blacks and Indians could not be changed either by education or by an improved environment. It made her feel ill. During her four days alone in New York Eliza found herself assailed by a "tremendous battery of entreaty, argument, and ridicule"[42] urging her not to marry a "savage."

While awaiting Peter's arrival, Eliza stayed with Francis Hall and his wife on John Street, the Halls having offered their home for the wedding. Eliza at first regarded the North American custom of marrying at a private home as rather bizarre. "So wedded are we to old customs and local habits," she wrote, "that I could not easily be persuaded it would be agreeable."[43] But after her four anxious days alone in New York the detail no longer seemed important. Peter and Eliza arranged to be married at the Halls' the very day of his arrival, 8 September.

New York took note of the rare interracial union. A scurrilous article appeared in a major New York newspaper shortly after the wedding, entitled "Romance in Real Life." It began with a familiar literary reference:

On Sunday evening last, we were, fortuitously, witnesses of an incident equally interesting and painful. Many people have denounced Shakespeare's Othello, as too unnatural for probability. It can hardly be credited that such a fair, beautiful and accomplished woman, as Desdemona is represented to have been, could have deliberately wedded such a black a moor as Othello. But if we ever entertained any incredulity upon the subject, it has all been dissipated by the occurrence of which we are to speak.

Having introduced the two marriage partners, the tall, muscular Indian and the "light, fragile, delicate" Englishwoman, the anonymous journalist continued:

Our emotions were tumultuous and painful. A stronger contrast was never seen. She all in white, and adorned with the sweetest simplicity. . . . She a little delicate European lady—he a hardy iron-framed son of the forest. . . . A sweeter bride we never saw. We almost grew wild. We thought of Othello—of Hyperion and the satyr—of the bright-eyed Hindoo and the funeral pile! She looked like a drooping flower by the side of a rugged hemlock! We longed to interpose and rescue her . . . we heard the Indian and herself pronounced man and wife! It was the first time we ever heard the words "man and wife" sound hatefully.[44]

News of the libelous article reached Peter and Eliza only on 19 September, in Upper Canada. Eliza noted in her diary on that day: "breakfasted with my dear husband at Mr. Armstrongs heard that much had been written about our union in a New York paper—this is a cruel world. I felt much grieved that any one should find pleasure in amusing the world by misrepresentations and direct falsehoods." Then the next day—the very day that Peter and Eliza left for the Credit Mission—the story received a wider distribution, being carried in colonial newspapers from Brockville and Kingston in the east to York and St. Catharines in the west.[45] Every newspaper had its own opinion on interracial marriages. "Improper and revolting," declared the Kingston *Chronicle and Gazette;* "we believe that the Creator of the Universe distinguished his creatures by different colours, that they might be kept separate from each other." Similarly, the *British Colonial Argus* of St. Catharines pronounced against "the amalgamation system," "overstepping the line of demarkation which God and nature seem to have drawn between nations as it respects colour, features, etc." The York *Patriot* termed Eliza an "unhappy, deceived woman." But the Niagara *Gleaner* took up the couple's defense: Eliza would be well provided for by the Christian Indian farmers, for "the Indians and even Negroes are looked upon and treated as human beings within all the dominions of Great Britain. Not so in the republican states of America (who have declared all equal) to their everlasting disgrace."[46]

Eliza, an intensely private person, hated this attention—first the newspapers, then individual men and women she had never met

Matilda Jones, an English portrait artist, made at least two paintings of Peter Jones from sittings at her studio at 8 Coleman Street in London. The first was completed in November 1831 and the second six months later, in April 1832, after he had become engaged to Eliza. In the second his hair is shorter and neater and he has a more settled, composed look. Eliza selected this second portrait to take to Canada with her, along with the one painted of her, also in April 1832.

11. Portrait of Kahkewaquonaby, Reverend Peter Jones (1802–56). National Gallery of Canada, Ottawa. Matilda Jones, 1831.

12. Portrait of Kahkewaquonaby, Reverend Peter Jones. Peter Jones Collection, Victoria University Library, Toronto. Matilda Jones, April 1832.

13. Portrait of Eliza Field. Peter Jones Collection, Victoria University Library, Toronto. Matilda Jones, April 1832.

14. Nawahjegezhegwabe, "sloping sky," in English Joseph Sawyer. Peter Jones's uncle, elected head chief of the Mississaugas of the Credit River in 1829, was one of the strongest advocates of Methodism and of Europeanization among his people. He also remained a determined champion of the Mississaugas' land claims at the western end of Lake Ontario. The Reverend James Spencer, a Methodist minister, painted the portrait in 1846. Metropolitan Toronto Library, J. Ross Robertson Collection, T 30694.

15. Nahnebahwequay, "upright woman," in English Catherine Brown Sunegoo, Peter Jones's niece. She was named after Catherine Brown, a remarkable Cherokee Christian convert. Born in 1824, she attended the Credit Mission school and later married William Sutton, an English farmer. County of Grey–Owen Sound Museum, Owen Sound, Ontario.

16. Shahwundais, "sultry heat," in English John Sunday. This veteran of the War of 1812, a chief among the Mississaugas at the eastern end of Lake Ontario, became the greatest Mississauga orator of all. Peter Jones converted him to Christianity in 1826. From the March 1839 issue of the *Wesleyan-Methodist* magazine, published in London, England.

17. Pahtahsega, "one who makes the world brighter," in English Peter Jacobs. He was the first Mississauga Indian at the eastern end of Lake Ontario to become interested in Methodism and later became a missionary to the Anishinabeg in Rupert's Land, in the area of present-day northwestern Ontario and Manitoba. The photograph is dated 1864 and is in the possession of the County of Grey–Owen Sound Museum, Owen Sound, Ontario.

18. Kahgegagahbowh, "he who stands forever," in English George Copway. Born in 1818, George Copway later became a missionary among the Anishinabeg in present-day Wisconsin, Minnesota, and later Upper Canada. This Mississauga from Rice Lake became in the late 1840s and early 1850s a very successful writer and lecturer in the United States. The illustration appears as the frontispiece of Copway's *The Life, History and Travels of Kahgegagahbowh*, 2d ed. (Philadelphia: James Harmstead, 1847).

19. Shahwahnegezhik, known in English as Henry B. Steinhauer, a young Ojibwa boy of about ten from the Lake Simcoe area. John Neagle painted this portrait in the spring of 1829 when a party of Methodist Indians visited Philadelphia on a fundraising tour. The boy received his name from a Henry Steinhauer of Philadelphia who paid for his education. Henry B. Steinhauer later became a missionary in present-day Manitoba and Alberta. Collection of the Glenbow Museum, Calgary, Alberta.

20. An engraving of Peter Jones probably made about the time of his second British tour, 1837–38. On 14 September 1838 Lord Glenelg, the colonial secretary, acknowledged in the presence of Queen Victoria that the Credit River Mississaugas should receive tithe deeds to their lands. They never did. The engraving appears as the frontispiece of Peter Jones's *History of the Ojebway Indians* (London: A. W. Bennett, 1861).

21. Non-Christian Indian graves at
Munceytown. The non-Christians
believed that the soul lingered
around the body for some time before taking its departure. Before
they placed the body of the deceased within the coffin, the relatives bored several holes at the
head of the coffin. They believed
that this would allow the soul to go
in and out at pleasure. From an illustration in Peter Jones, *History of
the Ojebway Indians*, opposite p.
99.

coming up and telling her that decent white women never married Indians. When Eliza accompanied Peter among white settlers, the new bride discovered (she wrote on 6 September 1834, one year after their marriage) that "my peculiar situation in connection with my dear husband excites much unpleasant curiosity." She found "the gaze of the vulgar very annoying and disturbing."[47]

The whites' reaction to his mixed marriage also affected Peter, even before the New York newspaper article appeared. A chance meeting between him and Patrick Bell, a graduate of St. Andrew's University in Scotland and later an ordained Presbyterian clergyman, reveals this. Bell met Peter and his bride on their way back to Canada on an Erie Canal boat. The Scot's comments, recorded in his diary, reveal Peter's disturbed mental state. Bell wrote of a talk the native minister made to his fellow passengers: "The first thing that disappointed me was—the hesitating manner in which he got on—as if he did not know what sentence was to follow the one he had concluded. . . . The Indian had either forgotten his address or he has not been much accustomed to make such speeches before a mixed audience."[48] Aware of many white Americans' hatred of him for marrying a white woman, Peter had temporarily lost his self-confidence. But two years earlier the English newspapers had commented on his eloquence and his fine presentation.

The white settlers' opposition was only one of Eliza's problems. She came from a sheltered and privileged background and had never lived in straitened circumstances. Nor did the young Englishwoman know the rigors of a Canadian winter, with its intense cold and snow. She had always lived in well-heated, comfortable houses and from childhood had been attended by servants who prepared the meals and stoked the fires. Eliza also faced the difficult task of adjusting to the culture and society of her husband's people. The Credit Indians had accepted Christianity only a decade before, and the old people in particular still lived in a different psychological world. To them the forests and rivers were living things just like persons, with their own moods and feelings. There were places in the forest many did not go.

In England Eliza had resisted all the arguments of her father, her family, and several of her friends that she should end her engagement. Peter had always admired her inner strength, her resistance to conforming. It came from two sources. First, she deeply loved her Indian husband, and second, she strongly believed in her "mission" to come to Canada and help carry Christianity throughout the world.

From a British army officer's account we know how the village looked when Eliza first arrived. Captain J. E. Alexander visited about 1830 and later wrote: "We found ourselves on an elevated plateau, cleared of wood, and with three rows of detached cottages, among fields surrounded with rail fences; below, a clear stream, abounding in fish, rushed over its rocky bed to join the waters of Lake Ontario. We rode into the open space in the centre of the village, and found . . . a pole, on which fluttered the Union Jack: on the top was a small house for the martens [martins] to build in, whose presence is considered fortunate in Canada."[49]

The ride from York (in 1834 the town again became Toronto) had taken the newly married couple five hours on horseback. They had ridden through a forest bright with the colors of fall—reds, yellows, and greens—arriving at five o'clock in the afternoon. In her diary Eliza noted enthusiastically: "My heart was full, too big for utterances. I felt that now I had entered the scene of my future labours." They went first to the home of Peter's brother, where John's wife Christiana "received me kindly" and "numbers came in to welcome us." Well versed in English and familiar with white people, Christiana became in the weeks to follow Eliza's closest female friend at the mission. Peter was delighted to see how the Indian women welcomed Eliza and how well she and Christiana got along.

Mrs. Peter Jones's introduction to her new life at the mission station came that evening when her husband took her to their modest dwelling, built of squared logs chinked with plaster. She later described it: "My first Canadian home, was one room, which my dear husband called his study—a bedstead, a writing desk, a table, & a few chairs, Indian mats on the floor, & round the bedstead—an open fire place."[50] But its modest appearance in no way dampened Eliza's spirits. The next day, the twenty-first, she wrote in her fine hand in her diary: "Rose this morning with a grateful & a happy heart, felt as contented in my humble dwelling as tho' I had risen surrounded by the splendours of a Palace." The next week Eliza, a trained artist, sketched the cabin, the school, and the church, which stood close to each other, and sent the drawing to her friends in England.

On her first Sabbath (her third day) at the mission, Eliza attended the eleven o'clock church service. The women sat opposite the men in Methodist fashion with the children and young people immediately in front of the preacher and the settlement's elders. While singing everyone stood, and during prayer they all, including the children, knelt. On being dismissed the women retired first, commencing with the first row. The men followed in the same order, then the children, some of whom were no more than two years old.[51] During the service Eliza noticed the different form of Indian etiquette. The congregation never stared at the minister in the pulpit, considering that "to fix their eyes on the speaker would be a mark of rudeness." Later she also noticed that the Mississaugas at their councils looked to see who was going to speak, then lowered their eyes again.[52]

On Monday Eliza visited the Indian school, attended by forty Indian children. A contemporary description of the school exists, written by William Lyon Mackenzie, editor of the *Colonial Advocate*, the same energetic little man who later became renowned as the leading instigator of the Upper Canadian rebellion of 1837. Seven years before his rebellion he reported on the Credit Mission schoolhouse, a large building containing "tiers of raised benches (like a gallery) in the rear; on one division of which sit the girls, and the boys on the other." Around the schoolroom lay Bibles and New Testaments, English and American books, a handsome map of the world, "attractive alphabets on pasteboard," a picture of Elijah fed by ravens, arithmetic figures, colored pictures of birds, fish, and animals, and "the figure of a clock, in pasteboard, by which to explain the principles of the time-piece." Mackenzie added that "the walls of the School are adorned with good moral maxims; and I perceived that one of the rules was rather novel, though doubtless in place here: It was, 'No blanket to be worn in School.' "⁵³

Eliza saw firsthand the impressive results of the Methodists' first decade of work with the Mississauga children. After her visit on 23 September she wrote in her diary: "the children sang well, their writing very good, the boys have made good progress in reading." She also noted one shortcoming: the "want of neatness in the school & cleanliness about the children" appalled the soap manufacturer's daughter. Later that same week, on 26 September, she mentioned to their teacher that arrangements should be made about "getting aprons made for the children & washing apparatus that they may present a cleaner & neater appearance at school."

In her first weeks at the village Eliza adjusted well. She loved her first canoe ride with Peter, as she noted in her diary on 19 October: "had my first paddle in a canoe, enjoyed it much my husband very handy." Eliza spent her days visiting, discussing and then helping Peter copy out his translations, and making clothes for the needy Indian children. Tuhbenahneequay, Peter's mother, warmly accepted her son's English bride. On 1 October she gave her new daughter the appropriate gift, a washing basket. And in those first few weeks Eliza frequently visited Christiana, then in her ninth month of pregnancy. The young bride seemed to be on a cloud of euphoria. In the first week of October Eliza hired a servant girl at York, no doubt with the help of a stipend from her father, to help with her work at the Indian village.

Eliza's spirits altered in the second month as she slowly realized the vast cultural differences separating her from her husband's people. She discovered, for example, that the Indian custom was to walk right into one's house without knocking. On the morning of 15 October she suddenly felt a presence, then saw a shadow fall across the floor. That day she wrote in her diary, "This morning without ceremony before I was dressed an Indian man came in, this is common." Other habits of the Indians surprised her. After several

Indian men came to talk to Peter, Eliza recorded, "they annoyed me much by spitting, this is a dirty habit, but it is a little trial I must bear patiently." Her greatest frustration, though, came not through the lack of privacy or her concern with cleanliness, but on account of her inability to speak Ojibwa. The entry for 28 October reads: "Several Indian women came and sat with us, oh! how I long to understand their language and converse with them." Although she apparently never became fluent, her husband taught her many Ojibwa words.[54]

Eliza's resources of strength—physical and spiritual—were tested when in her sixth week in the village Peter left on a missionary tour to the Grand River, over one hundred kilometers away. All that spring, summer, and fall the village of slightly over two hundred Indians had been stricken with ague, or malarial fever, carried by mosquitoes in the marshland of the valley. Then more serious illnesses developed. During Eliza's first month in the village four Indians—including the tall, robust Chief John Crane—suddenly died. Then only a day after giving birth to a baby boy Christiana Jones fell ill. On 1 November John Jones came to ask Eliza for a bottle of castor oil for his wife. By 2 November, Christiana's condition had deteriorated still further. To help John with the baby and to comfort her stricken friend, Eliza sat with her all night.

The entry for Sunday 3 November begins, "a night of most painful anxiety." Christiana, in "great agony, high fever and inflammation," appeared "fast hastening to another world." And all night John lay writhing on the floor from the agony of his finger, festering from blood poisoning. Eliza had never experienced this kind of life before—a dear friend dying before her eyes, a brother-in-law tortured by pain, and the constant crying of a four-day-old child. Eliza stayed and helped all she could until 5:30 A.M., when she left the "house of mourning." "As I walked alone to my solitary dwelling," she wrote in her diary, "I felt that I was in circumstances different to any I had ever experienced before, now I thought my trials are beginning."

Christiana died later that day. Eliza offered to keep house for John. No longer was there time for reading. Then two days later another blow fell—John and Christiana's newborn son died. Eliza then called upon her last reserves of strength. By 18 November we know that she had conquered her depression, for the entry that day is triumphant: "I am where my God hath led me & altho' very far from so many loved ones, I have a kind husband and many undeserved comforts—& if I have but the love of God in my heart all must be well."

The following months passed quickly. Many days proved so busy that for long periods Eliza neglected her diary. She and Peter moved on 14 December into the larger house he had built for her. There Eliza taught the Indian girls the same household skills she had herself so hastily learned, instructed them in religion, and helped Peter complete and copy out his translation of the Bible. Years later one of her early visitors, Catherine Brown Sunegoo, Peter's niece, wrote expressing her gratitude: "Dear sister when I was a child you gave me clothes to were [wear] . . . you taught little Indian girls in that little house a cross the road and you taught them how to sew and many other things. . . . When I look back in days that are past and gone how good you were to CB Sunegoo who once lived at Credit what a naughty girl she was not to [k]now you[r] kindness."[55] Eliza saved the letter for the rest of her life.

Those villagers who unconditionally supported Peter Jones befriended Eliza. They slowly warmed to this white woman who had come to live among them. They called her Kecheahgahmequa, "the lady from beyond the blue waters."[56] Perhaps Mrs. Jones's own tragedies helped endear her to them. At the Credit Mission she suffered two miscarriages and bore two stillborn babies between 1834 and 1836.[57] After Eliza lost her first two babies her friend Mrs. John Keshegoo offered to allow her to raise (in Eliza's words) "her oldest little girl, a child I have taken a great fancy to, as being quick and interesting." But still hoping to bear her own children, Eliza reluctantly turned down the generous offer of her Mississauga friend.[58]

Throughout their first years of married life Peter and Eliza knew that many white settlers watched them closely. Eliza had no sympathy for those so perversely curious. As the well-bred Englishwoman wrote in her diary on 6 September 1834, "I desire to be enabled to feel charity to such who from the want of education or refined delicacy towards the feelings of a stranger make me an object of general observation." Her appreciation of the Indian people grew. After a year or so at the Credit River she wrote: "Many of the people in this country do not seem to know what good manners mean, they have nothing like the natural refinement & delicacy & modesty of Indian women."[59]

"All Out of Tune"

Chapter 10

"By an inalienable law of our nature such a temperament is liable to great reverses. As the ebb-tide succeeds the flood, and the calm a storm, so naturally a feeling of depression follows a high degree of exhilaration."[1] So Joseph Holdrich, a popular American Methodist writer in the mid-nineteenth century, remarked about the religious condition. His observations certainly apply to Peter Jones after his wedding on 8 September 1833. His depression came not from his marriage—Egerton Ryerson would later write of Peter and Eliza, "I question whether a happier marriage than theirs, on both sides, was ever experienced—truly in life they were of one heart and one soul"[2]—but from his new perceptions of the world around him.

The newspaper report about his marriage, printed in one New York paper, then reprinted in another and finally spread throughout Upper Canada, had wounded him. The ugly racial prejudice, presented so openly and without apology, angered the young minister, who believed that "character alone ought to be the distinguishing mark in all countries."[3] Certain newspapers had long attacked him—the York *Courier*, for example, for several years had labeled the "son of Mr. Augustus Jones the surveyor, by a Mississagua Squaw" an impostor.[4] The *Courier* argued that he was white and not an Indian at all.[5] But the New York articles cut much, much deeper. Peter expected the anti-Methodist editor of the *Courier* to be hostile to him, but he had not expected the treachery of a trusted friend. In New York the cruel and insulting article had first appeared in the

Commercial Advertiser and the *Spectator,* both owned and edited by Francis Hall.[6] They had been married in his home! Whom could he trust?

Eliza became a strength to her husband at this very difficult time. Her assessment of her husband's worth paralleled that of Peter Jacobs, a fellow Mississauga preacher, who later described him as a man "who has not been excelled in usefulness to the Indians of Canada by any Missionary of our own or any other Church."[7] Even the Roman Catholics recognized as much. In 1836 she noted that Father Nicolas Wiseman, to become England's Cardinal Wiseman only four years later, specifically mentioned Peter in his lecture "On the Practical Success of the Protestant Rule of Faith in Converting Heathen Nations":

> there has been, to all appearance, a most important change in this part of the [Great Lakes] missionary district; in consequence of the work having been undertaken among some of the tribes, by half-natives who have had the benefit of European education, while they possessed the confidence of their fellow-countrymen. Among these is the Wesleyan Missionary Jones; and, it is certain that he has succeeded in bringing a considerable number to the profession of Christianity; probably the first instance in which the labours of any Protestant missionary have been successful.

When Eliza saw the published lecture, she carefully copied out the passage.[8]

Peter's wife perceived that the Methodists kept her husband subordinate to others in the mission work, treating him like an inferior. In late 1833, for instance, the Methodists in Upper Canada finally united with the Wesleyan Methodists in Britain, largely to forestall a threatened Wesleyan invasion of their own congregations. The Wesleyans, deemed politically safer than the "American" Methodists, had been encouraged to come to Upper Canada by Sir John Colborne. Shortly after the union the Reverend Joseph Stinson, a British Wesleyan with no previous experience with North American Indians, became the head of the Methodists' Canadian Indian mission work with, as his second-in-command, William Case, the new "General Missionary to the Indian tribes, who will also pay attention to the Translation of the Sacred Scriptures into the Indian Languages."[9] It seemed totally ridiculous—the Indian missions turned over to a man who had never served on one and the supervision of translations given to a man who could not speak Ojibwa.[10]

Every day Eliza saw William Case, her husband's immediate supervisor, since the Credit Mission became Case's new headquarters. She would not be impressed, for the veteran American circuit rider had a poor reputation as a preacher[11]—as one clerical observer politely expressed it, he had "a style of preaching not the best suited to ordinary congregations of educated whites."[12] Eliza's most exasperating moments with William Case came at their weekly class meeting, when the members confessed to each other the state of their souls. The sophisticated Englishwoman found it "strange and new"[13] to recount her innermost religious thoughts before William and his new bride, Eliza Barnes Case (Hetty had died in 1831, and two years later William had married Hetty's bridesmaid). Out of "duty" she prayed publicly,[14] but "I may truly say to utter a word was indeed a trial"[15]—an exercise that had "rather the effect to destroy than to increase devotional feeling."[16]

Peter's "best earthly friend"[17] pointed out to him his strengths. She encouraged him in his work, to make his people the perfect equals of the whites. Absolutely color-blind, to her a person's race meant nothing, environment being everything. What in her opinion the Indian children needed were "the same privileges and blessings that English children enjoy, to make them equally clever and useful members of society."[18]

Through Eliza's insights about the workings of white society, Peter became more critical of the Methodist church. Always compliant, Peter had closely followed Case's instructions and done his bidding since his conversion. On all matters great and small, the superintendent gave him lengthy advice and constant directives.[19] Now Peter began to resent his own lack of responsibility. Then, shortly after the union of the British and Canadian Methodists,

William Case antagonized his most important native worker still further. Without first consulting Peter, he instructed James Evans, a white Methodist minister, to continue his own biblical translations. With the help of a native assistant Evans was to retranslate the very hymns that Peter Jones had already translated.[20]

James Evans, a young English immigrant in his thirties, had served before his ordination as a schoolteacher at Rice Lake in the late 1820s. Linguistically talented, he had learned Ojibwa. In the spring of 1835 he first preached in that tongue, one of the few white Methodist ministers ever to do so.[21] The confident young man now promised Case and Stinson that he would develop a more accurate orthography for transcribing Ojibwa words. The Jones brothers, he argued, put down the Ojibwa words as they sounded to them. Since, he wrote, "almost every writer has a method of notation perculiar to himself . . . none have presented us with a complete system in which each sound is rendered invariable by a distinct and appropriate character."[22]

Once Peter and Eliza learned of the new translations early in 1836, Peter began to reconsider his role in the church. On 21 January Case reported to James Evans, then resident missionary at the St. Clair mission: "What will you think if we should lose our Bro. Jones. I fear he is not much longer with us. He seems to construe everything unfavourably. His wife has no taste for Methodist [?] actions, & speaks against them, I fear the consequences in this Mission and perhaps elsewhere. He thinks Mr. Stinson & others have misused him . . . a dissatisfied spirit. I think it has existed some time . . . we must prepare ourselves for the worst."[23] Similarly, in a letter of 22 March 1836 the "King Bird," as the Indians termed Joseph Stinson,[24] told Evans, "Translating—you are the person to whom we shall chiefly look in future for this very important part of our work as Br. Jones is all out of tune, more of this when we meet—I have done all I can to save Him, but his mind is in a most unhappy state."[25]

Other problems beset Peter at this time. His father had overextended himself in an attempt to build a grist- and sawmill on his farm by the Governor's Road, and by the summer of 1835 he was nearly bankrupt. The financial pressures weighed heavily on the elderly man, in his late seventies and in poor health, no doubt contributing to his death in November 1836. As Eliza wrote, the loss of his father, "for whom he had a strong affection," came as a serious blow to her husband.[26] Peter now felt a direct obligation to assist his stepmother and his young stepbrothers. After his father's death Peter invited his stepmother Sarah Tekarihogen Jones and his two half-brothers Augustus and Joseph to come and live at the Credit Mission.[27] His welcoming his Iroquois relatives to the mission must have antagonized some Credit band members, concerned that Peter's half-sister Polly and her husband Jacob Brant already lived at the Credit.

The difficulties with Case and Stinson, his father's poor health, and financial problems troubled Peter early in 1836. For several years his own health had not been good; another serious illness in the winter of 1832–33 had forced him temporarily to give up his translations of the Gospels.[28] Additional stress came upon him in 1835–36 when an opposition group in his own band openly attacked him.

Although many years had passed since Augustus Jones had secured the band's promise of a tract of land for his two Mississauga sons, twenty years later they had still not received it. Having served as one of his surveyors Augustus knew well John Graves Simcoe's policy of presenting his executive and legislative councilors, and other leading citizens in Upper Canada, with free grants of some three thousand to five thousand acres, and further grants of twelve hundred acres to their children (who in a number of cases were very numerous).[29] Augustus believed that the Mississaugas should be allowed to be as generous with their own friends (and blood relations). Both Peter and John Jones had been taught by their father that they had a right to their land grants of nearly thirteen hundred acres each at the Credit River. The two brothers had petitioned Lieutenant Governor Maitland in August 1825 for their promised four square miles on the eastern bank of the Credit. They pointed out to the governor that the "Messessague Indians say, that when they surrendered their lands to His Majesty Government, they particularly reserved the said tract for the use of the said Tyantenagen [John Jones] and Kagawakanaby [Peter] their heirs and assigns." Eighteen Credit men had signed the Joneses' petition of 1825.[30]

Not being "purely Indians," the Joneses claimed the same right as the children of Stuart McTefferty and Robert Kerr, white men who had married Iroquois women and whose offspring had all received title to their Indian lands on the Grand River.[31] But the Executive Council of Upper Canada refused, and they did the same with the Joneses' second request, now reduced to four hundred acres, which they submitted in February 1833.[32] The Executive Council replied to the Joneses that the lands claimed "had been surrendered by the Credit Chiefs to Government in the year 1820, and that in their surrender they made no reservation of the Lands."[33]

Peter and John refused to give up their claim, but before petitioning a third time they called a council of the Credit men in March 1835. To their surprise Lawrence Herkimer and a group at the meeting refused them more than a hundred acres each. The heated discussion continued to two o'clock the next morning and resumed six hours later. Anxious to secure a land base for themselves, the Joneses refused to make any concessions until later that second day. Then, "entirely from motives for the good of the tribe, that divisions might be prevented, and that union and peace might continue amongst us as a people, so that the mission might be preserved," the Joneses accepted, as tradition required, the consensus of the meeting. They took the one hundred acres each on the lakeshore, east of the river.[34]

This time the new petition to the Executive Council worked. In May 1836 the government approved the band's request to give the native minister title to one hundred acres, in light of his contributions to the band, and later John also received his land.[35] The government's action notwithstanding, William Herkimer, Lawrence's brother, still contended that the Joneses' two hundred acres ultimately belonged communally to the Credit band, as did all of the reserve land. Peter, though, refused to surrender his economic independence. When William Herkimer later questioned the Jones brothers' titles in 1842, Peter informed him that "the Council had no right to meddle with their lands as they were private property and had Deeds for them from the Government which they had granted to them on account of their claims founded on a grant from our fore-fathers made many years ago."[36] That the Jones brothers removed their land grant from the reserve meant to at least one band member that they had "severed their connection with the band."[37]

With important tribal matters like this Eliza, limited by her own experiences and background, could not help Peter. While sympathizing with the Mississaugas over past injustices, she could not understand why they might wish to remain Indians. She always believed that the Christian Indians must abandon their old ways for "civilization." By strengthening Peter's belief in private property, she increased friction on a reserve where many still cherished the old communal ideal.

The Herkimers and their faction had other grievances against the Joneses. Shortly after his return from Britain in 1832, Peter had tried to put more order into the Credit Indians' lives. The children must be prepared for the discipline of farming. On Christmas Day 1832 he preached to the adults "the importance of family government in order to train up their children in the path of duty and virtue, and to have them in complete subjection, and not to suffer them to cry and scream for every trifling thing." But the children objected to such talk. As Peter humorously added, "Whilst I was on this subject the children cried and bellowed as if Satan himself had got into them!"[38]

On the Jones party's suggestion, the council in June 1836 decided to discipline all children who "ill behaved" at the mission. The Herkimer group immediately protested by refusing to serve on the committee "to look after the conduct of the children and to punish them whenever they deserve it by whipping them."[39] In fact, while none of the Herkimers' names or those of their known supporters— the Johnsons, Keshegoos, and Tobecos—appear in the list of the group's eleven members, five of the eleven on the discipline committee can be closely linked to the Jones faction: Peter Jones, Joseph Sawyer, Peter's brother-in-law James Chechok, Chechok's brother

John Peter, and the Joneses' loyal follower James Young.[40] The committee, quite likely Peter and Eliza Jones's idea, had not impressed his opposition. In the old egalitarian society no one had the right to command another—parents could not even do so with their own children. The second resolution Peter's party sponsored, "that James Tobeco be required to put away his fiddle," was also opposed. In addition to the principle involved, James Tobeco was William and Lawrence Herkimer's nephew.[41]

Peter Jones wanted above all to make his people economically self-supporting. He realized, of course, that much had been accomplished at the Credit by the late 1830s. In just ten years the Indians, with their own labor, had built a hospital, a mechanic's shop, and eight barns and had added over twenty houses to the original twenty. They had enclosed for pasture and farming nine hundred acres, or nearly one-third of their reserve. On their farms they raised wheat, oats, peas, Indian corn, potatoes, and other vegetables; several cut hay and had small orchards. The band ran two sawmills. Even at the mouth of the river they had made many improvements. The village of Port Credit had been laid out, and they had sold town lots. With £2,500 of their annuity money the Mississaugas purchased two-thirds of the shares of the Credit Harbour Company. Under their direction as its majority stockholders, the company had constructed a port that could accommodate any ship on Lake Ontario.

After more than a year's residence as the band's missionary, the Rev. Benjamin Slight had commented on the settlement's affluence. Slight, one of the Wesleyan Methodist ministers from Britain, who arrived in Upper Canada after the union of the British and Upper Canadian churches, was very impressed by the Credit Mission. In his diary on 30 August 1837 he wrote, "a great proportion of the peasantry of even happy old England, might envy many in this villiage [sic]."[42]

Appearances aside, however, Peter realized that much of the old culture had not disappeared but had just become less visible. The first two white ministers, Egerton Ryerson and James Richardson, had themselves recognized this. During his year with the Missis-

saugas Egerton praised the Indians' rapid adjustment to a settled way
of life but added, "in some respects they are Indian, though they have
become Christians."[43] The Indians' priorities were quite different.
When building the parsonage at the Credit in late 1827, for example,
Richardson had difficulty keeping them at work during the fall hunt
and the fall salmon run: "But oh! the task I had to get these children
of nature out every morning, and keep them at work several hours
each day. They appeared willing and began cheerfully, but then they
would fly off at a tangent, or loiter at intervals, so that winter was at
hand ere my house showed itself erect."[44] The revolt of the Herkimer party also showed that many on the reserve had kept intact their
old attitudes about landownership.

In the mid-1830s Peter Jones no longer enjoyed the band's univer-
sal support. Some Mississaugas, including a number of staunch
Christians, felt that he talked, acted, and lived too much like a white
man. A small group left the reserve, allying themselves with Bluejay,
a former convert who had rejected Peter Jones and the Methodists.
Until his death in 1837 Bluejay apparently led the encampment just
west of Toronto—the men and women Peter Jones referred to in his
diary as the "wicked Indians at the Humber."[45]

One can divide the converts remaining at the Credit into three
groups: the traditionalists, the moderates, and the reformers. The
traditionalists dropped out of the church but stayed at the mission.
The Herkimers and other moderates remained church members and
willingly adjusted to many of the changes, but they resisted the
introduction of more and more white codes of behavior. The Jones
party—the reformers or progressives as they would be termed a
generation or so later—sought to eradicate many of the surviving
Indian characteristics of the Credit Mission. One-third of the band
belonged to the traditionalist group, a greater number—almost
half—sided with the reformers, and the remainder, say one-sixth,
were moderates.[46]

In their campaign to "Europeanize" the Credit people, Peter Jones
and his supporters encountered major obstacles. The Ojibwa language proved perhaps the most formidable, for despite the ever-

increasing employment of English in the school,[47] the villagers universally used Ojibwa. Through their parents' tongue the young acquired the old concepts. As George Copway, a Mississauga preacher, later wrote, "our language perpetuates our own ideas of civilization, as well as the old usages in our nation."[48] Indeed, even in the Christian religious services the native preachers occasionally relied on the terms of their former observances, thus keeping their memory alive. The difficulty of translating European theological expressions into Ojibwa encouraged this dependence. *Sahsahgewejegun*, for example, the name of the pre-Christian painted-pole feast, remained in use. As Peter states in his *History of the Ojebway Indians*, the term, which signified "the spreading out to view [of] the desires of the supplicants," was "still often used by the Christian Indians in making their wants known to God."[49]

Language and lifelong associations provided effective barriers to change. The white people's explanations puzzled the old people, who still believed implicitly that the spirit beings controlled events. In 1831 Peter Jones reported how puzzled they had been after their minister explained thunder and lightning. All their lives the Credit people had never questioned that the thunderbirds, large eagles, created lightning and thunder. The whites' principles of cause and effect seemed quite implausible to many of the older band members.[50]

At the Credit school the native and white teachers worked to break down the Indian children's traditional outlook. In the classroom John Jones, who taught until his poor health forced him to retire in 1830, took particular pains to explain the phenomena of nature to the students. He explained that the great thunderbird's flapping his wings did not make the thunder, nor did the flashing of his eyes cause the lightning. Similarly, he worked to convince the students that the world was a sphere and not an island, instructing them about "the diurnal and annual revolutions of the earth, its shape and dimensions."[51] But, some Ojibwa children asked, if the earth were globular, would not the lakes be emptied?[52]

The white and Indian schoolteachers failed to destroy their students' Indian habits and beliefs. Over ten years after the first schools had been established, Peter Jones recognized their shortcomings. Since the pupils lived at home, their parents and grandparents neutralized the effect of each day's schooling, for the older Mississaugas, "a number of whom are good pious christians, . . . nevertheless retain many of their old habits."[53] Writing in February 1835, the Indian missionary recommended that "all the children be placed entirely under the charge and management of the teachers & missionaries; so that their parents shall have no control over them."[54] Peter Jones wanted the schools eventually to be run by Indians, to produce duplicates of himself: men and women able to compete with the white people, able to defend their rights in English, under English law.

The absence of several of his most competent followers at distant missions greatly weakened Peter's attempts to modernize the reserve. In April 1840 he wrote that he could not send James Young or David Sawyer, his first cousin, away to other mission stations, for if he did he feared "our people here will go to destruction, as there will be no one left who has any great influence among them."[55] That very year ten Credit band members labored in different parts of Upper Canada.[56]

The death of a number of the first generation of educated "progressive" Indians also hurt Peter Jones's modernization program, depriving him of valuable allies. In 1828 Joseph Quinipeno, the grandson of Chief Golden Eagle, died very young. The bright, promising boy of twelve was attentive and punctual at school and was devout. He "always knelt down night & morning & offered up a private prayer to God." After he died his friends, knowing how much he had loved school, had placed his prized books:—his Bible, his Ojibwa hymnbook, and his spelling book—on top of his coffin.[57]

Another loss came when tuberculosis claimed the life of Sahgahgewagahbaweh, baptized as John Summerfield. Trained at the Credit school and later at Cazenovia Seminary in New York State, the young man, then about twenty, had completed and published a *Sketch of Grammar of the Chippeway Language* in 1834, the first ever to appear. The American Methodists had wanted him to direct the school they planned to establish among the Menominees, or "wild rice people," as the Ojibwas termed the Algonquian tribe near Green Bay on Lake Michigan. He died at the Credit River on 1 August 1836.[58]

One of the most promising Credit Indian students of all was William Wilson, born, like Joseph Quinipeno and John Summerfield, about 1815. Wilson, in Peter's words "an Indian youth of superior abilities," completed the Credit school, then attended Upper Canada College and the Methodists' Upper Canadian Academy (later Victoria College) at Cobourg. Egerton Ryerson took great interest in the young man, paying his tuition and lending him his copies of the letters of "Junius," a late eighteenth-century English political author, Lord Kames's *Elements of Criticism*, and Gisborne's *Enquiry into the Duties of Men*. At the academy Wilson made rapid progress in classics, wrote poetry with ease, and headed his class. On leaving Cobourg, though, he went to New York, contracted smallpox, and died about 1838.[59]

The continued deaths discouraged many new Christians. Bunch and Polly Sunegoo, loyal supporters of Peter Jones, lost all but two of their several children to disease. Their only surviving son drowned in the millrace at the Credit River.[60] John Jones's wife Christiana and their five children all were carried away.[61] The Credit exhorter Thomas McGee's seven children all died in infancy.[62] Over a two-year period in the mid-1830s David Sawyer lost seven of his relatives: his mother, her two sisters, his mother-in-law, a brother, his only sister, and his only child.[63] So affected was his father by these losses that for some time he drank once again. When caught intoxicated, Joseph Sawyer was expelled from the church, but after his repentance the chief gained readmission.[64]

Peter's knowledge of contemporary events in the United States led him to act hurriedly. He wanted the Anishinabeg to hold onto their land, unlike the situation in the United States, where the Americans forced the Indians westward. In December 1835 the American government reached an agreement with a small minority of some three to five hundred Cherokees out of a total population of more than seventeen thousand. The Americans claimed that by this agreement the Cherokees had agreed to removal beyond the Mississippi. They must all be gone by 23 May 1838.[65] But this treaty had not been negotiated with John Ross, the principal chief of the Cherokee Nation, and no official of the Cherokee Nation had signed it. What would happen in Upper Canada, Peter asked himself, if the lieutenant governor enacted a similar removal policy? In less than a year Sir Francis Bond Head, Colborne's replacement, did exactly that.

Before his arrival Sir Francis had met Indians not in Upper Canada, but on the Pampas of Argentina, where he had spent several years in the 1820s.[66] A romantic, Bond Head believed the Indians could never adapt to agriculture and a settled life regardless of what one did for them. He believed they were a race doomed to extinction. The British government's civilization policy adopted by Sir John Colborne in Upper Canada in 1830 was in his opinion a total waste of time, a policy that "implanted many more vices than it has eradicated."[67] The short man, with luxuriant curly gray locks crowning his small head,[68] had quickly made up his mind about the Indians' future. After only a few months in the colony he advised shipping "the few remaining Indians who are lingering in Upper Canada" to Manitoulin Island on the north shore of Lake Huron or "elsewhere toward the North West."[69] This approach would solve the "Indian problem" and at the same time provide additional lands for settlers.

This hasty suggestion angered the Methodist Indians. True, the government-sponsored farming settlements at the Narrows and at Coldwater had advanced slowly, but some progress had been made.[70] And certainly the Mississaugas had made solid gains at the Credit River, Grape Island, and now at Alderville, the Grape Islanders' new reserve on Rice Lake. Head Chief Joseph Sawyer of the Credit band protested against the new lieutenant governor's harebrained relocation scheme:

Now we raise our own corn, potatoes, wheat . . . we have cattle, and many comforts and conveniences. But if we go to Maneetoolin, we

could not live; soon we should be extinct as a people; we could raise
no potatoes, corn, pork, or beef; nothing would grow by putting the
seed on the smooth rock. We could get very few of the birds the
Governor speaks of, and there are no deer to be had. We have been
bred among the white people, and our children cannot live without
bread, and other things, to which they are now accustomed.[71]

In 1836 only one large tract of fertile land remained in Indian
hands: the Saugeen. Augustus Jones, who had been present at many
of John Graves Simcoe's councils, must have told his son of the
lieutenant governor's promises about Indian land titles. In speeches
such as that made at Niagara on 22 June 1793, Simcoe told his Indian
allies: "no king of Great Britain ever claimed absolute power or
Sovereignty over any of your Lands or Territories that were not fairly
sold or bestowed by your ancestors at Public Treaties."[72] The Proclamation of 1763 had categorically stated that a majority of the members of a band must agree to a surrender before it could be considered
a legal document. Bond Head, though, knew nothing of these procedures. In his haste to obtain the Saugeen Tract, he summoned the
Saugeen Ojibwas to his council at Manitoulin Island in August 1836
before he had even read the Proclamation of 1763.[73]

The Reverend James Evans attended the council at Manitoulin
and later described how the governor had secured the transfer, which
left the Indians only "the granite rocks and bog land," of the northern Saugeen or Bruce Peninsula. Bond Head began by telling the
Saugeens that "he could not protect them in the possession of their
land;—that the white man *would* settle on it; and that if they did
not give it up the would *lose* it." They refused. In a subsequent
interview he applied more pressure. Then, without even any written
promise of financial compensation, the spirit of resistance of the few
Saugeen Indians present broke. They gave up the tract. If denied the
protection of the government, they knew they could not retain the
land against tens of thousands of land-hungry white settlers. On
their return from the meeting place they told Evans that "they were
ruined, but it was no use to say any thing more, as their Great Father
was determined to have their land,—that they were poor and weak

and must submit, and that if they did not let him have it his own way, they would lose it altogether."[74]

At the Saugeen some of the warriors refused to accept their leaders' capitulation. Thomas Hurlburt, the Methodist missionary to the band, whom Peter had known on Grape Island years before, later recorded their discontent. The Indians talked of a general uprising, and for perhaps the last time in the southern portion of Upper Canada, they sent wampum belts from band to band inviting them "to take up the hatchet." When the Ojibwa-speaking Hurlburt told them they could never win against the numerous whites, they replied: "We know that very well; but don't you see we are all doomed to die; all our land is taken from us, and we think if we kill a few of the white people that they will come and kill us off, and then there will be an end of us."[75]

"Every Man always feels best when he is in his own house and stands on his own ground."[76] Peter knew that the Indians could never adjust if the threat of relocation hung constantly over their heads. To John Sunday, then on a missionary tour of Britain, he wrote on 9 December 1836 a short urgent note in Ojibwa: "Now the Indians have given up all the land at Sah-gung, on Lake Huron, as the governor had begged it from them . . . also the Narrows and Coldwater Indians. They all give up their lands, the whole of them. I do not know what would become of them, and where they should go now I know not . . . I am afraid all of them will be destroyed."[77]

A united front formed to fight the removal policy, bringing Peter firmly back into his church, side by side with Stinson, Evans, and Egerton Ryerson. In England the Wesleyan Methodists and John Sunday approached for support the newly formed Aborigines Protection Society, successor to the British Anti-Slavery Association, which had played an important role in abolishing slavery in the empire. Two leading members of the society became the Anishinabeg's champions: Thomas Hodgkin, a medical doctor who was the first to describe the disease that now bears his name; and Sir Augustus d'Este, Queen Victoria's first cousin.[78]

Early in October 1837 the Credit band decided that Peter Jones

must present their land petition directly to Queen Victoria. Lawrence and William Herkimer and the moderates approved, closing
ranks with the reformers.[79] The Mississauga chief left with Stinson's and Case's blessing, to advance the cause of the Christian
Indians in Britain.

Bond Head immediately set to work. As soon as he heard of the
mission the governor sent a hasty letter to Lord Glenelg, the colonial
secretary, informing him of the Indian chief's origins: "Mr. Peter
Jones who in the power of Attorney of which he is the bearer has the
double title of *Chief* and *Missionary* of the Mississagua tribe of the
Chippewa nation of Indians is the son of an American surveyor who
having in open adultery had children by several Indian Squaws
deemed it admirable to bring up one of them as a Missionary!"[80] But
despite Bond Head's letter the colonial secretary did meet his Indian
visitor.

Shortly after Peter left Upper Canada, Bond Head's administrative incompetence precipitated a short-lived uprising of several
thousand white settlers led by William Lyon Mackenzie. A somewhat larger rebellion in Lower Canada, led by Louis-Joseph Pa-
pineau, also quickly suppressed, made it difficult for Peter to secure
an immediate interview. The harried Lord Glenelg had thirty colonies to administer in addition to the troublesome Canadas. The two
men finally met in early March 1838—by coincidence the same
month Sir Francis Bond Head left Toronto, having resigned his post
as lieutenant governor.[81]

In the interview, Glenelg's concern for the Indians impressed
Peter.[82] Silently he listened as the Ojibwa explained to him: "So long
as they hold no written document from the British Government to
show that the land is theirs they fear that the white man may at
some future day take their lands away from them, and the apprehen-
sion is constantly cherished by observing the policy pursued by the
United States Government."[83]

Peter did not know that Glenelg, a vice-president of the powerful
Church Missionary Society,[84] a predominantly Church of England
organization, was already predisposed to help. His Lordship had

always believed the Indians could be converted and civilized. "Our forefathers the ancient Britons," he told Peter, "were once as barbarous as the North American Indians are; and as Christianity has made our nation what it is, surely it will do the same for the Indian tribes."[85] The colonial secretary wanted to help, and later that month he promised to work to secure proper title deeds for the Christian Indians.[86]

Peter rejoiced. Unlike their American brethren, the Canadian Indians would not be removed. Believing that the Indians' ownership of their lands had been recognized, he spent his last months in Britain undertaking a lengthy speaking tour to raise money for the Canadian mission work. Throughout Cornwall, strong Methodist country, he attracted huge crowds; at Penzance, for example, the Falmouth *Packet* reported: "The chapel was crowded to excess long before five o'clock the hour appointed for the meeting, and scores of persons were obliged to go away unable to get admission." In tiny St. Ives, 4 to 5,000 people came to hear the 'Red Indian' preacher. Later at Bristol hundreds, including his own wife, could not obtain seats for his talk in the crowded St. Philip's Chapel. When the doors closed in Leeds they left hundreds outside, the chapel which had a capacity of 3,500 persons being completely filled.[87] From England Peter went to Wales and Ireland and passed through Scotland. The Wesleyan Methodists drove him at a furious pace. As he told Eliza in one letter, "we have not only missionary & preaching meetings, but *breakfast* meetings, *dinner* meetings, *tea* meetings, *supper* meetings, *calling* meetings, & so on, & so on."[88] Throughout the British Isles the novelty of a North American Indian preacher again, as in 1831–32, brought out huge congregations—and collections.

Peter's interview with the queen completed his exhausting tour. Glenelg probably had first scheduled it for late July, since Eliza recorded in her diary of 18 July: "at home all day preparing Peter for an interview with the Queen." But the court postponed the call until 14 September. Finally the day for his presentation to Her Majesty arrived, and Peter left for Windsor Castle. An amusing incident preceded the audience.

On the appointed day Peter presented himself at Windsor Castle at 12:30 P.M. As arranged, he had arrived early to discuss with Lord Glenelg how he should dress for the ceremony. But His Lordship became nervous when he mentioned his Indian costume. "Is it like the Highland Scotch dress?" the colonial secretary asked. "It is not like the Highland costume," Peter replied and assured him, "It is a perfect covering." Lord Glenelg immediately excused himself to consult Lord Melbourne, the prime minister.

For several minutes two of the world's most powerful leaders discussed the Ojibwa national costume. The colonial secretary asked Lord Melbourne whether he thought the Canadian Indian costume was court dress.[89] But the leader of the British Empire, fearing any impropriety before the young queen, advised a cautious policy—the Indian should present himself dressed in his English tailored suit.

But now Glenelg was curious. Returning to the room where he had left Peter, he asked him to bring the Indian costume to the castle. Back he went by carriage to the inn where he was staying. When the Indian and the Reverend Robert Alder returned, Glenelg, seeing the costume, deemed it quite proper and counseled Peter to wear it. The colonial secretary gave him the use of his room at the castle to change. Twenty minutes later Peter emerged, ready to meet his sovereign. Away went he and Alder, led by Lord Glenelg, to the queen's reception room.

Although it lasted only a few minutes, Peter remembered his interview with Queen Victoria for the rest of his life.[90] Back at his father-in-law's house in Lambeth, he recounted to Eliza and her family each minute detail of his afternoon at Windsor Castle. Most important, Queen Victoria had approved her colonial secretary's recommendation to grant title deeds. The interview with Her Majesty, and the promised cooperation of Lord Glenelg, made Peter more of an anglophile than ever. Britain stood in the vanguard of moral progress. It had led the world in abolishing the slave trade and ending slavery in its colonies. Now it promised justice to its North American Indian allies.

Despite the frantic pace, Peter enjoyed many aspects of his year abroad. He walked into the future in England, experiencing developments that would come to Canada in the decades to follow. He had traveled in 1831–32 from Manchester to Liverpool by railway, a distance of fifty kilometers, in an hour and a half.[91] Six years later he found almost all of England's major cities linked by railway lines. He could even take a train from London to a point very near Windsor itself.[92] As Eliza, Peter, and his niece Catherine Sunegoo, who had accompanied them to England, traveled through Britain, Peter marveled at the nation's rural strength—its fairs and markets, its fat cattle, and its fields tilled, in many cases, for over fifty generations. When they passed through Worcestershire in early May 1838 and saw the orchards in bloom, he commented in his diary: "When will my poor native land assume such a garden of paradise?"[93] Rural and industrial England became his ideal.

Another England existed, of course. Britain's wealth, based on rapid economic growth, had been achieved at a very high social cost: dreadful living conditions existed in the new factory towns of the North and the Midlands. Undernourished children of seven or eight worked in coal mines. Women became old and infirm by the age of thirty after two decades of unhealthy work in cotton mills. Men could be seen in city streets with legs crooked or shoulders twisted from working for years in cramped quarters in mines or on dangerous industrial jobs. One could not help but notice these scenes.

Peter did see another negative side of English life. A North American Indian named La Grasse had been imprisoned at London's Clerkenwell prison. (How he arrived in England or was arrested for assault, though, is unknown.) Peter visited La Grasse in the dingy prison to give him religious instruction.[94] But Clerkenwell prison aside, Peter was shielded from much of the harshness of English life. On their travels through Britain, Peter and Eliza stayed in the homes of prosperous Methodists,[95] and in the London area they lived with Eliza's parents.

In London Peter met powerful, affluent individuals like the Duke of Sutherland, who controlled as his personal property the entire

Scottish county of Sutherland, roughly two thousand square miles in extent.[96] He conferred with Sir George Simpson,[97] governor of the Hudson's Bay Company, a man in charge of Rupert's Land, a domain that included the watersheds of all the rivers draining into Hudson Bay and James Bay, as well as all of British North America westward to the Pacific. Frequently he also called upon Sir Augustus d'Este of the Aborigines Protection Society.

Sir Augustus d'Este became one of Peter's closest English friends. Then in his early forties, Sir Augustus had long been interested in North American Indians. Just four years earlier he had helped Maconse, "little bear," or Francis Eshtonoquot, "clear sky," to use his English name, an Ojibwa from the American side of Lake St. Clair.[98] Maconse had come to Britain enticed by the promises of an English theatrical entrepreneur, who had then abandoned him and his troupe of six Indians. While in Britain Maconse lost his wife, his nephew, and a warrior in his dance troupe to smallpox.[99] Sir Augustus befriended him and he, with the help of Dr. Hodgkin, sent Maconse and the three survivors back to Michigan with farm tools and with books to begin a school for their people, the Swan Creek band.[100] Prominently on display in his home in London Sir Augustus had a full-length portrait of Maconse.[101]

The English aristocrat had been to North America. In 1815 he had participated in the unsuccessful British assault on New Orleans in the War of 1812.[102] The chief advocate of the American government's Indian removal policy had commanded the American forces at New Orleans: General Andrew Jackson. Perhaps this helps to explain Sir Augustus's hatred of the relocation scheme.

Sir Augustus's interest in Indians came in part from his father, the Duke of Sussex, and his maternal grandfather, the Earl of Dunmore. In 1823–24 the duke had befriended John Dunn Hunter, the author of an intriguing book, *Memoirs of a Captivity among the Indians of North America, from Childhood to the Age of Nineteen.* Hunter claimed to have been kidnapped as a child by the Kickapoos, captured by the Pawnees and then by the Kansas, and raised to manhood by the Osages in the Arkansas country. The duke, the youngest son of King George III, welcomed Hunter to his home, Kensington Palace, and introduced him to many important and influential people,[103] including Sir Augustus.[104] After Hunter's return to the United States the Duke of Sussex became the vice-patron of the Reverend Thaddeus Osgood's Society for Promoting Education and Industry among the Indians and Destitute Settlers in Canada.[105]

An even stronger family link existed between Sir Augustus and the Indians, one that helps explain his interest. The most poignant recorded speech of a North American Indian had been addressed to his maternal grandfather, John Murray, the fourth earl of Dunmore, the last royal governor of Virginia. In October 1774, at the close of Dunmore's war against the Lenni Lenapes, Shawnees, and Mingos (Ohio Iroquois), the governor summoned a treaty meeting. Conspicuously absent was Chief John Logan, an important Mingo leader. When invited again to appear, Logan sent a message to Lord Dunmore.

I appeal to any white man to say if he ever entered Logan's cabin hungry, and he gave him not meat; if ever he came cold and naked, and he clothed him not. During the course of the last long and bloody war Logan remained idle in his cabin, an advocate for peace. Such was my love for the whites, that my countrymen pointed, as they passed, and said, "Logan is the friend of the white man." I had even thought to have lived with you, but for the injuries of one man. Colonel Cresass [Cresap], the last spring, in cold blood and unprovoked, murdered all the relations of Logan, not even sparing my women and children. There runs not a drop of my blood in the veins of any living creature. This called on me for vengeance. I have sought it; I have killed many; I have fully glutted my vengeance. For my country, I rejoice at the beams of peace; but do not harbour the thought that mine is the joy of fear. Logan never felt fear. He will not turn on his heel to save his life. Who is there to mourn for Logan? Not one.

Peter Jones included the entire speech in his *History of the Ojebway Indians*, adding that it had "become familiar wherever the English language is spoken."[106]

Most likely it was through the good offices of Sir Augustus d'Este that Peter secured his audience with the queen. Not only was Sir Augustus on his father's side a first cousin of the queen, but also on his mother's side he was the first cousin of Charles Augustus Murray, master of the queen's household.[107] Peter had visited Sir Augustus the day before he left for Windsor.[108]

As a parting gift Sir Augustus gave Peter a beautiful steel peace pipe to use at the opening of Indian councils in Upper Canada.[109] He also sent a short note: "I wish both to your wife and yourself Calmseas, and Right-winds for your Passage across the Great Salt waters."[110] From Canada Peter sent back a strange gift—a small bottle of bear grease.[111] Concerned perhaps about his hairline, Sir Augustus had asked for it, one of the uses of bear grease being to prevent baldness.[112]

Peter's esteem for Britain increased enormously after he and Eliza passed through New York City in late October 1838 on their way home. Though the objects they brought with them were destined for distribution at Canadian Indian missions, the American customs officials charged exorbitant duty on these goods.[113] In New York Peter also heard distressing news about the brutal treatment of the Cherokees. American troops armed with rifles and bayonets had rounded up nearly fifteen thousand Indians for eviction west of the Mississippi to Indian Territory (present Oklahoma), a journey that in Cherokee memory became known as the Trail of Tears.[114]

The very day before his interview with Queen Victoria, Peter Jones had written down his dreams for the Ojibwas of Upper Canada. Immediately, he wanted title deeds for all the existing reserves, and later he desired an Anishinabeg homeland in Upper Canada in the Saugeen Tract:

I beg to suggest the great importance of Her Majesty's Government Reserving a Sufficient Tract of Land on what is called "the Saugeen Territory" as the future home of all the Canadian Indians, for any who may come over from the United States to settle in Canada.

I am of opinion that the time will come when many of those Tribes located in the midst of the white settlements will see the necessity of forming one general community, and I know of no place (unoccupied by the white population) better calculated for this purpose than the Saugeen Territory.[115]

Peter sought a place of refuge for those Great Lakes Indians in the United States trying to escape removal and a homeland, separate from the whites, for the future surplus population of the tiny Ojibwa reserves around Lake Simcoe and on the north shore of Lake Ontario.

On the eve of his thirty-seventh birthday, on 1 January 1839, Peter Jones's dreams for his people appeared on the point of realization: the Ojibwas had united, the white Canadian and British Methodists had strongly supported them, and the colonial secretary and the queen herself had promised title deeds. Perhaps the greatest accomplishment of his life occurred the following year in late January 1840, when several hundred chiefs and warriors from across Upper Canada gathered for a grand council at the Indian village on the Credit. At this, the first modern Indian political meeting in present-day Ontario, he hoped that Upper Canada's Indian bands would formulate a joint position on landownership, education, and a future Anishinabe homeland.

Land and Education

After the victory of the Anishinabeg over the People of the Long-house about 1700, the tribes had made a pact of friendship. They renewed that treaty on 21 January 1840, for the fifth time. Fifteen Iroquois chiefs faced two hundred Ojibwa chiefs and warriors across the council fire at the Indian village on the Credit River. They came together for the treaty that, once made, was so strong "that if a tree fell across their arms it could not separate them or cause them to unloose their hold."[1]

Joseph Sawyer rose. In his hand the Credit River head chief, then in his early fifties, carried an ornate steel peace pipe tomahawk, about two-thirds of a meter long, with twelve ornamental silver bands on its fine-grained wooden stem. As he smoked the pipe the chief prayed that the smoke of the calumet would ascend straight upward to the Great Spirit.

At the Grand River, the master of ceremonies at the Six Nations' councils acted in a similar manner. He rose to his feet, filled the pipe of peace, and then lighted it from his own fire. One after another he drew three puffs from the pipe, blowing the first toward the sky directly overhead, the second toward the ground, and the third toward the sun. By the first action he returned thanks to the Great Spirit for preserving his life over the past year and for his being permitted to be present at this council. By the second he returned thanks to the earth, his mother, for her bounty. And by the third he returned thanks to the sun for his never-failing light, which shone on all.[2]

At the Credit River council the Ojibwas' peace pipe tomahawk, once it had been properly lit and presented, was passed around the council ring. All the chiefs smoked it. The silver blade, inscribed "From Augustus d'Este to Ka-kiwe-guun-ebi, 1838," flashed in the light of the fire. As the smoke ascended upward the Great Spirit would witness it mingling together as one body. The ceremony had deep significance, ratifying as it did the lasting peace concluded between the two once hostile groups. By the 1840s the roughly 10,000 Anishinabeg and Iroquois had become a tiny minority in this new colony of some 450,000,[3] which made it ever more imperative for the Ojibwas and the Iroquois to renew their alliance and to stay together.

In early 1840 the thoughts of many Indians in Upper Canada were directed southward. Conditions for Indians in the eastern United States had become desperate. Rumors must have reached the Mississaugas and the Iroquois in late 1838 and 1839 of the brutal treatment of the Cherokees. Lurid stories of the harshness and inhumanity of the soldiers' rounding up of the Indians appeared in the American press.[4] On the forced march westward at least one-tenth, perhaps one-third, of the nearly 15,000 Cherokees died as a result of malnutrition, exposure, and cholera.[5] Meanwhile, in Florida the Americans brought in bloodhounds from Cuba to track down the last fugitive Seminole Indians in the swamps and everglades.[6]

The American removal policy also affected Upper Canada. Several thousand Ojibwas, Ottawas, and Potawatomis emigrated from the American side of the Great Lakes to avoid relocation. Maconse of Lake St. Clair, Sir Augustus d'Este's friend, settled for new lands in Kansas, but the vast majority of Indians wanted to remain by the Great Lakes. By 1840 an estimated 2,000 had already reached Upper Canada, most of them Potawatomis, as Peter Jones later wrote, "in a most deplorable state of poverty and degradation." In the early 1840s nearly 500 Oneidas from New York State, followed, and they purchased land just south of the Ojibwas and Munsees at Muncey-town.[7]

Sakayengwaraton, "the haze that rises from the ground in an

autumn morning and vanishes as the day advances,"[8] or John Smoke Johnson as the Mohawk chief was known in English, spoke for the Iroquois to the Ojibwas and Lenni Lenapes (Delawares and Munsees) before him. An interpreter translated from Iroquois into English, then Peter translated the English into Ojibwa. The important Ojibwa chiefs—William Yellowhead of Lake Simcoe, John Sunday of Alderville, George Paudash of Rice Lake, John Assance of Coldwater, Joshua Wawanosh of Lake St. Clair, and John Riley of Munceytown—listened intently, as did their warriors. Peter Jones had invited chiefs and delegates from all the settled bands in Upper Canada to the council; Indian Methodists stood beside Anglicans, Roman Catholics, Moravians, and even Indian traditionalists.[9]

The speaker of the Six Nations council had an agreeable voice and an interesting, dramatic presentation.[10] "All the Indian tribes ought to unite in obtaining titles to their lands," he told the Anishinabeg, to prevent any additional losses. He also counseled the Ojibwas to be more assertive in their negotiations, to call the governor "Brother" and not "Father," so "that they might feel themselves equal with the Governor, and so speak more freely with him."[11] If John Smoke Johnson had been the only speaker from the Six Nations the unity of the moment might have been preserved.

Peter's dream had been exactly this: Indian unity. "Be united in all your important matters, Union is Strength,"[12] he had told Joseph Sawyer only two years earlier. Wise in the ways of the settlers' political system, the perceptive Indian missionary knew that pressure must be constantly applied until they had the promised title deeds in hand.

Peter had met George Arthur, Bond Head's successor, immediately after his return from England in November 1838.[13] Unfortunately, though, Lord Glenelg had resigned as colonial secretary in February 1839.[14] With no one in the Colonial Office to prod him, Arthur did nothing about the title deeds.[15] In December 1839 Peter met Arthur's superior, the newly appointed governor general of Canada, Charles Poulett Thomson, to ask that the Indian reserve at the Credit River be recognized as the Indians' in perpetuity. He also informed him of the grand council to be held at the Credit River the following month.[16]

The first day of the Ojibwa-Iroquois meetings went well but, as Peter had feared, the second did not. The talks collapsed, and it proved impossible to forge a pan-Indian front in 1840. The hereditary enemies still distrusted each other too much. Even Benjamin Slight, the white missionary at the Credit, caught the note of contempt of the Iroquois toward the Ojibwas.[17] On the second day a dispute arose over the meaning of an important symbol on ancient wampum belts.

The disagreement arose out of a statement made the first day by Skanawiti, "beyond the river," known to the whites as John Buck, an Onondaga chief and the official keeper of the wampum belts of the confederacy.[18] At the council Skanawiti presented four wampum belts and explained their symbols. The bowl appearing on the first, he claimed, "represented that the Ojebways and the Six Nations were all to eat out of one dish—that is to have all the game in common."[19] William Yellowhead, head chief of Lake Simcoe, protested what he believed was an outrageous statement. On the second day Yellowhead produced a historic belt given to the Ojibwas by the Iroquois themselves, which contained the details of the peace concluded between the two groups. The dish marked on it meant "that the right of hunting on the north side of the Lake was secured to the Ojebways and that the Six Nations were not to hunt here only when they come to smoke the pipe of peace with their Ojebway brethren."[20] The meeting broke up.

After the Iroquois chiefs departed, the Ojibwa chiefs continued their meetings. The failure to build an Iroquois-Ojibwa alliance effectively cut the Upper Canadian Indians' strength in half. The Ojibwas alone sent an important petition, one of several proposed by Peter Jones, to George Arthur. It asked that the lieutenant governor of Upper Canada "secure to us and to our children, as soon as convenient, the lands on which we reside, as expressed in Lord Glenelg's dispatches."[21]

To meet their request Arthur must ensure that the Royal Proclamation of 1763 henceforth be scrupulously observed. Just the previous year the Aborigines Protection Society had reprinted the document whose key phrase read: "any lands whatever which not having been ceded to or purchased by us . . . are reserved to the said Indians, or any of them." The Indians, "with whom we are connected, and who live under our protection, should not be molested or disturbed."[22] But the lieutenant governor, preoccupied with achieving peace and stability among the white settlers after the Rebellion of 1837, did nothing.

Arthur had come to the colony well versed in the problems of interracial conflict. He had served for twelve years as the governor of Van Diemen's Land (Tasmania), where the settlers' treatment of the aborigines made even the Americans' policies look gentle. The whites in Van Diemen's Land had literally massacred the Tasmanians, almost exterminating them. Poisonings, trappings, and ambushes occurred, as they did later to an even greater degree in other parts of Australia: in western Victoria, western New South Wales, and most of Queensland.[23] While George Arthur admitted that injustices had been committed against the Indians,[24] to this veteran of Tasmania these injuries seemed minor. He devoted his time instead to what he considered to be more pressing matters and left Indian affairs entirely to Samuel P. Jarvis, the new Indian superintendent, James Givins's replacement.

Francis Bond Head had named S. P. Jarvis, scion of a well-established Loyalist family at Toronto, chief superintendent of Indian affairs in June 1837, considering him "an active, intelligent humane person."[25] Peter Jones differed with this assessment. In his eight-year term of office from 1837 to 1845, never once did the chief superintendent give the Credit Indians a report on their band funds. They had no idea whether they had received the full amount of their annuity, and they obtained no financial statement at all on the sale of their lands at Twelve Mile Creek and Sixteen Mile Creek and on the Credit River. Joseph Sawyer and John Jones termed Jarvis's behavior "uncourteous and repulsive."[26]

Regardless of the number of times Peter Jones and the Credit

Indians explained the nature of the title deeds they sought, their Indian superintendent failed to listen. He told the Indians assembled at the Credit Mission in January 1840, for example, that his opposition to deeds "arose from the good-will he had towards them, as he feared if they had deeds many of them would soon dispose of their lands."[27] But he had totally missed the point. As Joseph Sawyer, Peter Jones, and John Jones later explained: "we have never asked for, nor desired patents in fee simple, as we all well know, that under present circumstances it would be unwise to give the Indians the power to alienate their lands. But our prayer to her Majesty's Govt. has been for the obtaining of a Govt. Document securing the lands to our Tribe and their posterity for ever."[28]

Arthur had not acted, but the Credit Indians hoped in 1840 that Governor General Charles Poulett Thomson would. Named Lord Sydenham in August 1840, Thomson had just skillfully negotiated Upper Canada's acceptance of the plan of union with Lower Canada, a union achieved early in 1841. During the grand council at the Credit in January 1840, Peter Jones had formulated the strategy to follow: the Ojibwas must apply great pressure to obtain title deeds, and they must work to gain back the Saugeen Tract, or at least some portion of it, to be used as an Indian homeland in Upper Canada. Unfortunately, though, the unity of the Ojibwa bands proved only temporary. Within six months the community had split down the middle.

Less than half a year after the council, the Wesleyan Methodist church in Canada was on the point of breaking apart. Ever since the union of 1833 Egerton Ryerson and a number of the Canadian preachers had resented the fact that the British Wesleyans held all the power in the new church. The conflict between the British and the Canadian factions intensified throughout 1840. As early as June, the British party approached Peter promising him that his "salary would be permanent, & my *usefulness* greatly extended" if he sided with them.[29] The imminent collapse of the Methodist union led both the British and the Canadian parties to begin recruiting Indian allies.

The threatened breakup of their church totally confused the Christians of the Credit. In council Thomas Smith, Jr., stated that he was "greatly puzzled to know why there should be two kinds of Methodists." As to the distinctions between the two bodies, David Sawyer, a veteran of several missionary campaigns, confessed he could not identify them. In fact, he told the council that he "saw no differences between the British and Canada Methodists. The preachers in Canada were as proud as the British. They love ease and were afraid to go into the backwoods for fear [of] wetting their feet."[30]

Without any clear guidance from the band, Peter, once the inevitability of division approached, had to decide which group to support. William Case's and John Sunday's decision to stay with the British placed him in a quandary, for temperamentally he felt far more at home with the impoverished Canadians led by his close friend Egerton Ryerson. Peter implicitly trusted Egerton—"a friend," he once wrote to Eliza, "in whom I have the greatest confidence."[31] Their friendship, dating back nearly fifteen years, finally led Peter into the Canadian Conference. Once he had made known his preference the Credit Mission unanimously followed,[32] as did Lake Simcoe (Rama),[33] Mud (Curve) Lake, Munceytown, and the Saugeen. Against them stood George Paudash at Rice Lake and, more important, John Sunday at Alderville—the new Grape Island Mission. The British also held on to St. Clair, where James Evans had worked in the mid-1830s. With the Indian missions divided into two opposing camps, little pressure could be applied for title deeds or the return of the Saugeen Tract.

In mid-October 1840 Peter rode from the Credit to neighboring Oakville, ten kilometers to the west. The morning air was chill and sharp, the leaves had changed hue, and patches of many colors—pale yellows, reds, and browns—made the countryside look like one of the splendid quilts Eliza enjoyed making at the mission.[34] In Ojibwa the Indians called September the fading-leaf moon, October the falling-leaf moon, and the approaching November the freezing moon.[35]

Peter knew he had lost. The white settlers would occupy the Saugeen Tract, just as they had the entire lakefront at the western end of Lake Ontario—apart from the "very small dot"[36] represented by the Credit Mission. Already the white settlers had begun surveying a road stretching northward from Oakville to Owen Sound on Georgian Bay,[37] which would allow the first white farmers in the Saugeen Tract to ship out their wheat.

The developments at Oakville amazed Peter. Only twenty years earlier a forest had stood here with Indian cornfields on the flats by the river mouth. Now the former Indian reserve had a harbor and shipyards and a population of 450. It had become an important shipping center for white oak and for grain. Thanks to its prosperity the village in 1840 had regularly laid out streets and lots. Peter had come to help open the new Wesleyan Methodist church.[38]

The exterior of the new building, the second Wesleyan church in Upper Canada to be provided with a steeple and bell, was impressive. The tin spire glistened in the sunlight high over the one- and two-story shops on the main thoroughfare, Colborne Street, named after the former governor. Peter dedicated the chapel with the help of the Reverend Anson Green.[39]

As his text the Indian minister took the eighty-ninth Psalm, "Blessed is the People that know the joyful sound."[40] Bravely Peter struck a positive note, but it could not change reality. Two weeks later the Canadian Conference and the British Wesleyans formally dissolved their union. The split caused the Oakville congregation irreparable damage; in fact, the divided local group soon could no longer keep up the payments on the expensive chapel. They sold it in 1841 to the Anglicans, who renamed it St. Jude's.[41]

An increased denominational rivalry in the 1840s hurt both the white and the Indian Methodists. The reentry of the Jesuit fathers to Canadian mission work in the early 1840s effectively ended any further Methodist advances on the north shore of Lake Huron. The thoroughness of the Jesuits' training, their ability with languages, and their persistence made them the divided Methodists' greatest rivals.[42] Similarly the Anglicans made advances, in the 1840s winning over influential Methodists into their church. The church's ties with the Indian Department helped, since several Indian leaders noted their close connection. William Yellowhead, for example, joined the Church of England in the early 1840s, as the important Chief Shingwahkoons (Little Pine) at Sault Ste. Marie, had done several years earlier.[43]

Interdenominational rivalry had caused enormous confusion among the Anishinabeg and had hurt the Methodists at the Sault. The Methodists competed with the Baptists, the Anglicans, and the Roman Catholics.[44] When Peter Jones had visited the Sault in the summer of 1833 he had found that "many of the Indians who are inclined to become Christians, did not kneel during prayer, and kept their seats when singing, on account of the different modes of worship pursued by the too numerous sects and parties in this place."[45] Shingwahkoons, being at a complete loss as to which denomination to support, had asked Lieutenant Governor John Colborne, who had replied: "Your great father, King George, and all his people in the far country across the sea, follow the English religion (the Church of England). I am a member of this Church. I think it right that you Chippeways, who love the English nation, and have fought under the English flag, should belong to the Church of England."[46]

It must have pained Peter greatly that the Methodists failed to win Shingwahkoons and the Anishinabeg of the Sault over to their side. Henry Schoolcraft, the American Indian agent at the Sault in the 1820s and early 1830s, had witnessed their strong beginning. As the husband of Susan Johnston, granddaughter of Waub-o-jeeg, "the white fisher," an important Ojibwa chief at La Pointe on the southwestern shore of Lake Superior,[47] he knew the native response to the Methodist Anishinabe preachers. Schoolcraft attributed their large number of conversions at the Sault in the early 1830s, "to John Sunday and his companions, who enjoy extraordinary advantages in the use of their vernacular tongue in speaking to the Indians."[48] But with the marriage in 1833 of Charlotte Johnston, Susan Schoolcraft's sister, to the Reverend William McMurray, of the Sault, the

Anglicans gained a native voice,[49] and they soon stopped the Methodists' advance.

In the early 1840s Peter Jones failed to receive the long-promised title deeds; he saw the Anishinabeg divide into Roman Catholic, Anglican, Methodist, and traditionalist factions; and he witnessed the destruction of his own church. Just to consider the five most prominent ministers who had served at the Credit, only one, Egerton Ryerson, remained in 1840 in the Canadian Conference; another, James Richardson now adhered to the Methodist Episcopal church, a splinter group that had broken away in the early 1830s; a third, George Ryerson, had joined the Irvingite movement, a new sect that favored speaking in tongues or the spontaneous outpouring of the Holy Spirit;[50] the band's most recent ministers, William Case and Benjamin Slight, had sided with the British Conference. In addition to at least three kinds of Methodists and George Ryerson's Irvingites, the Indians knew of the Roman Catholics, the Anglicans, and now the Mormons who appeared at the Credit Mission in the late 1830s.[51]

The most auspicious moment had passed for an Ojibwa offensive to obtain title deeds and to win back the Saugeen Tract, or a significant portion of it, for a future Anishinabe homeland. The Indians stood weakly divided into several camps and so could not constitute an effective lobby. On 14 September 1840 the government gave the Saugeens an annuity equal to that accorded other tribes,[52] but they never regained their lost lands. (They retained only the rocky Bruce Peninsula, separating Georgian Bay from Lake Huron.) The government took no action at all on the question of title deeds.

As George Arthur had done, Lord Sydenham delegated all responsibility for Indians to Chief Superintendent Jarvis. In reality Indian matters occupied so little of the governor general's attention that the Act of Union of 1841 joining the two colonies omitted to provide for the annuities to which the Indians were entitled. Only in 1844 did the government discover and rectify this.[53] After union, Sydenham showed little interest in Indians. Like Bond Head, he termed Colborne's civilization policy a failure, "a waste of resources of the province, and injury to the Indians themselves."[54] All attempts to civilize the Indians were useless, he argued; they would best be left in their native state. He had no time to hear otherwise and flatly refused to see Peter Jones on 22 July 1841, pleading that he was "so much engaged at present."[55]

Lord Sydenham's term of office ended abruptly two months later, on 19 September 1841. On the fourth he badly shattered his right leg when his horse stumbled. Infection set in, and the unlucky governor died in the agonies of lockjaw.[56] Had he lived, this opponent of the civilization policy might have tried to reintroduce Bond Head's removal policy.

Sydenham's replacement, Sir Charles Bagot, proved much more sympathetic to the Christian Indians. Without making any hasty judgments or relying solely on Jarvis's advice, Bagot established a royal commission of inquiry into Indian affairs, appointing three special commissioners to review departmental records, receive briefs, and question the Indian superintendents.[57] The appointments pleased Peter immensely.[58]

In his submission to the Bagot Commission Peter brought forward the ideas about his people's future that he had long ago formulated. Five years earlier, in a letter to the Aborigines Protection Society, he had summarized his position: "I am of opinion that all the Christianized and civilized Indians, ought to be (as soon as they are sufficiently instructed) considered in all points as Her Majesty's subjects, and so be invested with all the civil privileges enjoyed by the English Settlers, such as voting for members of parliament, voting at Township meetings, the right of sitting as jurors, & the holding of situations & offices under the Government." Peter believed that they must pursue this route of equality, for they had no alternative, "scattered & surrounded by the White people as the Indians are, it would be in vain for them to attempt to keep up a separate form of Government from their neighbours, who form the largest population."[59]

The Indian missionary expanded upon these thoughts in his letter to the commissioners. To improve the Indians' condition, "all the civil and political rights of British subjects ought to be extended to them so soon as they are capable of understanding and exercising such rights." While becoming full citizens, the Indians and "their posterity" must retain the security of owning their reserve lands, forever. The granting of title deeds to the respective bands would dispel the Indians' fear of one day being removed, a fear that "acts as a check upon their industry and enterprise." Always the Indians must have detailed financial reports on their annuities and sales. Three concepts—civil rights, land rights, and financial responsibility—summarize his position. Finally, to prepare his people for citizenship and the wise administration of their lands, Peter urged "the importance of establishing schools of industry as soon as possible, that there may be no further delay in bringing forward the present rising generation."[60]

From Peter's point of view the timing of the Bagot Commission proved inopportune. The Ojibwa bands were completely disunited, at sixes and sevens with each other, and the old feud at the Credit Mission between the Jones and the Herkimer parties, the progressives and the moderates, had just broken out again. If only the spirit of the first day of the grand council between the Ojibwas and the Iroquois in January 1840 had held! The Indians of Upper Canada could have addressed the commissioners with strength, as one entity. Who would listen to a group of fragmented bands?

That a significant number of his own band opposed him allowed Samuel Jarvis to claim that Peter Jones did not speak for the Credit Indians. Openly the chief superintendent encouraged the Herkimer party. The clash this time came over removing to the rich farming area near Munceytown, a decision Peter and Joseph Sawyer had reluctantly made after the failure to secure title deeds at the Credit. The Herkimer party, at most twelve families out of the fifty in the band,[61] refused to move. Although the band as a whole had approved the decision to relocate, Jarvis refused to sanction it as long as the dissidents held out. In despair the band abandoned the idea in February 1844 "on account of the difficulties thrown in the way of their removal by Mr. Jarvis and his agents."[62]

Already attacked by the Herkimer party at the Credit and by the Ojibwa British Wesleyans,[63] Roman Catholics, Anglicans, and traditionalists, Peter suffered another reversal in 1843. It came from an unexpected source, a fellow member of the Methodist Canadian Conference. Having spent most of his adult life in distant mission stations, the Canadian-born Thomas Hurlburt, a strong, rugged-looking man,[64] had become resentful of what he felt was his church's favoring of Peter Jones. As early as 1838, after only several years' acquaintance with the Ojibwa language, he openly challenged the validity of Peter's numerous translations of the Scriptures. In the *Christian Guardian* he acidly commented that "all the translations that had been made are deficient" and "need revising." He recommended the new Ojibwa hymnbook recently completed by James Evans and the Credit Indian George Henry.[65]

As the first person to reduce the language to written form, Peter Jones himself admitted the imperfections of his work. "After more mature experience and knowledge, I see many defects in my own translations. I have, however, this satisfaction, that I did my best, and I am happy to say that the errors are not of vital importance."[66] The experts agreed. At the general council at the Credit in January 1840, the chiefs and principal warriors had voted one hundred to five "to have the Old Ojibwa hymns reprinted, together with such others, as our Brother Peter Jones may translate, for the use of ourselves and families."[67] Nearly a century and a half later Peter Jones's hymnal remains in use.[68]

Three experienced non-Indian Ojibwa-speakers recognized the uniqueness of Peter's work. Captain Charles Anderson, a retired Indian Department officer who had an Ojibwa wife (two simultaneously, according to one report), regarded Peter's translation of the first seven chapters of Matthew "as good as the Chippeway language will admit of."[69] Sherman Hall, an Ojibwa-speaking missionary for the American Board of Commissioners for Foreign Missions at La Pointe on Lake Superior, termed the Jones brothers' translation of the Gospel of John, "as good [as] could be made at present. The language is generally simple and intelligible."[70] Joseph Howse, a retired Hudson's Bay Company trader of twenty years' experience in Rupert's Land, wrote of the same translation, "it is a well executed performance—the Style is of course perfectly Indian & the choice of terms except in some two or 3 unimportant instances—very correct."[71] But Thomas Hurlburt remained unsatisfied.

The controversy began again in the spring of 1843 when Hurlburt elaborated his opinion of the "savages" in an address to the Toronto branch of the Missionary Society. In an abbreviated form, the *Christian Guardian* reported what the outspoken white missionary had told his audience: "The Indians, unchristianized were destitute of fellow-feeling, were superstitious, immoral, imbecile in mind, and degraded in social habits. On these topics his facts were startling, especially two: That the Indians are cannibals, and that the intercourse of the White man does not corrupt the Indian, but that the Indian corrupts the white man, except in the case of ardent spirits."[72]

"Startled and astonished" by such ridiculous, insulting comments, Peter Jones rose to vindicate the character of his people. Hurlburt had claimed in his lecture that they were "destitute of fellow-feeling," yet, Peter said, "their hospitality is proverbial, as all who have travelled in the Indian country will readily acknowledge." As for the charge that they practiced cannibalism, they "have a common rule amongst them, that, when an Indian is known to have eaten human flesh through starvation, it is right to put such to death as soon as possible." The final assertion that the Indians had corrupted the white man baffled the Mississauga missionary. "Who taught the Indian to swear, which he could not do in his own language. He [Hurlburt] knows well that almost the first words he learns to speak in English is to take the name of God in vain."[73]

The headstrong Hurlburt replied in the *Christian Guardian*. Jones, he claimed, "has not travelled extensively among the Indians."[74] From this second letter the explanation of the white minister's strange conduct becomes apparent—jealousy: "while others, besides their regular labour, have been directed to employ all their spare time in performing manual labour, with and for the Indians,

and have built mission-houses with their own hands, others—
among whom is Br. J.—have been directed to pursue their studies,
make translations, etc."[75]

At the annual conference that summer Thomas Hurlburt continued to bait Peter Jones. He claimed before all the assembled
ministers that his translations contained many "absurdities." As
Peter told Eliza on 18 June, "I am getting sick of such proceedings,
and if I am to be thus annoyed and attacked by my ministerial
brethren, the sooner I withdraw from them the better, for I cannot
co-operate with a body who look upon me with a jealous or sus-
picious eye."[76]

Hurlburt's antics annoyed the influential members of the Canadian Conference. The meeting, in fact, condemned "the proceedings
of a certain person." On 23 June Peter happily informed his wife,
"The report made by the Committee on the Ind. translations was
altogether in my favor, indeed they were praised up a great deal more
than I think they deserved."[77] The Reverend Mr Hurlburt was finally
silenced.

Not surprisingly, this factionalism led to the disillusionment of
many native Christians. George Henry had been the first to go.
Although he presented himself as Peter's "second cousin," the blood
connection was a stronger one. Evidence in the Credit Mission
Church Registry reveals that George Henry, ten years younger than
Peter, was actually his half-brother.[78] But unlike Peter's, George's
father was an Indian. His parents, Mesquacosy and Tubenahneequay, had raised George entirely as an Indian before his conversion
to Christianity about 1825 at the age of fourteen or so.

As a young man George was one of the Methodists' most promising native candidates for the ministry. He had taught at the Credit
Sunday school, accompanied a missionary party to the Sault, and
acted as a mission interpreter at Munceytown. In the late 1830s he
had worked as James Evans's interpreter and as the assistant missionary at the St. Clair.[79] Among his own people he enjoyed wide
respect. Although he decided to remain at the St. Clair, the Credit
band had invited him back in 1837 as their third chief.[80]

The white ministers also appreciated his abilities. The Reverend Benjamin Slight found him "a clever, respectable looking young man, a good speaker, said to be a good divine, a tolerable poet, and an excellent translator."[81] In 1838 Jonathan Scott, another white missionary, publicly referred to him as one of the foremost Indian preachers, writing in the American Methodist newspaper the *Christian Advocate* that "Jones, Sunday, Henry, and Jacobs, are at the head of our chosen pioneers."[82] Then in 1840 the "good divine" and respected man suddenly resigned from the church.

In disgust George Henry left the Methodists, who were too strict for his liking. A few months later he went one step further in his personal revolt against his half-brother and his movement. In the summer of 1844 he helped organize a dance troupe, consisting of his family and several Walpole Island non-Christians, to tour England. The thought of this party flamboyantly dressed in silver brooches, beads, seashells, and necklaces of bear claws—"for the sole object of dancing and shewing of the wild Indian before the British public for the sake of gain"—horrified Peter. "I feel for the honor of my nation & am much mortified where any thing is done calculated to lower the Indian character in the estimation of the religious public."[83] The native missionary also knew the fate of Maconse's troupe—three out of seven had died overseas. George Henry, or Maungwudaus, "a great hero,"[84] as his public knew him, left despite Peter's protests, and as a further insult he joined the Roman Catholic church during his tour of Britain.[85]

The mid-1840s definitely were a transitional period for Peter Jones, one in which his focus changed. Concerns that in the 1830s had great urgency for him, such as the completion of his history of the Ojibwas, no longer seemed so immediate. After 1845[86] he apparently gave his manuscript history little attention, and indeed it was only through Eliza's efforts that his notes eventually were collected and published several years after his death.[87] Even his diary suffered in the 1840s—in 1848, for instance, he made only one entry for the entire year.[88] The split in the Methodist church, the discouragements of the Hurlburt affair, his troubles with the Herkimers, his own half-brother's defection, all disheartened him.

During these difficult years Peter's health deteriorated. The Reverend Anson Green reported in February 1843 that his native colleague was "in a very precarious state."[89] By 1844 his strength had so declined that the conference made him a supernumerary in the church. The description of the post in *The Doctrine and Discipline of the Methodist Episcopal Church* reads: "A supernumerary preacher is one so worn out in the itinerant service as to be rendered incapable of preaching constantly; but at the same time, is willing to do any work of the ministry which the Conference may direct and his strength enable him to perform."[90] Still Peter carried on considerable work for his church, on missionary tours and at the Munceytown mission.

In the 1840s Peter's greatest joys came from his growing family and from his important work at Munceytown. Eliza and Peter had rejoiced in April 1839 on the birth of their son Charles Augustus, named after both their fathers. After two miscarriages and two stillbirths, Eliza understandably idolized their first living child. She recorded with great care his first tooth at the age of ten months, the second at eleven months, and the date when he ran on his own—fourteen months. Wanting him to have an Indian name, Charles Augustus's parents approached Joseph Sawyer. The boy's greatuncle called him Wahweyakuhmegoo, "the round world, or he who encircles the world."[91]

With the birth of Charles Augustus, Peter more than ever before disliked his lengthy trips away from home. Immediately after the breakup of the union with the British Methodists in late 1840, the Canadian Conference had sent their leading Indian preacher on a fund-raising tour of eastern Upper Canada. Peter left in the middle of winter for a journey of two and a half months to local gatherings in Port Hope, Belleville, Kingston, Bytown (to become Ottawa several years later), and many points en route. In Kingston a young lawyer of twenty-six with political ambitions chaired the missionary meeting—John A. Macdonald.[92]

In hindsight this meeting in Kingston potentially was the most important of Peter's life. Who could have foreseen in 1840 the subsequent career of the young Scottish immigrant, who had come to Upper Canada with his parents at age five? Macdonald soon entered politics. He first served as an alderman in Kingston, then ran the next year for the Legislative Assembly of the Canadas. Winning his seat in 1844, the young man rose to become attorney general of Upper Canada and then joint premier of the Canadas. His would be the dominant creative mind that produced the British North America Act and the confederation of the Canadas (Ontario and Quebec), New Brunswick, and Nova Scotia that became Canada in 1867. As Canada's first prime minister in 1867–73 and 1878–91, he added Manitoba, the North West Territory (present-day Saskatchewan and Alberta), British Columbia, and Prince Edward Island to the new Union.[93] From 1878 to 1885 he served as superintendent general of Indian affairs as well as prime minister.[94] Few individuals have ever had more power and influence over Canadian Indian affairs than John A. Macdonald.

Unfortunately, at that meeting in early February 1841 Peter failed to convince the chairman that the Indians, if supplied with the necessary education, the proper housing and equipment, and the security of title to their lands, could become the equals of the whites. Nearly forty years later, as prime minister, John A. Macdonald summarized his own opinion: "The general rule is that you cannot make the Indian a white man. . . . You cannot make an agriculturalist of the Indian. All we can hope for is to wean them, by slow degrees, from their nomadic habits, which have almost become an instinct, and by slow degrees absorb them or settle them on the land."[95] In these opinions Peter Jones would hear echoes of Sir Francis Bond Head and of Lord Sydenham. Just as had happened in Upper Canada, Macdonald wanted the Indians pushed off the arable lands of the prairie west and replaced by white farmers.

The speaking tour, though financially successful, troubled Peter. One month after it began Eliza, then seven months pregnant, had written to her husband of Charles Augustus's sudden, very serious illness. Peter felt it imperative that he return to his family and to his congregation at the Credit River, among whom sickness was then general. He first consulted his fellow preachers: "they all say that under present circumstances they conceive it would be my duty to attend to the calls of the church, even if my friends were to die. Now this view is shocking to my views and feelings. I have yet to learn how to lose those *tender domestic feelings* which in my opinion ought ever to reign around the family circle, for the sake of gratifying the *curiosity* of a few hundred persons."[96]

Fortunately Peter learned in Eliza's next letter that the health of Charles Augustus and others at the Credit had improved.[97] He could continue. With his fellow ministers the Indian missionary completed the tour—in all, sixty-four meetings and two thousand kilometers of traveling.[98]

Peter's domestic happiness increased yet again shortly after his return. Only days after his arrival, Eliza gave birth to a second healthy son, to be named Frederick, no doubt after Eliza's beloved fifteen-year-old half-brother Frederick Field. The tiny child, who was given the Indian name Wahbegwuna, "a white lily or flower," would accompany his parents and his two-year-old brother to Peter's new mission station at Munceytown that fall. At Munceytown their third son arrived on 30 October 1843, Peter Edmund in English, or Kahkewaquonaby (Sacred Feathers—his father's name). Their third son's first name in English came of course from his father, and his second came from Eliza's youngest half-brother, Edmund Field, who had been born eleven years earlier, in January 1832, during Peter's courtship of Eliza.[99]

The names selected for her sons indicate Eliza's closeness to her younger brothers. When she left England in August 1833 Fred, then seven, had penned a little poem to his sister:

> *I'm a very little boy*
> *But will wish my sister joy;*
> *This is all that can be said*
> *By her little brother Fred.*[100]

In the early 1840s Fred began his studies in the laboratory of the Polytechnic Institution in London (he later became a well-known chemist, a fellow of Britain's Royal Society). In letters from home

Eliza learned from Edmund about his growing collection of animals at Norwood. By 1845 Edmund, then thirteen, kept fifteen chickens and five ducks at his parents' country home.[101]

At Munceytown, about thirty kilometers southwest of London, the Jones family initially lived on the lower floor of the two-story mission house, the upper level serving as a church on Sunday and as a schoolhouse during the week.[102] The mission house lay by the meandering Thames River, in the center of the settlement of over a thousand Indians, roughly half being Ojibwas and Munsees and the remainder Oneidas, members of the Six Nations Confederacy newly arrived from New York State.[103]

The Joneses' best friends at the mission included John Carey and his family, the first white schoolteacher at Munceytown, who still farmed there.[104] Next to the Carey farm at the townsite of Colborne lived Joseph Clench, the Indian agent, who had some Indian ancestry through his mother. Both Peter and Eliza liked him and his wife, Serena, a Jewish woman who had been born in Germany.[105] Another good friend, Abraham Sickles, a portly Indian Methodist preacher, lived on the opposite bank of the Thames on the Oneida reserve.[106]

Peter liked the challenge of Munceytown, a settlement in which many still refused Christianity. As he wrote Eliza just before their move from the Credit in 1841, "There is very much to do amongst these Indians, and there will be no danger of want of employment. I feel I am where I ought to be."[107] With its rich, fertile land Peter considered Munceytown "the most suitable place for an Indian colony in all Canada."[108] The Indian missionary wanted the Credit Indians to remove here (if title deeds could not be obtained at the Credit), but Samuel Jarvis, the Indian superintendent, had obstructed the move.

While Peter worked at Munceytown the Bagot Commission delivered its report in January 1844. Sir Charles Bagot had died in March 1843, and his replacement, Sir Charles Metcalfe, formerly provisional governor general of India and most recently governor of Jamaica, received it. Peter's concerns had been primarily fourfold: full Indian civil and land rights, full financial reporting in Indian trust funds, and educational reform. Unfortunately, the commission advised immediate action only on the last point: education.[109] Having failed by 1844 to secure title deeds to the existing reserves and to retain an Indian homeland in the good agricultural lands of the Saugeen Tract, Peter devoted much of his attention in the mid-1840s to education. He believed that only by learning the white people's way well, so well that they could acquire financial independence, could the Indians survive. If land can be said to have been Peter Jones's major concern in the 1830s, in the mid-1840s it became land and education. To compete, the Indians needed to know basic reading, writing, and arithmetic and to have a fund of general knowledge about the larger society. Once they had become self-reliant, they could protect their tiny reserves from outsiders' intrusions, defend the unsurrendered lands to the north and the west, and also participate in the settlers' world around them. The Indian missionary objected to the fact that "the Colonial Government assumed a parental authority over them, treating them in every respect as children."[110] He wanted the Indians to be what he had become, the equal of any white person.

In the late summer of 1839 an incident occurred that tells much about Peter Jones' desire to see his people educated. James S. Buckingham, an extraordinary Englishman who had gone to sea at the age of ten, founded a newspaper in Calcutta, and traveled to nearly every continent made a lecture tour of North America. While in Toronto he met the "celebrated Indian Kah-ke-wa-quo-a-bee," who attended his lectures on Egypt. Afterward the chief, in Buckingham's words, "expressed himself so pleased with them, that he sent up to the settlement to request as many of the Indians as could be spared from their labours to come down and attend with him the lectures on Palestine."[111]

Determined to build a manual labor school, or residential school, for Indian children, Peter first sought the approval of the Canadian Conference and of Governor General Metcalfe himself. To raise money for such a school and its accompanying model farm, he proposed that the bands donate one-quarter of their annuities to education. He also asked, and obtained, the Canadian Conference's permission to make another fund-raising tour of Britain. Before he left, however, he, Joseph Sawyer, and George Copway traveled to meet the governor in Montreal.

No doubt S. P. Jarvis sent warnings to Sir Charles Metcalfe about the Reverend Peter Jones. By the summer of 1844 Peter and the chief superintendent were no longer on speaking terms. The previous year Joseph Sawyer and Peter's brother John Jones had reported to the governor general's secretary the charge of several Lake Simcoe Ojibwas that the chief superintendent had fathered a baby by Harriet, a Snake Island woman.[112] Joseph Sawyer and John Jones themselves accused Nehkik, "the otter," as the Mississaugas called him, of financial irresponsibility.[113] Ever since Jarvis's appointment there had been "no balance sheet furnished us ... we do not know whether we get the full amount of our annuity, and the proceeds of the sale of our Reserves."[114]

S. P. Jarvis, a member of a highly influential Loyalist family at York, had in the past behaved very much as he pleased. As a young man in Cornwall, Upper Canada, he and several school friends had badly beaten up an Indian boy in a brawl. As a young man of twenty-five he had killed John Ridout in 1817 in a fatal duel at York. Nine years later in 1826 he had led the gang of men who had destroyed the radical William Lyon Mackenzie's printing press at York.[115]

Sir Charles Metcalfe took his own counsel. From the findings of the Bagot Commission he already knew of the validity of the charges about Jarvis's financial incompetence. The chief superintendent had kept few, if any, accounts of band revenues. In May 1844 he had been stripped of his official rank in all but name. One year later he would be ordered to return over four thousand pounds, a sum roughly eight times the Credit Indians' annual annuity. The government then officially dismissed him.[116]

It would be fascinating to have a firsthand account of the meeting in Montreal on 16 August 1844[117] between Peter, Joseph Sawyer, George Copway, and Charles Metcalfe. None, unfortunately, survives. Peter no doubt presented the case for the badly needed school at Munceytown. As he wrote only a few months later:

Our contemplated plans are to establish two Schools; one for one hundred boys, the other for one hundred girls. The boys to be taught in connection with a common English education, the art of Farming and useful trades. The girls to be instructed in Reading and Writing, Domestic Economy, Sewing, Knitting, Spinning; so as to qualify them to become good wives and mothers. It is also our intention to select from each School the most promising boys and girls, with a view of giving them superior advantages; so as qualify them for Missionaries and School teachers among their brethren.[118]

Metcalfe, once informed of Peter Jones's mixed ancestry, would want very much to meet him. At age sixteen young Charles had left England for India, where he had remained for thirty-seven years, rising quickly in the East India Company—reaching the post of acting governor general in 1835. During his early years in India he had spent over eight years at the court of Ranjit Singh in the Punjab. While resident there he apparently had a liaison with a wellborn Sikh woman. Few in Montreal knew his secret—that he, a bachelor, had fathered three Anglo-Indian sons, all of whom he had educated at his expense in England.[119]

Sir Charles Metcalfe, a portly, plain man, had a kindly face. But by the summer of 1844 he had a tortured look. The governor general was dying. Although the blinds had been drawn to protect his eyes from the light, one could make out the large swelling on his right cheek, a cancerous tumor that had already failed to yield to surgery and then to the agony of repeated external applications of zinc chloride.[120]

Greatly impressed by the soft-spoken native missionary and his dreams for his people, Sir Charles endorsed his Indian visitors' plea for a better system of Indian education. Approving of the establishment of a manual labor school at Munceytown, the governor himself made a financial contribution to it.[121] He went further. Judging the Credit River Indians to be sufficiently prepared, he entrusted their chiefs with the administration of their band's finances, the first time in Canadian history an Indian band had obtained financial control over its own trust funds.[122]

Peter Jones, who had met half a dozen colonial governors, never forgot the humanity and the decency of Sir Charles Metcalfe. No doubt the governor's personal bravery, his determination to continue even though in great pain, drew the native missionary to him. Out of a sense of duty the dying man kept on at his post for one more year until, hardly able to talk and half blind, he could no longer continue. In his last year in office Indian education became one of the issues preoccupying him. Several months before his departure from Canada the dying Metcalfe told his secretary Captain Higginson that one or more boarding schools must be established for Indian boys and girls, enabling them "to occupy a social position equal to that of their white fellow subjects."[123]

When Sir Charles returned to England in December 1845 Peter, then still on his British tour to raise funds for the proposed Indian residential school, visited him twice, meeting him in London for the last time in late February 1846. Lord Metcalfe (he had been raised to the peerage in January 1845) told Peter on his last visit that "his health was no better." Within six months he was dead.[124]

Peter Jones received more disappointing news that same summer. His promising native lieutenant George Copway was expelled from the church. The young Copway, then twenty-eight, had long been regarded as a promising mission worker. Years earlier, when the Rice Lake Indian had left in 1834 to work as an interpreter at the American Methodists' Lake Superior mission, Peter Jones had praised him as "an Indian youth of deep piety."[125] Similarly, the Reverend John Carroll, a prominent white Methodist minister, described the tall, handsome convert as "an exceedingly clever man and good speaker both in Indian and English."[126] In June 1840 Copway had married Elizabeth Howell, the eldest daughter of Thomas Howell, a respected Upper Canadian Methodist.[127] Badly in need of effective native preachers for the Canadian Conference, Peter Jones had invited him back in 1842 from the American Methodist Indian missions in Minnesota.

At first it had seemed that Copway's presence would greatly aid the Indian mission work. The Canadian Conference even appointed him to accompany Peter Jones and Joseph Sawyer when they called on Sir Charles Metcalfe.[128] That Peter Jones asked to have the younger man—sixteen years his junior—included in this important delegation to Montreal shows his respect for him as late as the summer of 1844.

George Copway's connection with the Methodists ended abruptly only two years later. The Saugeen band, among whom he had worked from 1843 to 1845, charged that their Indian minister had embezzled their funds. A similar accusation submitted by Chief George Paudash and John Taunchey, his uncle, came from his home mission of Rice Lake. Imprisoned for several weeks and immediately expelled from the Canadian Conference in June 1846, Copway left in disgrace for the United States.[129] Over fifty years later he would still be remembered at Rice Lake. Although half a century served to blend his initial departure for Lake Superior at about the age of fifteen and his hasty flight twelve years later, the essential details would survive unaltered. In 1902 the Rice Lake Indian agent learned from "all the older members of the band" that "about fifty years ago, George Copway then a lad of fifteen years of age, committed a forgery and fled from Justice to the United States and as far as [is] know[n], never returned to Rice Lake Reserve."[130]

From Edinburgh to Echo Villa

Edinburgh's David Octavius Hill and Robert Adamson had formed their photographic partnership in 1843, locating their studio at Rock House, Adamson's home, halfway up Calton Hill at the east end of Princes Street. After Mr. Hill had arranged the poses, Mr. Adamson took the pictures and developed the prints. On the morning of 4 August 1845 the two men had invited Sacred Feathers, the North American Indian, and his English wife to a sitting at Rock House.[1]

On his guests' arrival, Mr. Hill asked Peter's permission to photograph him in European dress as well as in his national costume, and with Eliza's consent they also took one photograph of her. Mr. Adamson shot at least five studies of the famous native missionary in European dress, wearing an Indian sash about his waist, and he took three studies of him in his deerskin coat, leggings, and upright feathered headdress. His shot bag appears, with its design of a thunderbird, and in his hands he holds the ornate peace pipe given him by Sir Augustus d'Este. Comparing this photograph with the oil portrait completed by Matilda Jones in 1832, one sees that thirteen years had taken their toll on his health. The forty-three-year-old missionary had gained considerable weight—the result of his repeated bouts of ill health.

Surprisingly, Eliza, who kept a full diary of their journey together in Scotland,[2] made no reference at all to their visit to Rock House, though only ten days later she devotes five pages to their dinner with the Duchess of Gordon at her mansion on the late duke's huge estate. She liked the duchess a great deal—"a commanding looking woman quite grey, most pleasing countenance; & her manners so kind." Four footmen attended them during dinner, served on silver plates. But of Rock House she says nothing. In fact, for 4 August Eliza wrote only one sentence in her diary: "Public breakfast in the Saloon of Royal Hotel in honor of my dear husband, several speeches, splendid breakfast, all delighted—dined at Dr. Woods." Ironically, a century and half later those Hill and Adamson calotypes of her husband are what is remembered: they are the oldest surving photographs of a North American Indian.[3]

Peter loved Edinburgh, a city he described on his first short visit in 1838 as "one of the most beautiful and romantic cities I have ever witnessed in all my travels."[4] The striking castle, atop a mass of rock a hundred meters high, dominated the ancient capital. Peter called the city "magnificent"[5] with its attractive sandstone buildings in the Old Town and New Town. A great walker, eager to see everything, he went up and down the city's hills. As he later wrote Eliza from Glasgow after extensively touring that city, "I have been walking about all day, & am fagged out."[6]

Edinburgh, in return, warmed to its visitor. "This good man," the Edinburgh *Witness* wrote of him. The Edinburgh's *Ladies' Own Journal* termed him "interesting."[7] His plea for financial support for an Indian residential school in Canada reached receptive ears. On 1 August 1845 he wrote from Edinburgh, "I have been most warmly received by the good citizens of this place, and I have already realized about £100 in this city with a prospect of getting more."[8] He found the Scots "more like my Ind. brethren than any people I had seen on account of their gravity and quiet spirit."[9] They enthusiastically supported his appeal—two-thirds of the thousand pounds that Peter raised in Britain on this fund-raising tour came from Edinburgh and his two months in Scotland: in Aberdeen, Inverness, Glasgow, and many smaller centers.[10]

The transformations that had taken place in Britain since his last visit seven years earlier amazed him. He wrote out his impressions at length for the *Christian Guardian* in Toronto. London with its "teeming population" had expanded in all directions. "Many of the old narrow streets had been widened, several streets paved with wooden blocks, and the toll gates that were once in the suburbs, but now in the town, have been taken down." Everyone seemed mad for the railways. "These are being made in every direction," allowing a traveler to visit any part of the kingdom in just hours, not days. Peter and Eliza journeyed from Liverpool to London, over three hundred kilometers, in nine hours. The Great Western Railway averaged a speed of fifty kilometers an hour. New roads, railways, and buildings arose everywhere. From the Fields' home in Lambeth Marsh he saw the new "great Council-House of the British nation,"[11] the Houses of Parliament, then under construction.

As on his previous trips, the Indian missionary was impressed by the country's technological developments. He had the opportunity, he explained to an audience in Greenock, Scotland, of examining through a telescope the sun, the moon, and the stars. "The very gods whom we used to worship!—you know all about them!"[12]

Peter visited many clergymen and friends of the North American Indians while in Britain. A sad meeting took place with Sir Augustus d'Este, with whom he had corresponded ever since his last visit. Sir Augustus had multiple sclerosis,[13] and the disease had greatly weakened him. As Peter reported back to Canada, "I found my excellent friend, Sir Augustus d'Este, as kind and as much interested for the welfare of the Aborigines of our country as ever; but, I regret to say, that he is quite an invalid, and is not able to walk without assistance."[14]

Sir Augustus no doubt put Peter back in touch with George Henry, whom he had many times invited to take tea at his home.[15] In any event, Peter's contact with his half-brother, broken by George Henry's departure from the Methodist church, was restored. Possibly Peter, temporarily setting aside his opposition to the idea of Indians' participating in wild West shows, even attended one of George's performances at Egyptian Hall in Piccadilly. To cite the handbill, he would have seen:

A Grand Indian Council
In front of the Wigwam, when
the whole Party will appear in
FULL, NATIVE COSTUME,
Displaying all the Implements
of War—the Chief will Address
the Council—and the whole of
the Forms of declaring War will
be gone through.
The INTERPRETER will Deliver
A LECTURE
Descriptive of Indian Character . . .

The lecture terminated with the "Dance of the Wabunnoog," the singing of a war song, the pipe dance, "a fac-simile of the operation of scalping! Never before attempted in this Country," and a war dance. In the middle of the performance Maungwudaus shot an apple off a boy's head.[16]

Later that year Peter received an extraordinary letter from Maungwudaus in Paris. In the fall of 1845 George Catlin, the famous American artist and promoter of Indian curiosities in Europe, had sponsored Maungwudaus's troupe in France. They made a great hit, as Maungwudaus told Peter in his letter dated 19 October 1845:

My Dear Brother,

. . . Last Saturday we saw the great chief of France, and his great chief woman; the great chief of Belgium, and his great chief woman; and some hundreds of their people. . . . These things we did for them:—We played the Indian ball-play, shot at marks with our bows and arrows, false scalping, war dance, paddled one of our birch-bark canoes in a beautifully made river, among swans, wild geese and ducks. After the two great chiefs and their great chief woman had much talk with us, they thanked us, got into their carriages covered with gold, drawn by six beautiful horses, and drove to the wigwam of the great chief of France. We followed them,

and the great chief's servant, who wears a red coat, and much gold and silver, and a hat in the shape of half-night sun, took us into one of the great rooms to dine. Everything on the table was gold and silver; we had twelve clean plates. Many came in while we were eating, and it was great amusement to them all.[17]

Peter himself visited Paris to obtain medical advice. He went to see Dr. Achille-Louis Foville, a renowned French medical specialist. The Indian missionary traveled with an English friend, a Mr. Richardson, who spoke French. From Boulogne he mailed Eliza a humorous note warning her that he had "already begun to learn French and I hope to be able by the time I return to you, to know more of this language than either you or Miss Boot [the Fields' governess]."[18]

Peter took special pains to locate George Catlin, still residing somewhere in the city. He failed to find him on his first day but succeeded on the second. His fears about George Henry's party had come true. Immediately after leaving Paris three members of the troupe had contracted smallpox in Belgium and died. Although a doctor in England had offered to vaccinate them before they left for the Continent, the three men had refused, saying that they carried the needed protection in their medicine bags. Fortunately George Henry and his family had been vaccinated, and they survived. Two years later, however, three of George's children died in Scotland, and his wife Hannah died in England.[19]

Catlin made a poor impression on Peter the day he and Mr. Richardson visited the artist in his rooms. Before coming to Europe the American artist had spent eight years traveling through the upper Mississippi valley, the Central Plains, and the Southwest. He had done hundreds of portraits and paintings of Indians, their ceremonies, and their hunts. But Peter felt he had little interest in Indians as human beings. In a note to Eliza on 7 March Peter described him as, "a thorough blue Yankee he makes great professions of attachment for the Indians." Catlin told him that never again would he stage wild West performances—the mortality of those participating appalled him, and in the end his financial costs had been astronomical. Badly needing cash to support his four small children, he explained that at the very moment he was trying to sell all his Indian paintings—those completed on his trips through the American West and those done from sittings with the Indians in his English and European shows.[20]

The distinguished French physician Achille-Louis Foville did meet with his Canadian visitor, who came with a letter of introduction from Dr. Hodgkin. Dr. Foville, a specialist in brain and nervous illnesses, had just published the first section of his magnum opus on the cerebrospinal nervous system. The French doctor recommended that Peter's nerves and general health could be improved without medicines. Peter reported the diagnosis in full to Eliza on 8 March 1846, the day after his appointment: "After a long consultation he told me I had a weak heart, & to increase its action he advised my sponging with cold water every morning, & rubbing before & after with coarse flannel. He does not recommend medicines, a little wine, but no spirits. He was very kind, & I trust my visit will be of use to me."[21]

After just a week in Paris, Peter longed to return to the English capital. "The public buildings & royal gardens, fountains etc. are splendid," but he found Paris's back streets "narrow, and filthy and the houses looked very dingy." Peter considered London's West End and the queen's palaces much superior to anything Paris had to offer.[22] His three trips to Britain and his English wife had made him a great anglophile.

Peter, Eliza, and the boys returned to Canada in April 1846 after a year's hard work to raise money for Indian residential schools. Throughout Britain the format of Peter's talks had remained rigidly the same.[23] In the seaside town of Hastings on the English Channel, for example, the native missionary spoke at the Swan Inn, the town's leading hotel, which hosted its most important assemblies, dinners, and meetings. The circular for the lecture read:

NORTH AMERICAN INDIANS.

A LECTURE
(in aid of the Indian Manual
Labor Schools) on the
MANNERS, CUSTOMS, & RELIGION,
of the above
INTERESTING PEOPLE,
by
KAHKEWAQUONABY,
(Peter Jones)
Indian Chief, from Canada, who has
laboured as a Missionary for
twenty years among his countrymen

Several specimens of Heathen Gods
and Indian Curiosities
will be exhibited. —
Lecture to commence at 7 o'clock.

Admission, 6d. each — At the
close of the meeting,
a collection will be made for the
subject above stated.

This was the winning formula, guaranteed to bring out the crowds: the Indian talk, the Indian costume, the specimens of "heathen gods," and the Indian curios.

Peter had detested having to appear as a curiosity to attract attention. At one point in his British travels he referred in a letter to his "*odious* Indian Costume."[24] Peter longed to be invisible, for once to have no one turn and look at him. The separations from his family had also been difficult. Apart from Eliza's joining him for his first Scottish visit in August, she and the children had stayed in Lambeth and for some time at Hastings. He missed them greatly, as he wrote to his wife during his second Scottish tour: "I long to be with you again & feel sometimes as if I could pack up, and leave my good Scotch friends and my begging and run away to the dear embraces of my beloved wife & children. Were it not for the hope of benefitting my poor countrymen I should certainly spare myself the toil & anxiety connected with this undertaking."[25]

On their arrival back in Canada one immediate problem faced them—should the Credit River band remove to Owen Sound? The old issue surfaced once again. The Indians still lacked a firm title to their existing lands, and they wanted security. A general council of the Upper Canadian Ojibwa communities, under Joseph Sawyer's leadership, had been held during his absence in July 1845. At the meeting the Saugeen and Owen Sound bands invited all the other Ojibwa bands in the province to settle in the Bruce Peninsula, all that remained to them of the Saugeen Tract.[26] Peter expressed caution. Unlike the fertile southern area of the Saugeen Tract lost in 1836, he viewed the rocky northern peninsula as "too frozen a region for Indians." "They and their cattle together will more than consume what they raise—then away they will wander to other regions for food."[27]

On his return Peter sensed his people's desire for change. The band, in Chief Sawyer's words, wanted to migrate to Owen Sound and the Bruce Peninsula provided the government "secure to the Indians who may settle there a positive and irrevokable right to that Tract for themselves and their descendants for ever."[28] If they could not secure title deeds to their Credit River reserve, remove they must to the northern Saugeen.

In twenty years the Credit River area had changed radically. The white population of the township surrounding the reserve had risen from eight hundred to over four thousand between 1821 and 1835,[29] a 500 percent increase. Operating farms now existed near the reserve. The land itself had changed. No longer was the reserve heavily forested—over twenty years the Indians had cut down all the trees immediately around their townsite for firewood, and white trespassers from the four villages around the reserve had freely removed wood elsewhere on the tract. Already the Indians feared that in ten years the small reserve at the Credit would contain no more timbered land.[30] Second, the salmon run, so dependable and abundant in the past, had almost ceased. *Smith's Canadian Gazetteer* reported in 1846 that as a result of "the great number of mills which have been erected on the river during the last four years, the fishing is destroyed, the salmon being unable to make their way over the dams."[31] Salmon could no longer pass on their way to the upper spawning grounds.

Yet at the same time the band had adjusted remarkably well to a new way of life. On a smaller scale they had duplicated the achievement of the Cherokees in Georgia, Tennessee, and North Carolina twenty years earlier. By the early 1840s the nearly 250 Indians provided nearly all their own bread and large quantities of potatoes, beef, and pork. They had milk and butter.[32] True, the Indians' anxiety in the 1840s that they might be driven from their homes led some farmers to neglect their fields.[33] If the government had guaranteed tenure, the Credit Indians could have improved and expanded their farms. Insecurity had checked their advancement.

Economically they had done much more than develop farms—the Credit Indians had helped pay the costs of developing the mouth of the Credit River into a harbor. Now two parallel piers ran out into the deep water on cribs—frames of timber filled with stones.[34] With Port Credit as its home port, the Indians had become part owners of a schooner captained by James McLean, a Scottish immigrant who at the age of sixteen had married a Mississauga woman. By the 1840s he had lived with the Credit River people for twenty years. Captain McLean carried lumber on the schooner from the Indians' new sawmill to Niagara and other points around the lake.[35]

The Credit Indians had made in two decades the same difficult transition that the Europeans had completed over centuries. The hunters and fishermen had become farmers, and a few were skilled craftsmen: the Credit Mission boasted two or three Indian carpenters and an Indian shoemaker.[36] Many band members had received a good education in the mission schools and could read and write—

which a number of the white settlers could not do. In the twenty years since the establishment of the mission, twenty-four Credit Indians had worked as missionaries, interpreters, and schoolmasters at their home mission and throughout Upper Canada.[37] At that very moment, the Reverend William Herkimer served on Georgian Bay and the French River; David Sawyer worked among the Owen Sound Indians; and the Reverend Peter Jacobs labored in distant Rupert's Land around the border of present-day Manitoba, Ontario, and Minnesota.[38]

In their adoption of the white man's ways, the Indians had in one respect certainly gone too far. They had acquired the whites' prejudice against blacks. While the Credit Indians did indeed sympathize with the blacks, whom they called "our fellow-suffering brethren" on account of the injustices the whites committed against them,[39] they opposed intermarriage with them. At a council at the Credit River on 12 September 1844, the band had passed a resolution "that no coloured person or persons shall be allowed to become resident within the bounds of our Reserve."[40] Five white men, including Captain James McLean and the English-born farmer William Sutton, who had married Jones's niece Catherine Sunegoo,[41] lived on the reserve, as did white women such as Eliza Field Jones and Mary Holtby Jones, John Jones's second wife.[42] But John Mike,[43] a black man who had married a Credit Indian woman named Catherine, was not welcome.

The general council at the Narrows of Lake Simcoe in late July 1846 brought Peter abreast of developments in Upper Canada during his absence. He had been back only several weeks when it began. Thomas G. Anderson, the veteran Indian agent who was S. P. Jarvis's replacement, welcomed the Ojibwa bands from across Upper Canada to the Narrows, where the townsite of Orillia now stood. The sixty-six-year-old Anderson, who spoke Ojibwa, had worked with the Anishinabeg for nearly half a century in the upper Mississippi valley, on Drummond Island, and on Manitoulin Island as well as at Lake Simcoe.[44] He was well respected by the Lake Simcoe Indians, who looked up to the former fur trader on the Mississippi River and long-time Indian Department official "as a king."[45] A very active man, Captain Anderson had the energy of someone half his age. One gesture shows the style of the man: twenty-five years after the council, at the age of ninety-two, he joined the YMCA and remained a member until his death in 1875 at the age of ninety-six.[46] Although the new superintendent had strongly opposed the Methodists at Coldwater a decade and a half earlier Peter viewed Anderson as a vast improvement over Jarvis.

To the hundred or so Indians before him, Captain Anderson explained the government's new Indian policy as developed by former governor general Metcalfe. The Indian superintendent urged the chiefs and principal men to abandon their tiny settlements and form larger ones, where residential or manual labor schools could be established. He added that the government would "secure, by written documents to you and your posterity for ever," all the new lands selected. Peter, who had urged the same policy for twenty years, praised the new superintendent's objective, "to raise you to the same rank in social life as your white brethren, and to make you an independent and happy people."[47] Before Chiefs Paudash, Sunday, Sawyer, Assance, Snake, and Yellowhead, Peter, in Ojibwa, urged the Anishinabeg to remove to a large settlement and to construct manual labor schools.

For financial support Peter urged the Indian bands to donate one-quarter of their annuities each year to support manual labor schools.[48] The Mississauga bands at the Credit, Alderville, Rice Lake, Mud Lake, and Scugog Lake all agreed. George Vardon, assistant superintendent general of Indian affairs, then repeated Superintendent Anderson's promise that "the Government will secure, by writings, such lands as the Indians repair to, with the consent of the Government."[49] The Ojibwas of Upper Canada, it seemed, could at last obtain a homeland, title deeds, and a manual labor school. Reluctant at first to accept the idea of a migration to the Bruce Peninsula, Peter Jones now advocated removal there as the only agricultural area left for a Christian Indian homeland.

One year earlier Peter had written Eliza from Scotland that we must "sometimes have stormy days and it is well it is so, as too much prosperity might make us forget ourselves & our Maker."[50] In late November 1846 the "stormy days" indeed arrived. He first heard bad news about Seth Crawford, his Methodist coworker at Davisville a quarter of a century earlier. Because he had looked after Chief Davis and his wife in their old age, the late Mohawk leader had deeded Seth part of his land near Augustus Jones's old farm on the Grand River. The government, though, had refused to accept this Indian deed, and Seth had lost the farm. Second, the poor man's wife had gone insane and needed constant care.[51]

Two months later misfortune struck Peter's own family at the Credit. The vaccination of band members against smallpox had reduced but not eliminated deaths from that source, and other diseases continued to be a terrible problem on the reserve. The spread of infectious diseases like tuberculosis ("consumption") and measles increased because the band members lived so close together in a settled village. In one year in the 1840s twenty people, roughly 10 percent of the entire band, died, most carried off by a measles epidemic.[52] In January 1847 Peter's second youngest Iroquois half-brother, Joseph Oneida Jones, contracted smallpox. Joseph's Mississauga wife, Catherine Jackson Jones, had been stricken with consumption. Both died on the same day that very month. About the same time Peter's Mississauga half-brother Wahbunoo, or in English Francis Wilson, then studying to become a medical doctor in Toronto, also caught smallpox and died.[53] Eliza, then four months pregnant, did her best to comfort her husband, also burdened by the recent news that his brother John, then serving as Colonel Clench's interpreter at London, Canada West, had a fatal illness.[54]

More distressing news followed in January 1847 when the Credit men who had gone north to survey the new lands returned. Peter wrote immediately to George Vardon, the deputy superintendent general:

There is quite a dissention amongst our people with regard to their removal to Owen Sound. Our young men who assisted in surveying

the boundary line of our intended tract there have brought an evil
report as to the quality of the soil. They say that the land is very
rocky and that there is not more than one third of the whole tract fit
for cultivation. In consequence of these tidings a large majority of
our Tribe are reluctant to remove to that tract of land. In my
opinion it will be necessary to send early next spring a deputation to
examine the real state of the land in order to satisfy the minds of
those who are prejudiced against it. If the land is really as poor as
they represent it I should be the last man to induce any of our people
to remove to it, as I am fully persuaded that when Indians emigrate
to another part of the country they ought to settle on a better tract of
land than that which they leave.[55]

Peter wanted to wait until spring before reaching a final decision—
but the Credit Indian men forced his hand. They wanted a council to
decide the issue immediately.

On 5 February the returning Indians reported on the barrenness of
Owen Sound. James Young, one of those in the surveying party, told
the council that when he saw the "stony and rocky" land his heart
sank "when he thought of the long winters and the quantity of
fodder it would take to feed his cattle and the scarcity of water on the
Tract." Thomas Smith, Jr., stated that even in those areas where the
soil appeared good "they found it was only from 6 to 12 inches deep."
In the vote that followed twenty-nine men opposed and only four
approved the proposed move.[56]

Suddenly the Credit band appeared to be breaking up. Since their
land had been surveyed and was now in the hands of the government
to be sold, they soon had to leave. Isaac Henry announced that he
would depart for Munceytown. John Sterling said he would leave the
reserve "and seek for work elsewhere." Those who remained were
terrified about what the future held for them and their families. John
Peter told the council he was afraid that after his death "his children
would be obliged to carry a woodsaw on their backs to saw wood for
the white people for a living."[57]

The decision greatly troubled Peter. Sir Charles Metcalfe had trusted the Credit band to become the first in the Canadas with control over its own funds.[58] How could he explain to the government that his band had suddenly changed its mind and that no manual labor school would be erected at Owen Sound? That the money spent on buying a schooner to move the band there might be lost? Perhaps the band's ultimate decision would be the same— Peter after all had been the first to have doubts about the agricultural potential of the rocky northern peninsula—but the final vote must be taken only after a full discussion of the alternatives. The Indian leader operated in two worlds and responded to the signals of both. To obtain greater independence the Credit band needed the full confidence of the government, and they must work to convince the white officials that they were acting responsibly. The council's rapid judgment negated all that Peter had spent twenty years working toward—proving that Christian Indians could govern themselves. After two general councils the Indians, with much care and deliberation, had reached their decision. To change their minds so abruptly would, from the government's viewpoint, prove that the Credit band was "incapable of trust and so totally devoid of that steadiness of purpose which is necessary to conduct all business."[59] Peter Jones and Joseph Sawyer called another council for 9 February.

For two decades Peter had successfully taken command in council meetings. He had the ability to assert himself and to convince others to support him. But on this occasion he failed. The Indians' uncertainty about the future and their resentment at having to leave the Credit River all surfaced. He could not obtain a consensus. At this second meeting James Young, one of Peter's most loyal supporters, denounced him. Speaking on behalf of a group of warriors, Pepoonnahba, "the god of the north, who makes the winter,"[60] stood up and protested: "My Chiefs, you are very great cowards indeed, in being afraid to speak to the government, you know our minds on the subject, and will not speak and tell the same."[61] He had used the most derogatory word in a warrior society: "coward."

The action Peter then took shows the stress he was under—he totally overreacted to this ridiculous charge. Exhausted, frustrated, tired of trying to bridge two cultures, he bluntly announced that if James Young's statement represented the spirit of the meeting he would resign as chief. The charge of cowardice, so ill founded, revealed the intensity of his people's pain. If only they had received secure tenure on their reserve they could have stayed—and a major Indian reserve would still be situated in the Toronto area today.

Within three days calmer spirits prevailed. The majority of the band realized they could not do without their most bilingual and bicultural member. Twenty-six principal men in the band, a majority of those attending the councils, signed a petition expressing "every confidence in our brother." Peter withdrew his resignation.[62]

That April help arrived from a most unexpected source. In one of their full councils the Six Nations—after indirectly hearing of the Mississaugas' dilemma—remembered that when their fathers had come from the Mohawk River the Mississaugas had kindly given them land. They now felt "a great pleasure in returning the compliment to their descendants."[63] After the full Iroquois council invited them to their reserve, the Credit band accepted. In 1847, the same year the two warring factions of the Methodist church finally reunited, "New Credit" was founded on a fertile tract in the southwestern corner of the Six Nations reserve.

In the late spring the Credit River Indians began their migration one hundred kilometers to the west.[64] Once they had announced their decision not to move to Owen Sound, all the other Mississauga bands abandoned their plans to relocate to the rocky Bruce Peninsula. No Ojibwa territory would be established in Upper Canada. No fertile tract remained in Ojibwa hands by the late 1840s. There could be no self-supporting Anishinabe homeland.

For Peter more misfortunes followed. His brother John, his trusted ally and loyal friend in the first years of the founding of the Credit Mission, died on 4 May in London.[65] Then in the summer came the distressing news of John Assance's death. The veteran chief, once a close associate, had become confused and bewildered, a chronic alcoholic. Forced to exchange his reserve four times, he had lost all his bearings. Twenty years before Peter Jones had described him as "a man of considerable thought and understanding." This same chief, while intoxicated, fell from his canoe near Penetanguishene and was found drowned in about three feet of water.[66] Another death that hurt Peter greatly came the following spring— Seth Crawford's—his end hastened no doubt by his wife's sickness and his failure to obtain the land given him by Chief Davis.[67]

The first positive news for the Joneses in that troubled year came during the summer. The Canadian Conference by a vote of eighty-eight to eight decided to accept the new terms of union with the British Conference, ending "seven years of fratricidal rivalry."[68] On 30 June came more welcome news: Eliza gave birth at the Credit to their fourth living son, George Dunlop, his second name being chosen in honor of John Dunlop, one of Peter's loyal Scottish friends. His Ojibwa name became Wuhyahsakung, "the shining one or sun." Egerton Ryerson, Peter's closest white friend, baptized the baby in August 1847.[69] A fifth son, Arthur Field Jones, named after Eliza's half-brother Arthur, who had gone to sea on East India ships, followed in July 1849. In Ojibwa he was called Wawanosh, after Peter's friend the chief at Lake St. Clair.[70]

With great sadness Peter and Eliza left their comfortable home at the Credit in late 1847 for the mission station at Munceytown. They had lived well at the Credit—their home was valued at £124, four times as much as William Sutton's, the second most valuable home on the reserve.[71] Peter and his family left in the fall of 1847. As he wrote from his new station the next year, "the reason of the Conference sending me here was to superintend the establishment of the Industrial School; otherwise I should have gone with my own people to the Grand River."[72] By May 1848 the school's two hundred acres had been surveyed, by July 1849 the cornerstone was laid, and the buildings were all completed by December.[73]

Unfortunately, Peter's health had subsequently deteriorated so much that he had to resign his position as superintendent just before the opening ceremony. His illness returned the following summer, and this time it almost proved fatal. Although retired in effect from the summer of 1849 on, Peter continued to undertake—when his health permitted—any work asked for by his church.[74] He bought property three kilometers west of Brantford, at Echo Place, where he could be closer to his people at New Credit. In 1851 his home, Echo Villa, was completed, and here he would spend his final years.[75]

The resignation of Peter Jones had a disastrous effect on the evolution of the school, Mount Elgin. After a year's supervision by S. D. Rice, the Reverend Samuel Rose, a minister of nearly twenty years' experience, took charge for a term of five years.[76] Rose's problems as an administrator arose from his ignorance of Indians. His negative and ill-informed view of their pre-Christian society dated back to the year he spent in 1831 as a missionary worker among the Lake Simcoe Ojibwas. In a letter from Lake Simcoe to his brother John he described how the Indians used to kill their old people who "could no longer provide for themselves." "Yea I have seen the old wooden mawl that was once used to kill the aged parent . . . who can hear those dreadful facts and not thank God for the conversion of this people."[77] At no point in any of his writings did Peter Jones even hint at the existence of such a practice.

Peter had intended that Mount Elgin should eventually come under the Christian Indians' control. It never did. White people fed, clothed, trained, and preached to the students, in English. Without apology Principal Rose stated, "they are never left alone, but are constantly under the eye of some of those engaged in this arduous work."[78] Not feeling part of the school, the students failed to become the legion of Indian missionaries, teachers, and interpreters— the symbols of power—that Peter Jones had prayed for. The three commissioners who investigated Indian affairs in the Canadas in 1857 themselves deemed Mount Elgin a failure and recommended that it become an Indian orphan asylum.[79] Peter Jones himself apparently thought very little of the institution he had worked so hard to establish. Not one of his sons attended.

The Final Years

After settlers had partially cleared the forest immediately northeast of the Six Nations reserve, the area resounded with strange echoes. The farmers consequently named their new hamlet, three kilometers east of Brantford, Echo Place.[1] Here in 1851 Peter and Eliza built their handsome brick house by the well-traveled road from Brantford to Ancaster and the Head of the Lake. They called their home, on its spacious thirty-acre lot, Echo Villa. The green lawns, well-kept gardens, stately trees, and flowering shrubs led one of Peter's fellow ministers to term the property an estate.[2]

Eliza and Peter had examined the English pattern books until they found the appropriate neoclassical design. No doubt Eliza supervised the construction, for throughout it bore evidence of her sophisticated taste, from the Venetian windows on the lower story to the Palladian window over the front entrance with its Doric columns. From the front door one entered a wide hall with a spacious living room to the right and a parlor to the left. The classical octagonal lantern on the roof lit the stairwell during the day, soft light glowing on the polished wood. Eight of the rooms had their own fireplaces, including the boys' rooms on the second floor.[3] Eliza's wealthy father must have supplied much of the capital to clear the land, landscape it, and finish Echo Villa.

A tragedy had struck the Jones family a year before their move to their new home. On 22 September 1850 they lost Arthur Field, their youngest son, only fourteen months old. A very bright child,

Wawanosh had been the delight of his parents and older brothers.[4] Probably Peter and Eliza built Echo Villa to help offset their sorrow. At Echo Villa Peter once again turned to his hobbies. He had always loved wood carving. In the summer of 1852 he submitted a bowl and ladle he had carved to the annual provincial exhibition in Toronto and won fifteen pounds, or nearly seventy-five dollars, a welcome prize. He also enjoyed carpentry. To store his books he made several walnut bookshelves, then built a round table to match them.[5] Peter also planted trees and culled the flowers in Eliza's gardens. With special care he planted seeds sent by an English friend, all of which flowered beautifully. Indian visitors commented to him on their scent, far greater than that of the local flowers.[6]

He read considerably in these years. Eliza once noted of her husband that "his was a mind that gained more from the study of men and things than from books, although whenever he got interested in a work it was difficult to divert his attention from it."[7] Peter particularly enjoyed religious and historical works. Surprisingly, biography was not a favorite: in his opinion, "persons are extolled too much."[8] In his *History of the Ojebway Indians*, published posthumously, he refers to many varied works on Indians—for example, Alexander Henry's *Travels and Adventures in Canada and the Indian Territories between the Years 1760 and 1776;* Jonathan Carver's *Travels through the Interior Parts of North-America in the Years 1766, 1767, and 1768;* and John Heckewelder's *An Account of the History, Manners, and Customs, of the Indian Nations Who Once Inhabited Pennsylvania and the Neighbouring States.* We know that he kept up his interest in the Cherokees, for he owned a copy of James Adair's early work, *The History of the American Indians, particularly those nations adjoining to the Mississippi, East and West Florida, Georgia, South and North Carolina, and Virginia,* first published in 1775. Through the publications of London's Aborigines Protection Society—their annual reports and their magazine *The Colonial Intelligencer; or, Aborigines' Friend*—he read about subject peoples in Australia, New Zealand, the Pacific, southern Africa, and especially California, where white miners and settlers had begun exterminating the Indians.[9] He himself acted as the society's correspondent in Canada.

Whenever requested, Peter joined in local and church events. The retired minister spoke, for example, in late November 1850 at the reinterment of the bones of Joseph Brant. Young warriors traveling in relays had carried the chief's body from Wellington Square at the Head of the Lake to the Mohawk chapel at Brantford. Before an audience of five thousand whites and Indians the son of one of Brant's executors recalled his late father's close friendship with the Mohawk war chief:[10] "By mutual consent, Brant settled at the northern extremity of the Burlington Bay beach, now called Wellington Square, and my father at the southern extremity, now called Stony Creek—the beautiful smooth beach forming a delightful natural sand-road, over which they travelled backwards and forwards in visiting and sharing each other's hospitality."[11] Among those present Peter was one of the few who, nearly half a century earlier, had known the man Brantford was named for.

The very year that Peter and Eliza settled into Echo Villa, 1851, the Methodist church asked him to visit the important Roman Catholic Indian mission at Lake of Two Mountains, immediately northwest of Montreal. The Algonquin Indians at the mission had joined with the Iroquois, also resident on this reserve, to dispute, unsuccessfully, the Sulpician priests' title to the mission. Peter, whose Ojibwa would be easily intelligible to the Algonquins, also spoke English, known by a number of the Iroquois. He agreed to go. For several days he tried to convince the Indians to become Protestants; and though his visit had no immediate effect, a generation later in the late 1870s the Iroquois did leave the Roman Catholic church and become Methodists.[12] This would have pleased Peter, since he considered the Roman Catholic Indians to be held in the grips of "idolatry, witchcraft, and drunkenness." As he wrote in his *History*, "I have never discovered any real difference between the Roman Catholic Indian and the pagan, except the wearing of crosses."[13]

The year of Peter's visit to Lake of Two Mountains, George Henry reappeared in Canada. During the spring of 1851 he and his troupe performed at Toronto's newly opened St. Lawrence Hall. The advertisement in the Toronto papers told at length of their many successes, of appearances "before most of the Kings, Queens, Nobility, Religious Ministers and people of Europe for the last seven years: also, the late President Zachary Taylor, and the Senators and Representatives of the United States, at Washington City."[14] After Toronto they also made other appearances, including performances in Cleveland in early July 1851.[15] When Maungwudaus's eldest son John Tecumseh Henry settled at Munceytown in 1852 and his younger brother George Henry, Jr., settled at New Credit in 1854, Peter learned more of their adventures.[16] The Henrys no longer considered themselves Roman Catholics; instead it appears that George Henry, Jr., at least, adhered to his reserve's small traditionalist faction. More than thirty years later, in 1889, the Oakville *Star* described "Saigitoo, the medicine man from the Mississaugas of New Credit . . . son of the well known Indian doctor Maungwudaus." Saigitoo had just visited Urquhart's Medical Hall in Oakville with "a full supply of medicines from his father's recipes."[17]

Peter worked hard to ensure the success of the New Credit settlement, visiting it often. He saw Maungwudaus's sons there and at Munceytown. At some point he must have glanced over his half-brother's pamphlets. On the cover of two of the three booklets Maungwudaus had proudly indicated that he was a "Second Cousin to Kakiwahquonaby,"[18] distancing himself but still admitting his blood tie with Upper Canada's most famous native missionary. The pamphlets were entertaining, with references such as that to Peter's favorite city in Britain—Edinburgh. In *An Account of the Chippewa Indians*, published in Boston in 1848, Maungwudaus held forth:

the new town is very handsome, but the old town is rather filthy. All the dirt is thrown in the streets before people get up, and carts take it away, but still the smell of it is most offensive all day. One of the chiefs told us that a Scotchman some years ago, who was born in the city, was away from it for some years, and returning to it he said,

"There is nothing like home"; and when he began to smell the streets, he said, "Ah! sweet Edinburgh, I smell thee now."[19]

The humor aside, Peter knew only too well the human cost of George's trip. Of the eleven Indians who left for Europe in early 1845, only seven lived to return in 1848: three Walpole Islanders had died, as well as Maungwudaus's own wife and their three children born overseas.

Peter's concern with New Credit affairs took up much of his time. He settled the band's accounts, attended its councils, and acted as its intermediary with the Indian Department.[20] He constantly gave or lent his own money to those in need.[21] The founder of the old Credit Mission realized the challenges they faced at their new location, living again in wigwams until they had chopped away the dense forest and built their new homes. By the end of the first year each family had cleared and prepared from two to seven acres. To support themselves many had to hunt or fish or return to selling baskets, leaving the reserve for up to ten months of the year.[22] How unnecessary, Peter must have thought to himself—if only the government had given them title deeds to the over eight thousand acres they had reserved in 1818 at the Credit River.

White squatters harassed the Credit River Indians at their new location. The trespassers cut timber on the tract and maintained farms there illegally even after the Mississaugas had taken possession of their new reserve. By the winter of 1851–52 many Indians had temporarily stopped making improvements. "We know not whether we shall be able to hold our land—we may be driven off to make room for the White Man."[23] In August 1851 an arsonist burned down the Indians' sawmill, a loss of $1,350.[24] All these adversities occurred at a time of great trial for the Indians, for disease, particularly consumption, reached an alarming level at New Credit. Twenty band members—seven adults and thirteen children—died in 1853 and 1854 alone.[25]

For several of the Indians the problems proved too great. Whiskey traders, active even in this isolated location, catered to the needs of the broken and defeated. The third winter at New Credit, for example, the body of one of the Johnson boys was found near Mackenzie Creek, at the edge of the Plank Road near the reserve. The coroner ruled that the death was caused "by intemperance and exposure to cold."[26] Later that same year Nowiqueyasika, "the noon day or shining sun," or Samuel Finger as he was known in English, died, while intoxicated, from a fall from a wagon.[27] He was forty-nine.

Others found consolation in their church and in the gospel. The resident white minister in the area, and Peter himself, made frequent visits. The native missionary rejoiced with his people when their new white frame church was completed in the summer of 1852. At the dedication service Peter Jones and the New Credit congregation welcomed several hundred visitors and well-wishers to a huge lunch, served on long board tables set with cutlery, plates, cups, and saucers. The New Credit women loaded down the tables for this modern *kahgahgeshee*, or crow feast, with bread and butter, cheese, milk, tea, and maple sugar. Behind the tables stood the attractive building with its handsome tin steeple. Five years earlier the Credit Indians had brought the bell from the old Credit River church.[28]

The vast majority of the New Credit people persevered, staying on their farms and clearing and cultivating more land. Finally the last white squatters left, though for years the theft of pine timber remained a serious problem. The band also rebuilt their burned mill.[29] By early 1855 the Indians ordered fruit trees to plant around their newly completed farmhouses.[30] Five years later the settlement was near completion when one of the Credit Indians' old friends, the Reverend Alvin Torry, called. The Credit Indians' first ordained minister found the reserve "twelve miles square, divided into farms which compare favourably with any I had seen among the whites; good houses, good fences and barns, everything in as good order as their white brethren."[31]

Only days after the opening of the New Credit church, Peter Jones had left on a long missionary tour to Sault Ste. Marie and Lake Superior, the legendary Kitchi-Gami, "the big water,"[32] the ancestral home of the Ojibwas. He had last visited the Sault nineteen years earlier. On this second trip he took his eldest son Charles, whom Chief Sawyer and a number of other Credit Indians hoped would one day succeed his father as one of their chiefs.[33]

Father and son traveled north along the very road that Charles's white grandfather and Mississauga great-grandfather had first surveyed over half a century earlier. Peter had often told his sons about the building of the famous road and about Chief Wahbanosay's extraordinary abilities as a guide. Before starting for Lake Simcoe Augustus Jones had asked the Mississauga chief to set the point of the compass from Toronto Bay to Holland Landing. "My father then followed the course set by the Indian, and came within twenty rods of striking the point aimed at, after running more than 30 miles through a vast wilderness."[34]

For Charles, then thirteen, the trip across Georgian Bay by steamer proved an exciting adventure. His father's Indian tales came alive, like the story about Pequahkoondeba Minis, or Skull Island, where the Anishinabeg had "killed a large body of the Nahdooways," about the time the French first came to this country.[35] Near Manitoulin Island Peter no doubt pointed out the La Croche hills composed of white flint, which from a distance had the appearance of snow-capped mountains. On these "mountains," he would tell his son, the old Indians "say the thunder-gods, or eagles, have their abode, and hatch their young."[36]

Charles met legendary Indian chiefs, like Shingwahkoons at the Sault, and at Manitoulin his father's great rival in the 1830s, Assiginack or Blackbird. In some respects, though, Charles must have found the meeting with Blackbird disappointing. As one of the leading Anishinabe war chiefs in the War of 1812 he was legendary among the Ojibwas.[37] This great orator, it was said, had many times spoken nonstop from sunrise to sunset.[38] But now Charles saw a spiritless old man in his early eighties. Lieutenant Governor Francis Bond Head had presented Manitoulin Island in the late 1830s as the promised land, leading the Blackbird and his people to settle there. The aged Odawa chief now regretted his decision, for he told Peter, "we don't get on at all: the weather is so cold here, that nothing grows to perfection."[39]

The trip north reminded Peter how Bond Head had ruined so many Indians' lives. At Coldwater, north of Lake Simcoe, he saw the fields the Ojibwas had cleared in the 1830s, now overgrown with underbrush and the log cabins fallen into decay. Forced from their lands by the governor, the Indians now "eked out a miserable existence on a comparatively barren spot in Rama or in the sandy banks of Island of Beausoleil" in the Georgian Bay,[40] or like the Blackbirds they had exchanged their farms at Coldwater for homes on rocky Manitoulin Island. Why had the Coldwater Indians and those at the Credit River not been given title deeds and protected from trespassers?

At Manitowaning Peter learned from Captain George Ironsides, the Indian superintendent on Manitoulin, of another broken promise. The imperial government had just decided to reduce Indian presents by one-fourth annually after the next issue, until they were extinguished. Yet as Peter wrote in the *Christian Guardian:* "I have heard many of our Chiefs declare in councils, that their great fathers, the Kings of England, had promised and pledged their faith to the Indian Nations, that the presents should be continued to them and their posterity 'as long as the sun should shine, the rivers flow, and the grass grow.' "[41] Oral promises meant nothing.

Almost two decades to the year had passed since Peter first landed at Sault Ste. Marie. At the Indian village he and Charles met Chief Shingwahkoons, now elderly, but still a man of a commanding presence.[42] From the old chief, a veteran of the War of 1812, and others he learned of the new treaties, signed only two years earlier, surrendering the north shores of Lakes Huron and Superior, treaties arranged by S. P. Jarvis's brother-in-law William Benjamin Robinson.[43]

Once again these new treaties denied the Indians the land base needed to form an Indian territory. But seven years earlier Peter had told a Scottish audience: "the Indian territories have been taken away till our possessions are now so small that you would almost require a magnifying glass to see them. We are surrounded on all sides by white settlers, still encroaching on us; and I am afraid that in a few years we will hardly have space enough left to lay down our bones upon, or ground enough to cover our bodies."[44] Peter also resented the courts' narrow legal interpretation of the Indians' title to their tiny parcels of land. Only eight years after the Robinson treaties the chief justice of Upper Canada—or Canada West, to use its official title after 1841—described the Indians' reserves as "such lands as Indians are merely permitted to occupy at the pleasure of the crown." The chief justice, incidentally, was John Beverley Robinson, William Benjamin's brother.[45]

Religion lifted Peter above these dismal thoughts. Three days later he and Charles reached the Indian camp meeting at Whitefish Point—about one hundred kilometers northwest of the Sault on the American side. The Reverend John Pitezel, an American Methodist present at the meetings, later commented on the "persuasive eloquence with which [Peter] preached Jesus and the resurrection."[46] For thirty years Jesus had given the veteran minister his source of power and his strength. One of the last hymns he translated was "Jesus, Lord, We Look to Thee."[47] He and the seven other preachers converted thirty of the two hundred Ojibwas at the Whitefish Point camp meeting.[48]

Peter had changed greatly since his last visit to Lake Superior. As he grew older his rigid Methodist outlook had widened and become more generous. On seeing Blackbird, for example, he forgot the past and greeted his great Roman Catholic rival as an "old friend."[49] Similarly, he had mellowed toward the Church of England. In the early 1850s probably his best friend in Brantford was the Reverend Abraham Nelles, the Anglican missionary to the Iroquois, whom he later named one of the two executors of his will.[50] Even toward the traditionalists he had a new tolerance. After the late 1830s he no longer thought it likely "that any of the men who had passed the middle period of life would ever be prevailed upon to change their religion,"[51] and he respected their wishes.

The cool weather and pure air of Lake Superior invigorated Peter, as did the warm fellowship at the camp meeting. The trip had brought him closer to his eldest son. Refreshed, Peter went back to Brantford ready for another church assignment. He also returned impressed by the Reverend George McDougall, the "excellent" white missionary at the Sault whom the local Indians called Uhyahbans, "the young male deer."[52] The energetic minister had previously served as William Case's assistant at Alderville. Within a decade the Methodist Conference would appoint George McDougall superintendent of all Methodist missions in Rupert's Land. Twenty years later George and his son John would reach the Stoney Indians 2,500 kilometers to the west, in the foothills of the Rocky Mountains.[53]

Around Sault Ste. Marie Indians still remained a distinct presence. This pleased Peter, for near Toronto they had almost disappeared, hidden away on reserves and submerged in number by hundreds of thousands of white immigrants in the 1830s and 1840s. Johann Georg Kohl, a German traveler who in 1855 visited Toronto—now a city of forty thousand not one thousand as thirty years earlier—noted that Indians

were numerous when the English founded here the town of York; and there are still people in Toronto who remember the fleets of bark-canoes and little skiffs, in which the Indians used to bring fish and other things to sell to the inhabitants—mostly encamping on that long sandy peninsula.

But the Indians have now vanished like a morning mist, and nothing remains to recall even their memory, but the well-sounding name they invented for the locality,—the sonorous Toronto.[54]

Only about fifteen thousand Indians lived in the Canadas, population nearly two million in 1850.[55] The Indians now lay completely at the Indian Department's mercy. In late 1852 Peter traveled to Quebec to meet the man delegated to supervise Indian affairs—Robert Bruce, Governor General Elgin's brother.[56] Peter urged the imperial government to continue the Indians' presents, and he reintroduced New Credit's land claims to landing spots and campgrounds at the western end of Lake Ontario, including the Toronto peninsula—claims they had first submitted over five years earlier. Predictably, Colonel Bruce had done nothing about the claims, and he offered little encouragement about any restoration of the imperial government's presents.[57] As Peter himself bitterly wrote in his manuscript history of the Ojibwas, at first Britain considered the Indians "allies with the British nation and not subjects . . . until the influx of emigration completely outnumbered the aborigines. From that time the Colonial Government assumed a parental authority over them, treating them in every respect as children."[58]

In 1854 the government of the Canadas—again desperate for land to settle the tens of thousands of immigrants arriving each year—pressured the Saugeen and Owen Sound (Newash) bands to surrender the Bruce Peninsula. The superintendent general of the Indian Department pointed out to the Indians that white landless squatters were already squatting on the Indians' land—the department could not protect the bands. They must surrender it. With such scare tactics the superintendent convinced a small number of Saugeen Indians to sign a treaty. On 13 October 1854 a minority of the bands consented, retaining "to ourselves and our children in perpetuity" five tiny parcels of land in the peninsula and opening up the remainder to settlement.[59]

Peter learned of this highly pressured purchase on his second visit to the Indian Department of Quebec City in mid-November 1854.[60] At the same time he heard firsthand of the latest scandal at the highest level of Indian administration in Canada West. The governor general had just dismissed Colonel Joseph Clench as visiting Indian superintendent—he was charged with embezzling Indian funds later estimated at nine thousand pounds, or roughly forty thousand dollars.[61] What a blow to learn that his good friend, his trusted adviser, was another S. P. Jarvis. Who, Peter wondered, could be trusted in the Indian Department?

Few native leaders in Canada West enjoyed the respect of as many bands as did Peter Jones. The Indian missionary served as the agent of three Indian communities: the New Credit Mississaugas, the

Indians of Munceytown, and the Delawares of Moraviantown.[62] The Six Nations trusted him, and in fact earlier that year their council had sent him to Albany, New York, to investigate all the English Indian treaties in colonial times.[63] In terms of experience he had few rivals—for thirty years as minister and chief he had dealt with lieutenant governors and governor generals, from Sir Peregrine Maitland to Lord Elgin. Not surprisingly, Peter Jones soon became publicly identified as the most likely candidate to replace Colonel Clench.[64] And he wanted the job.[65] From within, he could at last work to reform the Indian Department.

Egerton Ryerson immediately took affairs in hand. For ten years Peter's best white friend had served as superintendent of education in Canada West, a very senior civil service post. In his thirty-year term Ryerson would establish the modern public school system of Ontario. He knew the bureaucracy from the inside. On 22 November 1854 he wrote to the chief superintendent of Indian affairs:

Having understood that Col. Clench has been removed . . . I take the liberty of mentioning for the favorable consideration of His Excellency the name of the Reverend Peter Jones, as Col. Clenches successor. . . . I have known him from his boyhood. I was the first stationed Missionary among his tribe on their settlement at the Credit in 1826, and had the happiness of being their teacher in the first elements of domestic economy and agriculture, as well as in the doctrines and duties of Christianity; and Mr. Jones was my chief interpreter and most efficient assistant. Since then he has become an able Minister—a well educated man—a man of large and liberal views. . . . I know of no man whom I think better qualified for the office lately vacated by the removal of Colonel Clench . . . his appointment to the office referred to, will be an appropriate recognition of his merits . . . a great stimulus to Indian civilization and confer a very great benefit as well as give great satisfaction to the Indian tribes.[66]

Ryerson's suggestion of appointing an articulate, well-informed Indian leader as a senior official in the Indian Department failed to

22. Maungwudaus, "a great hero," in
English George Henry. He and his
family and several other Anishinabeg from Upper Canada left for Europe in 1844. They performed as a
dance troupe for several years, returning to North America in 1848.
This photograph, taken in 1851,
shows Maungwudaus, second from
the left, and several of his troupe.
They performed at Toronto's newly
constructed St. Laurence Hall in
that year. Chicago Historical Society, ICHi-08800.

Egyptian Hall,

PICCADILLY.

JUST ARRIVED,

ELEVEN NATIVE
CANADIAN NORTH AMERICAN

INDIANS!!

Of the O-JIB-WAY, O-DEAU-WAU, and MIS-SIS-SAGEE Tribes of Indians, from the
Western Wilds of North America,

HEADED BY TWO CHIEFS,

Will Perform at the above Hall, at

2 o'Clock in the Afternoon, & 8 o'Clock in the Evening,

COMMENCING ON

MONDAY NEXT, MAY 12,

AND SUCCEEDING DAYS.

The Performance will commence with

A Grand Indian Council

In front of the Wigwam, when the whole Party will appear in FULL NATIVE COSTUME,
Displaying all the Implements of War—the Chief will Address the Council—and
the whole of the Forms of declaring War will be gone through.

The INTERPRETER will Deliver

A LECTURE

Descriptive of Indian character; showing the habits and manners of the "Children of the Forest" on
the most elaborate scale, embracing a true picture of real Indian life, both in the wild and civilised state
—their mode of living through the northern winter, as well as under the burning sun of a southern
summer—their means of procuring food in the different seasons—hunting the deer in the depth of
winter—fishing on the great lakes through the ice—the interior of the wigwam—the "Papoose" in the
cradle—method of cooking in the woods—together with their various ceremonies, religious and superstitious—healing the sick by charms—appeasing the storm—funerals—rifle and bow and arrow shooting,
in which they will display great dexterity—various games, dances, &c.

The following are the Names, in Indian and English, their Ages and Height:

MAUNG-GWUD-DAUS—A great Hero, 40 years of age, 6 ft. 1 in. in height.
SAY-SAY-GON—Hail storm, 34 years of age, 6 ft. 3 in. in height.
KE-CHE-US-SIN—A mighty Rock, 27 years of age, 5 ft. 9 in. in height.
MISH-SHE-MONG—King of the Loons, 25 years of age, 5 ft. 8 in. in height.
A-WUN-NWABE—Bird of Thunder, 19 years of age, 6 ft. in height.
WAU-BUD-DICK—A Rein Deer, 18 years of age, 5 ft. 9 in. in height.
AU-NIM-MUCK-KWUH-UM—Thunder Bird, 21 years of age, 5 ft. 7 in. in height.
NOO-DIN-NO-KAY—Raging Storm, 4 years of age, Son of Chief.
MIN-NIS-SIN-NOO—A brave Warrior, 3 years of age, Son of Chief.
U-JE-JOCK—A Pelican, 10 years of age, Son of Chief.
UH-WUS-SIG-GEE-ZHIG-GOO-KWAY—A Woman of the Upper World, 38 years ...

23. Maungwudaus was Peter Jones's half-brother. The dances and displays he put on in Britain and Europe horrified the highly respected Indian missionary. This poster advertises the performance at the Egyptian Hall in Piccadilly, London, on 12 May 1845. Thomas Gilcrease Institute of American History and Art, Tulsa, Oklahoma.

25. David Octavius Hill and Robert Adamson took these two calotypes of Peter Jones in Edinburgh, on 4 August 1845. They have been identified as the oldest surviving portraits of a native North American. Note the image of a thunderbird on Peter Jones's shot bag. He is also carrying the pipe tomahawk given him by Sir Augustus d'Este, Queen Victoria's first cousin. National Galleries of Scotland, Edinburgh.

26. Eliza Field Jones, a calotype taken in Edinburgh, 4 August 1845, by David Octavius Hill and Robert Adamson. While Peter toured Britain raising money for the new Indian Industrial schools, Eliza looked after their sons in Lambeth, and in Hastings on the English Channel. She joined him, however, for his first series of lectures and sermons in Scotland in the late summer of 1845. National Galleries of Scotland, Edinburgh.

27. A circular advertising a talk during Peter Jones's second visit to Scotland in 1845. His performance was much more subdued than that of his half-brother Maungwudaus, who at the time of Peter's Scottish tour was in France. Among other performances Maungwudaus's troupe entertained the kings of France and Belgium at the palace of St. Cloud, near Paris. Peter Jones Collection, Victoria University Library, Toronto.

28. Oominewahjeween, "the pleasant stream," in English William Herkimer. The son of a white fur trader and Magiyakamigoqua, a Mississauga woman, William Herkimer had ancestors on both sides of the American Revolution. His father's father, Johan Jost Herkimer, had served as a Loyalist captain in the British forces. His father's uncle, Nicolas Herkimer, had risen to the rank of general in the American militia. He died at the Battle of Oriskany in 1777. But this meant little to William, who identified fully with his Indian heritage and not his white ancestry. At the Credit River he opposed Peter Jones's attempt to impose a hierarchical structure on the reserve and to destroy the old communal society. Arvilla Louise Thorp, Aldergrove, B.C.

PROGRAMME OF SOIREE

IN BEHALF OF THE

NORTH AMERICAN INDIANS,

IN THE TRADES' HALL,

On Thursday Evening, 30th Oct. 1845.

REV. DR. SMYTH IN THE CHAIR.

TEA.

CHAIRMAN'S ADDRESS.

JOHN DUNLOP, ESQ,
TO INTRODUCE THE INDIAN CHIEF.

KAHKEWAQUONABY, THE INDIAN CHIEF,
On the Customs, Manners, Religion, and Superstitions of the RED INDIANS.

REV. DR. KING,
On the Claims of the NORTH AMERICAN INDIANS on our Sympathy and Support.

SERVICE OF FRUIT.

REV. DR. BUCHANAN,
On Native Agency.

REV. DR. JOHN M'FARLANE,
On the utility of Mechanical Arts, as a handmaid to Christianity, in the Advancement of Civilization.

REV. ANDREW KING,
On the Present Condition of Canada.

REV. DR. EADIE,
On Education, and its special importance with reference to the youth of Heathen Lands.

D. MACDONALD, PRINTER.

.9. A photograph taken by Horatio Hale showing the chiefs of the Six Nations explaining their wampum belts, at the home of Chief George H. M. Johnson, 14 September 1871. The photograph shows George Johnson (the father of the famous Mohawk poetess Pauline Johnson), second from the left, and his father, John Smoke Johnson, fourth from the left. George and his father were close friends of Peter and Eliza Jones. Ontario Archives, Acc. 16659-6.

o. Echo Villa, Peter and Eliza's home near Brantford, Upper Canada, built in 1851. Peter died here on Sunday morning, 29 June 1856. Arvilla Louise Thorp, Aldergrove, B.C.

1. The last drawing made of Peter Jones, probably completed by Eliza in the early 1850s. Shortly before his death he wrote to a friend that he felt "like the *old oak tree*, whose top branches are fading and drooping, and the whole trunk bending towards the earth." The drawing appears as the frontispiece in Peter Jones's *Life and Journals of Kah-ke-wa-quo-na-by* (Toronto: Anson Green, 1860).

32. Dr. Peter Edmund Jones, the third son of Peter and Eliza Jones. On a visit to the Smithsonian Institution in Washington, D.C., in August 1898, he was photographed in his father's headdress (given to his father by a chief on the chief's conversion to Christianity) and suit of buckskin, ornamented with porcupine quills and decorated with the Eagle totem. In the photo he carries a war club and the tomahawk pipe Sir Augustus d'Este presented to his father. Dr. Jones also brought with him one of the eagle feathers that Wahbanosay had given his father at his naming feast almost a century earlier. W. J. McGee describes the objects in "Ojibwa Feather Symbolism," *American Anthropologist* 11(1898): 177–80. Smithsonian Institution photo no. 498-a-1.

gain official approval. Lord Elgin's replacement as governor general, Sir Edmund Head, a cousin of Sir Francis Bond Head,[67] passed over the veteran Indian missionary to select a man with no previous connection with Indians: Froome Talfourd, a magistrate, an associate justice of the peace for assizes at Sarnia, a commissioner in the Court of Request, a captain in the militia[68]—a safe choice to safeguard the status quo.

One of the reasons Peter had wanted the post was so he could introduce, while he was still physically able, the reforms in the Indian Department that he had argued for since the mid-1820s. He knew in 1854 that he would not live much longer. In fact, only the previous year he had purchased a grave plot in Brantford's Greenwood Cemetery.[69] His health remained very poor. During the winter of 1855–56 Peter handed over to the Missionary Society the diaries he had begun in 1825 as records of the early Indian work.[70] Disappointed in his application for Clench's post, he now applied his remaining energy to providing for his family's future. For his sons Fred and George he bought land at Munceytown, where he built a barn and fences and planted an orchard.[71] He also invested in the new Buffalo and Brantford Railway, a line linking the two centers.[72]

In the mid-1850s Peter's greatest happiness came from Eliza and his children. He wrote in 1849 after returning from a missionary journey, "I am such a home-body that I never feel happy, but when surrounded by my precious family."[73] All his sons remained at home in the 1850s except Charles, who during the school year attended Genesee College at Lima, New York. Peter and Eliza wanted their eldest son to get a good basic education before studying law.[74] They also hoped that Peter, their third son, would continue. At first the bright young boy had suffered serious lameness that forced him to use crutches, but he determinedly conquered his handicap, eventually walking unaided. He later studied medicine at the University of Toronto and at Queen's University in Kingston, graduating as a medical doctor in 1866.[75]

At home on the carpeted floors of Echo Villa Peter squatted for hours recounting Indian stories and legends to his youngest sons,

Fred, Peter, and George. Eliza's only criticism of her husband arose from his leniency with the boys, for "he ruled by love, perhaps too much like Eli." But she hastened to add, "in him his boys found a friend ever ready to give them advice, a father who joined in their amusements."[76]

In her diary of her trip to England in 1854 Eliza recorded an interesting story of one of the boy's feelings toward his father. She returned to Lambeth that year to see her dying father for the last time, and she took young Peter Edmund, then ten years old. On the boat from Canada a Methodist gentleman later told her what he had overheard Peter Edmund saying to another small boy: "My Papa does not read his prayers and sermons he prays what he feels in his heart."[77]

Through their father and the visits of their granduncle Joseph Sawyer, and most important of all through "Kokomis," their grandmother, the boys learned Ojibwa and much Indian lore. Now in her early seventies, Tubenahneequay had become feeble and partly blind.[78] She kept to her old customs and when visiting at Echo Villa slept on her blanket on the floor, never in a bed.[79] The four boys practiced their Ojibwa with her and on their visits to New Credit. Peter wanted his sons to be proud Indians. What would be said of his third son, Peter Edmund, could be applied to him—"Although he was married to a white lady, it was his wish to train his children to be Indian children."[80]

Peter and Eliza had hoped their boys would grow up in an Upper Canada free of anti-Indian bias. Yet twenty years after their own marriage, racial prejudice remained entrenched and pervasive. In 1852, for example, Mrs. Susannah Moodie wrote *Roughing It in the Bush*, a popular account of her own settlement experiences. In the book she reported that her own brother said to her at the time of Peter and Eliza's marriage, "I cannot think how any lady of property and education could marry such a man as Jones."[81] When Peter and Eliza's friend George H. M. Johnson, son of John Smoke Johnson the Mohawk orator, married Emily Howell, a well-bred English woman, in 1853, it also caused much discussion among Upper Canada's upper middle class.[82] Similarly, the interracial marriage in 1852 of Peter Jacobs's son Peter, who had become an Anglican missionary, and Susan Cooper, the daughter of a fellow Anglican clergyman, led to much comment for and against.[83]

On many fronts Peter's last years seem full of disappointments: his failure to become a superintendent in the Indian Department, the persistence of anti-Indian prejudice, his repeated illnesses. He continued, though, as best he could. In early March 1853 he had recovered enough to visit New York, where he spoke in the John Street Chapel and in several other Methodist churches.[84] He also returned to New York State in April 1854, this time to Albany to examine for the Six Nations all the records of colonial Indian land surrenders.[85] On these two American visits he learned of the extraordinary success an subsequent failure of George Copway, whose stage career had eclipsed even that of Maungwudaus.

How well the Methodists had taught their native workers basic organizational techniques: they could easily switch from organizing camp meetings to running wild West shows and lecture tours! In 1851 George Copway had become one of the best-known Indians of the day in the eastern United States. Peter pieced together his remarkable story from several accounts. For six months after his expulsion from the Methodist church the defrocked minister had wandered in the United States, surfacing in Albany, New York, in late December 1846.[86] Thanks in part, no doubt, to the literary assistance of Elizabeth Howell, his well-educated English-born wife,[87] George published his autobiography, *The Life, History, and Travels of Kah-ge-ga-gah-bowh (George Copway), a Young Indian Chief of the Ojebwa Nation, a Convert to the Christian Faith, and a Missionary to His People for Twelve Years*. It became a best-seller, running through six editions by the end of 1847.[88] He made, of course, no reference to his expulsion in the work and incorrectly claimed in the title to be an "Indian chief," which he was not. In the United States he wrote for a number of newspapers, and the *Saturday Evening Post* welcomed him to its pages.[89] Aided by his next book, *The Traditional History and Characteristic Sketches of the*

Ojibway Nation, which appeared in 1850, he secured a great following even among the intellectual community.[90] When the Indian lecturer brought out the first issue of *Copway's American Indian* on 10 July 1851, he obtained letters of support for his weekly newspaper from the eminent ethnologists Lewis H. Morgan and Henry Schoolcraft, the young historian Francis Parkman, and two distinguished novelists, James Fenimore Cooper and Washington Irving.[91] Then, after the last issue of his paper appeared in October 1851, he disappeared. What a disappointment to Peter that such a talented man had not devoted his life to improving the status of the Indians of Upper Canada.

A religious experience during his New York tour in 1853 did much to sustain Peter. He wrote to Eliza at Echo Villa immediately after it occurred:

> On Tuesday afternoon I attended one of Mrs. Palmer's meetings in her house. Dr. Bangs, and about forty others, were present. These meetings are held for the special purpose of promoting holiness of heart. Several rose and declared that the blood of Christ had cleansed them from all sin. Among those who spoke was a sailor, who said that the Lord had enabled him to enjoy this blessing on board his ship. My own soul was greatly blessed. Glory be to God for what I enjoy! My soul is happy. Of a truth God is love. I know that the precious blood of my dear Saviour cleanseth my poor heart from all sin. Join with me in praising God for what he hath done for my soul. My heart is full of Jesus. Little did I think when I came to this bustling city that I was going to obtain such a baptism from above. Continue to pray for me, that I may retain this simple power to believe what God has promised in his holy word.[92]

One of the greatest shocks Peter suffered in his last year of life arrived in October 1855, when news reached Brantford of the death of William Case at Alderville. With the passing of the Elder Case, Peter lost the religious mentor of his youth, a man who had the best of intentions for the welfare of the Anishinabeg. Throughout his later life the elder, as he told the Ojibwa general council at

Orillia in 1846, had held onto his dream: "You may indeed live to see some of your sons doctors, attorneys and magistrates. This is a thing not at all improbable. You have already lived to see your warriors become Ministers of the Gospel, Interpreters, and Teachers of your Schools."[93]

Peter, despite his poor health, struggled to achieve the same dream. A large meeting of three hundred to four hundred Indians at Rochester, New York, at the Onondaga reservation in 1854 had cheered him immensely. When Peter first visited this Genesee River country in 1811 on a bear hunt, Rochester had not even existed. Now in the summer of 1854, thanks to the Erie Canal, it was a thriving city. The Christian Union Convention of Indians attracted over two hundred Christian Indians from the Onondaga, Seneca, St. Regis, and small Oneida reservations on the American side, and about a hundred Christian delegates came from the Six Nations and New Credit reserves. The conference, lasting ten days, had been called by the American Iroquois to work for the conversion of the non-Christian tribespeople. Peter was impressed by the businesslike manner of the meeting: "They had their chairman, and all questions were decided by a majority of votes." These modern American Iroquois no longer sought to make decisions by the time-consuming consensus method, and in this respect "are far in advance of our Canadian Indians."[94]

Through a Seneca interpreter Peter spoke to the audience. The response was similar to that of his early missionary career. His address brought nearly forty forward to the penitents' seats. In Peter's words: "Towards the conclusion of this service, we had such a shower of Divine Grace poured upon us, that many shouted and praised the Lord aloud. Some of the Indian brothers fell upon each other's necks, and wept, and exhorted one another to be faithful in the service of the Great Spirit."[95]

Another happy moment came the following summer, in 1855, with the dispatch of two Methodist ministers, both in their mid-thirties, to mission posts in the distant North West. Henry B. Steinhauer, an Ojibwa from Lake Simcoe, left for the district northeast of Fort Edmonton, and the English-born Thomas Woolsey left for Fort Edmonton itself.[96] Steinhauer, Peter would remember well, had obtained his English name on the fund-raising tour of New York over a quarter of a century earlier. A loyal convert, he had later studied the classics at a church school in New York state, then at Victoria College in Cobourg, immediately east of Toronto.[97] By 1855 he had already served a decade and a half in distant Rupert's Land as a teacher, interpreter, and missionary at Rainy River, Norway House, and most recently Oxford House, a mission he founded near Norway House in present-day northern Manitoba. Later that year he would found the first permanent settlement of Indians in present-day Alberta and Saskatchewan, about two hundred kilometers northeast of Fort Edmonton.[98] A realist like Peter Jones, Steinhauer recognized the necessity of having Indian workers in the field, individuals who understood the Indians' nature and habits and knew firsthand their way of life; for in his words, "A foreigner, either as a Missionary or otherwise, will never take so well with the natives of this country, let him be ever so good and kind to them; there is always distrust on the part of the native to the foreigner, from the fact that the native has been so long downtrodden by the white man."[99]

In these final years of his life Peter also enjoyed his renewed contact with John Sunday. The Indian veteran of the War of 1812 had become one of the most successful Indian preachers. In his sermons John urged his Christian listeners to "be as wise as a red squirrel, who looks ahead and thinks of the approaching winter and provides food for his winter's use. So ought a Christian to prepare to meet his God; that now is the time to lay up the good words of the Great Spirit, and thus imitate the red squirrel."[100] Was John ever besieged by doubt? Yes, he would add: "Sometimes I find it very hard to get along—sometimes it just like when I was in a swamp surrounded by flies, had to make a fire and smoke them away: so in religion have to keep a good fire in my heart to keep away wicked thoughts and bad spirits."[101] John Sunday's faith inspired many other native Methodists, including Peter.

One of Peter's frequent visits over the rough thirty-kilometer road to New Credit occasioned his final illness. That December afternoon, after making the tiring journey in a lumber wagon, Peter felt very unwell. Determined to attend the council meeting the following day, however, he refused to return to Brantford. When the meeting ended he rode home through a drizzling rain. As soon as he reached Echo Villa he went immediately to bed, and his condition progressively declined.[102]

Peter Jones's Legacy

An "*old oak tree*, whose top branches are fading and drooping, and the whole trunk bending towards the earth."[1] So Peter described himself early in 1856. In late March the Reverend and Mrs. Kennedy Creighton had invited Peter and his family to stay at their home, the Methodist parsonage in Saint Catharines. The ailing minister should try the celebrated mineral baths in the town and consult local medical experts.[2] The Joneses both liked the kind, caring Irish preacher who loved music and played on the flute and violin the "most popular airs of his native land."[3] They spent a week with the Creightons in April. But the diagnosis of the local doctors proved discouraging—Eliza recorded it in her diary: "they found my dear P. had Bright's disease of the kidneys which if so is incurable."[4]

Only the remote chance of a misdiagnosis remained. On Eliza's insistence she and Peter traveled to Toronto in May to consult Dr. James Bovell, who had studied in London, Edinburgh, and Dublin and lectured at both the Toronto School of Medicine and the Trinity Medical College.[5] However, after a careful examination the eminent doctor candidly told Eliza that while he could alleviate Peter's suffering, no human power could cure the disease—"congestion of the stomach and liver, the kidneys were also much affected."[6] The next day Peter could still walk downstairs and visit the garden at Egerton Ryerson's, where they stayed, but the following morning he could not rise from his bed. He remained in this condition for a month, growing weaker every day, unable to eat and reduced to a skeleton.[7]

The Reverend John Hannah, a representative from the British Conference then visiting Toronto, saw him at the Ryersons' on 1 June. Hannah had met Peter years before during one of his English tours; but how the tall, robust Indian had changed: "He is thin and sunken both in countenance and body, and is dying of consumption. But love to Christ and to the churches of England beamed from his dark eyes, and irradiated his tawny face, as he said to us, 'Tell my friends of England that I die triumphing in the blood of a crucified Redeemer.' " At Peter's request the Reverend Dr. Hannah administered Holy Communion to him, his wife, and his friends.[8]

Now that she saw her husband's end draw near, Eliza approached Egerton: "I could not bear to think of his dying away from home." Immediately he had a litter made for a mattress, and on this, covered with blankets, Peter was carried to the railway station. The dying man traveled in a special compartment, the train stopping as near as possible to Echo Villa, about one kilometer away. Peter's friends then took him home. He reached Echo Villa the evening of 17 June.[9]

As long as his strength permitted, Peter thanked those who had come to see him. To one friend, who pressed both his hands, he said "I am going home—going to my Father's house above; all is well, meet me there." To another he whispered, "God bless you; be faithful unto death, and you shall receive a crown of glory." He asked John Carey, who had traveled all the way from Munceytown, to tell the Ojibwas, the Munsees, and the Oneidas, "if I had my life to live over again, I would wish to live as I have in the service of God."[10]

So many called: boyhood Mississauga and Mohawk friends, white clergymen and neighbors, and Peter's relatives, including his closest sister Polly Brant and his aged mother Tuhbenahneequay. His four boys surrounded him during his final hours: Charles Augustus, aged seventeen; Fred, fifteen; Peter Edmund, twelve; and George, on the eve of his ninth birthday. Most precious of all, his "best earthly partner" stood anxiously by his bedside.

Realizing his end was near, on 26 June he called his boys to him. To each he gave a parting gift, handing Charles one of his Bibles and his dressing case. To Fred, who like his father loved the outdoors, he

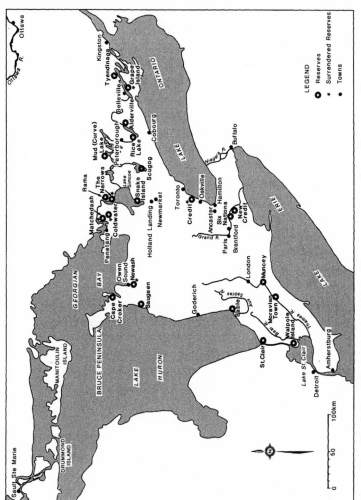

Map 3. Canadian Indian Mission Stations Visited by Peter Jones in the Mid-Nineteenth Century

presented another Bible and his gun. Touching Peter Edmund, he gave him a New Testament and his watch. George, after taking the hymnbook and two other books given him, cried and threw his arms about his father's neck. In the background two dozen Mississauga men and women sang, prayed, and wept aloud in an adjoining room."[11] Peter heard the grand old Wesleyan hymns he had translated into Ojibwa so many years before: "Let Your Joy Be Known," "Jesus My All to Heaven Is Gone," "Salvation, O, the Joyful Sound!" His eyesight failed that evening, but he still heard sounds distinctly and knew his friends by their voices. As he grew weaker all he could do was rest and dream.

Within two days, on 28 June, the approach of death was evident. He remained unafraid, confident of his trust in his God, knowing that death would only bring a passage into his presence. That morning Eliza had asked him, "How can I do without you, love?" Peter, holding her hand, replied, "Jesus will take care of you."

At one-thirty the following morning Eliza, seeing the long-dreaded event had arrived, called their four sons, Tuhbenahneequay, and Polly to his bedside. Minutes later his lips quavered one final time and his breathing ceased. Eliza believed she heard his spirit progress toward heaven:

As I tried to trace its progress, methought I heard shouts of victory resound through the vaults of New Jerusalem, as the redeemed Indian bands hailed with a fresh song of triumph the Benefactor of their race, the friend of suffering humanity; and the adorable Saviour who had prepared for him a seat in glory, purchased with his own precious blood, bid him welcome with the plaudit, "Well done, good and faithful servant, enter thou into the joy of thy Lord."[12]

The attendance at Peter's funeral illustrates the respect both white and Indian communities accorded him. The Toronto *Globe* commented that the funeral procession of "upwards of eighty carriages besides a great number of white people and Indians on foot" was the largest ever witnessed in Brantford. Eighteen clergymen of different religious denominations attended the funeral and heard the oration by the Reverend Egerton Ryerson. As the *Globe* added, "the text of the discourse on the occasion of his funeral was his truest portrait. 'He was a good man, and full of the Holy Ghost, and of faith.'"[13]

In his lifetime Peter Jones had accomplished much for his people. Before his conversion to Christianity in 1823 the band had appeared on the verge of complete extinction, weakened by disease and alcohol abuse, forced off its land by tens of thousands of white settlers, neglected by the Indian Department. The white immigration had pushed the Mississaugas' whole world out of equilibrium. Now, thanks to his intervention and that of the other native and white mission workers, the Anishinabeg on the north shore of Lake Ontario had adjusted to the European presence. Peter Jones, more than any other individual, had achieved this.

Tragically, the Canadian government in the late nineteenth and early twentieth centuries failed to follow Peter Jones's advice. The Mississauga chief had identified in the 1840s four conditions to be met before the Indians could obtain full partnership in Canadian society: first, security of ownership of their reserves; second, ample amounts of arable farmland; third, access to good schools; and fourth, the same civil rights for Indians as those held by all Englishmen. Had these been granted, the Mississaugas would have felt completely a part of the Canadas. Unfortunately, though, the government moved in the opposite direction: instead of enlarging the Christian Indians' liberties, they restricted them, instituting minute supervision of their activities. Only one year after Peter Jones's death in 1856, John A. Macdonald, then the attorney general for Upper Canada (Canada West), introduced and defended the Gradual Civilization Act.[14] Once passed by the Assembly of the Canadas, it became an integral part of Canadian Indian policy for over a century.

Canadian Indian policy sought the elimination of the Indians—their assimilation into the larger society. Group rights would not be recognized. Security of tenure and full civil rights would be granted individually upon enfranchisement—the giving up of one's Indian status. The Act of 1857, championed by John A. Macdonald, stipulated that any Indian judged by a special board of examiners to be educated, free from debt, and of good moral character could, upon application, be granted fifty acres of land and "the rights accompanying it." In short he could become "enfranchised," or legally equal to his white neighbors, with the same rights and privileges—but he must cut all his tribal ties and sign away his rights as an Indian forever. His land would be taken from the reserve, and he would be removed from band membership. The most successful Indians would be absorbed into the general population, and their links with their reserves would be broken. If the Act of 1857 had succeeded, in the space of several generations the reserve communities would have completely disappeared as individuals gradually became enfranchised.[15]

All his life Peter had fought this philosophy. He had sought the full participation of the Indians in the society around them. He wanted them to control their own lives, run their own communities, and have a voice in making their country's laws. "May the time soon come when my countrymen will be able to walk side by side with their white neighbours, and partake in all the blessings and privileges enjoyed by the white subjects of her most gracious Majesty the Queen!"[16] He wanted full civil rights, but not the ending of the Indians' land base or the assumption of complete government control over the reserves as introduced after Confederation in 1867—in the Act of 1869 and the Canadian Indian Act of 1876. These acts even stipulated that the children of Indian women and white men could not be considered Indian[17]—which meant that, had the government's interpretation been in effect in 1802, the year of his birth, Peter Jones would not even have been considered an Indian.

None of his sons ever applied to be enfranchised. Peter Edmund, a university-trained medical doctor, even returned to live on the reserve. Within the restrictions of the Indian Act of 1876, as amended by John A. Macdonald's Conservative administration in 1880, Dr. Peter E. Jones worked to achieve Indian self-government. His goal as a chief of the New Credit Mississaugas, like his father's, was to increase reserve independence, not increase Indian dependency.

Peter's objectives in education, as well as in band self-government, were not achieved after his death. His cherished goal of a first-class Indian school at Mount Elgin never materialized. The Commission to investigate Indian Affairs in the Canadas, chaired by Richard T. Pennefather, reported the school to be a "failure" in 1858. Although closed for three years in the mid-1860s, it opened its doors again in 1867,[18] but it never became what Peter Jones had envisaged. Over sixty years after its founding—immediately before World War I —a white principal and white teachers still ran the school that Peter had hoped in 1849 would soon be under the Christian Indians' control. At Mount Elgin the authorities, half a century after the school's founding, frowned upon the use of native languages. It was a white people's school, in one student's words, "trying to make Whitemen out of the Indians."[19]

After Peter Jones's death the zeal for church work declined among the Mississaugas. This was normal in part. Methodism had indeed performed a vital role in seeing the Indians through a crisis and now, the crisis past, the normal means of sustaining life returned.[20] But the ardor declined for another reason—the church's concern for Indian mission work diminished. The Methodists failed to send the same quality of men and women into the Indian mission field and to give it the same attention. The new workers lacked, for example, their predecessors' respect for the Ojibwa language. J. G. Kohl, the well-educated German traveler, meeting several white Methodist missionaries in the 1850s, discovered that they knew no Indian tongues: "Those good people are rather ignorant, and can unfortunately in general only communicate with and preach to the Indian through an interpreter. They do not learn their language when they have lived years among them. 'We English,' they say, 'have no talent for learning languages; with you Germans, and Poles, and Russians the case is different. You have it by nature.' "[21]

What a contrast between the generation of William Case, James Evans, and Thomas Hurlburt, and the one that followed. No attempt was made to adapt to the Christian Indians' culture. Both Evans and Hurlburt had learned the language. The Elder Case, several years before his death, had called for further translations of the Scriptures into Ojibwa. Peter Jones, of course, had devoted years of his ministry to making translations from English into Ojibwa. Yet only two years after Peter's death the resident white Methodist missionary at New Credit tried to destroy all Indian books and to end the speaking of Ojibwa at school. Within four years the goal had largely been achieved, English being "used almost exclusively in the play as well as the studies of the Indian children."[22]

Case, Ryerson, and the early Methodists had done all in their power to encourage a native clergy. This emphasis changed after Peter Jones's death. With the appearance of Darwin's *Origin of the Species* in 1859 the monogenists' theory triumphed, but a popular new hypothesis arose—all men might well issue from common ancestors, but the races themselves represented different stages of evolution. By the late nineteenth century the idea of "inferior" and "superior" races had become commonly accepted. Even in the Methodist church many believed in the pseudoscientific theory of white racial superiority. The Reverend Alexander Sutherland, for example, who served for nearly forty years as the Methodists' mission secretary, wrote of a native clergy in 1904, "it is better as a rule that Indians should be under the care of white men." Only in the mid-twentieth century would the false doctrines of what became known as race theory be discredited.[23]

The Credit band, which had sent forth several ordained ministers in the first half of the nineteenth century, produced none in the second. Even as staunch a Methodist supporter as David Sawyer lost much of his zeal for his old church. When the Reverend Edward F. Wilson, an Anglican clergyman, met him in 1868 at New Credit, he later wrote; "I called on Chief Sawyer, a tall, fine man, with a sensible-looking face. He said there were about 300 Ojebway Indians on the Reserve, and that many of them were most desirous of having a Church of England teacher." Peter Jones's third son, Dr. Peter E. Jones, became an Anglican.[24]

As long as those who had grown up in the pre-Christian era lived, intimate knowledge of the oral traditions and beliefs of the Mississaugas persisted. The widow Wahbanosay, who converted to Methodism in 1825, provides a case in point. Although well known as one of the settlement's most fervent Methodists,[25] she lived largely in her own universe, part aboriginal and part Christian. For example, in the early 1850s the old woman once joined a party from New Credit traveling to Toronto to sell baskets and brooms. In Toronto all went well. To speed their journey home the Indian women decided to take a train back to Hamilton. Once aboard, the widow, who had never been on a train before, sat perfectly still and said nothing until the train arrived in Hamilton. Then she immediately rushed out and threw herself on the ground. Running over to aid the woman, the conducter asked her friends to find out what ailed her. When they questioned her she calmly replied, "I am waiting for my soul to come."[26] Traditionally the Anishinabeg believed that the soul, housed in the heart, could travel outside the body for brief periods; but if it remained separate too long the body died.[27]

The behavior of the New Credit Christians during Peter's final illness showed their blend of old and new beliefs. They had indeed come to sing and to pray for Sacred Feathers's recovery, but at the same time they meant to secure adequate medical attention for him. As soon as they arrived and found him "so low" they dispatched a runner to obtain, at their expense, a noted Indian doctor from Rice Lake.[28] They had accepted Christianity but had not necessarily rejected all their traditional beliefs.

Even Peter Jones himself, without a doubt the Mississauga who had adjusted most successfully to the dominant society, with his English wife and an English home, proved incredibly resistant to change. While he rejected its supernatural qualities, he kept all his life one of the eagle feathers that Chief Wahbanosay had given him at his naming feast.[29] Proudly he decorated his buckskin suit and his shotbag with the eagle totem.[30] Before undertaking his important translations of the Gospels he fasted, just as a traditional Ojibwa warrior might do before an important hunt or war party.[31] To the despair of his wife, he freely lent money again and again to other Indians in need and made business arrangements orally.[32] Again to

Eliza's great annoyance, like a true Ojibwa father he gave his sons the greatest possible freedom in their childhood.[33] A true Indian, he believed in the superiority of many native recipes for medicines from barks, roots, and leaves[34]—he encouraged Eliza to take herbs during her sicknesses.[35] As an acute observer noted of the distinguished Indian missionary: "His whole intellect and demeanour, though somewhat marked by his English education and intercourse with different classes of society, were essentially of the Indian caste."[36]

Thanks largely to the intervention of this extraordinarily bilingual and bicultural man, the Mississaugas had adjusted to the new settler society around them. At New Credit, Alderville, Rice Lake and Curve Lake, and at the tiny reserve of Scugog, on the lake of that name near Port Perry, many band members now could read, write, and speak English. They wore the white people's clothes. Particularly at New Credit and Alderville, many farmed. Yet at the same time, a generation after Peter Jones's death an Indian identity remained. Dr. Peter E. Jones himself in the late nineteenth century led New Credit's struggle to resist the government's attempt to break up the reserves.

Welcome news arrived in 1885 from a strange source. In 1880 Prime Minister John A. Macdonald, who also acted as his administration's superintendent general of Indian affairs, had amended the Indian Act of 1876. Its repressive features, designed to control every aspect of life on the reserves and to encourage the "successful" Indians to enfranchise, remained on the statute books until 1951. Even today a number of the provisions of the Indian Act of 1880 still apply. But then in early 1885 the prime minister relaxed the government's hold in one small but significant way. Macdonald introduced legislation that gave the vote in federal elections to adult male Indians in Eastern Canada. The Indians who had the right property qualifications could now gain the franchise without giving up their Indian status. A jubilant Dr. Peter E. Jones wrote to congratulate the prime minister: "I now thank you on the part of the memory of my father and on the part of myself, as for many years we advocated and urged this step as the one most likely to elevate the aborigines to a position more approaching the independence of the whites."[37] (To Dr. Jones's great disappointment, the Liberal administration of Wilfrid Laurier in 1898 repealed this legislation—status Indians obtained the federal franchise again only in 1960.)

Many of the improvements at New Credit were due to the efforts of the energetic Peter Edmund Jones. With the two other New Credit chiefs, he worked for the construction of a new council house, completed in 1882, a church addition, finished in 1890, and a modern schoolhouse, completed in 1892.[38] Elected a band chief, he also served as the community's doctor, and for several years he was its Indian agent. As a result of the strict quarantines enforced by the band council, New Credit's infant mortality rate fell. By the late 1880s the population rose to more than 250, the highest figure in over half a century.[39] For a year the doctor published a newspaper, *The Indian*, which he distributed on reserves throughout the province.[40] Alfred A. Jones, a son of John Jones, complemented his cousin's work on the reserve, teaching Sunday school for thirty-five years, from 1875 to 1910.[41]

New Credit's success with agriculture continued. In the summer of 1890 David Boyle, curator of the Ontario Provincial Museum, called at the reserve while en route with Dr. Jones to a neighboring archaeological site. He later noted that he found the Mississaugas' farms well fenced and well cultivated. They owned fine livestock and lived in clean, comfortable homes; in fact, "no stranger driving through the settlement could observe anything to indicate that the land was farmed by others than white men."[42] Two decades later the *Handbook of Indians of Canada*, published in 1913, also commented on New Credit Indians' success, the Indians having "often won prizes against white competitors at the agricultural fairs."[43]

Not all farmed. Some preferred the old migratory pattern of living and traveled away from New Credit in the summer to help fruit growers in the Niagara peninsula. In the fall some Indians went on hunting parties to Muskoka, two hundred kilometers to the north. To earn money a number of the New Credit women joined their men during the fruit-picking season. Other New Credit men worked all year at the limestone quarry at neighboring Hagersville.[44]

Apart from Peter Edmund, none of Peter and Eliza's sons lived on the reserve, though all remained band members. Charles, in fact, on behalf of the Mississaugas, welcomed Edward, prince of Wales, to Brantford in 1860. After Genesee College, he had attended Victoria College at Cobourg, but he had to discontinue his studies in law when Eliza lost money in several property transactions. Charles instead went to seek his fortune in the United States, joining the American army in 1865. His unit served in the American South, then under military rule. Upon his discharge he worked for a newspaper in Sacramento, California, returning to Brantford in 1870. Shortly after his arrival home he married Hannah Ellis, granddaughter of a Loyalist captain in the American Revolution, and obtained a position with the federal Inland Revenue Department. Until his early death in 1882 he served as secretary of the Brantford committee to raise a monument to Chief Joseph Brant.[45]

Peter and Eliza's second oldest son Fred also left Brantford to seek his fortune. He went in 1862 to British Columbia, returned to Brantford in 1869 and then moved to Chicago in 1873, where he found work as a sign and ornamental painter. Becoming ill in the winter of 1875–76, he came back to Brantford with his Irish-American bride, and he died there in March 1876.[46]

Only Eliza's youngest son, George Dunlop, stayed all his life in Brantford, working as a painter in a local carriage factory. On 30 April 1882 George's wife Minnie delivered a baby boy, Eliza's first living grandchild. George died young, as did his two brothers. He died in 1894,[47] four years after his mother.

After Peter's death in 1856 Eliza did not know what she should do, her "spirits and energies so much depressed."[48] She thought at first of selling the house, it "being far beyond my management, and too large," and for the sake of the boys' education moving to Toronto.[49] Several months later she developed a new plan. Providing she could sell Echo Villa, at her price of three thousand pounds, she would build next summer at Munceytown and end her days there "among my Indian friends."[50] Then, on Peter's birthday, 1 January 1857, she had a visitor. Her diary entry reads, "Mr. Carey from Muncey also came, he had lately buried his wife."[51] By the end of the coming fall Eliza, distraught and confused, in haste married her late husband's good friend.

The second marriage proved a mistake. It simply did not work, as Eliza wrote in one of her notebooks:

It should seem strange that my two eldest sons Charles & Frederick should leave the maternal roof to seek their fortunes in foreign lands so soon after my second marriage, but alas when too late, I found to my grief, that their domestic happiness was blasted by the entire contrast they experienced in the conduct of a step-father in the room of the loved one they had lost ... my own tastes, & feelings & sympathies, were not and never could be in union with my husbands ... the dear departed was endeared to us all by natural refinement & amiable qualities.[52]

As if to bring her beloved back, Eliza assembled his notes for his *History of the Ojebway Indians*, published in 1861.

Peter's *History* is a marvelous book, a first-person account of what he saw and remembered about old tales, Indian religion, and government—about keeping time, playing games, and many other topics. Eliza presented it well. Throughout, she has preserved his indignation at the white majority's treatment of the Indian minority, the Europeans introducing to his people drunkenness; the habit of taking the name of God in vain ("in their own language they have no words by which they can blaspheme the name of the Lord"); contagious diseases ("such as smallpox, measles, whooping cough"); dishonesty, lying, and deception; and "the loss of their country and game, for a trifling remuneration."[53]

Eliza also helped assemble Peter's diaries for publication. They appeared as his *Life and Journals*, edited in 1860 by the Reverend Enoch Wood, the Methodist missionary superintendent. Immediately after Peter's death she had also led a public campaign to have a marble monument erected to him. It was unveiled at the Brantford

Public Cemetery in July 1857 and still stands. An Iroquois, Chief George H. M. Johnson, father of the future poet Pauline Johnson, paid tribute to the deceased. Having known Peter Jones for thirty years, he said he "had greatly profited by his example and advice, and his loss was deeply felt by the Indian tribes."[54]

In the mid-1860s either Eliza separated from John Carey or he died, for she definitely lived on her own after that time. Having sold Echo Villa, she moved into Brantford itself, to the home she called Lambeth Cottage on Brant Avenue.[55] To keep her mind active she taught drawing classes[56] and wrote. Her essay on the life of Joseph Brant won first prize in a contest sponsored in 1872 by the Montreal *Witness*.[57] She kept up with friends at New Credit[58] and her old acquaintances of years gone by, such as Elizabeth Howell Copway, the widow of George Copway.[59] From Mrs. Copway and her daughter Minnehaha Eliza no doubt learned the unhappy tale of George's debts, his drinking, and his eventual conversion to Roman Catholicism. He had died at Lake of Two Mountains Reserve outside Montreal in 1869.[60] Eliza became totally blind in 1882 but, determined woman that she was, by means of a writing board similar to those then in use at the Blind Institute she kept up her wide correspondence with her friends and relatives. Eliza outlived her two sons Fred and Charles. She died at age eighty-six in 1890, and her son Peter, the last surviving child, died in 1909.[61]

The reserve's two political parties of the mid-nineteenth century continued: that led by Dr. Peter E. Jones favored the new ways a little more than the second, led by Charles Herkimer, nephew of William and Lawrence Herkimer. Charles Herkimer, the leader of the New Credit church choir, himself served years on the council and once was chief. Dr. Jones effectively retired from reserve politics in the late 1880s, but as New Credit's Indian agent he remained a strong influence into the 1890s.[62]

New Credit supported the Canadian government in two world wars. Within a year and a half of the outbreak of World War I, twenty-five New Credit Mississaugas enlisted in the Canadian army.[63] Two and a half decades later, twenty-four New Credit men and one woman served in Canada's armed services in World War II.[64] The first Indian soldier to give his life in World War I was Peter Jones's great-grandnephew Lieutenant Cameron Brant, the great-grandson of Polly Jones Brant, Peter's favorite half-sister.[65] The Indian officer from New Credit died leading his unit in the second battle of Ypres—killed on the very day he was to have become a captain.[66]

The Great Depression proved disastrous for farming on the reserve. In the new era of mechanized agriculture the small Mississauga producers could not compete. As John A. Macdonald's amended Indian Act of 1880 stipulated, the legal title to the reserves belonged to the Crown. The band had no title deed, and consequently the Indians could not use their lands as collateral on loans from the banks. Many had to stop farming. No longer self-employed, the Indians began, particularly in the 1930s, to work for wages off the reserve.

After World War II the move into industry grew. The automobile made it possible to work in Brantford or Hamilton and commute. Those working in more distant centers returned home only in summer. Like the Iroquois, renowned for their skill in structural steel work, in the 1950s and 1960s a number of Mississaugas worked on major construction projects across North America. Peter Jones led the Anishinabe hunters and fishermen on the north shore of Lake Ontario through their first transformation. A century later the Indian farmers successfully responded to the second—the new challenge of industrialization.

If you travel to the New Credit Reserve today and visit the church, built in 1852, you will find close to the altar a marble tablet over a century old. It reads:

In Memory of

KAHKEWAQUONABY,

(Peter Jones),

THE FAITHFUL AND HEROIC OJIBEWAY MISSIONARY AND CHIEF:

THE GUIDE, ADVISER, AND BENEFACTOR OF HIS PEOPLE.

Born January 1st, 1802.
Died June 29th, 1856.
HIS GOOD WORKS LIVE AFTER HIM,
AND HIS MEMORY IS EMBALMED IN MANY GRATEFUL HEARTS.

Peter Jones lived in a period of oppression for Canada's native peoples, at a time when the Indians of present-day southern Ontario had lost their equality with whites. Without consultation the newcomers had begun to determine the original inhabitants' future. For three decades Peter Jones fought back: to obtain a secure title to the reserves, a viable economic land base for each band, a first-class system of education, and Indian self-government. The white politicians largely ignored him. I end this study of this remarkable man with the thought that others today fight the political battles that Peter Jones began. Through their voices his message still reverberates.

*And
there
are those
who receive
the seed in
good soil; they
hear the word and
welcome it; and
they bear fruit
thirtyfold,
sixtyfold,
or a
hundred-
fold.
Mark
4:20*

Peter Jones on the Ojibwas' and the Europeans' "Creeds and Practice"

Appendix 1

Lorenzo Dow (1777–1834), a well-known American evangelist, heard Peter Jones speak at the Methodist Church in Boston on 24 April 1829. He later recorded his impressions in his book, *The Dealings of God, Man and the Devil* (New York: Sheldon Lamport and Blakeman, 1854; first published 1833). The experienced American evangelist had a high opinion of Peter's abilities as a preacher. The passage also reveals Peter's belief in the similarity between the Ojibwas' and the Europeans' "creeds and practice."

1829. Visited Boston—heard an INDIAN *preach—he spoke some in Indian—it seemed more oratorical to me than any thing I ever heard!*

He related his experience of the Indian Creed, which cast more light on the subject of the Heathen Mythology, than any thing I had ever seen, as a key to the subject.

"The white man believes in one God—the Indian believes in the Great Spirit."

"The Indian believes in subordinate deities—and the white man believes in angels."

"The white man believes in a future existence—a heaven and a hell. The Indian believes in a future state of rewards and punishments."

"The white man get drunk, and Indian get drunk too—Indian steal; white man steal—white man lie; Indian lie!"

Thus when he compared their creeds and their practice, he could see no difference!

(My thanks to the Rev. William Lamb of Islington, Ontario, for this reference.)

Eliza Field Jones on the Character of Her Late Husband

Appendix 2

As a husband, he literally obeyed the command of the great apostle contained in Eph. v. from the 25th verse. In him I found combined everything that was amiable, tender, confiding, faithful, and judicious. I think it is Newton says, "A friend is worth all hazards we can run." I knew this when I united my destiny with his, notwithstanding the fearful forebodings, and the cruel things that were written and said. I knew that he was a man of God, a man of faith and prayer, a friend in whom I could trust, and I looked with pity on those who from ignorance and prejudice viewed the alliance with contempt; deeming them not worthy to tread in the shadow of my honoured husband. Never from the day of our happy espousals had I cause to lament that our destinies were united. Would that all who marry white men possessed in them the same lovely Christian graces that rendered my home with my noble Indian such an abode of peace and love. But he is gone! gone to his reward; and he who "turned many to righteousness, now shines as the stars for ever and ever."

Daily I need the present promise, 'My grace *is* sufficent for thee, my strength *is* made perfect in weakness.'

As a father, he ruled by love, perhaps too much like Eli; a little firmer rein might have been occasionally for the advantage of his sons; but in him his boys found a friend ever ready to give them advice, a father who joined in their amusements, instructing and helping them in every way that would promote their happiness or improvement. His children both loved and feared him, for lenient as he was, I never knew him pass over sin without severely punishing the guilty one. With filial confidence his boys trusted to his judgment, and reposed in his tender love. For hours have I seen them listen with delighted attention to the fund of anecdotes he had treasured up in his memory, particularly Indian stories. The loss of such a father is irreparable. May his mantle fall on each of them, and may "God bless the lads!"

As a master, he was mild and persuasive. Often have I marvelled at the patient forbearance he has displayed when greatly provoked to anger, but religion had wrought that change in his heart, which enabled him to "endure all things." He was "slow to anger," he knew how "to rule his spirit," and many times has his "soft answer turned away wrath." Those who served him faithfully always found in him a friend and kind adviser; but when he met with imposition or ingratitude he faithfully warned, and if that failed to produce the desired effect, they parted.

As the priest of his family, he always made it a rule to be short in reading and prayer, so as never to weary the children or servants. His prayers were very simple and devotional, offered up in strong faith. He often mentioned individuals by name as their circumstances required particular notice. The poor and the needy, the sick and the dying, the widow and the fatherless, were seldom omitted in his supplications at the throne of the heavenly grace; and I have often thought since his departure from our midst how much of our present comfort we owe through Jesus Christ to his intercessions at the mercy seat. I believe no sincere prayer is ever unanswered, although it may not be in accordance with our shortsighted desires; consequently how many needful blessings may his widow and fatherless boys expect to descend on them!

As a friend, he was firm in his attachments. He was a man whose friendship and society needed to be sought; he never courted the favour of any, and I often told him I believed he lost the intimacy of many who would have proved valuable friends, by his backwardness to intrude unsolicited into any society. His amiable and gentle manners rendered him a favourite with all who knew how to appreciate real worth. He was faithful in giving advice and reproof, but it was always done in so mild a manner it was impossible to take offence. His Indian brethren can bear testimony that "faithful were the wounds" of their friend, Peter Jones. He never saw sin in them without pointing out the evils resulting from it, and ever encouraged industry and virtuous deeds. They all looked up to him with respect, and consulted him as their *best friend*. May the Lord raise up another to fill his place!

His course of reading and study was desultory. His was a mind that gained more from the study of men and things than from books, although whenever he got interested in a work it was difficult to divert his attention from it. As his early education had not encouraged application or deep study, neither had formed a taste for mental culture, it could not be expected that in his later years with the cares of a family, very poor health, and a vast amount of business to transact for his tribe, that he should be able to devote much time to reading. I think I might mention history as his favourite subject of reading. He never took much interest in biography; and when I expressed my surprise, he would say, "Persons are extolled too much. Bible biography is honest." And I am certain nothing would have grieved him more than that his character should be set forth to the world as blameless. He was well informed on all the great events of the day.

As a correspondent, he was punctual and explicit, his style varying according to the subject and parties he addressed. He could be solemn, touching, and comforting, or humorous and loving. He never wrote (excepting purely on business matters,) without saying something of the Saviour. I believe those friends who have his letters will keep them for his sake.

In preparing his sermons, the Bible and prayer, with the teaching of the Holy Spirit, were his principal aids. Having several commentaries, he made use of them when he needed light thrown on any difficult passage. His notes were rather concise, depending more on the teaching of the Holy Spirit than any preparations for the pulpit. He often said he could never preach, however much time he took to prepare a sermon, unless the Lord helped him.

In summing up my dear husband's character, I should say his

actions, words, and looks, were governed by a principle of uniform consistency, humility, and moderation. Amidst popular applause, to which in the Old Country he was no stranger, he kept on his steady course, and never seemed the least inflated, even by the notice of monarchs, and the great and noble of the earth.

He was remarkable for integrity in all his dealings with his fellow creatures, never taking advantage of ignorance. This was one excellence that raised him so in the estimation of the Indians; they placed implicit confidence in all he said, and trusted the management of their temporal affairs in his hands. Not only was he Chief over the tribe to which he belonged, but the Munceytown and Moravian Indians made him Chief in their tribes, and urged him to do their business for them. In one instance he paid, I think, £200, which no law could have obliged him to do, but a sense of honour made him spurn the temptation to take advantage on that account.

I think the circumstance of his rising so superior to the generality of his countrymen should be noticed. Although he was evidently chosen by God to do a great work, and prepared by His Spirit for the accomplishment of the same; still the remarkable way by which he was guided through the wilderness, his preservation from the temptations so fatal to youth, and especially Indians; his never having the least desire for that accursed fire-water; the marked blessing that rested on all his lawful temporal undertakings, so that he rose by industry, honesty, and piety to a respectable and honourable station in society,—these and many other circumstances demand remark, not only to his own credit, but for the glory of that God who made him by His grace what he was.

(From Peter Jones, *Life and Journals of Kah-ke-wa-quo-na-by*, pp. 420–24.)

Mississauga Place-Names

On map 2 I have used, whenever available, Peter Jones's transcriptions of the Mississauga names, in preference to those of his father and son. The comments of Basil Johnston, a native Ojibwa-speaker and language teacher, follow. Since there is no standard method of transcribing Ojibwa words in English, the spellings of the various words vary.

As Currently Known in English	As Pronounced by the Mississaugas	Significance	Source
Don River	Won.Sco.ton.ach	Back burnt ground	Augustus Jones
Toronto Peninsula (now Toronto Islands)	Min.ne.sink Menecing	Island	Augustus Jones Peter Jones, *History*, p. 125
	Mi-ni-sing	On the island	Dr. P. E. Jones
Humber River	Co bec he nonk	Leave their canoes and go back	Augustus Jones
Etobicoke River	Ato.bi.Coake. A-doo-pe-kog	Black alder creek Place of the black alder	Augustus Jones Peter Jones, *History*, p. 164
	E-o-bi-coke	The place of the alders	Dr. P. E. Jones
Credit River	Mis.sin.ni.he	Trusting creek	Augustus Jones
Oakville (Sixteen-Mile) Creek	Ne.sau.ya.y.onh Nan-zuh-zau-ge-wa-zog	Having two outlets Two outlets	Augustus Jones Peter Jones, *History*, p. 164

As Currently Known in English	As Pronounced by the Mississaugas	Significance	Source
Bronte (Twelve-Mile) Creek	Es qui sink Ash-qua-sing	Last out creek That which lies at the end	Augustus Jones Peter Jones, *History*, p. 164.
Forty-Mile Creek (Grimsby)	Mos.squa.waunk	Salt lick where deer resort	Augustus Jones
Twelve-Mile Creek (St. Catharines)	Esquesink	Last creek in going down lake	Augustus Jones
Ten-Mile Creek	Me.kis.ewan.ce. nonk	Eaglesnest place	Augustus Jones
Niagara Falls	Kahkejewung	The water falls	Peter Jones, *History*, pp. 48–49

BASIL JOHNSTON'S COMMENTS

Don River, "Wonscotonach," *does not translate exactly* as "back burnt grounds" (Augustus Jones); probably means "burning bright point or peninsula," a point bright with fire, or made clear by fire.

> *from:*   waussae—bright
> ishkstae—fire
> naeyaush—point

Toronto, "Menecing," *agrees* with Dr. P. E. Jones "on the island."

> *from:*   minissing

Humber, "Cobechenonk," *does not mean* "leave the canoes and go back" (Augustus Jones); probably means "place of rest or refreshment."

> *from:*   kabae—entire, all, through
> ishinoo—to lie or rest
> inoong—at the place of

Etobicoke, "Adoopekog," *agrees* with Peter Jones and Dr. P. E. Jones, "place of the alders."

> *from:*   waedoopigook

Credit, "Missinnihe," *roughly translated* as "the trusting creek" (Augustus Jones); a better translation would be "to

write or give and make credit." The word should be
written "Mazinigae-zeebi."

from: mazin—image
ikae (igae)—to make
zeebi—river

Oakville (Sixteen-Mile Creek), "Nanzuhzaugewazog," "having two
outlets," *agrees* with Augustus and Peter Jones.

from: Nanauzh-zaugi-waezaug

Bronte (Twelve-Mile Creek), "Ashquasing," "that which lies at the end,"
agrees with Augustus and Peter Jones.

from: Ae-ishquae-issing

Forty-Mile Creek (Grimsby), "Mossquawaunk," "salt lick where deer
resort," *agrees* with Augustus Jones, but should be
written "Noossiquawung(k)."

Twelve-Mile Creek (St. Catharines), "Ashquasing," "that which lies at the
end"; this is the same word as that for Bronte (Twelve-
Mile Creek).

Ten-Mile Creek, "Mekisewancenonk," "eaglesnest place," *agrees* with
Augustus Jones.

from: migizi—eagle (black)
waussinoong(k)—the habitat of the black-headed eagle

Niagara Falls, "Kahkejewung," "the water falls," *agrees* with Peter Jones.

from: gau—that which
geedji—over slightly
wung—falls

SOURCES

Augustus Jones, "Names of the Rivers, and Creeks, as they are called by
the Mississauguas . . . ," dated 4 July 1796. Ontario Archives, Surveyors'
Letters, vol. 28, pp. 103–5.

Peter Jones, *History of the Ojebway Indians* (London: A. W. Bennett,
1861), pp. 48–49, 125, 164.

Dr. P. E. Jones, cited in "The Meaning of Place Names Asked by Mr. H. F.
Gardiner, Supplied by Dr. P. E. Jones, May 25, 1898," Anthropological
Archives, Smithsonian Institution, Washington, D.C.

Interview with Basil Johnston, Toronto, 30 May 1986.

ABBREVIATIONS

BR, MTL	Baldwin Room, Metropolitan Toronto Library
CA	*Christian Advocate*
CG	*Christian Guardian*
CO	Colonial Office, London, England
CMCR, UCA	Credit Mission Church Registry, United Church Archives
HP	Haldimand Papers
mfm	Microfilm reel
Miss. Soc. Report	*Annual Report of the Wesleyan Methodist Church Missionary Society*
MM	*Methodist Magazine*
OHSPR	*Ontario Historical Society, Proceedings and Records*
PAC	Public Archives of Canada, Ottawa
PJC, VUL	Peter Jones Collection, Victoria University Library, Toronto
RG 10	Record Group 10, Indian Affairs, Public Archives of Canada, Ottawa
RP	*The Correspondence of the Honourable Peter Russell*, ed. E. A. Cruikshank, 3 vols. (Toronto: Ontario Historical Society, 1932–36).
UCA	United Church Archives

Notes

Preface

1. The description of Peter Jones's audience with Queen Victoria is taken from three accounts. The fullest and most complete appears in his diary; see Peter Jones, *Life and Journals of Kah-ke-wa-quo-na-by* (Toronto: Published by Anson Green at the Wesleyan Printing Establishment, 1860), pp. 405–8. His wife included a reference to the interview in her diary; consult Eliza Field Jones, diary entries for 13 and 14 September 1838, Peter Jones Collection, Victoria University Library, Toronto (hereafter cited as PJC, VUL). A third account appeared in the London (England) *Watchman* on 19 September 1838 and was reprinted in an unidentified Canadian newspaper on 14 November 1838. The clipping is in the McCord Museum, Montreal. I describe the Reverend Robert Alder as "well fed" on the basis of John Carroll's description in John Carroll, *Case and His Cotemporaries*, 5 vols. (Toronto: Samuel Rose, 1867–77), 3:88. My thanks to Sir Robin Mackworth-Young, librarian of Windsor Castle, Berkshire, for his suggestion of sources for this interview. The "Court Circular" in the *London Times*, 15 September 1838, details the queen's activities on 14 September 1838.

2. Ronald N. Satz, *American Indian Policy in the Jacksonian Era* (Lincoln: University of Nebraska Press, 1975), p. 97. My thanks to Kay Graber for this reference.

3. Peter Jones to Robert Alder, 24 November 1837, Letter Book, 1825–42, RG 10, vol. 1011, p. 134. PAC.

4. The petition, dated 4 October 1837, is reprinted in Peter Jones, *History of the Ojebway Indians* (London: A. W. Bennett, 1861), pp. 265–67. For the English translations of the Indian names see the *History*, pp. 161–62.

5. The White Drawing Room is briefly described in Sir Owen Morshead's "The Private Apartments at Windsor Castle," *Country Life Annual*, 1952, p. 66. A photograph of the room appears on p. 58.

6. Although this statement was actually made to Robert Alder a year earlier, Sacred Feathers no doubt expressed the same sentiments to the queen; Peter Jones to Robert Alder, 24 November 1837, Letterbook, 1825–42, p. 1, RG 10, vol. 1011, p. 134. PAC.

7. Charles Augustus Murray, *Travels in North America during the Years 1834, 1835 and 1836: Including a Summer Residence with the Pawnee Tribe of Indians in the Remote Prairies of the Missouri, and a Visit to Cuba and the Azore Islands*, 3d ed. (London: R. Bentley, 1854), 1:iii, 1. H. O. S., "Sir Charles Murray's Adventures with the Pawnees," *Cornhill Magazine*, n.s. 3 (July–December 1897): 638–853. R. J. S., "The Right Hon. Sir Charles Murray," *Athenaeum*, 8 June 1895. While Peter waited in Lord Glenelg's apartment he spoke with Charles Murray, who "talked on Indian customs, languages, etc. He informed us that he had been in America, and had seen many of the western Indians. I found he understood a few Chippeway words"; Jones, *Life*, p. 406.

8. Royal Archives, Windsor Castle, Journal of Queen Victoria (typescript copy) 14 September 1838, quoted by the gracious permission of Her Majesty the Queen.

9. Jones, *History*, p. 218. His aspirations for his people are outlined on pp. 217–18.

10. Robin McGrath, *Canadian Inuit Literature: The Development of a Tradition* (Ottawa: National Museums of Canada, 1984), p. 3.

11. Karen Evans lists a number of Peter Jones's translations in *Masinahikan. Native Language Imprints in the Archives and Libraries of the Anglican Church of Canada* (Toronto: Anglican Book Centre, 1985), pp. 18, 200–201, 204, 209, 212.

1. An Indian Boyhood

1. Credit Mission Church Registry, United Church Archives, Toronto (hereafter cited as CMCR, UCA). Her age, place of birth, and father's name are given.

2. Catherine Parr Traill, *The Canadian Settler's Guide* (Toronto: McClelland and Stewart, 1969), p. 212. The book first appeared in 1855. The names of the seasons in Ojibwa appear in Jones, *History*, pp. 135–36.

3. Sonia Bleeker, *The Chippewa Indians: Rice Gatherers of the Great Lakes* (New York: William Morrow, 1955), pp. 12, 15. This popularly written account is helpful in conveying what a young Ojibwa's life would have been like. The recollections of his childhood by George Copway, a native Ojibwa writer, are very useful; see *The Life, History, and Travels of Kah-ge-ga-gah-bowh (George Copway)* (Albany: Weed and Parsons, 1847), particularly pp.

11–36. Other valuable study studies are Albert Ernest Jenks, *The Childhood of Ji-shib, the Ojibwa* (Madison, Wisc.: American Thresherman, 1900); and Timothy G. Roufs, *The Anishinabe of the Minnesota Chippewa Tribe* (Phoenix: Indian Tribal Series and the Minnesota Chippewa Tribe, 1975). A modern anthropological treatment is Robert E. Ritzenthaler and Pat Ritzenthaler, *The Woodland Indians of the Western Great Lakes* (Milwaukee: Milwaukee Public Museum, 1983), originally published in 1970. Edward Benton-Banai, a modern Ojibwa writer, has written *The Mishomis Book: The Voice of the Ojibway* (St. Paul, Minn.: Indian Country Press, 1979), a popular account of Ojibwa, or Anishinabeg, traditions. An excellent introduction to Indian religion in Ruth Underhill's *Red Man's Religion* (Chicago: University of Chicago Press, 1965); see particularly the chapter "Women Power," pp. 51–61.

4. Peter Jones notes, "The stature of the men averages five feet ten inches, that of the women five feet" (*History*, p. 62). On the basis of personal observation Robert and Pat Ritzenthaler estimate the average height of Woodland Indians in the Western Great Lakes to be 5'2" for women, and 5'7" for men. Ritzenthaler and Ritzenthaler, *Woodland Indians*, p. 16. Here I have followed Peter Jones's assessment.

5. Mrs. John Graves Simcoe, *The Diary of Mrs. John Graves Simcoe*, ed. J. Ross Robertson (Toronto: Ontario Publishing, 1934), p. 298. Marjorie Freeman Campbell, *A Mountain and a City: The Story of Hamilton* (Toronto: McClelland and Stewart, 1966), pp. 2–3, 18.

6. John Heckewelder's *History, Manners, and Customs of the Indian Nations Who Once Inhabited Pennsylvania and the Neighbouring States* (Philadelphia: Historical Society of Pennsylvania, 1876) provides a good account of Indian life in the eighteenth century; see pp. 191–92 for a reference to their weapons and tools. The "inland Indians" lived between Lakes Huron and Superior and Hudson Bay, are described by Peter Jones in Anecdote Book, Anecdote no. 59, PJC, VUL.

7. J. A. Cuoq, *Lexique de la langue algonquine* (Montreal: J. Chapleau, 1886), p. 263. William W. Warren, *History of the Ojibway Nation* (Minneapolis: Ross and Haines, 1957; first published 1885), p. 83; Jones, *History*, pp. 32, 111. Peter spelled the word "Nahdooways" and "Nahdoways." I have followed the first spelling.

8. William Dummer Powell to John Askin, Mount Dorchester, 7 May 1798, in *The John Askin Papers*, 2 vols., ed. M. M. Quaiffe (Detroit: Detroit Library Commission, 1928–31), 2:140.

9. Jones, *Life*, p. 2. Peter Jones is spelling it here, no doubt, as the Mississaugas pronounced the Iroquois word. It is usually spelled Thayendenagea in English.

10. The spelling of "Nesinnececonk" is Augustus Jones's, who also translated the word. See his "Names of the Rivers, and Creeks, as they are Called by the Mississauguas . . . ," dated 4 July 1796. Surveyors' Letters, 28, pp. 103–5. Ontario Archives. William Chewett to E. B. Littlehales, dated Newark, 31 August 1794, in *The Correspondence of Lieut. Governor John Graves Simcoe*, ed. E. A. Cruickshank, 5 vols. (Toronto: Ontario Historical Society, 1923–31), 3:24. Peter Jones, "Missionary Tour to Lakes Huron and Superior," *Christian Guardian* (hereafter cited as *CG*), 25 August 1852. For details on Jones's life see "Augustus Jones," *Annual Report of the Association of Ontario Land Surveyors, 1923*, pp. 112–21; and Donald B. Smith, "Augustus Jones," in *Dictionary of Hamilton Biography*, ed. T. Melville Bailey (Hamilton: Dictionary of Hamilton Biography, 1981), pp. 110–11. For Peter Jones's comments on his father's background see *Life*, pp. 1–2.

11. Jones, *History*, pp. 50–51, 210–11.

12. Pataquan used this expression at the council at the Credit River in October 1801; see CO 42, 332:16, Ontario Archives.

13. Enclosed in the Petition of Augustus Jones, 11 June 1832, a copy of the magistrate certificate of the marriage of Augustus Jones and Sarah Tekerehogen, Grand River 27 April 1798, RG 10, vol. 104, file 1832, Public Archives of Canada (hereafter referred to as PAC). For information on Augustus Jones's two wives, see Journal of the Reverend William Case, typed copy, Ontario Archives, entries for late May 1808; the Reverend Ezra Healey, quoted in Carroll, *Case*, 3:46; E. C. [Eliza Field Jones Carey], Obituary of Sarah Jones, *CG*, 13 March 1861; and Peter Spohn Van Wagner to F. H. Lynch-Staunton, Hamilton, 24 January 1895, in Campbell, *Mountain*, p. 22.

14. Dr. P. E. Jones, Hagersville, Ontario, to Dr. Lyman C. Draper, Madison, Wisconsin, dated 12 November 1882, Lyman Draper Papers, Joseph Brant Section, 12F14, State Historical Society of Wisconsin, Madison, Wisconsin.

15. The Credit Mission Church Registry gives John Jones's birthdate as 10 July 1798.

16. Jones, *History*, pp. 81, 2 (the quotation appears on p. 2).

17. Augustus Jones to Sir John Colborne, Cold Springs, Grand River, 11 June 1832, Grand River Claims, RG 10, vol. 104, file 1832, PAC. For information on the Coldens, particularly Cadwallader Colden II, see Joseph Bragdon, "Cadwallader Colden, Second, an Ulster County Tory," *New York History* 14(1933): 411–21. Evidence of Augustus Jones's presence at Coldenham in 1783 and 1784 appears in records of land transfers; see L. D. Scisco, "Onondaga County Records," *New York Genealogical and Biographical Record* 30(1899): 239–40; 31(1900): 38, 171. My thanks for this reference to Harold A. Senn of Victoria, British Columbia, a descendant of Augustus Jones.

18. "Augustus Jones," Ontario Archives Land Record Index, microfiche 24, p. 6368; copy of A. Joneses Lease 4800 acres 4 October 1797, Grand River Claims, RG 10, vol. 103, file 1797–1801, PAC; Lease Six Nations by Brant to Augustus Jones, 1200 acres of land for 999 years, Grand River Claims, RG 10, vol. 103, file 1802–7, PAC.

19. *Upper Canada Gazette*, 10 July 1794; *Annals of Forty* 1 (1950): 45. My thanks to Harold Senn for these references.

20. A Copy; deed from the Missisagui Nation to Tyantenagen and Kagawakenaby, 10 September 1805, RG 10, 1:293, PAC. Also see Augustus Jones's affidavit, 22 December 1822, RG 10, vol. 2238, file 45, 742, p. 86203.

21. The size of the Mississauga bands appears in Lord Selkirk, *Diary*, ed. P. C. T. White (Toronto: Champlain Society, 1958), p. 162—"50 or 60 individuals is considered as a large band." The description of the wigwam appears in Jones, *History*, p. 72. I have also benefited from reading Frances Densmore's useful summary, "Dakota and Ojibwe People in Minnesota," *Roots* 5, nos. 2–3 (Winter/Spring 1977): 14–15.

22. Jones, *History*, p. 138. A buffalo totem may seem surprising, but apparently buffalo existed at one time in the Great Lakes area; see John Witthoft, *The American Indian as Hunter* (Harrisburg: Pennsylvania Historical and Museum Commission, 1967), p. 17.

23. Jones, *Life*, p. 2; Jones, *History*, pp. 160–61 (for information on the naming ceremony); Jones, *History*, pp. 85–86 (on the thunders). Peter Jones translates Kahkewaquonaby, as Sacred Feathers on page 160 of his *History*. See also A. F. Chamberlain, "The Thunder-Bird amongst the Algonkins," *American Anthropologist*, o.s., 3 (1890): 51–54. An interesting modern statement about the naming ceremony appears in Benton-Banai, *Mishomis Book*, p. 9.

24. Jones, *History*, pp. 135–36.

25. Peter Jones mentions the annual gathering at the Credit River at the end of sugar making ("or about the first of May") in his *History*, p. 109. He adds that they then held their "grand pow-wow dances and various games." We know that all the smaller bands gathered then (and in the fall), for William Claus wrote to Lieutenant Governor Maitland on 1 May 1819, "they resort in numbers to the River Credit, in the Spring and Fall of the year at which times the salmon is plenty, when not less than Two hundred and eight resort to it," CO 42, 362:203. (In effect this meant that all the bands assembled at the Credit River, since the total population was only approximately two hundred in the late 1820s.)

26. William N. Fenton, "The Iroquois in History," in *North American Indians in Historical Perspective*, ed. Eleanor Burke Leacock and Nancy Oestreich Lurie (New York: Random House, 1971), p. 136.

27. CMCR, UCA; see the entries for Catharine Cameron, or Wechekeweka-pawiqua; George Henry, or Pemikishigon; Margaret Henry, or Sakagiwequa; and Francis G. H. Wilson, or Wahbunoo.

28. Densmore, "Ojibwe," p. 47.

29. Henry R. Schoolcraft, *Personal Memoirs of a Residence of Thirty Years with the Indian Tribes on the American Frontiers* (Philadelphia: Lippincott, Grambo, 1851), p. 678.

30. Jones, *History*, pp. 32–35. See also A. F. Chamberlain, "Nanibozhu amongst the Otchipwe, Mississagas and other Algonkian Tribes," *Journal of American Folk-lore*, o.s., 4 (July–September, 1891): 193–213.

31. Copway, *Life*, pp. 37–38.

32. The description of the Ojibwas' moral code and religious beliefs is taken from Jones, *History*, pp. 31, 57, 66, 68, 83, 92. The direct quotation in this paragraph appears on p. 83. A short useful summary of the Ojibwas' religion is contained in Maungwudaus [George Henry], *Remarks concerning the Ojibway Indians* (Leeds: C. A. Wilson, 1847), p. 4.

33. Diamond Jenness, *The Ojibwa Indians of Parry Island, Their Religious and Social Life* (Ottawa: King's Printer, 1935), pp. 18–21.

34. Jones, *History*, p. 104.

35. Ibid., p. 85.

36. Jones, *History*, p. 255; Patrick Campbell, *Travels in the Interior Inhabited Part of North America to the Years 1791 and 1792*, ed. H. H. Langdon (Toronto: Champlain Society, 1937), p. 161; William Case in CG, 14 August 1833; (on Niagara Falls) Jacob Mountain, "From Quebec to Niagara in 1794, Diary," *Rapport de l'Archiviste de la Province de Québec*, 1959–60, p. 158; Isaac Weld quoted in Donald Braider, *The Niagara* (New York: Holt, Rinehart and Winston, 1972), p. 146.

37. J. G. Kohl, *Kitchi-Gami: Wanderings Round Lake Superior* (London: Chapman and Hall, 1860; Minneapolis: Ross and Haines, 1956), p. 119.

38. Jones, *History*, pp. 84–85.

39. Ibid. pp. 156–57.

40. Ibid., pp. 159–60.

41. Kohl, *Kitchi-Gami*, p. 60.

42. Jones, *Life*, p. 3; Jones, *History*, p. 84.

43. Jones, *Life*, p. 3; Jones, *History*, pp. 94–96.

44. Maungwudaus, *Remarks*, p. 4.

45. Jones, *History*, p. 65.

46. Jones, *Life*, p. 5.

47. Jones, *History*, pp. 89–90.

48. Jones, *History*, pp. 87–88; Frances Densmore, *Chippewa Music* 2 vols. in 1 (Minneapolis: Ross and Haines, 1973; originally printed Washington, D.C.: Government Printing Office, 1910, 1913): 2:16, 1:1–3.

49. Ibid., p. 91; see also pp. 87–88.
50. Traill, *Guide*, pp. 232–33.
51. Jones, *Life*, p. 3; Jones, *History*, pp. 64, 71–72, 135.
52. Jones, *History*, p. 97; Ritzenthaler and Ritzenthaler, *Woodland Indians*, p. 37.
53. Jones, *History*, p. 135; Jones, *Life*, p. 3.
54. Jones, *Life*, p. 3.
55. Jones, *History*, p. 51.
56. The band member was Kezhegowinine, or David Sawyer (1811–89), Peter's first cousin. See David Sawyer's affidavit, prepared 6 February 1888, at the New Credit Reserve in the Report of A. Dingman, dated Stratford, 3 May 1888, RG 10, vol. 2238, file 45, 742, p. 5, PAC.

2. The Mississauga Indians

1. There is no universally accepted system of transcribing Ojibwa words into English. Here I follow the transcription of Gerald Vizenor in "The Anishinabe," *Indian Historian* 4, no. 4 (Winter 1971): 16–18. For other spellings see: Peter Jones, trans., *Collection of Hymns for the Use of Native Christians of the Chippeway Tongue* (New York: J. Collard, 1829), p. 86, "Ah ne she nah paig, Indian men." John Summerfield, *Sketch of Grammar of the Chippeway Language* (Cazenovia, N.Y.: J. Fairchild, 1834), p. 25; A. F. Chamberlain, *The Language of the Mississaga Indians of Skugog* (Philadelphia: MacCalla, 1892), p. 39; Cuoq, *Lexique*, p. 48.

In accepting the Potawatomis as Anishinabeg I follow John David Nichols, "New Introduction," in F. Chrysostom Verwyst, *Chippewa Exercises: Being a Practical Introduction into the Study of the Chippewa Language* (Minneapolis: Ross and Haines, 1971), p. 1; and Friedric Baraga, *A Dictionary of the Otchipwe Language, Explained in English. This language is spoken by the Chippewa Indians, and also by the Otawas, Potawatomis and Algonquins, with Little Difference* (Cincinnati: Jos. A. Hemann, 1853). William Warren also terms the Potawatomis Anishinabeg; see his *History*, pp. 81–82.

2. The location of the Algonquian and Iroquoian groups is given in Conrad Heidenreich, "Map 24. Indian Groups of Eastern Canada, ca. 1615–1640 A.D.," in *Huronia: A History and Geography of the Huron Indians, 1600–1650* (Toronto: McClelland and Stewart, 1973).

3. A brief sketch of this troubled period is provided in Bruce G. Trigger's *The Indians and the Heroic Age of New France*, Booklet 30 (Ottawa: Canadian Historical Association, 1977). For a full account see Trigger, *The Children of Aataentsic: A History of the Huron People to 1660*, 2 vols. (Montreal: McGill-Queen's Press, 1976) and his *Natives and Newcomers: Canada's "Heroic Age" Reconsidered* (Montreal: McGill-Queen's Press, 1985).

4. Donald B. Smith, "Who Are the Mississauga?" *Ontario History* 67 (1975): 215.

5. Jones, *Life*, p. 5.

6. *Jesuit Relations*, ed. R. G. Thwaites, vol. 18 (1640), p. 230; quoted in E. S. Rogers, "Southeastern Ojibwa," in *The Northeast*, ed. Bruce G. Trigger, vol. 15 of *Handbook of North American Indians*, gen. ed. William C. Sturtevant (Washington, D.C.: Smithsonian Institution, 1978), p. 769.

7. Allan Salt, "A Short History of Canada, according to the traditions of the Mississagues and Chippewas," Muncey 1874; Notebook, 1872–1901, M 29 H 11, in PAC.

8. For a reference to the two dialects of the Mississauga see David Sawyer's journal, translated by John Jones, in CG, 13 February 1833. The journal describes a missionary tour by several Credit Indians to Sault Ste. Marie. During the tour Thomas McGee, David Sawyer, and James Young sent a note back to Peter Jones (the letter is now in the Peter Jones Collection, Victoria University Library): "The Indians at Pahwitig [Sault Ste. Marie] told us they could understand us more than they could them which were there last summer [John Sunday and two Mississaugas from the Bay of Quinte]. Therefore the Credit dialect must be more genuine."

9. Jones, *History*, pp. 138, 164. For a fuller discussion of the name Mississaugas, see Smith, "Who Are the Mississauga?" pp. 211–22.

10. The Ojibwa names for Lake Superior, Lake Erie, and the Thames River, the translation of Toronto, and the pronunciation of Niagara in Ojibwa are given in Jones, *History*, pp. 40, 48, 163–64. For the translation of Niagara from Iroquois, see Oronhyatekha, "The Mohawk Language," *Canadian Journal of Science, Literature and History*, n.s., 10(1865): 194; and for the translation of the Iroquois word "Ontario," consult Paul A. W. Wallace, *The White Roots of Peace* (Port Washington, N.Y.: Ira J. Friedman; first published 1946), p. 12.

11. The English translations of the Ojibwa names for the Grand and Credit rivers appear in Augustus Jones, "Names of the Rivers and Creeks, as they are Called by the Mississagues . . . ," dated 4 July 1796, Surveyors' Letters, 28, pp. 103–5, Ontario Archives. The Ojibwa word for Toronto appears in Jones, *History*, p. 125, and is translated by his son, Dr. P. E. Jones, in "The meaning of place names asked by Mr. H. F. Gardiner. Supplied by Dr. P. E. Jones, May 25, 1898," p. 3, National Anthropological Archives, Smithsonian Institution, Washington, D.C.

12. William Claus to Lieutenant Governor Maitland, York, 1 May 1819, CO 42, 362:203, PAC.

13. Mrs. Simcoe, *Diary*, pp. 120, 184. Mrs. Simcoe writes that she could see the "spray of the Falls of Niagara rising like a cloud. It is 40 miles distant" (p. 120).

14. Peter Jones to the Indian Department, Brantford, 13 February 1855, in *Mississaugas of the Credit* (Toronto: Warwick Brothers and Rutter, 1895), p. 38 in RG 10, vol. 2357, file 72, 563, PAC.

15. The best source on the Toronto Carrying Place is Percy J. Robinson, *Toronto during the French Regime, 1615–1793,* 2d ed. (Toronto: University of Toronto Press, 1965). The reference to the wampum belt appears in Jones, *History,* p. 121.

16. The Indian names are given in P. E. Jones, "Place Names," p. 3 (the Forks); Andrew F. Hunter, *A History of Simcoe County* (Barrie: Historical Committee of Simcoe County, 1948; first published 1909), p. 12 (Lake Simcoe); Robert Paudash, "The Coming of the Mississagas," *Ontario Historical Society: Proceedings and Records* (hereafter cited as OHSPR) 6(1905): 10 (Rice Lake). The time needed for traveling these distances appears in Jones, *History,* pp. 62, 75; Mrs. Simcoe, *Diary,* pp. 158, 308. See also Alexander Henry, *Travels and Adventures,* cited in Robinson, *Toronto,* p. 150.

17. Pierre-François-Xavier de Charlevoix, *Histoire et description générale de la Nouvelle France* (Paris: Giffart, 1744), 3:207.

18. Ives Goddard, "Central Algonquian Languages" in *Northeast,* ed. Trigger, p. 587; Peter Jones to Wawanosh, River Credit, 7 December 1838, Wawanosh Correspondence, box 4382, no. 6, University of Western Ontario, London, Ontario. For use of the French word, *bonjour* in Ojibwa, see Kohl, *Kitchi-Gami,* p. 191.

19. Robinson, *Toronto,* p. 78.

20. Ibid., p. 96.

21. Jones, *History,* p. 216.

22. Guy Carleton to the Earl of Dartmouth, secretary of state, Quebec, 14 August 1775, CO 42, 34:174, PAC; and references in the Haldimand Papers (hereafter cited as HP) in PAC, B107, 21767, p. 683, microfilm reel (hereafter cited as mfm) A-683; B111, 21771, pp. 204, 207, mfm A-684; B127, 21787, pp. 54, 56, 139, 243, mfm A-688. "The Petition of Wabakenyne's Sons," OHSPR 26(1930): 359. My thanks to Jane Graham of Toronto for this reference.

23. Claus Papers, Memoranda and Diary, 1771–73, entry for 25 July 1772, MG19, F 1, p. 3, PAC. "The Interpr. St. Jean observed to me that the Missageys in that Quarter are in great Awe and have a great Respect for Sr. Wm. Johnson." The statements made at Fort Oswego were remembered by Mary Jemison, the famous white captive who was raised as a Seneca; see James E. Seaver, *A Narrative of the Life of Mrs. Mary Jemison* (Canandaigua, N.Y.: J. D. Bemis, 1824; New York: American Scenic and Historical Preservation Society, 1949), p. 66.

24. Carolyn Gilman, *Where Two Worlds Meet: The Great Lakes Fur Trade* (St. Paul: Minnesota Historical Society, 1982), p. 25.

25. Lieutenant Governor John Graves Simcoe also (until 1794) favored the

creation of an Indian buffer state in the Indian lands immediately south of the Great Lakes; consult S. F. Wise, "The Indian Diplomacy of John Graves Simcoe," *Canadian Historical Association Report, 1953*, pp. 36–44. See also Robert F. Berkhofer, Jr., "Barrier to Settlement: British Indian Policy in the Old Northwest, 1783–1794," in *The Frontier in American Development*, ed. David M. Ellis (Ithaca: Cornell University Press, 1969), pp. 249–76.

26. W. J. Eccles, "Sovereignty-Association, 1500–1783," *Canadian Historical Review* 65 (1984): 498. George S. Snyderman, "Concepts of Land Ownership among the Iroquois and Their Neighbors," in *Symposium on Local Diversity in Iroquois Culture*, ed. William N. Fenton, Smithsonian Institution Bureau of American Ethnology Bulletin 149 (Washington, D.C.: United States Government Printing Office, 1951), pp. 15–34, particularly p. 28. John Witthoft's *The American Indian as Hunter* (Harrisburg: Pennsylvania Historical and Museum Commission, 1967), pp. 1–2, and Allen W. Trelease's *Indian Affairs in Colonial New York: The Seventeenth Century* (Ithaca, N.Y.: Cornell University Press, 1960; Port Washington, N.Y.: Kennikat Press, 1971), p. 12, are also very useful. For Peter Jones's comments on the Mississaugas' system of land use see his *History*, pp. 40, 71.

27. Quinipeno quoted at a meeting with the Mississaugas at the River Credit, 2 August 1805, RG 10, 1:299, PAC.

28. Return of the Missesayey Nation of Indians, 23 September 1797, RG 10, 1834:197, PAC. The "Distribution of Arms, Ammunition and Tobacco," 27 September 1787, lists seven bands, RG 10, 1834:195, PAC.

29. Guy Johnson to Frederick Haldimand, Niagara, 9 May 1781, HP, B 107, 21767, p. 179, mfm A-683, PAC. A full account of all the early land surrenders appears in Donald B. Smith, "The Dispossession of the Mississauga Indians: A Missing Chapter in the Early History of Upper Canada," *Ontario History* 73(1981): 67–87. Guy Johnson to Frederick Haldimand, Niagara, 20 April 1781, HP, B 107, 21767, p. 173, mfm A-683, PAC; *Canada, Indian Treaties and Surrenders*, 3 vols. (Ottawa: Queen's Printer, 1891–1912), 3:196–97.

30. Captain William R. Crawford to Sir Johnson, Carleton Island, 9 October 1783, HP, B 128, 21818, p. 366, mfm A-746, PAC. For references to Crawford as a leader of Mississauga raiding parties in the Revolution see HP, B127, 21787, pp. 119, 139, 243, mfm A-688, PAC.

31. Joseph Sawyer in reply to T. G. Anderson on his visit to the Indians under his superintendence, Indian Village, Credit, 25 October 1845, RG 10, 1011, Entry Book, 1831–48, p. 128, PAC; and RG 10, 410:74. mfm C-9615.

32. Extract from the Minutes of the Land Committee held at the Council Chamber, Quebec, 30 April 1791, in Provincial Archives of Ontario *Report*, 1905, p. 454.

33. Indenture, 22 May 1784, Simcoe Papers, envelope 1, Ontario Archives.

34. For the "surrender" of 1787 see Dorchester to John Collins, Quebec, 19 July 1787 in Provincial Archives of Ontario *Report*, 1905, p. 379. Indenture, 23 September 1787, in Canada, *Treaties*, 1:32–33. Since so little information has survived, the nature of Colonel Butler's agreement in 1788 is unclear. See John Butler to Sir John Johnson, Niagara, 28 August 1788, enclosed "c" in Robert Prescott to Peter Russell, Quebec, 21 October 1797, RG 10, 15:413, mfm C-1224, PAC. For a summary of the 1787 and 1788 agreements Percy J. Robinson's "The Chevalier de Rocheblave and the Toronto Purchase," *Transactions of the Royal Society of Canada*, 3d ser., 31, sect. 2 (1937): 138–46, is helpful.

35. Letter of John Ferguson, 1 August 1794, Letters Received by the Surveyor-General, RG 1, A-I-1, 50:520–21, Ontario Archives. Since the boundaries (like those of the Crawford Purchases of 1783 and 1784) were never accurately specified, the cessions of 1787 and 1788 were eventually ruled invalid. The Toronto section was surrendered again and a proper deed secured in 1805. Only in 1923, however, did the Canadian government obtain a proper deed for the section from Toronto to the head of the Bay of Quinte (the two Crawford Purchases of 1783 and 1784 have still not been executed correctly). John Sunday et al., Memorial, dated Alderville, 21 June 1847, RG 10, 439:408–10. mfm C-9635.

36. Bruce Wilson, *As She Began: An Illustrated Introduction to Loyalist Ontario* (Toronto: Dundurn Press, 1981), p. 95.

37. John Butler, Head of Lake Ontario, 16 October 1790, Simcoe Papers, envelope 4, Ontario Archives; *Upper Canada Gazette*, 30 December 1797.

38. Quinipeno quoted at a Meeting with the Messissagues at the River Credit, 1 August 1805, RG 10, 1:294; PAC. A slightly different version is in CO 42, 340:51, PAC. J. B. Rousseau was the interpreter. Basil Johnston, Department of Ethnology, Royal Ontario Museum, translates Quinipeno, or Kineubenae into English as Golden Eagle.

39. Jones, *History*, p. 27.

40. The details of Wabakinine's murder are taken from three sources: Peter Russell to J. G. Simcoe, Niagara, 28 September 1796, *The Correspondence of the Honourable Peter Russell*, ed. E. A. Cruikshank, 3 vols. (Toronto: Ontario Historical Society, 1932–36), 1:50 (hereafter cited as RP; "State of Case the King vs. Charles McCuen. For murder committed on the Body of Waipykanine an Indian Chief," RG 22, 7 Home, vol. 35, Ontario Archives; and the Council of the Mississauga at Navy Hall, 8 September 1796, RG 8, 249:369–73, PAC.

41. Jones, *Life*, p. 228.

42. The members of Wabakinine's family are mentioned in "The Petition," OHSPR 26 (1930): 359; Isaac Weld, *Travels through the States of North*

America and Provinces of Upper and Lower Canada during the Years 1795, 1796, and 1797 (London: John Stockdale, 1799), pp. 294–95.

43. Peter Russell to J. G. Simcoe, Niagara, 31 December 1796, *RP*, 1:117.

44. The population of York and surrounding area in 1797 appears in *The Town of York, 1793–1815*, ed. Edith Firth (Toronto: Champlain Society, 1962), p. lxxvii. The number of troops is listed in Peter Russell to the Duke of Portland, Niagara, 20 August 1796, Russell Papers, Letterbook 1796–1806, Baldwin Room, Metropolitan Toronto Library (hereafter cited as BR, MTL).

45. Canada, *Indian Treaties and Surrenders*, 1:251–52; 1:7–8. C. H. Torok, "The Tyendinaga Mohawks," *Ontario History* 57(1965): 76.

46. Dr. P. E. Jones, "Place Names," p. 3.

47. Peter Russell to the Duke of Portland, York, 21 March 1798, *RP*, 2:122.

48. Col. D. Claus to General Haldimand, Montreal, 15 December 1783, HP, B 114, 21774, p. 344. mfm A-685, PAC.

49. Lord Selkirk, *Diary*, p. 306.

50. In 1787 Wabakinine was reported to command "at the Head of the Lake 506, of which one hundred and forty two can make use of Arms." Return of the Mississayey Nation of Indians assembled at the Head of the Bay de Quinte and Toronto, 23 September 1787, RG 10, 1834:197, PAC. Quinipeno gave the population figures at a meeting with William Claus, [Burlington] Beach, 3 November 1798, *RP* 2:306. Claus mentions that there were also three families at the Credit, *RP*, 2:304. On smallpox see Diary of Lieut. Governor Simcoe's Journey, entry for 1 October 1793, in *The Correspondence of Lieut. Governor John Graves Simcoe*, 5 vols., ed. E. A. Cruikshank (Toronto: Ontario Historical Society 1923–31), 2:73; William Osgoode to Ellen Copley, Niagara, 25 September 1793, in "Three Letters of William Osgoode: First Chief Justice of Upper Canada," ed. A. R. M. Lower, *Ontario History* 57(1965): 185; extract of a letter from Nathaniel Lines, Interpreter for the Indian Department, Kingston, 17 October 1796, RG 8, 249:215, PAC; Augustus Jones to D. W. Smith, Saltfleet, March 1797, Surveyors' Letters 28, p. 131, Ontario Archives.

51. For the implications of such a sudden population loss, see Kai Erikson, "Foreword," in Anastasia M. Shkilnyk, *A Poison Stronger Than Love: The Destruction of an Ojibwa Community* (New Haven: Yale University Press, 1985), pp. xiii–xviii.

52. William T. Hagan, *American Indians* (Chicago: University of Chicago Press, 1961), p. 52. My thanks to Franz Koennecke, a graduate student at the University of Waterloo, for this important point.

53. George Quimby, *Indian Life in the Upper Great Lakes* (Chicago: University of Chicago Press, 1967), p. 154.

54. Major Ross to Capt. Mathews, Cataraqui, 2 October 1783, HP B 124,

21784, p. 14, mfm A-688. The Indians admitted their addiction in their "Memoreal of Differant famley of the Massesagoe Indeans," Winter 1793 (see note 61 below).

55. For an excellent study of the effects of malnutrition consult "Ecology and Nutritional Stress in Man," *American Anthropologist* 64 (1963): 22–34.

56. Reginald Horsman, *Matthew Elliott, British Indian Agent* (Detroit: Wayne State University Press, 1964), pp. 123–24.

57. "Proclamation to Protect the Fishing Places and the Burying Grounds of the Mississagas," *Upper Canada Gazette*, 30 December 1797; also *RP*, 2:41.

58. Proceedings of a Garrison Court Martial Held by Order of Captain Mackenzie, 19 August 1801 in *Kingston before the War of 1812*, ed. R. A. Preston (Toronto: Champlain Society, 1959), p. 363.

59. John Cameron to [unknown], York, 16 December 1806, MG 19, F 1, 9:155, PAC.

60. Mrs. Simcoe, *Diary*, p. 115.

61. The Memoreal of Differant famley of the Massesagoe Indeans to his Excellancy John Graves Simco, North side of Lake Onteareo the winter 1793, Simcoe Papers, Canada, Loose Documents, 1793, envelope 17, Ontario Archives. Royston J. Packard, forensic consultant, Barrie, Ontario, has identified David Ramsay as the transcriber of this document; letter to D. B. Smith, 10 March 1979. For information on Ramsay see Donald B. Smith, "The Mississauga and David Ramsay," *Beaver* 305, no. 4 (Spring 1975): 4–8.

62. Quinipeno quoted at a meeting with the Mississaugas at the Credit River, 1 August 1805, RG 10, 1:295–96, PAC.

63. Jones, *History*, p. 164; P. J. Robinson to M. Richardson, Toronto, 16 April 1951, P. J. Robinson Papers, V, Indian Languages, envelope 1. Ontario Archives. In error the government also named the third township on the lakefront (the one through which the Credit River flows) Toronto—the Iroquois word referred, of course, to the area around the Humber River, approximately twenty kilometers to the east.

64. Upper Canada *Gazette*, 19 May 1825, p. 163, col. 2. At this date the *Gazette* was also called the *Weekly Register*.

3. Sacred Feathers Becomes Peter Jones

1. The account of the War of 1812 at the Head of the Lake is taken from two sources, Campbell, *Mountain*, pp. 32–48, and Pierre Berton, *Flames across the Border, 1813–1814* (Toronto: McClelland and Stewart, 1981), pp. 72–80.

2. Jones, *Life*, p. 5.

3. Obituary of Joseph Sawyer in *CG*, 16 December 1863.

4. Jones, *Life*, p. 376. A Return of the Mississgue Indian Nation, residing at the River Credit taken 5 July 1827, J. Givins, RG 10, 499:31639, mfm C-13341, PAC.

5. Ibid., p. 6.

6. Jones, *History*, p. 164; Berton, *Flames*, p. 208.

7. Jones, *History*, p. 91.

8. Ibid., p. 255.

9. On Possessor of Day or John Cameron, consult Jones, *Life*, pp. 185–86; Jones, *History*, p. 199. See also references in A Meeting with the Mississagues at the River Credit, 1st August 1805, CO 42, 340:51, and William Claus to Lieut. Governor Gore, dated Fort George, 11 September 1806, RG 10, 27:417–18, PAC. Possessor of Day had two Indian names, Okimapenasse, and Wageezhegome (Possessor of Day).

10. Jones, *History*, p. 102; Peter Jones, Anecdote Book, anecdote no. 93, "Indians' future state—River of Poles," PJC, VUL.

11. Jones, *Life*, pp. 185–86.

12. On Quinipeno, or Golden Eagle, see Proceedings of a Meeting with the Mississauges at the River Credit, 31 July 1805, CO42, 340:49–53; Quineppenon's Speech and the Deputy Superintendent General's Answer, 6 September 1806–8 September 1806, RG 10, 27:420–21; William Claus to Major Halton, Head of Lake Ontario, 22 September 1806, RG 10, 27:438; Proceedings of a meeting with the Missisawque Indians at the River Credit, October 3, 1810, RG 10, 27:n.p., PAC.

13. Peter Jones, Anecdote Book, anecdote no. 53, "Powwowiska Quenebenaw's death," PJC, VUL. Consult also Jones, *History*, pp. 88, 90–91.

14. Berton, *Flames*, pp. 298–99; Campbell, *Mountain*, p. 48.

15. Campbell, *Mountain*, p. 54.

16. Malcolm MacGregor to Henry Goulburn, Clatterford, Isle of Wight, 11 February 1819, CO 42, 363:135; The Return of the Indians on the Grand River, 17 February 1817, MG 19, F 1, 11:7, PAC; Charles Durand, *Reminiscences* (Toronto: Hunter, Rose, 1897), p. 30; Campbell, *Mountain*, p. 22.

17. Jones, *Life*, 4, 7–8; Jones, *History*, 30, 142. On p. 167 of his *History* Peter Jones recalls the children's reactions during the "drunken frolics." The story about Joseph Sawyer appears in Conrad Van Dusen, *The Indian Chief* (London: William Nichols, 1867), p. 23.

18. A paper talk of the River Credit Indians, laid before the Governor General, Port Credit, 5 December 1844, Entry Book, 1831–48, RG 10, 1011:105–6, PAC.

19. Francis Gore to the Earl of Bathurst, York, 10 April 1817, CO 42, 359:141.

20. Malcolm MacGregor to Henry Goulburn, Clatterford, Isle of Wight, 25 October 1818, CO 42, 361:351.

21. Ajetance quoted, Minutes of the proceedings of a council held at the Rivière au Credit, 27, 28, 29 October 1818, RG 10, 790:64, PAC.

22. Return of the Missesayey, 23 September 1787, RG 10, 1834:197; W. Claus to Lieutenant-Governor Maitland, York, 1 May 1819, CO 42, 362:203.

23. See maps, "Plan of the Tract of Land Purchased from the Mississagua Indians in 1806," Canada, *Treaties*, vol. 1, following p. 58, and see pp. 50–54.

24. William Claus at the council held with the Messessague Nation of Indians, 28 February 1820, RG 10, 790:125, PAC. The New Credit band currently claims the two hundred acres; see Diana L. Rankin, Indian Land Claims Researcher, Office of Indian Resource Policy, Ministry of National Resources of Ontario, "The Mississaugas of New Credit Indian Band Claim to 200 Acres Adjacent to the Credit River," research report, mimeographed, 20 February 1985.

25. Joseph Sawyer, John Jones to Sir John Colborne, River Credit, 3 April 1829, RG 10, 5:47, PAC.

26. Peter Jones to S. Y. Chesley, Brantford, 25 November 1854, RG 10, vol. 2225, file 43,957, part 2. The indenture of 28 February 1820 mentions a payment of fifty pounds that must have been used to pay for these presents; Canada, *Treaties*, 1:53–54.

27. Joseph Sawyer, John Jones to Sir John Colborne, River Credit, 3 April 1829, RG 10, 5:47, PAC.

28. Henry Stommel and Elizabeth Stommel, "The Year without a Summer," *Scientific American* 240, no. 6 (June 1979): 176–85; "Climate of the United States," *Niles' Weekly Register* (Baltimore), 10 August 1816; Thomas G. Ridout to Thomas Ridout, letter dated 1816, Ridout Papers, Ontario Archives.

29. John Jones to James Givins, Port Credit, 22 February 1837, Upper Canada Land Petitions, "J" Bundle, 20, no. 34, RG 1, L 3, vol. 260, PAC.

30. Jones, *Life*, pp. 6–8; Peter Jones, *The Sermons and Speeches of the Rev. Peter Jones: Leeds, September 25th, 26th and 27th, 1831* (Leeds: H. Spink, 1831), p. 12.

31. For the importance of the verb in Ojibwa, see Verwyst, *Chippewa Exercises*, p. 1; Fred Wheatley, Ojibwa Language Class, Toronto Native Friendship Centre, 26 January 1972 (the importance of placing the Ojibwa verb before the noun); Fred Wheatley, Ojibwa Language Class, Toronto Native Friendship Centre, 26 October 1971; "Character and Customs of Indian Tribes, Muncey Town, 11 March 1842, CG, 15 June 1842 (on the lack of a word for good-bye in Ojibwa).

32. Paulette Jiles, "Reverend Wilson and the Ojibway Grammar," *This Magazine* 10, no. 1 (February–March 1976): 15. A very perceptive article by the winner of the 1984 Governor General's Award for poetry in English.

33. George Copway, *The Traditional History and Characteristic Sketches of the Ojibway Nation* (London: C. Gilpin, 1850), p. 125.

34. Basil Johnston, *Ojibway Language Course Outline for Beginners* (Ottawa: Supply and Services Canada, 1978), p. 10; Kohl, *Kitchi-Gami*, p. 16; J. Steinbring, "Culture Change among the Northern Ojibwa," *Historical and Scientific Society of Manitoba*, 3d ser., 21 (1964–65): 15.

35. H. Christoph Wolfart and Janet F. Carroll, *Meet Cree: A Guide to the Language* (Edmonton: University of Alberta Press, 1981), p. xi.

36. Campbell, *Mountain*, pp. 59–60. The details supplied about Peter Jones's first year of schooling, and his years on the Grand River, are taken from his *Life*, pp. 6–8.

37. Peter mentioned that he was sent to the school, "along with some of my sisters," in the *Banner* (Aberdeen, Scotland), 15 August 1845.

38. The details on Augustus's Iroquois family are taken from several sources: on sister Catherine, National Archives, Washington, Archibald Russell, 147 Regiment (Wood's) New York Militia (1812). My thanks to Harold Senn of Victoria, British Columbia, for this reference; on sister Mary, known as Polly, Notes of conversation with Molly Jones Brant, Information gathered 26 September 1879, Draper Collection, Brant MSS. 13F23, Wisconsin Historical Society; on sister Rachel, Peter Jones to David Thorburn, Brantford, 21 October 1851, RG 10, 822:306–8, mfm C-15107, PAC. I have guessed her age from the fact that she was already married by 10 January 1826; see "entry for Rachel Parker" (Dekacharyax) in "A list of names of the members of the Methodist Society at the Upper Mohawks, Grand River, January 10, 1826" in Credit Mission Church Registry, United Church Archives (hereafter cited as CMCR, UCA); on sister Sally, Petition of Sally Henes Jones to Sir John Colborne, Cold Springs, 11 June 1832, Grand River Claims, RG 10, vol. 104, file "1832," PAC; on brother Henry, Henry Jones to J. T. Gilkison, Hartford, 12 December 1863, RG 10, vol. 1974, file 5620/1, PAC; on brother Joseph, Petition of Sarah Jones to Sir John Colborne, Cold Spring, 11 June 1832, Grand River Claims, RG 10, vol. 104, file "1832," PAC; on brother Augustus, Jr., Henry Jones to J. T. Gilkison, Hartford, 12 December 1863, RG 10, vol. 1974, file 5620/1, PAC.

39. Peter Spohn Van Wagner to F. H. Lynch-Staunton, Hamilton, 24 January 1895, in Campbell, *Mountain*, p. 22; Ezra Healey quoted in Carroll, *Case*, 3:46. The point about no longer eating with his fingers, and using plates instead of bowls is taken from Jones, *History*, p. 74.

40. Peter Jones to Eliza Field, River Credit, 6 May 1833, in the Letter Book, PJC, VUL.

41. Van Wagner to Lynch-Staunton in Campbell, *Mountain,* p. 22. Sir Francis Bond Head to Lord Glenelg, Toronto, 18 October 1837, CO42, 439:271.

42. Nathan Bangs, *An Authentic History of the Missions under the Care of the Missionary Society of the Methodist Episcopal Church* (New York: J. Emory, 1832), p. 183; William Case, "Journal of William Case," 6 April 1808–19 August 1809, United Church Archives, see entry for late May 1808.

43. Von Wagner to Lynch-Staunton, in Campbell, *Mountain,* p. 22.

44. Anson Green, *The Life and Times of the Reverend Anson Green* (Toronto: Methodist Book Room, 1877), pp. 32–33; obituary of Joseph Sawyer, *Annual Report of the Wesleyan Methodist Church Missionary Society* (hereafter cited as *Miss. Soc. Report*), 1863, p. xvi.

45. Donald A. Smith, *At the Forks of the Grand* (Paris: Walker Press, 1956), pp. 4–6.

46. Jones, *History,* pp. 134–35.

47. Jones, *Life,* p. 6.

48. Jones, *History,* p. 211. Peter Jones spells it Sagondensta. The translation of "De sagondensta" is by Reg Henry, Woodland Indian Cultural and Educational Centre, Brantford, Ontario, May 1984. My thanks to David Roberts of the *Dictionary of Canadian Biography* for this reference.

49. S. R. Mealing, ed., *Robert Gourlay's Statistical Account of Upper Canada* (Toronto: McClelland and Stewart, 1974), p. 196.

50. Gerald Craig, *Upper Canada: The Formative Years, 1784–1841* (Toronto: McClelland and Stewart, 1963), p. 131.

51. Isabel Thompson Kelsay, *Joseph Brant, 1743–1807: Man of Two Worlds* (Syracuse: Syracuse University Press, 1984), p. 40; Barbara Graymont, *The Iroquois in the American Revolution* (Syracuse: Syracuse University Press, 1972), p. 10; Sally M. Weaver, "Six Nations of the Grand River, Ontario" in *Northeast,* ed. Trigger, pp. 525–26.

52. Kelsay, *Brant,* p. 23.

53. Ibid., p. 372.

54. Peter never gained complete fluency in Mohawk; Jones, *Life,* p. 95.

55. Kelsay, *Brant,* pp. 529, 536; Jones, *Life,* p. 6.

56. Jones, *Life,* p. 191. For Oneida Joseph's loyalty to the Church of England, see Petition of Oneida Joseph et al., 17 October 1830, Strachan Papers, reel 2, Ontario Archives. Henry A. Hill and Oneida Joseph both served as witnesses to the marriage of Augustus Jones and Sarah Tekarihogen on 27 April 1798. See copy of the magistrate certificate of the marriage of Augustus Jones and Sarah Tekerehogen, Grand River, 27 April 1798, RG 10, vol. 104, file 1832 (the document accompanies Augustus Jones's petition of 11 June 1832).

57. Kelsay, *Brant,* pp. 280–81, 653.

58. Deed from the Chiefs and Principal Men and Women of the Mississauga Indians to Catherine Brant of a Certain Tract or Land, 7 May 1803, Miscellaneous Manuscript Collection, 1803, Ontario Archives; Kelsay, *Brant*, pp. 531, 279; Testimony of Mrs. Charlotte Smith, postmarked Tuscarora, Ontario, 23 November 1877, Lyman Draper Papers, Joseph Brant Section, 14 F 63, State Historical Society of Wisconsin, Madison, Wisconsin. Charlotte Brant Smith, a daughter of Jacob Brant, was Joseph Brant's granddaughter.

59. Kelsay, *Brant*, pp. 275, 277, 280, 658; Oronhyatekha to Lyman Draper, London, Ontario, 29 April 1879, Lyman Draper Papers, Joseph Brant Section, 1 F 145, State Historical Society of Wisconsin, Madison, Wisconsin.

60. W. C. Bryant to Lyman Draper, Buffalo, 28 May 1878, Lyman Draper Papers, Joseph Brant Section, 15 F 32, State Historical Society of Wisconsin, Madison, Wisconsin. "I was informed some twenty years ago by the late Peter Jones that Mrs. Joseph Brant was a half-breed"; Jones, *Life*, p. 191.

61. Kelsay, *Brant*, pp. 51, 128.

62. Jones, *Life*, pp. 6–7. The description of the deer is from Copway, *Life*, pp. 28–29.

63. Peter Jones, "The Indian Woman's Regret," Anecdote Book, anecdote no. 1, PJC, VUL.

64. Jones, *Life*, pp. 6–7.

65. Ibid., p. 7.

66. See the references in note 38 above for the marriage partners of Catherine, Polly and Rachel. I am assuming that Rachel's husband was not Indian—he was not listed as an Iroquois. Sally never married (see Jones, *Life*, p. 353). Henry's marriages are mentioned in John A. Noon, *Law and Government of the Grand River Iroquois* (New York: Viking Fund Publications in Anthropology, 1949), p. 183. Joseph's wife Catherine Jackson is listed with her husband in the Credit Mission Church Registry, UCA. In the 1851 census (mfm C-949), Tuscarora Township, p. 21, Augustus, Jr.'s, wife's name is listed as Hannah Jones and her birthplace as England.

67. Kelsay, *Brant*, p. 576.

68. For an excellent overview of the history of the Six Nations on the Grand River in the late eighteenth and early nineteenth centuries, see the introduction by Charles M. Johnston in his *Valley of the Six Nations: A Collection of Documents of the Indian Lands of the Grand River* (Toronto: University of Toronto Press, 1964), pp. xxvii–xcvi; and Sally M. Weaver, "Six Nations of the Grand River, Ontario," in *Northeast*, ed. Bruce G. Trigger, pp. 525–28.

69. For the different tribal locations see, "Plan of the Grand River and Location of Six Nations of Indians as found settled by the Revd. R. Lugger," 20 February 1828, and fig. 2 in Johnston, *Valley*, following p. lxxxvi.

70. Anthony F. C. Wallace's *Death and Rebirth of the Seneca* (New York: Alfred A. Knopf, 1970) provides an in-depth review of the rise of the longhouse religion—see p. 317 for a capsule summary; "Indian Prophet," *Niles' Weekly Register* 9, no. 5 (30 September 1815): 77. For the tensions a century later between the two groups see Arthur C. Parker, "The Code of Handsome Lake, the Seneca Prophet," in *Parker on the Iroquois*, ed. William N. Fenton (Syracuse: Syracuse University Press, 1968), p. 14. The phrase "whitemanized" is Parker's.

71. Lord Selkirk, *Diary*, pp. 245–46.

72. Jones, *Life*, p. 11.

73. Ibid., p. 8.

74. My thanks to Cynthia Bunnell for supplying me with information on her family, residents of Brant County for nearly two centuries: Cynthia Bunnell to Donald B. Smith, Brantford, 1 July 1980; "Bunnell Family One of Oldest," *Brant News*, 21 June 1978, p. 9.

75. Charles and James C. Thomas, "Reminiscences of the First Settlers in the County of Brant," OHSPR 12 (1914): 68–69. The school stood on a lot later deeded by the Crown to Enos Bunnell. Peter provides the fullest description of his education in Jones, *The Sermons and Speeches of the Rev. Peter Jones . . . Leeds, September 25th, 26th and 27th*, pp. 12–13; "Speech . . . Leeds," pp. 12–13.

76. Eliza Field Jones, Diary, 1834–35, entry for 23 August 1834, PJC, VUL.

4. Born Again

1. The description of March and April in Upper Canada is taken from Traill, *Guide*, pp. 213–15.

2. On Chief Davis see John Norton to Lieut. Col. Addison, Grand River, 17 February 1817, RG 8, 261:28, mfm C-2853, PAC; Eliza Field Jones, Diary, 1834–35, entry for 25 August 1834, PJC, VUL; Carroll, *Case*, 2:415, 3:53; George Ryerson to the British and Foreign Bible Society, 21 April 1828, British and Foreign Bible Society, Swindon, England; Chief Thomas Davis to Sir John Colborne, Davis's Hamlet, 30 December 1833, RG 10, vol. 104, "file 1834," PAC; John West, *The Substance of a Journal during a Residence at the Red River Colony, British North America: And Frequent Excursions among the North West American Indians*, 2d ed. (London: L. B. Sealey, 1827), pp. 279–81.

3. George Ryerson to the British and Foreign Bible Society, 21 April 1828, British and Foreign Bible Society, Swindon, England. Ryerson, in reporting Davis's words, uses the phrase "*to his heart*," which I have altered here "*to my heart.*"

4. On Edmund Stoney see Carroll, *Case*, 2:459–60; George F. Playter, *The History of Methodism in Canada* (Toronto: Wesleyan Printing Establishment, 1862), p. 217; Jones, *Life*, p. 9.

5. Jones, *Life*, p. 8.

6. Alvin Torry, *Autobiography of Rev. Alvin Torry*, ed. William Hosmer (Auburn: William J. Moses, 1864), p. 290.

7. Thomas Davis quoted in the Reverend William Case's letter dated 17 March 1824, *Methodist Magazine* (hereafter cited as *MM*) 7(1824): 463.

8. Carl F. Klinck and James J. Talman, eds., *The Journal of Major John Norton 1816* (Toronto: Champlain Society, 1970), p. 91.

9. On Seth Crawford see Jones, *Life*, p. 8; Carroll, *Case*, 2:410, 414; Alvin Torry, "Grand River Mission," *MM* 7(January 1824): 33.

10. My thanks to Robert Whitelock of Calgary for his discussion of religious conversion, 12 December 1979.

11. Wilcomb E. Washburn briefly summarizes James's interpretation in *The Indian in America* (New York: Harper Colophon Books, 1975), p. 115. The American philosopher presents his theory of conversion in his classic *The Varieties of Religious Experience* (New York: New American Library, 1958), pp. 112–206. The book is based on James's lectures at the University of Edinburgh in 1901/2.

12. Arthur Kewley, "The Location of Peter Jones' Conversion," manuscript kindly lent to me by the Reverend Mr. Kewley.

13. Rupert E. Davies, *Methodism* (London: Epworth Press, 1976), p. 84. Lovett Hayes Weems, Jr., *The Gospel According to Wesley* (Nashville: Discipleship Resources, 1982), pp. 1–19. A helpful short summary of Methodist theology appears in Goldwin French, "The Evangelical Creed in Canada," in *The Shield of Achilles*, ed. W. L. Morton (Toronto: McClelland and Stewart, 1968), pp. 18–21. Cyril Davey provides a popular survey of Methodism in his beautifully illustrated *John Wesley and the Methodists* (Basingstoke, Hampshire: Marshall Pickering, 1985). Rupert Davies's *Methodism* is a more detailed summary.

14. John Wesley, *The Works of the Reverend John Wesley, A.M.*, ed. T. Jackson, 3d ed. (London, 1829), 8:270–71, quoted in Goldwin French, *Parsons and Politics: The Role of the Wesleyan Methodists in Upper Canada and the Maritimes from 1780 to 1855* (Toronto: Ryerson, 1962), p. 7.

15. Carroll, *Case*, 2:129.

16. Wesley's *General Rules*, quoted in R. Carlyle Buley, *The Old Northwest: Pioneer Period, 1815–1840*, 2 vols. (Bloomington: Indiana University Press, 1978), 2:450. Buley provides an excellent summary of early American Methodism on pp. 447–61.

17. John Webster Grant, ed., "Introduction," in *Salvation! O the Joyful*

Sound: The Selected Writings of John Carroll (Toronto: Oxford University Press, 1967), pp. 14–21; Craig, *Upper Canada*, pp. 165–67; French, *Parsons*, pp. 1–42; John Wesley quoted in Wade Crawford Barclay, *Early American Methodism* (New York: Board of Missions, 1950), 2:375.

18. Carroll, *Case*, 1:120.

19. Charles A. Johnston, *The Frontier Camp Meeting* (Dallas: Southern Methodist University Press, 1955), p. 42.

20. Johnston, *Camp Meeting*, p. 40; Jones, *Life*, pp. 7–8.

21. Johnston, *Camp Meeting*, pp. 45–46.

22. The basic source on William Case is John Carroll's five-volume study *Case and His Cotemporaries* (the description of his appearance appears on 1:314). A short summary is available in John Carroll's chapter "The Father of Canadian Missions" in *Past and Present* (Toronto: Alfred Dredge, 1860), pp. 220–34. A. Burnside provides a review of Case's life in his B.D. thesis for Emmanuel College (a copy is deposited in the United Church Archives, Toronto), "The Work of William Case, 1780–1855," prepared in 1957. Case's height is given in Nathan Bangs's letter, dated New York, 30 October 1855, in William B. Sprague, *Annals of the American Pulpit* (New York, Robert Carter, 1859), 7:426. The baptism of John Jones, "son of Augustus Jones and Tubenaniqua" is listed in CMCR, UCA.

23. The quotations describing Peter Jones's conversion to Methodism are all taken from his recollection of the camp meeting; see Jones, *Life*, pp. 9–14.

24. One of the best descriptions that Peter Jones gives of his faith and his understanding of Christianity appears in his sermon at Ebenezer Chapel, Bristol, 5 February 1832, printed in *Wesleyan Preacher* 1 (1832):422–27.

25. Jones, *Sermons . . . Leeds*, p. 14.

26. For the fullest description of this Ojibwa belief see the speech of Pazhekezhikquashcum in *CG*, 27 February 1830, and in Jones, *Life*, 247–48, and the speech of Kanooting in Jones, *Life*, pp. 123–24.

27. This was a popular Methodist song in the mid-1820s; Carroll, *Case*, 2:454.

28. Jones, *Life*, p. 13.

29. Carroll, *Case*, 2:349; Torry, *Autobiography*, p. 60.

30. Alvin Torry quoted in Carroll, *Case*, 2:402–3; Torry quoted in William Case to Rev. Thomas Mason, 12 April 1823, MM 6(1823):233.

31. Torry, *Autobiography*, pp. 79–81.

32. Peter Jones, Anecdote Book, anecdote no. 33, PJC, VUL.

33. Jones, *Life*, pp. 15–16; Carroll, *Case*, 2:443–46; Torry, *Autobiography*, p. 97.

34. Jones, *Life*, p. 15; Obituary of Sarah Henry in *Miss. Soc. Report*, 1873–74, p. xxvii; Peter Jones's Anecdote Book, anecdote no. 2, PJC, VUL.

35. Peter Jones, Muncey Mission, 25 April 1843, CG, 10 May 1843.

36. Jones, "Speech . . . Leeds," p. 15.

37. Jones, *Life,* pp. 15–17; Alvin Torry, letter from the Grand River, 26 January 1825, MM 8(1825): 200.

38. Seth Crawford quoted in a letter from Rev. William Case, Saltfleet, Upper Canada, 17 March 1824, MM 7(1824): 236.

39. William Case to Seth Crawford, Stoney Creek, 18 January 1825 (should read 1826), in Jones, *Life,* p. 50.

40. John Cameron quoted in Jones, *Life,* p. 187.

41. Torry, *Autobiography,* pp. 99–100; Alvin Torry, letter from the Grand River, 26 January 1825, MM 8(1825): 200; Jones, *Life,* pp. 17, 36, 186. Catharine Cameron, Wechekewekapawiqua, was born in 1807, the daughter of Tuhbenahneequay; see CMCR, UCA. Her husband John Cameron, born about 1764, was over forty years her senior.

42. Peter's license to exhort is in PJC, VUL; Johnson, *Camp Meeting,* p. 20.

43. William Case, speech at the Genesee Conference Missionary Anniversary, Lansing, N.Y., 17 August 1825, in Carroll, *Case,* 3:43.

44. William Paley, *A View of the Evidences of Christianity* (New York: Griffin and Rudd, 1814). Flyleaf ink inscription: "Peter Jones's Book—June 28th, 1825." Title page inscription: "Augustus Jones's Book." I am grateful to Al Hiebert of Vernon, British Columbia, for this information.

45. Jones, *Life,* p. 13.

46. Peter Jones quoted in Rev. J. Ryerson, York, August 1826, *Miss. Soc. Report,* 1826, p. 18. See also his comment in his diary, Jones, *Life,* p. 398. Entry for 5 April 1838.

47. Jones, *Life,* pp. 21–23, 35.

48. Peter Jones to James Givins, Grand River, 17 June 1825, Letter Book, 1825–42, RG 10, 1011, PAC.

49. Ezra Healey, quoted in Carroll, *Case,* 3:45; William Case, Hallowell, Upper Canada, 31 August 1824, quoted in Carroll, *Case,* 2:496; Playter, *Methodism,* pp. 229, 245.

5. The Mississaugas' Cultural Revolution

1. Kahkewaquonaby to James Givins, Grand River, 17 June 1825, Letter Book, 1825–42, RG 10, 1011:86203, mfm T-1456, PAC.

2. The best summary of Givins's life appears in Sir Francis Bond Head to Lord Glenelg, Toronto, 5 May 1836, CO 42, 430:14.

3. Charles Durand, *Reminiscences* (Toronto: Hunter, Rose, 1897), p. 50.

4. Jones, *Life,* pp. 35–36.

5. *Collection of Hymns for the Use of Native Christians of the Iroquois.*

To Which Are Added a Few Hymns in the Chippeway Tongue: Translated by Peter Jones (New York: Printed at the Conference Office by A. Hoyt, 1827), pp. 38–39. Jones, *Life*, pp. 35–36.

6. She was then married to the Mississauga warrior Mesquacosy. See the records of baptism for George Henry (Pemikishigon), born 1811, and Margaret Henry (Sakagiwequa), born 1814, CMCR, UCA.

7. Jones, *Life*, pp. 3–4. For the identification of Captain Jim, and James Ajetance as the same person see Donald B. Smith, "The Mississauga, Peter Jones, and the White Man: The Algonkians' Adjustment to the Europeans on the North Shore of Lake Ontario to 1860" (Ph.D. thesis, University of Toronto, 1975), p. 159, n. 68.

8. Peter Jones quoted in Egerton Ryerson to John Ryerson, August 1826, reprinted in *Miss. Soc. Report*, 1826, p. 18.

9. The following quotations are all taken from Egerton Ryerson's summary of Peter Jones's two sermons, 23–24 July 1826, given in his letter to John Ryerson, dated August 1826, and reprinted in *Miss. Soc. Report*, 1826, pp. 17–18.

A full study of Peter Jones's theology could be made. The Victoria University Library in Toronto has hundreds of his sermon outlines. The titles of his six published sermons—all given in Britain in the years 1831–32—are listed in the bibliography. An Ojibwa speaker could also examine his translations of the Christian Gospels into Ojibwa.

10. Henry Steinhauer quoted in Slight, *Researches*, pp. 88–89. For another reference to the good and bad places referred to by the Anishinabeg, see John McLean, *Notes of a Twenty-five Years' Service in the Hudson's Bay Territory*, ed. W. S. Wallace (Toronto: Champlain Society, 1932), p. 160.

11. David Sawyer quoted on the back cover of Peter Jones's Anecdote Book, PJC, VUL. For John Wesley's interpretation of the Holy Spirit, see Davies, *Methodism*, pp. 92–93. My thanks to Stan Cuthand of Saskatoon for his comments on this section. Any errors remain, of course, my responsibility. Edward Benton-Banai mentions the role of Waynaboozhoo, or Nanahbozho, as the Great Spirit's messenger in *Mishomis Book*, p. 50.

12. Peter Jones to William Case, River Credit, 10 November 1825, MM 9 (1826): 157. For comments on Peter Jones's ability as a speaker in 1825, see Rev. Thomas Madden, Niagara, 4 July 1825, MM 8(1825): 321. For Indian responses to his sermons, see Jones, *Life*, pp. 36, 46, 53, 67, 77, 83, 88, 95, 133, 139.

13. Jones, *Life*, p. 237.

14. Jones, *History*, p. 189.

15. Jones, *Life*, p. 38.

16. On the Mississaugas' dress (Christian and non-Christian) see Jones,

History, pp. 75–77; Slight, *Researches,* pp. 54–55; Maungwudaus [George Henry], *Remarks concerning the Ojibway Indians* (Leeds: C. A. Wilson, 1847), p. 5. The precise time references in Peter's diary indicate that he carried a watch; see *Life,* pp. 38–39.

17. Peter Jones supplies the full details of the present-giving ceremony in *Life,* pp. 38–39.

18. Descriptions of councils at which presents were given appear in Jones, *Life,* p. 164; see also J. E. Alexander, *Transatlantic Sketches,* 2 vols. (London: Richard Bentley, 1833), 2:160, 162–63.

19. John Strachan, *Claims of the Churchmen and Dissenters of Upper Canada Brought to the Test in a Controversy between Several Members of the Church of England and a Methodist Preacher* (Kingston, 1828), pp. 19–20, 13; French, *Parsons,* p. 112. Strachan sincerely believed that great injustices had been committed against the Indians; see Report on Observations by the Archdeacon of Toronto, the Revd. Dr. Strachan on the Subject of a Protestant Missionary at Manatonwanning, in S. P. Jarvis to Sir George Arthur, 20 August 1838, RG 10, 502:120–21, mfm C-13, 342, PAC.

20. Jones, *Life,* p. 38; Peter Jones to J. Givins, Grand River, 8 August 1825, Letter Book, 1825–42, RG 10, 1011, PAC; Smith, "Mississauga," p. 162, n. 80; Jones, *History,* pp. 223, 230.

21. Jones, *History,* p. 174; Jones, Anecdote Book, anecdote no. 9, PJC, VUL.

22. The Credit Mission Church Registry gives Cameron's date of birth as 1764 and James Ajetance's, or Captain Jim's, as 1769; CMCR, UCA.

23. Jones, *Life,* pp. 62–64, 76; Smith, "Mississauga," p. 169.

24. The quotations from Warren are taken from his *History of the Ojibway Nation,* pp. 65, 70. For possible similarities raised by Peter Jones in his sermons I am indebted to Stan Cuthand of Saskatoon, in an interview 1 September 1983. Any errors in this presentation remain, of course, my responsibility.

25. *Collection of Hymns for the Use of Native Christians,* p. 50.

26. Jones, *History,* p. 237; Rev. James McGrath, Report on the River Credit, March 1829, CO 42, 388:281.

27. Jones, *Life,* p. 23. Gertrude Prokosch Kurath has suggested that perhaps Ojibwa converts saw Jesus appear as they saw a guardian spirit in a vision quest. See her study *Michigan Indian Festivals* (Ann Arbor: Ann Arbor Publishers, 1966), p. 47.

28. Jones, *History,* p. 233.

29. Jones, Anecdote Book, anecdote no. 7, "Polly Ryckman's Happy Death," PJC, VUL; Jones, *Life,* p. 132; entry under "Mary Ryckman," CMCR, UCA.

30. Jacobs, *Journal,* p. iii.

31. Thomas William Magrath to Rev. Thomas Radcliff in *Authentic Letters from Upper Canada,* ed. Rev. T. Radcliff (Dublin: William Curry, 1833), p. 210.

32. Jones, *History,* p. 200.

33. Jones, *Life,* p. 194.

34. Slight, *Researches,* pp. 162–64; Jones, *History,* p. 234.

35. Francis Hall, "Trafalgar, U.C., August 18, 1828," *Christian Advocate* (hereafter cited as *CA*), 5 September 1828. John Muskrat was born in 1781; CMCR, UCA.

36. Jones, *Life,* p. 167.

37. Jones, Anecdote Book, anecdote no. 58, "Conversion and happy death of old Tunewah," PJC, VUL.

38. Slight, *Researches,* p. 166.

39. Peter Jacobs, Sault de Ste. Marie, 12 May 1836, *CA,* 17 June 1836.

40. For the sources of these identifications of names, see Smith, "Mississauga," pp. 170–72.

41. Ontario Department of Planning and Development, *Credit Valley Conservation Report, 1956* (Toronto: Department of Planning and Development, 1956), p. 88; Jones, *History,* p. 72.

42. Jones, *History,* pp. 60, 71; Maungwudaus [George Henry], *Remarks,* p. 5.

43. Weld, *Travels,* p. 294.

44. Reminiscences of William Hewson of Big Bay Point, Lake Simcoe, in W. L. Smith, *The Pioneers of Old Ontario* (Toronto: George N. Morang, 1923), p. 81.

45. Jones, *Life,* pp. 152–53, 155; Jones, *History,* p. 78.

46. Peter Jones to Samuel Martin, River Credit Mission, 18 January 1830, PJC, VUL.

47. John Butler, Head of Lake Ontario, 16 October 1790. Simcoe Papers, envelope 4, Ontario Archives; Petition of the Messessague Nation to Sir Peregrine Maitland, Credit River, 16 November 1825, Lieutenant-Governor's Correspondence, RG 7, G14, vol. 2, PAC.

48. Petition of the Missisaga Indians to Sir Peregrine Maitland, River Credit, 14 December 1826, Lieutenant-Governor's Correspondence, RG 7, G14, vol. 3, PAC; "An Act the better to protect the Mississaga tribes, living on the Indian reserve of the river Credit, in their exclusive right of fishing and hunting therein," *Statutes of Upper Canada,* 10 Geo. IV, Cap. 3(1829): 28–30. My thanks to Bruce Clark of London, Ontario, for this reference. For the price of salmon at the Credit see Francis Hall, "Trafalgar, U.C., August 18, 1828," *CA,* 5 September 1828; and James Richardson to George Ryerson, Niagara, 2 October 1829, Ryerson Papers, UCA.

49. Jones, *Life*, pp. 70–71.

50. The following information on Peter's allies at the Credit Mission is taken from Smith, "Mississauga," pp. 167–70. John Jones's complaint is summarized by the Reverend James Magrath in his "Report on the River Credit," March 1829, CO 42, 388:285.

51. John West, *The Substance of a Journal*, 2d ed. (London: L. B. Seeley, 1827), p. 292.

52. CMCR, UCA; Kelsay, *Brant*, p. 609.

53. [Eliza Jones] Ke-che-ah-gah-me-qua, "Sketch of the Life of Captain Joseph Brant, Thayendanagea," *New Dominion Monthly*, November 1872, p. 282.

54. CMCR, UCR; entry under Lucy Brant; Peter Jones, Anecdote Book, no number given, "Lucy Brant," PJC, VUL.

55. George Sterling Ryerson, *Looking Backward* (Toronto: Ryerson, 1924), p. 30.

56. Rev. James McGrath, Report on the River Credit, March 1829, CO 42, 388:282. Three-quarters of the men and almost all of the women could not speak English.

57. Egerton Ryerson, "Brief Sketch of the Life, Death, and Character of the Late Rev. Peter Jones," CG, 23 July 1856.

58. Egerton Ryerson, *"The Story of My Life" (Being Reminiscences of Sixty Years' Public Service in Canada)*, ed. J. Hodgins (Toronto: William Briggs, 1883), p. 59.

59. Peter Jones, "Removal of the River Credit Indians, Muncey Mission, Dec. 22, 1847," CG, 12 January 1848; Egerton Ryerson, letter dated 18 April 1827, MM 10(1827): 313.

60. Jones, *Life*, p. 228.

61. Ryerson, "Story," pp. 73, 65–66, 59.

62. Ibid., pp. 66–67.

63. Basil Hall, *Travels in North America in the Years 1827 and 1828*, 3 vols. (Edinburgh: Printed for Cadell, 1829), 1:259.

64. Jones, *History*, pp. 227–28; Jones, Anecdote Book, anecdote no. 63, PJC, VUL.

6. *"Go Ye into All the World"*

1. Jones, *Life*, p. 77.

2. Catherine Parr Traill, *The Backwoods of Canada: Being Letters from the Wife of an Emigrant Officer* (London: Charles Knight, 1836; facsimile edition, Coles Canadiana Collection, Toronto, 1971), p. 197; Traill, *Settler's Guide*, p. 211.

3. Ibid., pp. 218–19.

4. Jones, *Life*, p. 78.

5. *The Valley of the Trent*, ed. Edwin C. Guillet (Toronto: Champlain Society, 1957), p. 36.

6. *Valley*, ed. Guillet, p. 304; Carroll, *Case*, 2:491; 3:237.

7. Samuel Strickland, *Twenty-seven Years in Canada West*, ed. Agnes Strickland, 2 vols. (London: Richard Bentley, 1853), 2:34, 38.

8. At Earnestown, near Kingston, the white settlers had almost mobbed him, so eager were they to hear him; see Jones, *Life*, p. 54, entry for 12 February 1826.

9. Jones, *Life*, pp. 264, 18, 34, 40, 4.

10. Ibid., pp. 86, 16, 33.

11. Jones, *History*, p. 29.

12. Alvin Torry, Grand River, 28 September 1825, *MM* 9(1826): 37–39. Very little has been written about the Munsees. To my knowledge the only study specifically about the Munsees at Munceytown is Roberta Miskokomon's "Migration Route of the Munsees to Ontario," mimeographed, March 1983. Available from the author, R.R. #1, Muncey, Ontario, N0L 1Y0.

13. Jones, *Life*, pp. 24–26.

14. Heckewelder, *History*, pp. xli, 52–53, 84–85.

15. Ives Goddard, "Delaware," in *Northeast*, ed. Trigger, pp. 213–16.

16. C. A. Weslager, *The Delaware Indians: A History* (New Brunswick, N.J.: Rutgers University Press, 1972), p. 31; Heckewelder, *History*, p. xli.

17. A number of Dutch words in their language confirm this; see Ives Goddard, "Dutch Loanwords in Delaware," in *A Delaware Indian Symposium*, ed. Herbert C. Kraft (Harrisburg: Pennsylvania Historical and Museum Commission, 1974), pp. 153–60.

18. Goddard, "Delaware," p. 221; the maps provided on pp. 214 and 215 are very useful.

19. Jones, *History*, p. 116; Heckewelder, *History*, pp. 96, 124.

20. Peter Jones himself did not know why the Anishnabeg called the Lenni Lenapes "grandfathers"; Jones, *History*, p. 116. The explanation given here is that of the anthropologist Frank Speck; see the reference in C. A. Weslager, *The Delawares: A Critical Bibliography* (Bloomington: Indiana University Press, 1978), p. 1.

21. John Norton, "Names of Some Chiefs and Warriors Whose Conduct Has Been Meritorious," "C" Series, RG 10, 261:218, mfm C-2853, PAC.

22. William Case, letter, Grape Island, 20 December 1829, *CA*, 19 February 1830.

23. John Carey, letter, Munceytown, 2 May 1825; Alvin Torry, letter, Grand River, 28 September 1825, *MM* 9(1826): 37.

24. Jones, *Life*, p. 26.

25. Ibid., p. 27.

26. Weslager, *Delaware*, pp. 316–17.

27. The two Munsee chiefs and Peter Jones are quoted in Alvin Torry, letter, Grand River, 28 September 1825, *MM* 9(1826): 38. See also Weslager, *Delaware*, p. 342, for a reference to the Delawares' memories of the massacre.

28. Peter Jones, quoted in Torry, letter, *MM* 9(1826): 38.

29. Abraham Luckenbach, diary entry for 5 April 1828, Moraviantown Diary, Moravian Archives, Bethlehem, Pennsylvania. Margaret Wilde provided the translation from the German; Jones, *Life*, pp. 121–22, 129–30, 250. For details on Abraham Luckenbach, see his "Autobiography" in Harry Emilius Stocker, *A History of the Moravian Mission among the Indians on the White River in Indiana* (Bethlehem: Times, 1917).

30. Torry, letter, *MM* 9(1826): 37–38; Jones, *Life*, p. 30; John Carey to John Strachan, York, 20 January 1828, Strachan Papers, reel 2, Ontario Archives; John Carey to Major Hillier, dated Muncee, 15 April 1828, *RG* 10, 791:194, PAC.

31. Principal Men of the Thames River Ojibwa quoted in Torry, letter, *MM* 9(1826): 39.

32. William Case, letter, River Credit, 27 November 1827, *CA*, 4 January 1828; Peter Jones, Diary, entry for 30 April 1830, *CG*, 12 June 1830. We know that Tomiko was his uncle, from the reference in *History of Middlesex* (Toronto: W. A. and C. L. Goodspeed, 1889), p. 729, which states that Tomiko was the uncle of Nelson Beaver—who was in turn the brother of Peter Beaver; see CMCR, UCA, entry for "Nelson Beaver," baptized 25 November 1827.

33. William Case, letter, Grape Island, 20 December 1829, *CA*, 19 February 1830.

34. William Case, letter, Munceytown, 6 April 1830, *CG*, 10 April 1830.

35. Kanootong, quoted by Peter Jones in *Life*, p. 123.

36. *Middlesex*, p. 20.

37. C. H. Torok, "The Tyendinaga Mohawks," *Ontario History* 57(1965): 76.

38. P. G. Selden, J. Lockwood, Joint Secretaries, Report of the Bellville [*sic*] Branch Missionary Society, August 1826, *Miss. Soc. Report*, 1826, p. 15.

39. Goldwin S. French, "Pahtahsega," *Dictionary of Canadian Biography*, vol. 9 (1881–90), p. 660.

40. Peter Jacobs, letter, 12 May 1836, *CA*, 17 June 1836.

41. Address of Peter Jacobs, Ninth Annual Report of the Missionary Society of the Methodist Episcopal Church, *CA*, 2 May 1828.

42. Ibid.

43. Peter Jacobs, *Journal of the Reverend Peter Jacobs, Indian Wesleyan*

Missionary, from Rice Lake to the Hudson's Bay Territory, and Returning, Commencing May, 1852, 2d ed. (Boston: George C. Rand, 1858), p. 27.

44. Pahtahsegay [Peter Jacobs], Exeter Hall, London, England, *cg*, 12 July 1843.

45. Jones, *Life*, p. 53.

46. Pahtahsegay [Peter Jacobs], Exeter Hall, London, England, *cg*, 12 July 1843. See also the address of Peter Jacobs, Ninth Annual Report of the Missionary Society of the Methodist Episcopal Church, *ca*, 2 May 1828.

47. Jones, *Life*, p. 57.

48. William Case quoted in Jones, *Life*, p. 58.

49. John Maclean, "Shawundais," in *Vanguards of Canada* (Toronto: Missionary Society of the Methodist Church, 1918), p. 17 (on the English translation of his name); Lucy Richards, "Memoirs (1830) of John Sunday and Other Indians," *Indian*, 17 March 1885, p. 55 (on John Sunday's three woɪds in English); "Veterans of the War of 1812," Miscellaneous Collection, no date, package 4, item 26, ca. 1875, Ontario Archives (on his presence at the Battle of Chrysler's Farm in the War of 1812); John Sunday, Plymouth, England, 1837, quoted in Robert Alder, *Wesleyan Missions: Their Progress Stated and Claims Enforced* (London: Wesleyan Missionary Society, 1842), pp. 36–37.

50. John Sunday, Grape Island, 30 September 1834, *cg*, 22 October 1834; Jones, *Life*, p. 59.

51. John Sunday, Grape Island, 30 September 1834, *cg*, 22 October 1834; Jones, *Life*, p. 67.

52. Peter Jones, *Life*, p. 68; William Case, letter dated Kingston, 30 June 1826, *mm* 9(1826): 394–96.

53. William Beaver quoted in William Case, letter, Kingston, 30 June 1826, *mm* 9(1826): 395. I have changed the word "squaws" to "women," since it is unlikely that Beaver would have used that word, a pejorative one to the Ojibwas; see Jones, *History*, p. 164.

54. William Case, letter, Bellville [sic], 10 January 1827, *mm* 10(1827): 227. This is the procedure generally followed by Peter Jones and the native workers; see Jones, *Life*, pp. 48, 76, 77–78, 91, 99, 134; William Case, "Account of Alnwick Mission," *Wesleyan Missionary Notices*, n.s., 13 (August 1855): 141.

55. William Case in *cg*, 19 September 1838.

56. John Sunday and John Moses quoted in Jones, *Life*, p. 73.

57. Jones, *Life*, p. 73. His age appears in the list of "Baptisms of native converts at Lake Simcoe, Baptised at the Yonge Street Camp Meeting on the 18th June 1827," by the Reverend William Case, *cmcr, uca*.

58. Peter Jones quoted in Thaddeus Osgood, communication dated

Montreal, 21 November 1827 in *The Canadian Visitor, Communicating Important Facts and Interesting Anecdotes Respecting the Indians and Destitute Settlers in Canada and the United States of America* (London: Hamilton and Adams, 1830), p. 38. For background on Osgood see W. P. J. Millar, "The Remarkable Rev. Thaddeus Osgood: A Study in the Evangelical Spirit in the Canadas," *Histoire Sociale/Social History* 10(1977): 59–76.

59. Jones, *Life,* 147; Canada, *Treaties,* 1:47 (the provisional agreement of 17 October 1818).

60. Charles Fothergill, *Upper Canada Gazette and Weekly Register,* 2:56, quoted in Paul Martin Romney, "A Man out of Place: The Life of Charles Fothergill; Naturalist, Businessman, Journalist, Politician, 1782–1840" (Ph.D. thesis, University of Toronto, 1981), p. 262.

61. *History of the Town of Newmarket* [1969?], pp. 55–57. Hunter, *Simcoe County,* 2:1–12; John Corkery, "The Irish Immigrations," in *Kawartha Heritage,* ed. A. O. C. Cole and Jean Murray Cole (Peterborough: Peterborough Historical Atlas Foundation, 1981), p. 150.

62. *CA,* 23 September 1826; Peter Jones, "Conversion of the Rice Lake Indians," Anecdote Book, anecdote no. 18, PJC, VUL. William Case cites Peter Jones's memories of the introduction of Christianity among the Rice Lake Mississaugas in his *Jubilee Sermon Delivered at the Request of and before the Wesleyan Canada Conference, Assembled at London, C.W., June 6th 1855* (Toronto: G. R. Sanderson, 1855), pp. 23–25; Carroll, *Case,* 3:94–95 (Carroll mentions George Paudash's conversion at the meeting); William Case, letter, 18 January 1827, *CA,* 14 April 1827; George Copway, *The Life, History, and Travels of Kahgegagahbowh* (Albany: Weed and Parsons, 1847), pp. 74–75. George Copway is the "young witness" referred to at the end of this sentence.

63. Copway, *Life,* pp. 76–77.

64. William Case, letter, 16 January 1827, *CA,* 7 April 1827; William Case, letter, Belleville, 10 July 1827, in Osgood, *Visitor,* p. 43.

65. Jacobs, *Journal,* p. 2.

66. William Case, 4 July 1828, cited in "Genesee Conference Missionary Society," *CA,* 31 October 1828. The estimate of the total population of Indians in Upper Canada appears in L. Mudge, Civil Secretary, to Messrs. George Ryerson and F. Metcalfe, dated York, 16 July 1830, British Wesleyan Methodist Missionary Correspondence, box 14, file 88, no. 2, UCA. The estimate must have been made about 1830. Mudge committed suicide in early June 1831; see "Death of Mr. Mudge," *Canadian Freeman,* 16 June 1831.

67. Carroll, *Past and Present,* p. 59.

68. Jones, *Life,* p. 165.

69. Ibid., p. 166.

70. Ibid., pp. 275–76.

7. *Opposition*

1. Jones, *Life*, p. 104.

2. C. P. Stacey, *The Battle of Little York* (Toronto: Toronto Historical Board, 1977), pp. 13, 15. For a lively popular account of the "Capture of Little York" see Pierre Berton, *Flames across the Border, 1813–1814* (Toronto: McClelland and Stewart, 1981), pp. 37–61.

3. Edith G. Firth, ed., *The Town of York, 1815–1834* (Toronto: University of Toronto Press, 1966), p. lxxxii.

4. William Kilbourn includes a fine description of York in the mid-1820s in *The Firebrand: William Lyon Mackenzie and the Rebellion in Upper Canada* (Toronto: Clarke, Irwin, 1956), pp. 3–7. See also R. Louis Gentilcore, "Ontario Emerges from the Trees," *Geographical Magazine* 45 (1972–73): 387.

5. Peter Jones gives the population figures in "Report of the Select Committee to which was referred the petition of Buckley Waters and Others," in *The Journals of the House of Assembly, Upper Canada*, 9th Parliament, 4th Session, vol. 4, 15 January–25 March 1828 (hereafter cited as "Report of the Select Committee"). Peter Jones testified 23 February 1828. The size of Grape Island appears in "Schedule of Islands Claimed by the Band of Alnwick Indians," RG 10, 731:165, PAC.

6. For a reference to Givins as "the Wolf," see Minutes of a Council held with the Messessague Nation of Indians at the Garrison of York on Monday, 18 February 1820, RG 10, 790:124, PAC.

7. G. F. G. Stanley, "The Significance of the Six Nations Participation in the War of 1812," *Ontario History* 55(1963): 224; Firth, *Town of York, 1793–1815*, p. xc; E. S. Coatsworth, "When Muskoka Defended Toronto," *York Pioneer and Historical Society, Annual Report, 1954*, pp. 18–19. In Joseph Sawyer's record of baptism, CMCR, UCA, his mother's name is given as "Pakakis." Her name is transcribed as "Puhgashkish" in Peter Jones, *Life*, p. 5.

8. Stacey, *Battle*, pp. 17–22.

9. Jones, *Life*, pp. 82, 93, 177; Peter Jones, *Report of a Speech, Delivered by Kahkewaquonaby, the Indian Chief, in the Wesleyan Chapel, Stockton-on-Tees* (Stockton, England: John Beach, 1831), p. 5.

10. John Sunday cited in the Minutes of a Council held at the Post of York on 30 January 1828, RG 10, 791:102. An account of the speech also appears in Jones, *Life*, pp. 104–5.

11. Ryerson, "*Story*," p. 74 (Ryerson describes the physical appearance of Paudash); Jones, *Life*, pp. 77, 87.

12. Jones, *Life*, p. 105.

13. For James Ajetance's speech see Minutes of a Council held at the Post of York on 30 January 1828, RG 10, 791:105, and also Jones, *Life*, p. 105; Peter

Jones quoted in "Report of the Select Committee." Peter Jones's statement was made 23 February 1828 (see Jones, *Life,* p. 113).

14. Jones, *Life,* p. 106.

15. Sir Francis Bond Head to Lord Glenelg, Toronto, 5 May 1836, CO 42, 430:14.

16. J. Ross Robertson, *Landmarks of Toronto,* 6 vols. (Toronto: J. Ross Robertson, 1894), 1:2; William Halton to James Givins, BR, MTL (the letter gives the name of his home as "Pine Grove," where he died on 5 March 1846; see the Toronto *British Colonist,* 10 March 1846, p. 3).

17. "Statement of the losses sustained by Major Givins from the enemy on the capture of York, the 27th of April 1813," James Givins Papers, BR, MTL; Firth, *Town of York, 1793–1815,* pp. 301–2.

18. James Givins to Major Hillier, York, 28 March 1828, cited in Francis Michael Quealey, "The Administration of Sir Peregrine Maitland, Lieutenant-Governor of Upper Canada, 1818–1828" (Ph.D. thesis, University of Toronto, 1968), p. 325.

19. Quealey, "Maitland," p. 18.

20. Quealey, "Maitland," pp. 18–23; H. Manners Chichester, "Sir Peregrine Maitland," *Dictionary of National Biography,* 35:367–68. See also the recent sketch of Maitland by Hartwell Bowsfield in the *Dictionary of Canadian Biography,* vol. 8, 1851–1860 (Toronto: University of Toronto Press, 1985), pp. 596–605.

21. John Beverley Robinson, "Early Governors—Reminiscences," Toronto *Mail and Empire,* 23 March 1895, in *Kingsford Scrapbook,* 4:201, Ontario Archives.

22. Quealey, "Maitland," p. 106. Stacey quotes Strachan referring to Robinson as his adopted son in *Battle,* p. 14.

23. Firth, *Town of York, 1815–1834,* p. 17, n. 47; Robertson, *Diary of Mrs. John Graves Simcoe,* p. 304.

24. Jones, *Life,* pp. 75, 222.

25. Jones, *Life,* pp. 106–7; Peter Jones and John Strachan quoted in "Report of the Select Committee," 23 February 1828.

26. Jones, *Life,* p. 75.

27. H. M. Stephens, "Sir John Colborne," *Dictionary of National Biography,* 11:253–54.

28. John Colborne to Lt. General Sir James Kempt, York, 7 May 1829, CO 42, 388:277–79.

29. Davies, *Methodism,* p. 121; Davey, *Wesley,* pp. 33–34; French, *Parsons and Politics,* pp. 134–42. In 1820 the British Wesleyans had agreed to divide the work in the Canadas with the Methodist Episcopalians. The British Wesleyans would restrict their work to Lower Canada, leaving Upper Canada to the American-based Methodists; see French, *Parsons and Politics,* p. 73.

30. Peter Jones to Eliza Field Jones, Coldwater, 29 July 1835, Letter Book, PJC, VUL. (Here Peter explains that the Ojibwas called the chief's medals "hearts.") Jones, *Life*, p. 223.

31. Samuel Wahbeneeb quoted in Jones, *Life*, p. 223. His Indian name, Metwechings, appears in CMCR, UCA.

32. When Samuel Wahbeneeb himself became a chief in 1836 he was given "the Chief's Medal and flag"; Council Minutes, 1835–48, p. 22, RG 10, 1011, PAC.

33. Sir John Colborne quoted in Jones, *Life*, p. 227, entry for 26 June 1829.

34. Jones, *Life*, p. 277; entry for 25 June 1830.

35. Sir John Colborne to T. G. Anderson, Government House, 29 September 1830; W. H. Merritt Papers, package 6, Indian Affairs [T. G. Anderson], Ontario Archives.

36. James Currie, Mahjedusk Mission, 24 March 1830, CG, 3 April 1830; William Law to James Richardson, Whitchurch, 6 February 1831, CG, 14 March 1832; George Ryerson, CG, 17 July 1830.

37. Mrs. S. Rowe, "Anderson Record, from 1699 to 1896," OHSPR 6 (1905): 128–29.

38. William Law to James Richardson, Whitchurch, 6 February 1831, CG, 14 March 1832.

39. Samuel Rose to James Richardson, Narrows, Lake Simcoe, 4 February 1832, CG, 14 March 1832. For Egerton Ryerson's comments on T. G. Anderson's complicity, see Egerton Ryerson to James Givins, York, 9 March 1832, CG, 21 March 1832. Anderson apparently took over the Methodists' Coldwater school in 1832; see Gilbert Miller, Coldwater, 29 May 1837, CG, 14 June 1837.

40. Egerton Ryerson to Colonel Givins, York, 9 March 1832, CG, 21 March 1832: "I am aware that most of the Indian converts, on their first embracing christianity, have supposed that there was but one kind or denomination of christians."

41. Rev. John McIntyre to T. G. Anderson, Orillia, 26 September 1845, RG 10, 409:752–53, mfm C-9615, PAC. In 1845 the Indians used the term "queen's religion," Victoria having come to the throne in 1838.

42. Rev. Adam Elliot, Journal for July 1834, in W. J. D. Waddilove, ed., *The Stewart Missions: A Series of Letters and Journals* (London: J. Hatchard, 1838), p. 54.

43. For a review of Roman Catholic missionary work in the Upper Great Lakes, see Mary William Owen, "The establishment of the l'Arbre Croche Mission" (M.A. thesis, University of Notre Dame, 1950).

44. Olivier Maurault provides a short history of this important mission in "Les vicissitudes d'une mission sauvage," *Revue Trimestrielle Canadienne* 16(1930): 121–49.

45. John Sunday, Diary, 11 July 1831, CG, 29 October 1831.

46. *Annales de la Propagation de la Foi*, no. 16 (janvier 1829): 344.

47. T. G. Anderson to Colonel Givins, Drummond Island, 4 October 1827, RG 10, 499:31901, mfm c-13, 341, PAC.

48. Andrew J. Blackbird, *History of the Ottawa and Chippewa Indians of Michigan* (Harbor Springs, Mich.: Babcock and Darling, 1897), p. 46.

49. Ibid., p. 47.

50. A. C. Osborne, "The Migration of *Voyageurs* from Drummond Island to Penetanguishene in 1828," OHSPR 3(1901): 124, 138.

51. James Evans, St. Clair Wesleyan Mission, 8 August 1836, CG, 9 November 1836.

52. Peter Jones, Journal, Penetanguishene, 26 June 1830, CG, 31 July 1830.

53. Peter Jones, Penetanguishene, 12 July 1832, CG, 8 August 1832.

54. Jean Baptiste Otagaonini à Monsieur l'Eveque McDonnel, la Rivière froide 28 juillet 1832, in *The Archives: Roman Catholic Archdiocese of Toronto* on microfilm, Ontario Archives.

55. Jones, *Life*, p. 163.

56. Peter Jones to Eliza, Coldwater, 3 August 1835, Letter Book, PJC, VUL. This "grandmother" would be a second wife of Chief Wahbanosay. In the CMCR, UCA, the mother of Sarah Henry (Peter's mother) is listed as "Naishenum"—not "Pakakis" or "Puhgashkish"—the grandmother mentioned as having being killed at York (Jones, *Life*, p. 5) and who is given in the CMCR as Joseph Sawyer's mother.

57. Peter Jones recounts the incident in full in his *Life*, p. 167, entry for 15 August 1828; see also *History of the Town of Newmarket*, p. 67.

58. John Assance quoted in Jones, *Life*, p. 167.

59. Jones, *Life*, p. 237.

60. Jones, *History*, p. 208.

61. William H. Smith, *Smith's Canadian Gazetteer* (Toronto: H. and W. Roswell, 1846), p. 202.

62. Affidavits of John McDonald, January 1880; Louis Tromblay, 7 November [1880]; Kahpagishgo[quay], 3 December 1878; Lombard Yax, 7 November 1878; Eber Yax, 24 January 1880; in RG 10, 2022, file 8520, PAC.

63. Pazhekezhikquashkum quoted in Jones, *Life*, p. 246.

64. Heckewelder, *History*, p. 104.

65. Peter Jones fully describes the encounter in his *Life*, pp. 246–49.

66. Pazhekezhikquashkum quoted in Jones, *History*, p. 230.

67. Jones, *History*, p. 144.

68. Canadian, *Hamilton Spectator*, reprinted in the CG, 5 February 1862.

69. James Evans, St. Clair Mission, 2 March 1835, CG, 2 March 1835, CG, 18 March 1835.

70. James Evans, St. Clair, 17 March 1835, *CG,* 15 April 1835.

71. Jones, *Life,* p. 272, entry for 5 May 1830.

72. William Case, Grape Island, 10 May 1830, *CA,* 28 May 1830.

73. Jones, *Life,* p. 240.

74. Ibid., p. 268; Peter Jones, Anecdote Book, anecdote no. 11, PJC, VUL.

75. La Cloche, Hudson's Bay Company Post Journal, 1830–31, entry for 18 May 1831. H.B.C.A., P.A.M., B. 109/a/4 fols. 37, 47, Hudson's Bay Company Archives, Winnipeg. My thanks to Jim Morrison for this reference.

76. Of a Speech from the Chief, John Aisence to his Lordship Bishop McDonald [*sic*], Coldwater, 28 February 1832 in the *Courier,* 14 March 1832; Substance of a speech from the Chief John Aismer [Assance] to Bishop McDonnell, Coldwater, 28 February 1832, in *Canadian Freeman,* 5 April 1832; Lawrence A. Keeshig, "Historic Sketches of the Cape Croker Indians," *Canadian Echo* (Wiarton, Ontario), 8 January 1931. William Case contended that Kegadoons had drowned; see *CG,* 14 August 1833.

77. Jones, *History,* p. 147.

78. Peter Jones to Samuel Chubb, River Credit, 3 November 1829, Methodist Archives, John Rylands Library, Manchester, England.

8. Fund-Raising

1. For a description of New York in 1828, see James Stuart, *Three Years in North America,* 2 vols. (New York: J. J. Harper, 1833), 1:21–32. The population statistics appear on p. 24. The information on the blossom times on the lower Hudson River (at Newburgh, seventy-five kilometers north of New York) appears in E. M. Ruttenber, *History of Orange County, New York* (Philadelphia: 1881), p. 42.

2. G. P. Disoway, "Wesley Chapel or the Old John-Street Church," *CA,* 8 February 1833 (part 3 of a three-part series); Arthur Bruce Moss, *John Street Methodist Church, 44 John Street, New York, N.Y., Oldest Methodist Society in America, 1766–1966* (New York, 1966), pp. 1–7.

3. Ira Rosenwaike, *Population History of New York City* (Syracuse: Syracuse University Press, 1972), p. 33.

4. In 1831 A. R. M. Lower estimated that the population of Upper Canada was 250,000; see A. R. M. Lower, *Colony to Nation* (Toronto: Longmans, Green, 1946), p. 181.

5. Caroline D. Emerson, *Old New York for Young New Yorkers* (New York: E. P. Dutton, 1932), pp. 219–20.

6. Goddard, "Delaware," in *Northeast,* ed. Trigger, pp. 220–24.

7. D. G. Brinton, "Lenape Conversations," *Journal of American Folk-lore* 1(1888): 38.

8. Heckewelder, *History*, p. 142.

9. William C. Smith, "Francis Hall," in *Pillars in the Temple; or, Sketches of Deceased Laymen of the Methodist Episcopal Church* (New York: Carlton and Lanahan, 1872), pp. 100–104; "Francis Hall," *Appleton's Cyclopaedia of American Biography* 3(1888): 40.

10. D. M. Reese to the Corresponding Secretary of the Missionary Society of the Methodist E. Church, CA, 2 October 1835.

11. Jones, *Life*, p. 217; entry for 4 May 1829, "Missionary Meeting," CA, 15 May 1829. On Bangs see Carroll, *Case*, 1:27–32, 125, 272. The Reverend Bangs's reference to Augustus Jones appears in his *Authentic History of the Missions under the Care of the Missionary Society of the Methodist Episcopal Church* (New York: J. Emory, 1832), p. 183. A physical description of Bangs appears in Carroll, *Case*, 5:67.

12. "Tenth Annual Report of the Missionary Society of the Methodist Episcopal Church," CA, 15 May 1829; "Canada Missions," CA, 12 August 1831 (mentions the $700 annual grant).

13. Dale Van Every has provided a popularly written summary of Cherokee history in *Disinherited: The Lost Birthright of the American Indian* (New York: Avon Books, 1967), pp. 20, 48, 52, 87, 88. For a scholarly study of the Methodists' Cherokee missions see William G. McLoughlin, *Cherokees and Missionaries, 1789–1839* (New Haven: Yale University Press, 1984), pp. 164–79. McLoughlin (on p. 25 of his study) provides the missionaries' estimate that as many as one-quarter of the Cherokees had some white ancestry. For the Methodists and the Cherokees see also Wade Crawford Barclay, *Early American Methodism, 1762–1844*, 2 vols. (New York: Board of Missions and Church Extension of the Methodist Church, 1950), 2:126–34.

14. Jones, *History*, p. 187.

15. CMCR, UCA, entry under Catherine Brown Sunego. A biography exists of Catherine Brown; consult Rufus Anderson, *Memoir of Catherine Brown: A Christian Indian of the Cherokee Nation*, 2d ed. (Boston: Crocker and Brewster, 1825).

16. Jones, *Life*, p. 217, also p. 204 (for the children's routine); "Missionary Meeting," CA, 15 May 1829. The ages of several of the children appear in William Case, York, 11 February 1829, in CA, 6 March 1829. The complete hymn sung by the children appears in Maungwudaus, *An Account of the Chippewa Indians* (Boston: Published by the author, 1848), p. 14.

17. D. M. Reese in CA, 2 October 1835.

18. Robert Steinhauer to Mrs. J. J. Moore, dated Saddle Lake, 24 July 1931. Sheilagh Jameson Correspondence re: Steinhauer Family, Glenbow Museum Archives, Calgary, Alberta (D 266.3.J31). Robert Steinhauer was the son of Henry Steinhauer.

19. The portrait is now in the Art Department, Glenbow Museum, Calgary, Alberta. The oil painting bears an inscription by the artist.

20. Jones, *Life*, p. 217.

21. Jones, *Life*, pp. 204, 207, 210; Peter Jones to John Jones, New York, 17 March 1829, PJC, VUL.

22. Van Every, *Disinherited*, pp. 113–14.

23. Howard B. Furer, comp. and ed., *New York: A Chronological and Documentary History, 1524–1970* (Dobbs Ferry, N.Y.: Oceana Publications, 1974), pp. 21–24; Charles H. Haswell, *Reminiscences of an Octogenarian of the City of New York (1816 to 1860)* (New York: Harper, 1896), p. 237.

24. Jones, *Life*, p. 208, entry for 28 March 1829.

25. Jones, *Life*, p. 253 (he names the nine stations); editorial, *CG*, 27 March 1833; Acknowledgements of the receipts, *CA*, 9 February 1830, 26 March 1830. In June 1832 the dollar was exchanged at the rate of four dollars for one pound; *CG*, 20 June 1832.

26. Jones, *Life*, p. 56.

27. Jones, *Life*, p. 218.

28. Peter Jones quoted in the Rev. George Cookman's "Speech . . . April 19, 1830," *CA*, 21 May 1830.

29. Peter Jones to Eliza Case, Brantford, 28 October 1855, PJC, VUL.

30. Carroll, *Past and Present*, p. 226.

31. Jones briefly describes the wedding in his *Life*, p. 217. For a physical description of William Case see Carroll, *Past and Present*, p. 222; for one of Hetty Hubbard, see Carroll, *Case*, 3:228.

32. Solomon Waldron, "A Sketch of the Life, Travels and Labors," manuscript, p. 14, UCA.

33. Jones *Life*, p. 282.

34. Peter Jones, "Speech Delivered in the Brunswick Chapel, September the 27th," in *The Sermons and Speeches of the Rev. Peter Jones . . . Leeds, September the 25th, 26th, and 27th, 1831* (Leeds: H. Spink, 1831), p. 21. Peter wrote, "my circuit is about eight hundred miles long."

35. Jones, *Life*, p. 205.

36. Peter Jones, Private Journal, 13 September 1829 to 1 November 1829, manuscript, UCA.

37. Jones, *Life*, pp. 219–81; John Carroll describes the Indian preacher's outfit in *Past and Present*, p. 228.

38. The best visual description of Grape Island appears in the anonymous article "A Visit to the Mohawk and Missisaqui Indians," *Children's Friend* 14, no. 157 (January 1837); 8–14; see also Philander Smith, "Visit to Grape Island, Bay Quinty, Nov. 1830," *CG*, 27 November 1830. A good review of Grape Island's history is Terence T. Whyte, "Grape Island: Methodist Mis-

sionary Station, 1827–1837" (B.D. thesis, Emmanuel College, University of Toronto, 1965).

39. J. B. Benham chronicles the rigorous schedule in "Grape Island Mission, Grape Island, January 22, 1830," *CG*, 13 February 1830. The anonymous visitor to Grape Island states that the missionary blew the cow's horn; see "A Visit to the Mohawk and Missisaqui Indians," p. 12. Case always rose early according to Carroll, *Case*, 2:44.

40. W. Case, Grape Island, 27 December 1829, *CA*, 12 February 1830.

41. John Sunday, Report, translated by Peter Jones, 6 August 1830, *CG*, 30 October 1830. Peter Jones was so excited by John's tales of his journey that he stayed up to two o'clock in the morning of 20 October 1830, translating them into English; Jones, *Life*, p. 290.

42. Schedule of Islands Claimed by the Band of Alnwick Indians, Surveyed . . . October 2, 1861," RG 10, 731:165; Grape Island Lease, in Playter, *History*, p. 292.

43. Francis Hall, "Grape Island Mission," New York, 10 October 1828, *CA*, 24 October 1828; Peter Jones to Alfred Jones, Bristol, 17 May 1831, John Rylands Library, Manchester, England; Grape Island Lease, in Playter, *History*, p. 292.

44. Obituary, "Eliza Jane Hurlburt Case," *CG*, 16 January 1858. My thanks to William Lamb for this reference.

45. Jones, *Life*, p. 101.

46. An extract; Peter Jones to John Jones, dated Grape Island, 13 August 1830, PJC, VUL.

47. Jones, *Life*, p. 272, entry for 8 April 1830.

48. Ibid., pp. 284–86.

49. Jones, *Life*, p. 279, entry for 24 July 1830.

50. Extracts from letters received by the Treasurer of the New England Company from the Revd. Richard Scott, CO 42, 424:145–60.

51. Z. Paddock, "Appendix—Rev. William Case,: *Memoir of Rev. Benjamin G. Paddock* (New York: Nelson and Phillips, 1875), p. 327; Aaron Hurd to his father, Rice Lake, 23 April 1831, in Joseph Holdrich, *The Wesleyan Student; or, Memoirs of Aaron Haynes Hurd* (Middletown, Conn." E. Hunt, 1839), p. 42.

52. William Case to Peter Jones, Belleville, 26 February 1832, PJC, VUL.

53. The Tenth Annual Report of the Missionary Society of the Methodist Episcopal Church, *CA*, 15 May 1829, lists the income (year ending 30 April 1829) as $14,176.11, or roughly £3,500. Peter Jones lists the annual receipts for the British Wesleyan Missionary Society in *Life*, p. 296 (entry for 2 May 1831), as £50,017 18s. 8d.

54. Ryerson, "*Story,*" p. 76.

55. Jones, *History*, p. 208.

56. Jones, *Life*, p. 295.

57. Satz, *Indian Policy*, pp. 9, 31, 64–73.

58. Peter Jones, Kingston, Upper Canada, 23 August 1830, CA, 10 September 1830.

59. George Dewey Harmon, *Sixty Years of Indian Affairs, 1789–1850* (Chapel Hill: University of North Carolina Press, 1941), p. 366.

60. Thurman Wilkins, *Cherokee Tragedy: The Story of the Ridge Family and of the Decimation of a People* (New York: Macmillan, 1970), pp. 227, 241. My thanks to Marion McKenna of Calgary for referring me to this volume.

· 61. Jones, *Life*, p. 296; Peter Jones, Liverpool, 15 August 1831, CG, 1 October 1831; Robert Sears, *A New and Pictorial Description of England, Scotland, Ireland, Wales and the British Islands* (New York: Robert Sears, 1847), p. 270; Arthur Bryant, *English Saga (1840–1940)* (London: Collins, 1940), pp. 1–3.

62. Peter Jones, Liverpool, 15 August 1831, CG, 1 October 1831; Mrs. James Wood quoted in Jones, *History*, p. 22.

63. Bryant, *Saga*, pp. 3, 5; Peter Jones, Liverpool, 15 August 1831, CG, 1 October 1831.

64. "Wesleyan Methodist Missionary Society," CG, 15 July 1831.

65. Jones, *Life*, pp. 296–300; London *Times*, 13 May 1831 (gives the number at the London Missionary Society meeting).

66. Peter Jones to John Jones, Bristol, 30 May 1831, in CG, 6 August 1831.

67. Jones, *Life*, pp. 322, 325.

68. Peter Jones to John Jones, London, 30 December 1831, CG, 22 February 1832; Peter Jones to William Case, London, 13 February 1832, CG, 18 April 1832.

69. One of the best descriptions of his Indian costume appeared in *Felix Farley's Bristol Journal*, 28 May 1831. Also, see Thomas William Magrath to the Reverend Thomas Radcliff, Dublin, in *Letters*, ed. Magrath, p. 210.

70. Jones, *Life*, p. 347.

71. Peter Jones, Anecdote Book, anecdote no. 69 (the Saugeens), immediately below no. 69 (the description of hellfire); no. 44 (the comparison of prayer to an arrow—attributed to Bishop Hall), PJC, VUL.

72. Peter Jones to John Jones, Manchester, 3 October 1831, CG, 11 January 1832. Peter Jones described his illness as "an inflammation of the mucus [mucous] membrane," in a letter dated Liverpool, 15 August 1831, CG, 1 October 1831.

73. Jones, *Life*, p. 303. Thomas F. Gossett, *Race: The History of an Idea in America* (Dallas: Southern Methodist University Press, 1963), pp. 54–56, 67.

74. Jones, *Life*, pp. 314, 336–37 (Adam Clarke); p. 312 (Richard Watson); p.

330 (Samuel Drew); pp. 306–7, 315 (Hannah More). For a sketch of Clarke's life see Frederick Jeffrey, "Adam Clarke," in *The Encyclopedia of World Methodism*, ed. Nolan B. Harmon (Nashville: United Methodist Publishing House, 1974), 1:517–18. For information on More, consult Stephen Leslie, "Hannah More," *Dictionary of National Biography*, 38:414–19. References to Watson and Drew appear in John McLean, "Peter Jones: Kahkewaquonaby," *Indian*, 29 December 1886.

75. Jones, *History*, p. 98.

76. Peter Jones to the Editor of the *Christian Guardian*, London, 30 December 1831, *CG*, 22 February 1832.

77. Jones, *Life*, pp. 290, 295; "Chippewa Translations," *CG*, 11 January 1832.

78. Peter Jones to the Editor of the *Christian Guardian*, London, 30 December 1831, *CG*, 22 February 1832.

79. Peter Jones to the Editor of the *Christian Guardian*, Liverpool, 15 August 1831, *CG*, 1 October 1831.

80. Peter Jones, "Farewell Sermon, at City Road Chapel [London], April 7, 1832," *Wesleyan Preacher* 2(1832): 115.

81. Jones, *Life*, p. 324, entry for 23 November 1831. Three Burkites were executed in London early in 1832; see "Burkites," York *Canadian Freeman*, 16 February 1832.

82. Jones, *Life*, p. 308.

9. Eliza

1. Peter Jones to Eliza Field, River Credit, 6 May 1833, Letter Book, PJC, VUL.

2. Peter Jones, letter, Muncey Mission House, 6 February 1843, in *History*, p. 241.

3. Eliza's son, Dr. Peter E. Jones, still had this issue of the *Times* in 1899. He said it had been collected by his mother "when she was a girl." Catalogue of articles loaned to the Canadian Historical Exhibition by Dr. P. E. Jones, Hagersville, June 1899, Women's Canadian Historical Society of Toronto Collection, Ontario Archives. My thanks to Leon Warmski for this reference.

4. Aileen Denise Nash, *Living in Lambeth, 1086–1914* (London: Truslove and Bray, n.d.), pp. 57–58; Valentina Hawtrey, "Lambeth," in *The Victoria History of the County of Sussex*, ed. H. E. Malden, 4 vols. (London: Constable, 1912), 4:51–52.

5. For information on the Field family see Montague S. Giuseppi, "Industries," in *Victoria History of the County of Sussex*, 2:408. My thanks to Bernard ffield for forwarding me the Field family tree, prepared in the late

nineteenth century; P. E. Sangster provides the most complete summary of Rowland Hill's work in his "Life of the Reverend Rowland Hill (1744–1833) and His Position in the Evangelical Revival" (D. Phil. thesis, Oxford, 1964). Surrey Chapel could seat 2,500 people, and on special occasions 3,000 were packed in; Sangster, "Hill," pp. 132, 294.

6. J. Corbet Anderson, *The Great Northwood* (London: Blades, East and Blades, 1898), pp. 12–13; Alan R. Warwick, *The Phoenix Suburb: A South London Social History* (Richmond: Blue Boar Press, 1972), pp. 17, 99; F. H. W. Sheppard, ed., *Survey of London*, vol. 26, *The Parish of St. Mary Lambeth*, part 2, "Southern Area" (London: Athlone Press, 1956), p. 167.

7. Eliza Field, Diary for 1829, entry for 31 August 1829, PJC, VUL. Charles Field mentions the pony in a letter dated Holly Cottage, Norwood, 30 May 1826 to Eliza, then at Mrs. Stone's, High Street, Hastings, PJC, VUL. Holly Cottage is mentioned in Sheppard, *Survey of London*, vol. 26, part 2, p. 186.

8. Eliza Field's Album, in the possession of Arvilla Louise Thorp, Vancouver, contains a sketch of the "house in which I spent eight happy years as a schoolgirl at Peckham Surrey, England." Miss K. Brown ran the school. For references to Monsieur Bocquet, see Eliza's diary for 1832, entries for 8 May and 9 June. An attractive watercolor by her drawing master appears in the album. A brief sketch of M. Bocquet appears in E. Benezit, *Dictionnaire critique et documentaire des peintres, sculpteurs, dessinateurs et graveurs* (Librairie, 1948), 1:719. Eliza's visit to Gloucestershire is mentioned in her Diary for 1829; see entries for the period 25 April to 24 June. For the visit to Brighton and neighboring towns see the same diary, entries from 7 October to 3 December.

9. Eliza's Sunday school teaching is mentioned in her Notebook for 1823, entry for 21 November, and her Diary for 1832, entry for 11 March 1832. The references to her visits to a sick woman and her family in Lambeth Marsh appear in her Diary for 1832, entries for 28 March to 4 April, PJC, VUL.

10. Eliza Field, Notebook for 1823, entry for 11 January, PJC, VUL.

11. Robert Southey (1774–1843), quoted in James Sherman, *Memorial of the Rev. Rowland Hill, M.A.* (London: Charles Gilpin, 1851), pp. 24–25.

12. Ibid., pp. 146–48, 196–97, 247–49.

13. Eliza Field, Notebook for 1823, PJC, VUL. She later wrote above, "Rules of Daily Use" from "The Life of Mrs. John Bickerstith."

14. Eliza Field, Diary for 1829, entries for 16, 23, 25, 26, 27 October and 17 January 1829. Sketches of Theophilus Jones appear in Sangster, "Hill," p. 273, and Edwin Sidney, *The Life of the Rev. Rowland Hill*, 5th ed. (London: Wertheim, Macintosh and Hunt, 1861), p. 329.

15. Mrs. Woods's observations respecting Kahkewaquonaby during his visit at her house in the summer of 1831, PJC, VUL; also reprinted in Jones, *History*, pp. 22–23.

16. Sheffield *Courant*, 7 October 1831; Liverpool *Courier*, 31 August 1831; Halifax and Huddersfield *Express*, 10 September 1831.

17. Eliza Field's Album, in the possession of Arvilla Louise Thorp, Aldergrove, B.C.

18. Eliza Field, Diary for 1832, entry for 9 November (recalling a meeting with Peter at Lambeth exactly one year earlier), also entries for 2, 10, 11, 28, 29, 30, 31 January, 1, 2, 3, 4, 7, 10, 14 February, PJC, VUL; Jones, *Life*, pp. 324, 329.

19. Peter Jones to the Editor of the *Christian Guardian*, London, 30 December 1831, *CG*, 22 February 1832.

20. Eliza Field, Diary for 1833, entry for 10 January. Peter was at Lambeth that day. Eliza Field, Diary for 1832, entry for 10 January, PJC, VUL.

21. Eliza Field, Diary for 1832, entry for 28 January, PJC, VUL.

22. Peter Jones to the Editor of the *Christian Guardian*, London, 30 December 1831, *CG*, 22 February 1832; also reprinted in Jones, *History*, pp. 220–22, and introduced as a letter to his brother, John Jones.

23. Thomas Allen, *The History and Antiquities of the Parish of Lambeth* (London: Published for J. Allen, 1826), pp. 332–35. Eliza Field's Album, now in the possession of Arvilla Louise Thorp, Aldergrove, B.C., contains an engraving of Carlisle House taken from Allen's *Lambeth*. Eliza has written beneath the caption, "Where my dear father M. Charles Field went to school when kept by Mr. Gibson at the end of Royal Row where I was born." The building was torn down in 1827 and the site and grounds were covered with about eighty small houses; see Edward Wedlake Brayley, *A Topographical History of Surrey*, 5 vols. (London: David Bogue, 1848), the volume on Lambeth, pp. 336–37.

24. Giuseppi, "Industries," 2:402–9; *Still the Candle Burns* (London: Price's Patent Candle Company, 1947), pp. 16–17; Charles Booth, *Life and Labour of the People in London*, 2d ser., Industry, vol. 2 (London: Macmillan, 1903), pp. 112–15.

25. Jones, *Life*, p. 338, entry for 23 February 1832.

26. Eliza Field, Diary for 1833, entry for 14 February. For her father's reaction see Eliza's Diary for 1832, entries for 14 February to 15 March.

27. Charles Field to Eliza, then at Mrs. Stone's, High Street, Hastings, Holly Cottage, Norwood, 30 May 1826, PJC, VUL.

28. Apparently the Fields had at least four servants: see Eliza's Diary for 1832 entries for 29 and 30 May; and the Diary for 1838–39, entries for 11 August 1838 and 16 September 1838. Joe King, a servant, worked with Charles Field's family from age thirteen to seventy-seven—sixty-four years (see the entry for 11 August 1838, PJC, VUL). The family also had Ellen Lyons as a home governess; see note dated March 1833 in Peter Jones's Album, 1831–32, now in the possession of Arvilla Louise Thorp, Aldergrove, B.C.

29. Eliza Field, Diary for 1832, entries for 24 and 26 October, PJC, VUL.

30. Eliza Field, Diary for 1832, entries for 27 March, 18 and 24 July, 28 August, and 8 September; Diary for 1833, entries for 27 January, 4, 15, 17, 18, 20 February, 6 March, 29, 30 July, PJC, VUL.

31. Eliza Field, Diary for 1833, entry for 15 February 1833, PJC, VUL.

32. Basil Hall, *Travels in North America* (Graz, Austria: Akademische Druck- und Verlagsanstalt, 1965), 1:258.

33. Jones, *Life*, pp. 328–29, 336. He preached at Surrey Chapel on 1 and 29 January 1832.

34. Jones, *Life*, pp. 340–44; Eliza Field, Diary for 1832, entries for 4 and 6 April. The ring is mentioned in the will of Eliza Field Jones Carey, Surrogate Court, will no. 1433, Brantford, Brant County, 1891, Ontario Archives—"The ring with King William's likeness (presented to Mr. Jones at Windsor)."

35. *Post Office London Directory for 1832*, p. 136.

36. Jones, *Life*, p. 324. The Archives of Victoria University, University of Toronto, now owns the miniatures that Peter and Eliza selected to bring to Canada. On the back of the portrait of Peter the inscription reads, "Kahkewaquonaby or Revd. Peter Jones—Painted by Matilda Jones 8 Coleman Street London April 1832." I am indebted to Nesta Marshall, of Wellington, New Zealand, for the information on her great-grandaunt Matilda Jones (b. 1799, fl. 1826–43). Mrs. Marshall had in her possession the other portrait of Peter Jones completed by Miss Jones. In June 1833 the *Wesleyan-Methodist Magazine* (London, England) published an engraving of the Matilda Jones portrait selected by Peter and Eliza. Later three hundred prints of it were sent to Canada for distribution (Jones, *Life*, p. 356, entry for 23 November 1832), hence it has become the most widely used representation of Peter Jones. The earlier version retained by the artist (11.3 × 8.7 cm) is now in the National Gallery in Ottawa, and is signed, "M.J./1831."

37. J. G. Dowling, *The Effects of Literature upon the Moral Character: A Lecture Delivered at the Tolsey, Gloucester, September 19, 1839.* (London: J. G. F. and J. Rivington, 1840), p. 27. He repeated the same thoughts in a note (entry dated 17 December 1830) in Eliza Field's Album, in the possession of Arvilla Louise Thorp, Aldergrove, B.C. A sketch of J. G. Dowling (1805–41), appears in the *Dictionary of National Biography*, 5:1295–96.

38. Eliza Field, Diary for 1832, entry for 28 June, PJC, VUL. All the subsequent entries from Eliza's diaries are taken from this journal, or that for 1833, as specified.

39. "Romance in Real Life," New York *Commercial Advertiser*, 12 September 1833.

40. Eliza Field, Diary for 1833, entry for 5 September 1833, PJC, VUL.

41. Eliza Field, Diary for 1832, entry for 11 June 1832, PJC, VUL.

42. "Mrs. Peter Jones," New York *Sun*, 26 May 1837.

43. Eliza Field, Diary for 1833; entry for 15 August 1833, PJC, VUL.

44. New York *Commercial Advertiser,* 12 September 1833.

45. "A Romance in Real Life," reprinted in Brockville *Recorder,* 20 September 1833; Kingston *Chronicle and Gazette,* 21 September 1833; Hallowell *Free Press,* 23 September 1833; York *Patriot,* 27 September 1833; St. Catharines, *British Colonial Argus* 28 September 1833. My thanks to Michael Dicketts of the Kingston Public Library for the Kingston reference.

46. Kingston *Chronicle and Gazette,* 21 September 1833; "Kee-ka-kwon-a-by," *British Colonial Argus,* 28 September 1833; "Romance," York *Patriot,* 27 September 1833; Niagara *Gleaner,* 28 September 1833. Ironically, in the same issue the *Gleaner,* seemingly so liberal on the question of interracial marriages, applauded the decision of the British House of Commons to deny Jews the right to be elected to Parliament.

47. Eliza Field Jones, Diary for 1834–35, PJC, VUL.

48. Patrick Bell, Journal, 1833, copied from originals in the University of Aberdeen, Scotland, pp. 118–19, MG 24 H, PAC (my thanks to Bennett McCardle of Ottawa for this reference). For information on Patrick Bell (1799–1869), see the entry on him in the *Dictionary of National Biography,* 2:171–72, and in *Fasti ecclesiae Scoticanae* (rev. ed., 1915–61), p. 434. My thanks to Colin McLaren and Dorothy B. Johnson, Department of Special Collections, Aberdeen University Library, King's College, Aberdeen, Scotland, for helping me with the identification of Patrick Bell. Before his ordination Bell invented a reaping machine, one of the first in the world.

49. J. E. Alexander, *Transatlantic Sketches, Comprising Visits to the Most Interesting Scenes in North and South Americà, and the West Indies,* 2 vols. (London: Richard Bentley, 1833), 2:162. The word "martin" is spelled "marten" in the original. I have corrected it since the bird is no doubt the purple martin. I am indebted to Mairi Babey of Calgary for this identification.

50. This quotation appears at the end of the Diary for 1833, as an appendix; see p. 137, PJC, VUL.

51. The seating arrangement in the Credit Chapel is explained by a Quaker visiter, Thomas Shillitoe, in his *Journal,* 2 vols. (London: Harvey and Darton, 1839), 2:199–200, entry for 13 January 1827; Francis Hall, Trafalgar, Upper Canada, 18 August 1828, CA, 5 September 1828.

52. [Eliza Jones], *Memoir of Elizabeth Jones, a Little Indian Girl, Who Lived at the River Credit Mission, Upper Canada* (London: John Mason, 1838), p. 20.

53. William Lyon Mackenzie, December 1830, reprinted in *Documentary History of Education in Upper Canada,* 28 vols. (Toronto, 1894–1910), 2:122.

54. Peter used Ojibwa words in many of his letters to Eliza; for examples,

see his Letter Book, PJC, VUL, for the letters of 1 June, 7 July, 16 July 1837, 4, 6, 21 April 1838, 31 January 1839, 26 January 1841, 23 October 1845, and 11 February 1846.

55. Catherine Sutton to Mrs. Peter Jones, Sah Keeng [Owen's Sound], 26 March 1847, PJC, VUL.

56. Eliza used her Indian name Ke-che-ah-gah-me-qua as her signature for her *Sketch of the Life of Captain Joseph Brant, Thayendanegea* (Montreal: Dougall, 1872). Her son Charles Jones translated the name in his letter to Lyman Draper, Brantford, 6 September 1877, Draper Papers, Joseph Brant, 13F6, Wisconsin Historical Society, Madison, Wisconsin.

57. Eliza Jones, Diary for 1834–35, entries for 1, 30 June and 13 July 1834 and 22 August and 6 September 1835; William Case to James Evans, Credit, 17 December 1834, James Evans Papers, University of Western Ontario, microfilm copy, Glenbow Museum, Calgary; Eliza Jones, Diary for 1845, entry for 21 August 1836, reads, "our second child born dead."

58. Eliza Jones, Diary for 1834–35, entry for 23 February 1835, PJC, VUL.

59. A quotation taken from p. 2 of the fragment of a manuscript by Eliza Jones describing a fall trip to the Niagara peninsula, probably written in 1835(?), PJC, VUL.

10. "All Out of Tune"

1. Holdrich, *Wesleyan Student*, p. 104.

2. Egerton Ryerson, "Brief Sketch of the Life, Death, and Character of the late Rev. Peter Jones," *CG*, 23 July 1856.

3. Peter Jones to Eliza Field, River Credit, 1 May 1833, Letter Book, PJC, VUL.

4. *CG*, 29 October 1831; Jones, *Life*, p. 330, entry for 12 January 1832; Peter Jones to John Jones, London, 14 January 1832, in *CG*, 30 May 1832.

5. "Ke-ke-kwa-quonaby!" York *Courier*, 6 June 1832.

6. In Upper Canada the Brockville *Recorder* (20 September 1833) and the Kingston *Chronicle and Gazette* (21 September 1833) reprinted the article, "Romance in Real Life," which had originally appeared in the New York *Commerical Advertiser* (12 September 1833); the St. Catharines *British Colonial Argus* reprinted the same article, "Romance in Real Life" from the New York *Spectator*.

7. Peter Jacobs, "Speech of Pah-tah-se-gay," *CG*, 12 July 1843.

8. A sketch of "Nicholas Patrick Stephen Wiseman," by Charles Kent, appears in the *Dictionary of National Biography*, 62:243–46. The actual passage cited in the quotation appears in Nicolas Wiseman, *Lectures on the Principal Doctrines and Practices of the Catholic Church, Delivered at St.*

Mary's Moorfields, during the Lent of 1836 (London: Joseph Booker, 1836), pp. 192–93. In her miscellaneous papers, PJC, VUL, Eliza's transcription appears under the entry "Testimony of Cardinal Wiseman as to the usefulness of my dear husband. Extract from Cardinal Wiseman's VI lecture on Catholic Doctrine, vol. 1, page 192."

9. Carroll, *Case*, 3:416–17.

10. See Case's statement in *Miss. Soc. Report*, 1847–48, p. xxii: "To the Indians we preach twice on the Lord's day, once in the English, and generally once through the medium of an Interpreter."

11. Green, *Life and Times*, p. 54, entries for 11, 16, 17 October 1824.

12. The Reverend Fitch Reed, quoted in 1820 in Carroll, *Case*, 2: 354.

13. Eliza Jones, Diary for 1833, entry for 16 September 1833, PJC, VUL.

14. Eliza Jones, Diary for 1833, entry for 2 February 1834, in the Diary's appendix, pp. 120–21; see also 28 September, 10 October, 3 and 10 November 1833, PJC, VUL.

15. Eliza Jones, Diary for 1833, entry for 7 February 1834, in the appendix, p. 121, PJC, VUL.

16. Eliza Jones, Diary for 1833, entry for 16 September 1833, PJC, VUL.

17. Peter Jones to Eliza Jones, Coldwater, 12 August 1835, Letter Book, PJC, VUL.

18. [Eliza Jones], *Memoir of Elizabeth Jones*, p. 17.

19. Carroll, *Case*, 3:30, 62; also see several of the letters from Case to Jones reprinted in this volume, pp. 151–54, 230–31, 317–19, 322–24. Before his missionary tour to Lake Huron in the summer of 1829 Case even went to the extreme of warning him: "Be careful of your health, and be cautious, especially, to dry after getting wet"; see Case to Jones, Grape Island, 13 June 1829, in Carroll, *Case*, 3:231.

20. Jones, *History*, pp. 383–84, entry for 12 July 1837.

21. Egerton Ryerson Young, *The Apostle of the North Rev. James Evans* (Toronto: William Briggs, 1900), pp. 9–36; James Evans, "St. Clair, March 17, 1835," CG, 15 April 1835 (he mentions his first sermon in Ojibwa).

22. James Evans, *The Speller and Interpreter, in Indian and English, for the Use of the Mission Schools, and Such as May Desire to Obtain a Knowledge of the Ojibway Tongue* (New York: D. Fanshaw, 1837), p. 4. A century and a half later there still is no universally accepted system of transcribing Ojibwa words into English.

23. William Case to James Evans, 20 January 1836, with note dated 21 January 1836, James Evans Papers, University of Western Ontario, microfilm copy, Glenbow Museum, Calgary.

24. Peter Jones, Anecdote Book, PJC, VUL. Me-ge-sun-e-nee-seh, "the king bird," was a name given to Joseph Stinson by John Sunday.

25. Joseph Stinson to James Evans, Kingston, 22 March 1836, James Evans Papers, University of Western Ontario, microfilm copy, Glenbow Museum, Calgary.

26. Eliza Jones, Diary for 1834–35, entry for 26 August 1834, PJC, VUL; Augustus Jones, Cold Springs, Grand River, to William Hepburn, 12 January 1835, RG 10, vol. 107, file January 1835, PAC; Augustus Jones to G. H. Markland and W. Hepburn, 8 June 1835, RG 10, vol. 107, file "1835, 1 June–22 June," PAC. Eliza Jones in Jones, *Life*, p. 380, entry for 18 November 1836; Augustus Jones died on 16 November 1836.

27. Henry Jones to William McDougall, Supt. Gen. Indian Affairs, Grand River, Hartford P.O., 18 March 1863, RG 10, vol. 1974, file 5620/1, PAC. Joseph Jones later married Catherine Jackson, a Credit Indian woman, CMCR, UCA.

28. Jones, *Life*, entry for 24 August 1832; Peter Jones to British and Foreign Bible Society, York, 28 February 1833, British and Foreign Bible Society, London, England.

29. Craig, *Upper Canada*, pp. 33, 12.

30. Petition of Tyantenagen, i.e. John Jones and Kagawakanaby, i.e., Peter Jones to Sir Peregrine Maitland, Grand River, 8 August 1825, Lieutenant-Governor's Correspondence, RG 7, G 14, 2:992, PAC.

31. John Jones to James Givins, Port Credit, 22 February 1837, Upper Canada Land Petitions, "J" Bundle, no. 34, RG 1, L 3, 260, PAC.

32. John Strachan, in Council, 21 February 1833, note written on the Petition of Joseph Sawyer, John Crane to Sir John Colborne, Upper Canada Land Petitions, "I–J" Bundle, 17, no. 46, RG 1, L 3, 259, PAC.

33. Manuscript Diary of Peter Jones, August 23–September 19 1828, entry for 3 September 1828, PJC, VUL.

34. Council, 2–3 March 1835, Minutes, 1835–48, pp. 10–11, RG 10, 1011, Council, PAC.

35. (Copy) Peter Jones to Sir Francis Bondhead, 30 April 1836, RG 10, vol. 2226, file 43, 957, pt. 4, mfm C-11183, PAC; marked "granted." The original document, endorsed 9 May 1836 by James Givins, is in the Upper Canada Land Petitions, "I–J" Bundle 19, no. 44, PAC. John had not received his grant at the moment of his petition to James Givins, dated Port Credit, 22 February 1837, Upper Canada Land Petitions, "J" Bundle 20, no. 34, RG 1, L 3, 260, PAC, but Peter Jones referred to John's grant in a Council, 3 October 1842; Council Minutes, 1835–48, p. 119, RG 10, 1011, PAC. John received his land between 1837 and 1842.

36. Peter Jones quoted in Council, 3 October 1842, Council Minutes, 1835–48, p. 119, RG 10, 1011, PAC.

37. Testimony of David Sawyer, given 6 February 1888, RG 10, vol. 2238, file 45, 742, PAC.

38. Jones, *Life*, p. 356, entry for 25 December 1832.

39. Council, 6 June 1836; Council Minutes, 1835–48, p. 34, RG 10, 1011, PAC.

40. For a list of the prominent members of the Herkimer party see Petition of Lawrence Herkimer to S. P. Jarvis, River Credit Mission, 5 July 1843, RG 10, vol. 132, file H (1-811), PAC. For information on the members of the Jones party: James Chechalk married Peter Jones's sister Catherine, the widow of James Cameron, who had died in 1828; CMCR, UCA. John Peter's full name was "John Peter Anchechak; CMCR, UCA. Peter Jones stated his trust in James Young in a letter to James Evans, Credit Mission, 18 April 1840, in Carroll, *Case*, 4:275.

41. Council, 6 June 1836; Council Minutes, 1835–48, p. 34, RG 10, 1011, PAC. *Miss. Soc. Report*, 1861–62, p. xviii, states that "Betsey Tobeco" was a sister of the Reverend W. Herkimer. CMCR, UCA, contains the following baptismal entry for James Tobico: "James Tobicoo son of John and Betsey Tobecoo was born at York in the year 1816."

42. Slight, *Researches*, pp. 152–53; Jones, *History*, p. 236. Memorandum for Mr. Hepburn, by Mr. Gifford, Indian Affairs, probably written in 1836, W. Dummer Powell Collection, BR, MTL; Joseph Sawyer, Peter Jones, John Jones, Chiefs to Sir George Arthur, River Credit, 7 May 1839, Letter Book, 1825–42, p. 163, RG 10, 1011, PAC; Benjamin Slight, Diary, vol. 1, entry for 30 August 1837, UCA.

43. Ryerson, "*Story*," p. 70, entry for 15 April 1827. For an interesting article on cultural persistence among the Ojibwas, see A. I. Hallowell, "Some Psychological Characteristics of the Northeastern Indians," in "Man in Northeastern North America," ed. Frederick Johnson, *Papers of the Robert S. Peabody Foundation for Archaeology* 3 (1946): 195–225.

44. James Richardson quoted in Thomas Webster, *Life of Rev. James Richardson: A Bishop of the Methodist Episcopal Church in Canada* (Toronto: J. B. Magurn, 1876), p. 116.

45. Peter Jones to Eliza Jones, Credit, 23 September 1837, Letter Book, PJC, VUL; Jones, *Life*, p. 352, entry for 24 July 1832.

46. The division of the numbers in these three groups, of course, is only an approximation. One can reach an estimate of the number of "traditionalists" in this manner: At the beginning of the 1830s nearly all the adults, roughly one-half of the total population of the mission (110 out of 220 persons), were church members (*Miss. Soc. Report*, 1829–31, p. 6). By the late 1830s, however, only approximately 70 to 75 remained on the register (*Miss. Soc. Report*, 1836, p. 13; Benjamin Slight quoted in a letter from the Reverend Joseph Stinson, Kingston, 5 April 1838; CO 42, 453:334; *Miss. Soc. Report*, 1839, p. 19). Since the band's population stayed roughly the same, one can state that

one-third of the adults had left the church by 1840. It is more difficult to arrive at an accurate estimate of the "moderates" and the "reformers." In the late 1830s (this can be determined from the numerous petitions of the band to the government) all three chiefs belonged to the "reform" group: Joseph Sawyer, Peter Jones, and John Jones. Their group must have been the largest of the three at the Credit, for they controlled the elective offices.

47. *Miss. Soc. Report,* 1829, p. 3.

48. Copway, *History,* p. 260.

49. Jones, *History,* p. 97.

50. Peter Jones, *Report of a Speech Delivered by Kahkewaquonaby, the Indian Chief, in the Wesleyan Chapel, Stockton-on-Tees, September 20th, 1831* (Stockton, England: J. Beach 1831), p. 10.

51. *CG,* 10 April 1830.

52. This example is taken from a young white schoolteacher's report on his school at Fond du Lac, at the western end of Lake Superior; see Edmund F. Ely to David Greene, 31 December 1835, American Board of Commissioners for Foreign Missions, MS. 74, no. 110 A.L.S., typescript in the Grace Lee Nute Papers, CBX.9 N976, box 4, Minnesota Historical Society, St. Paul, Minnesota. This is a fascinating letter pointing out the problems faced by a non-Indian teaching Ojibwa children.

53. Peter Jones to the Hon. Commissioners appointed to enquire into Indian Affairs, Muncey Mission House, 21 November 1842, in *History,* p. 276.

54. Peter Jones, "Memorandum, Thoughts on Indian Schools, delivered at Toronto—February 1835," Sermons and Addresses, PJC, VUL.

55. Peter Jones to James Evans, Credit Mission, 18 April 1840, in Carroll, *Case,* 4:275.

56. *Miss. Soc. Report,* 1840–41, p. 9.

57. CMCR, UCA, entries for "John Quenibinaw" and "Joseph Quinibina"; Jones, *History,* pp. 197–98; "Joseph Quenebenaw's happy death," Peter Jones, Anecdote Book, anecdote no. 16, PJC, VUL.

58. John Summerfield, *Sketch of Grammar of the Chippeway Language, to Which is Added a Vocabulary of Some of the Most Common Words, by John Summerfield, alias Sahgahgewagahbaweh* (Cazenovia: J. F. Fairchild and Son, 1834); Copway, *History,* p. 127; B. M. Hall, *The Life of John Clark* (New York: Carlton and Porter, 1857), p. 162; Jones, *Life,* pp. 376–77, entry for 1 August 1836. The Ojibwa origin of the name Menominee appears in Louise S. Spindler, "Menominee," in *Northeast,* ed. Trigger, p. 723.

59. CMCR, UCA, entry for "William Willson"; Jones, *History,* p. 191; George Dickson and G. Mercer Adam, comps. and eds., *A History of Upper Canada College, 1829–1892* (Toronto: Roswell and Hutchinson, 1893), pp.

297, 295; William Wilson to Egerton Ryerson, Cobourg Academy, 5 March 1838, Ryerson Papers, UCA.

60. Jones, *History,* p. 224, CMCR, UCA.

61. [Eliza Jones], *Memoir of Elizabeth Jones,* p. 13.

62. Jones, *History,* p. 224.

63. David Sawyer to Henry Snake, Muncey Town, 24 August 1835, James Evans Papers, University of Western Ontario, microfilm copy, Glenbow Museum, Calgary.

64. "Mrs. Joseph Sawyer," Peter Jones, Anecdote Book, no number, PJC, VUL; Jones, *Life,* p. 367; "D. S. Praying over his penitent father," Peter Jones, Anecdote Book, anecdote no. 3, PJC, VUL; Peter Jones to Eliza Jones, 4 June 1837, Letter Book, PJC, VUL.

65. Barclay, *Early American Methodism,* 2:132–33.

66. John Walker, "From the Argentine Plains to Upper Canada, Sir Francis Bond Head: Gaucho Apologist and Costumbrist of the Pampa," *North South: Canadian Journal of Latin American and Caribbean Studies* 9 (1980): 103–6.

67. Sir Francis Bond Head to Lord Glenelg, Toronto, 20 November 1836, CO 42, 431:263.

68. Anna Jameson, *Winter Studies and Summer Rambles in Canada,* 3 vols. (London: Saunders and Otley, 1838), 1:153. For a good summary of the lieutenant governor see Ged Martin, "Sir Francis Bond Head: The Private Side of a Lieutenant-Governor," *Ontario History* 73, no. 3 (1981): 146–69. A portrait appears on p. 148 and a reference to his gray hair on p. 146.

69. Sir Francis Bond Head to Lord Glenelg, Toronto, 20 November 1836, CO 42, 431:268. John Leslie provides a short overview of early Canadian Indian policy in "Buried Hatchet: The Origins of Indian Reserves in Nineteenth Century Ontario," *Horizon Canada* 4, no. 40 (1985): 944–49.

70. Peter Jones felt they had advanced well at Coldwater; Peter Jones to Eliza Jones, Lake Simcoe, 10 July 1834, Letter Book, PJC, VUL; Jones, *Life,* p. 384, entry for 24 July 1837.

71. Joseph Sawyer, quoted in Slight, *Researches,* p. 111.

72. Speech of Colonel Simcoe to the Western Indians, Navy Hall, 22 June 1793; *Simcoe Papers,* ed. Cruikshank, 1:364.

73. James Givins to Lieut. Col. Napier, sec. for Indian Affairs, Quebec, 20 August 1836, Chief Superintendent's Office Letter Book, 20 January 1835–10 April 1837, RG 10, 501:177, mfm C-13342, PAC.

74. James Evans, St. Clair, 24 March 1838, CG, 11 April 1838.

75. Thomas Hurlburt, St. Clair, 22 October 1858, CG, 3 November 1858. Peter Jones states that Thomas Hurlburt could preach a sermon in Ojibwa as early as May 1835; see *Life,* p. 373, entry for 30 May 1835.

76. Peter Jones to Lord Goderich, Colonial Secretary, London, 26 July 1831, CO 42, 395:259.

77. Peter Jones to John Sunday, 9 December 1836, translated from the Ojibwa to English by John Sunday, quoted in Irish University Press Series of British Parliamentary Papers; Report from the Select Committee on Aborigines (British Settlements) with Minutes of Evidence, Appendix, and Index, Anthropology Aborigines 2 (Shannon, Ireland: Irish University Press, 1968), p. 28.

78. Robert Harrison, "Sir Augustus Frederick d'Este (1794–1848)," *Dictionary of National Biography* 5:867–868; G. E. H. Foxon, "Thomas Hodgkin, 1798–1866: A Biographical Note," *Guy's Hospital Reports* 115 (1966): 243–61.

79. Lawrence and William Herkimer's signatures appear on the Credit River Indians' petition to Queen Victoria, dated 4 October 1837; see Jones, *History*, p. 267.

80. Sir Francis Bond Head to Lord Glenelg, Toronto, 18 October 1837, CO 42, 439:271.

81. Glenelg and Peter met on 3 March 1838; see Jones, *Life*, p. 395. Bond Head left York on 23 March 1838; see Martin, "Private Side," p. 163.

82. Jones, *Life*, p. 395, entry for 3 March 1838.

83. This quotation actually comes from a letter written three days later, but no doubt Peter Jones expressed the same sentiments to Lord Glenelg on 3 March. Peter Jones to Lord Glenelg, London, 6 March 1838, CO 42, 453:321.

84. Eugene Stock, *The History of the Church Missionary Society: Its Environment, Its Men and Its Work* (London: Church Missionary Society, 1899), 1:256.

85. Lord Glenelg quoted in Peter Jones, Muncey Mission, 25 October 1843, *Miss. Soc. Report*, 1842–43, p. 6.

86. Dispatch of Lord Glenelg to Sir George Arthur, 28 March 1838, in Jones, *History*, pp. 261–62.

87. Jones, *Life*, pp. 396–404; Falmouth *Packet*, 7 April 1838 (Penzance); Cornwall *Royal Gazette*, 6 April 1838 (St. Ives). Eliza Jones, Diary for 1838–39, entries for 6 May 1838 (Bristol) and 20 May 1838 (Leeds).

88. Peter Jones to Eliza Jones, Falmouth, 6 April 1838, PJC, VUL.

89. This comical scene is fully described in Jones, *Life*, pp. 405–6. Kathleen V. Moore has written a short version of the incident, "Young Indian Chief Proved Outstanding Methodist Preacher," London *Free Press*, 4 February 1956.

90. Over five years later Peter still loved to tell of his audience with the queen: "He delights frequently to revert to this honour, and relates with extreme minuteness and amusing simplicity the details of the ceremony; the

humour with which he does this forming a singular contrast to his general austere and dignified bearing"; James R. Brown, *Views of Canada and the Colonists* (Edinburgh: Adam and Charles Black, 1844), p. 15. Peter Jones also spoke of the audience with the queen at Sault Ste. Marie in 1852; see the entry for 12 July 1852 in Peter Jones, "Missionary Tour to Lake Huron and Superior," *CG*, 25 August 1852.

91. Jones, *Life*, pp. 316, 346, entries for 17 August 1831 and 19 April 1832. The travel time appears in Patrick Shirriff, *A Tour through North America* (New York: Benjamin Blom, 1971; first published 1835), p. 2, entry for 22 April 1833.

92. Jones, *Life*, p. 405, entry for 14 September 1838.

93. Jones, *Life*, p. 399, entry for 11 May 1838. Catherine Sunego is mentioned in Jones, *Life*, pp. 382, 389.

94. Jones, *Life*, p. 394, entry for 12 February 1838; Sir Augustus d'Este to Thomas Hodgkin, Friday, 15:13:27–28, Papers of Thomas Hodgkin, microfilm copies on deposit at the Countway Library, Harvard Medical School, Boston. The citation refers to the reel and item as cataloged under the direction of Dr. Edward H. Kass, Channing Laboratory, Harvard Medical School. The first nineteen reels of the Hodgkin Papers in the same order are also on deposit at Friends' House Library, London, where they are numbered MS. 178 to MS. 196. My thanks to Amalie M. Kass of Boston for this reference.

95. For one example, see Eliza Jones, Diary for 1838–39, entries for 18, 22, 24 May 1838, PJC, VUL.

96. Jones, *Life*, p. 396, entry for 21 March 1838. On the Duke of Sutherland, consult Brian Masters, *The Dukes* (London: Blond and Briggs, 1975), pp. 329–35.

97. Peter Jones recalls the visit in a letter, dated Muncey Mission, 25 April 1843, *CG*, 10 May 1843.

98. For a review of Maconse, or Francis Estonoquot's, life see John Sturm, "A Farewell to Anchor Bay: History of Bay Area Indian tribes," *Anchor Bay Beacon*, 24 March 1982; Joseph Romig, "The Chippewa and Munsee (or Christian Indians) of Franklin County, Kansas," Kansas State Historical Society *Collections* 11(1909–10): 314–23; Joseph B. Herring, "The Chippewa and Munsee Indians: Acculturation and Survival in Kansas, 1850–1870," *Kansas History* 6(1983): 212–20.

99. "Death and Funeral of the Wife of the Michigan Chief," London *Times*, 22 January 1835; "Funeral of the Chippewa Indian," London *Times*, 11 February 1835; "The Indian Chief," London *Times*, 26 March 1835. "Police Intelligence. Mansion-House. The Indian Chief," London *Evening Chronicle*, 14 April 1835. My thanks to Ken Thomas for this reference.

100. Thomas Hodgkin to Friend, no date, 19:6:10–13, Papers of Thomas Hodgkin; microfilm copies on deposit at the Countway Library, Harvard Medical School, Boston. My thanks to Amalie M. Kass for this reference.

101. Thomas Hodgkin to Ephrain Evans, 25 June 1835, James Evans Papers, University of Western Ontario; Jones, *Life*, p. 394, entry for 7 February 1838. Later Peter must have learned that Maconse was the brother-in-law of Chief Wawanosh of St. Clair—Wawanosh's wife being Maconse's sister; William Jones to James Givins, St. Clair, 21 September 1835, Letter Book of William Jones, Indian Agent, Ontario Archives.

102. Robert Harrison, "Sir Augustus Frederick d'Este (1794–1848)," in *Dictionary of National Biography*, 5:868; Samuel Eliot Morison, *The Oxford History of the American People*, 3 vols. (New York: New American Library, 1972), 2:126.

103. Richard Drinnon, *White Savage: The Case of John Dunn Hunter* (New York: Schocken Books, 1972), pp. 6–9, 34, 147, 261.

104. John Hodgkin to Thomas Hodgkin, Tottenham, 22 April 1824, 14:44:91:94, Papers of Thomas Hodgkin, microfilm copies on deposit at the Countway Library, Harvard Medical School, Boston. My thanks to Amalie M. Kass for this reference.

105. *The First Annual Report of the Society for Promoting Education and Industry among the Indians and Destitute Settlers in Canada* (London: J. Hatchard, 1826) p. 3. My thanks to Tony Hall, Laurentian University, Sudbury, Ontario, for this reference.

106. Jones, *History*, p. 204. Peter Jones has taken the speech from the version printed in William L. Stone, *Life of Joseph Brant–Thayendenegea*, 2 vols. (New York: Alexander V. Blake, 1838), 1:46. The exclamation mark at the end of the passage does not appear in Stone's citation. For a discussion of the Logan speech see Edward D. Seeber, "Critical Views of Logan's Speech," *Journal of American Folklore* 60(1947): 130–46.

107. The Murray family was very close; see Mollie Gillen, *Royal Duke: Augustus Frederick, Duke of Sussex (1773–1843)* (London: Sidgwick and Jackson, 1976), p. 199. Charles Augustus Murray was the second son of the fifth earl of Dunmore; see "Sir Charles Murray's Adventures with the Pawnees," *Cornhill Magazine*, n.s., 3 (July–December 1897): 638.

108. Eliza Field Jones, Diary, 22 March–20 September 1838, entry for 13 September 1838, PJC, VUL.

109. Jones, *Life*, pp. 393, 394, 396, 400; Donald B. Smith, "Historic Peace-Pipe," *Beaver* 315, no. 1 (Summer 1984): 4–7.

110. Augustus d'Este to Kakiwequonabi, 19 September 1838, PJC, VUL.

111. Peter Jones to Robert Alder, Toronto, 13 February 1840, Wesleyan Methodist Church, Missions, box 24, file 168, UCA.

112. Copway, *Life*, p. 31: "The oil of the bear is used for various purposes. One use is, to prevent the falling out of the hair."

113. Peter Jones to Robert Alder, Niagara, 17 December 1838, in *Wesleyan Missionary Notices* 11 (1839): 29.

114. Satz, *Indian Policy*, p. 101.

115. Peter Jones to Lord Glenelg, Upper Lambeth Marsh, 13 September 1838, CO 42, 453:336.

11. Land and Education

1. Jones, *History*, p. 119. The council is described on pp. 114–28 of the *History*. For the manuscript account (which is more complete), see the Council Minutes, 1835–48, pp. 72–104, RG 10, 1011. Peter mentioned the number attending in the *Banner* (Aberdeen, Scotland), 15 August 1845.

2. Lewis H. Morgan, *League of the Ho-de-no-san-nee or Iroquois* (New York: Dodd, Mead, 1901), vol. 2, appendix B, sect. 62, p. 232, cited in Hartley Burr Alexander, *The World's Rim: Great Mysteries of the North American Indians* (Lincoln: University of Nebraska Press, 1967; first published 1953), p. 5.

3. The population of Upper Canada is taken from J. M. S. Careless, *The Union of the Canadas: The Growth of Canadian Institutions, 1841–1857* (Toronto: McClelland and Stewart, 1967), p. 4. The estimate of the Indian population appears in Anthony J. Hall, "The Red Man's Burden: Land, Law, and the Lord in the Indian Affairs of Upper Canada, 1791–1858" (Ph.D. thesis, University of Toronto, 1984), pp. 207–9.

4. Peter Jones certainly would have known of the atrocities, for as Eliza later wrote, "He was well informed on all the great events of the day"; see Jones, *Life*, p. 423. Francis Paul Prucha, *The Great Father: The United States Government and the American Indians*, 2 vols. (Lincoln: University of Nebraska Press, 1984), 1:240.

5. Francis Paul Prucha, *Indian Policy in the United States: Historical Essays* (Lincoln: University of Nebraska Press, 1981), pp. 7–8; Prucha, *Father*, 1:241; Satz, *Indian Policy*, p. 101.

6. Jones, *History*, p. 240.

7. Kelsay, *Brant*, p. 370; James A. Clifton, *A Place of Refuge for All Time: Migration of the American Potawatomi into Upper Canada 1830 to 1850* (Ottawa: National Museums of Canada, 1975), p. 70. Details on Maconse's westward migration are contained in Joseph Romig, "The Chippewa and Munsee (or Christian) Indians of Franklin Country, Kansas," Kansas State Historical Society *Collections* 11 (1909–10): 314–15; Jones, *History*, p. 238; Alex F. Ricciardelli, "The Adoption of White Agriculture by the Oneida

Indians," *Ethnohistory* 10(1963): 314. Approximately 150 Oneidas stayed in New York State. The rest of the tribe had already emigrated to Wisconsin.

8. Horatio Hale, ed., *The Iroquois Book of Rites* (Toronto: University of Toronto Press, 1963; originally published 1883), p. 39.

9. See the list of names on the first petition to the governor general, 24 January 1840, Council Minutes, p. 96, RG 10, 1011, PAC; Slight, *Researches,* p. 72.

10. Betty Keller, *Pauline: A Biography of Pauline Johnson* (Vancouver: Douglas and McIntyre, 1981), p. 10.

11. John Smoke Johnson cited in Jones, *History,* p. 120.

12. Peter Jones to Joseph Sawyer, Leeds, 22 May 1838, in Jones, *History,* p. 263.

13. Peter Jones to Robert Alder, Niagara, 17 December 1838, reprinted in *Wesleyan Missionary Notices* 11 (1839): 30.

14. Edith Dobie, "The Dismissal of Lord Glenelg from the Office of Colonial Secretary," *Canadian Historical Review* 23 (1942): 284.

15. Peter Jones to Robert Alder, 13 February 1840, Wesleyan Methodist Church (London Correspondence), box 24, file 168, copy in UCA.

16. (Copy) Peter Jones to Sir Augustus d'Este, River Credit, 30 December 1839, Letter Book, p. 171, RG 10, 1011, PAC.

17. Slight, *Researches,* p. 24.

18. Hale, *Rites,* p. 41.

19. John Buck cited in the Minutes of a General Council held at the Credit River, 21 January 1840, Council Minutes, 1835–48, p. 82, RG 10, 1011, PAC.

20. William Yellowhead cited in the Minutes of a General Council held at the Credit River, 22 January 1840, Council Minutes, 1835–48, p. 87, RG 10, 1011, PAC.

21. Jones, *History,* p. 126.

22. The Royal Proclamation of 1763, excerpts of which are reprinted in Aborigines Protection Society, *Report on the Indians of Upper Canada, 1839* (Toronto: Canadiana House, 1968), p. 3.

23. Lyndall Ryan, *The Aboriginal Tasmanians* (Vancouver: University of British Columbia Press, 1981), p. 3.

24. Sir George Arthur to the Bishop of Montreal, Toronto, 18 December 1838, *The Arthur Papers,* ed. C. R. Sanderson, 3 vols. (Toronto: University of Toronto Press, 1957), 1:465.

25. Francis Bond Head to Lord Glenelg, Toronto, 24 June 1837, Jarvis Papers, BR, MTL.

26. A paper talk of the River Credit Indians (signed Joseph Sawyer, John Jones Chiefs) laid before the Governor General, Port Credit, 5 December 1844, Entry Book, 1831–48, pp. 107–8, RG 10, 1011, PAC; see also Peter Jones

to Rawson W. Rawson, Muncey Mission, 17 January 1843, Entry Book, pp. 52–53, RG 10, 1011, PAC.

27. Samuel P. Jarvis's remarks summarized in Jones, *History*, p. 115.

28. Joseph Sawyer, Peter Jones, John Jones to Col. S. P. Jarvis, Credit, 24 February 1842, Letter Book, 1825–42, p. 190, RG 10, 1011, PAC.

29. Peter Jones to Eliza Jones, Belleville, 10 June 1840, Letter Book, RG 10, 1011, PAC. Goldwin French provides a good summary of the final months of the union in his *Parsons and Politics*, pp. 184–89.

30. Thomas Smith, Jr., and David Sawyer, quoted in Peter Jones, Anecdote Book, anecdote no. 4, PJC, VUL.

31. Peter Jones to Eliza Field, Credit Mission, 10 April 1833, Letter Book, PJC, VUL.

32. Council, 28 September 1840, Council Minutes, 1835–48, n.p., RG 10, 1011, PAC.

33. The Ojibwas at the Narrows of Lake Simcoe went to Rama on Lake Couchiching after the disbanding of the first settlement in 1837.

34. A beautiful example of her quilts is now in the Brant County Museum, Brantford.

35. Jones, *History*, p. 136.

36. Joseph Sawyer and Peter Jones to Lord Sydenham, 28 June 1841, Letter Book, p. 184, RG 10, 1011, PAC.

37. Hazel C. Mathews, *Oakville and the Sixteen: The History of an Ontario Port* (Toronto: University of Toronto Press, 1953), pp. 164–69.

38. Ibid., pp. 27–30, 60, 97, 177.

39. A photograph of the church appears in Matthews, *Oakville*, between pp. 102 and 103—a good description of Colborne Street about 1850 appears on p. 223; Green, *Life and Times*, p. 239.

40. See the sermon "The Joyful Sound" Ps. 89:15, 16. Sermon Collection, PJC, VUL. Peter always marked in the margin of his sermon outlines the place and date that he preached the text. Between 1838 and 1854 he preached this sermon twenty-two times, or on the average once a year.

41. Green, *Life and Times*, p. 239; Mathews, *Oakville*, pp. 103, 105.

42. For a very complete account of the Jesuits' missions see Lorenzo Cadieux, ed., *Lettres des nouvelles missions du Canada, 1843–1852* (Montréal: Editions Bellarmin, 1973).

43. William Yellowhead to Capt. Anderson, Rama, 1 October 1845, RG 10, 407:502, mfm C-9614, PAC; W. J. D. Waddilove, ed., *The Stewart Missions: A Series of Letters and Journals* (London: J. Hatchard, 1838), p. 104. Shingwahkoons and seven of his family were baptized into the Anglican Church on 19 January 1834.

44. Peter Jones to Eliza Jones, Sault Ste. Marie, 10 June 1833, Letter Book, PJC, VUL.

45. Jones, *Life*, p. 362, entry for 9 June 1833.

46. John Colborne's words recalled by Augustin Shingwank, or Shing-wahkoons, "Little Pine's Journal," *Algoma Missionary News and Shing-wauk Journal* 1, no. 3(1 September 1877): 18. Augustin accompanied his father to York to ask the governor's advice. He would have been about thirty at the time. For a sketch of his life see "Death of Augustin Shingwauk," *Canadian Indian* 1, no. 5(February 1891): 153–54.

47. Warren, *History*, pp. 447–48.

48. Henry Schoolcraft to William Case, 1 March 1833, cited in William Case in *CG*, 8 May 1833.

49. Hugh D. Maclean, "An Irish Apostle and Archdeacon in Canada," *Journal of the Canadian Church Historical Society* 15(1973): 52.

50. William Canniff, "George Ryerson," *United Empire Loyalists Association of Canada, Transactions* 6(1914): 128; Graham Allan, "A Theory of Millennialism: The Irvingite Movement as an Illustration," *British Journal of Sociology* 25, no. 3(1974): 305–10.

51. Benjamin Slight, letter, Credit, 18 December 1837, "Mormonism," *CG*, 20 December 1837.

52. George Arthur to Lord Russell, Toronto, 11 July 1840, CO 42, 471:129.

53. John E. Hodgetts, *Pioneer Public Service: An Administrative History of the United Canadas, 1841–1867* (Toronto: University of Toronto Press, 1955), p. 205.

54. Lord Sydenham to Lord John Russell, Kingston, 22 July 1841, in Canada, *Journals of the Legislative Assembly*, Sessional Papers, appendix EEE, "Report on the Affairs of the Indians in Canada," Montreal, 1844–45, no page number.

55. (Copy) R. W. Grey to Revd. Peter Jones, Government House, 21 July 1841, Letter Book, p. 187, RG 10, 1011, PAC.

56. Careless, *Union of the Canadas*, p. 56.

57. John Leslie, "The Bagot Commission: Developing a Corporate Memory for the Indian Department," Canadian Historical Association *Historical Papers, 1982*, p. 31.

58. Peter Jones to Rawson S. Rawson, Muncey Mission House, 6 February 1843, Entry Book, p. 70, RG 10, 1011, PAC.

59. Peter Jones to the Aborigines Protection Society, Lambeth, 22 January 1838, Letter Book, p. 141, RG 10, 1011, PAC.

60. Peter Jones to the Commissioners, Muncey Mission House, 6 February 1843, in Jones, *History*, pp. 242–45.

61. Peter Jones claimed that only five of the fifty families refused to move; Peter Jones to the Commissioners, Muncey Mission, 6 December 1842, Entry Book, p. 47, RG 10, 1011, PAC. Samuel Jarvis believed that twelve families opposed the removal to Munceytown. Samuel P. Jarvis's Report on

the Removal of River Credit Indians to Muncey Town, Indian Office, Kingston, 26 July 1843, RG 10, 137, part 1, file "(660–77G)R," PAC: "forty-four souls or twelve men—thirteen women and nineteen children."

62. Peter Jones to Eliza Jones, 1 February 1844, Letter Book, PJC, VUL.

63. George Paudash, John Crow, John Copoway, John Taunchy, to the Editor of the Wesleyan, Rice Lake Mission, 2 February 1841, *Wesleyan*, 18 February 1841, "Rev. Peter Jones's Reply to the Rice Lake Chiefs," CG, 7 April 1841.

64. Carroll, *Past and Present*, p. 305.

65. Thomas Hurlburt, St. Clair Mission, CG, 2 May 1838.

66. Jones, *History*, p. 190.

67. General Council, 23 January 1840, Council Minutes, p. 90, RG 10, 1011, PAC.

68. Helen Hornbeck Tanner, *The Ojibwas: A Critical Bibliography* (Bloomington: Indiana University Press, 1976), pp. 18, 55. The hymnal was republished in 1969 for the Methodist Indians of the Saginaw Chippewa Reservation, Mt. Pleasant, Michigan.

69. Waldron, "Life," p. 30. A short biographical sketch of Charles Anderson appears in W. D. Reid, "Johan Jost Herkimer, U.E., and His Family," *OHSPR* 31(1936): 225; Charles Anderson quoted in the Report of the Committee of the York Auxiliary, Upper Canada Bible Society in *Twenty-seventh Report of the British and Foreign Bible Society, 1831* (London: British and Foreign Bible Society, 1831), p. lxviii; see also Jones, *Life*, p. 269, entry for 9 February 1830.

70. Sherman Hall to David Greene, La Pointe, 12 September 1837, American Board of Commissioners for Foreign Missions, MS. no. 115-A.L.S; Typescript in the Grace Lee Nute Papers, Minnesota Historical Society, St. Paul, Minnesota.

71. Joseph Howse to the British and Foreign Bible Society, Cirencester, 9 September 1832, Foreign Correspondence Inwards, 1832, no. 3, British and Foreign Bible Society, London, England. For a short sketch of Joseph Howse's life, see H. Christoph Wolfart, "Joseph Howse," *Dictionary of Canadian Biography*, vol. 8, *1851–1860* (Toronto: University of Toronto Press, 1985), pp. 411–14.

72. CG, 15 March 1843.

73. Peter Jones, Muncey Mission, 23 March 1843, CG, 12 April 1843.

74. Thomas Hurlburt, Whitchurch, 13 April 1843, CG, 19 April 1843.

75. Thomas Hurlburt, Lake Simcoe, 16 May 1843, CG, 24 May 1843.

76. Peter Jones to Eliza Jones, Hamilton, 18 June 1843, Letter Book, PJC, VUL.

77. Peter Jones to Eliza Jones, Hamilton, 23 June 1843, Letter Book, PJC, VUL.

78. George Henry described himself as a second cousin of Peter Jones on the cover of his pamphlet *Remarks concerning the Ojibway Indians, by one of Themselves Called Maungwudaus* (1847). I am convinced that he was actually Peter Jones's half-brother. An entry in the Credit Mission Church Registry, United Church Archives, clearly reads: "George Henry (Pemikishigon) son of Mesquacosy and Tubinaniqua his wife, was born at the 40 Mile Creek in the year 1811, and baptised in the year 1824, by Rev'd Henry Ryan." "Tubinaniqua" was Peter's mother. Tubinaniqua's name in English was Sarah Henry. George Henry always acknowledged his Credit River origins. As he wrote to S. P. Jarvis on 11 October 1843 (RG 10, vol. 132, file 812-1103H, PAC): "All my relations and forefathers came from the River Credit." Apparently Maungwudaus was George Henry's second Indian name, the first being Pemikishigon. This is confirmed by an article in the Oakville *Star* in 1889: "Saigitoo, the medicine man from the Mississaugas of New Credit . . . son of the well-known Indian doctor Maungwudaus," has just visited Oakville. "Saigitoo" would have been George Henry, Jr., the only son of Maungwudaus's to live at the Credit in the late nineteenth century. George Henry, Jr., stated on 16 May 1888 (RG 10, vol. 2238, file 45, 742, PAC): "My father was a member of the Band at the old Credit." The reference to Saigitoo's visit to Oakville appears in Hazel Mathews, *Oakville and the Sixteen* (Toronto: University of Toronto Press, 1953), p. 407.

79. Joseph Sawyer to S. P. Jarvis, River Credit, 1843, Entry Book, p. 92, RG 10, 1011, PAC; Peter Jones to Eliza Jones, Toronto, 16 June 1837, Letter Book, PJC, VUL.

80. Council, Credit, 25 September 1837, Council Minutes, p. 53, RG 10, 1011, PAC.

81. Slight, *Researches*, p. 43.

82. J. Scott, Lake Simcoe, 3 August 1838, CG, 12 September 1838, Entry Book, pp. 103–4, RG 10, 1011, PAC.

83. Peter Jones to George Vardon, Port Credit, 5 September 1844, Entry Book, 1831–48, p. 103, RG 10, 1011, PAC.

84. George Catlin, *Catlin's Notes of Eight Years' Travels and Residence in Europe* (London: The Author, 1848), p. 279.

85. Eliza Jones to Joseph Clench, Lambeth, England, 2 March 1846, RG 10, 438:698, mfm C-9634, PAC.

86. The last reference to "a book he [Peter Jones] had written," appears in a letter of Samuel Jarvis to J. M. Higginson, Toronto, 28 August 1844, RG 10, 508:388, mfm C-13 344, PAC.

87. Jones, *History*, p. iii.

88. Jones, *Life*, p. 411.

89. Anson Green, St. Thomas, 3 February 1843, CG, 22 February 1843, p. 70, c. 3.

90. Peter Jones to Eliza Jones, Kingston, 15 June 1844, Letter Book, PJC, VUL; *The Doctrine and Discipline of the Methodist Episcopal Church*, 12th ed. (New York: Methodist Society, 1804), p. 16 n, quoted in Arthur E. Kewley, "Three Monuments to the Reverend Peter Jones (Kah-ke-wa-quo-na-by, 1802–1856)," *Canadian Journal of Theology* 11 (1965): 196.

91. Eliza Jones in the notebooks marked "Extracts, Jan. 8, 1828," and "Exercises," PJC, VUL; Peter Jones, Anecdote Book, PJC, VUL. Chief Sawyer named his greatnephew on Christmas Day 1839.

92. Peter Jones to Eliza Jones, Brockville, 8 February 1841, Letter Book, PJC, VUL. John A. Macdonald's name is also announced as the chairman of the meeting in the Kingston *Chronicle and Gazette*, 30 January 1841.

93. A good summary of John A. Macdonald's career appears in the short sketch by J. K. Johnson in *The Canadian Encyclopedia* (Edmonton: Hurtig, 1985), pp. 1050–52.

94. Frank Pedley, Deputy Minister, Department of Indian Affairs, "Department of Indian Affairs" in *Handbook of Indians of Canada* (Geographic Board, Canada, 1912; Ottawa: King's Printer, 1913; New York: Kraus Reprint, 1969), p. 223.

95. John A. Macdonald, in Canada, House of Commons Debate, 5 May 1880, p. 1991.

96. Peter Jones to Eliza Jones, Brockville, 8 February 1841, Letter Book, PJC, VUL.

97. Peter Jones to Eliza Jones, Moulinette, 11 February 1841, Letter Book, PJC, VUL.

98. Peter Jones to Eliza Jones, letter begun Shillington, 23 February 1841, entry for 9 March Letter Book, PJC, VUL.

99. Fred was born 29 March 1841 at the Credit Mission, CMCR, UCA; Peter Edmund at Munceytown, 30 October 1843, Eliza Jones's Album and the Jones Family Bible held by Arvilla Louise Thorp, Aldergrove, B.C.

100. A sketch of Frederick Field (1826–85), by W. Jerome Harrison appears in the *Dictionary of National Biography*, 18:404–5. His poem to Eliza appears in Eliza Jones's Album, in the possession of Arvilla Louise Thorp, Aldergrove, B.C.

101. Edmund's birthdate appears in Eliza Field's Diary for 1832, entry for 10 January PJC, VUL. Edmund tells of his chickens and ducks in a letter to Arthur Field, his brother, then aboard the ship *John Line* of Calcutta. This letter is in the possession of Bernard ffield, England.

102. Young, *Evans*, pp. 43–44.

103. *Miss. Soc. Report*, 1840–41, p. 14; Ezra Adams, Muncey Mission, 11 October 1834, *CG*, 31 December 1834.

104. Eliza Jones, Diary for 1838–39, 1841, entry for 4 August 1841, PJC, VUL.

105. Daniel Brock, "Joseph Brant Clench," *Dictionary of Canadian Biography,* vol. 8, *1851–1860,* pp. 161–63.

106. Carroll, *Case,* 4: 384–85.

107. Peter Jones to Eliza Jones, Muncey, 12 July 1841, PJC, VUL.

108. Peter Jones, Muncey Mission, 20 September 1841, CG, 29 September 1841.

109. John Leslie, "The Bagot Commission: Developing a Corporate Memory for the Indian Department," Canadian Historical Association *Historical Papers, 1982,* p. 40.

110. Jones, *History,* p. 217.

111. James S. Buckingham, *Canada, Nova Scotia, New Brunswick, and the Other British Provinces in North America* (London: Fisher, 1843), pp. 44–45.

112. Joseph Sawyer and John Jones to Rawson W. Rawson, Jarvis Papers, SP 125, B 28, pp. 487–89, BR, MTL; Samuel P. Jarvis to Rawson W. Rawson, 17 November 1842, RG 10, 506:227, mfm C-13343, PAC.

113. At age two (in 1794) Sam Jarvis had been given (at his father's request) an Indian name, "Nehkik," by a band of Mississauga Indians at Newark; see Austin Seton Thompson, *Jarvis Street* (Toronto: Personal Library Publishers, 1980), pp. 27–29; Joseph Sawyer and John Jones to Rawson W. Rawson, Jarvis Papers, SP 125, B 28, pp. 487–89, BR, MTL.

114. A paper talk of the River Credit Indians (signed Joseph Sawyer, John Jones, Chiefs) laid before the Governor General, Port Credit, 5 December 1844, Entry Book, p. 107, RG 10, 1011, PAC.

115. Thompson, *Jarvis Street,* pp. 53, 91.

116. Douglas Leighton, "The Compact Tory as Bureaucrat: Samuel Peters Jarvis and the Indian Department, 1837–1845," *Ontario History* 73, no. 1(March 1981): 47–49.

117. Copway, *Life,* p. 185. Peter Jones and George Copway, Montreal, 14 August 1844, RG 10, 142, nos. 1–100, p. 81771, PAC; (copy) Peter Jones to Sir George Metcalfe, Montreal, 17 August 1844, Entry Book RG 10, 1011, PAC; J. M. Higginson, the governor's secretary, mentions the meeting in a letter to Samuel P. Jarvis, 20 September 1844, RG 10, 510:76, mfm C-13344, PAC.

118. Peter Jones, London, 26 December 1844, in *An Address to the Christian Public of Great Britain and Ireland in Behalf of the Indian Youth in Upper Canada* (1845), p. 2.

119. Edward Thompson, *The Life of Charles, Lord Metcalfe* (London: Faber and Faber, 1937), pp. 12, 101–2, 178–79, 234–35, 340, 353–54, 412.

120. Ibid., pp. 400–401. His physical appearance is described by his niece Emily, Lady Clive Bayley, in *The Golden Calm,* ed. M. M. Kaye (Exeter, Devon: Webb and Bower, 1980), p. 60. His offices at the Chateau de Ramezay are mentioned in Jacques Monet, *The Last Cannon Shot: A Study of French-*

Canadian Nationalism, 1837–1850 (Toronto: University of Toronto, 1969), p. 220.

121. Peter Jones, *Address to the Christian Public of Great Britain and Ireland*, p. 1.

122. George Vardon to Thos. G. Anderson, 19 February 1847, RG 10, 512:107, mfm C-13345, PAC.

123. J. M. Higginson to Col. Clench, T. G. Anderson, 19 August 1845, RG 10, 511:52, mfm C-13344, PAC.

124. Peter Jones to Egerton Ryerson, London, 2 March 1846, Ryerson Papers, UCA; Lord Metcalfe died on 15 September 1846; Thompson, *Metcalfe*, p. 412. Peter Jones left for New York in April; Eliza Jones to Joseph Clench, Lambeth, England, 2 March 1846, RG 10, 438:696B, mfm C-9634, PAC.

125. Peter Jones, Anecdote Book, anecdote no. 15, PJC, VUL.

126. Carroll, *Case*, 4:372.

127. Carroll, *Case*, 4:372, CMCR, UCA.

128. Copway, *History*, p. 201; Peter Jones and George Copway to J. M. Higginson, Montreal, 14 August 1844, RG 10, 142, no. 1–100, p. 81771. J. M. Higginson to S. P. Jarvis, 20 September 1844, RG 10, 510:76, mfm C-13344, PAC.

129. T. G. Anderson to George Copway, Toronto, 12 January 1846, RG 10, 532:120, PAC; George Paudash, John Crow, and John Taunchy, Rice Lake, 13 May 1846, RG 10, 409:953–54, mfm C-9615, PAC; T. G. Anderson to J. M. Higginson, Toronto, 9 June 1846, RG10, 532:249, PAC; George Vardon to T. G. Anderson, 17 June 1846, RG 10, 511:380, mfm C-13345, PAC. Copway mentions that Taunchey was his uncle in his *History*, p. 133, and that Paudash was his grandfather in George Copway, "Missionary Meetings—Eastern Division; Consecon, January 5, 1843," CG, 18 January 1843.

130. William McFarlane, Keene, Ontario, 13 October 1902, RG 10, 3058, file 251780, PAC.

12. From Edinburgh to Echo Villa

1. The following sketch of the two famous Scottish photographers is based on Marina Henderson, "Introduction," in *Hill and Adamson Photographs*, ed. Graham Ovenden (London: Academy Editions, 1973), pp. 5–11; Sara Stevenson, *David Octavius Hill and Robert Adamson* (Edinburgh: National Galleries of Scotland, 1981), pp. 6–20. Copies of all of the calotypes of Peter and Eliza Jones are now held in the collection of the Scottish National Portrait Gallery, Edinburgh. They are dated 4 August 1845.

2. Eliza Jones, "Journey in Scotland, 1845," PJC, VUL.

3. David Bruce, *Sun Pictures: The Hill-Adamson Calotypes* (London: Studio Vista, 1973), p. 120; Colin Ford, ed., *An Early Victorian Album: The Photographic Masterpieces (1843–1847) of David Octavius Hill and Robert Adamson* (New York: Alfred A. Knopf, 1976), p. 34.

4. Jones, *Life*, p. 403, entry for 12 July 1838.

5. Peter Jones to Eliza Jones, Edinburgh, 30 June 1845, Letter Book, PJC, VUL.

6. Ibid; Peter Jones to Eliza Jones, Glasgow, 23 October 1845, Letter Book, PJC, VUL.

7. Edinburgh *Witness*, 26 July 1845; *Ladies' Own Journal and Miscellany* (Edinburgh), 2 August 1845. The UCA has a file containing press clippings on Peter Jones's Scottish tour in 1845 (PPJ4).

8. Peter Jones to George Vardon, Edinburgh, 1 August 1845, George Vardon Papers, MG 19 F23, PAC.

9. Peter Jones to Eliza Jones, Edinburgh, 30 June 1845, Letter Book, PJC, VUL.

10. Peter Jones, Lambeth, England, 2 January 1846, to an unidentified party, File of Preachers' Letters, Methodist Archives, John Rylands Library, Manchester. He states he collected £650 in Scotland. The total amount raised was £1,002; see Peter Jones, River Credit Mission, 12 October 1846, *Miss. Soc. Report*, 1845–46, p. ix.

11. Peter Jones, Lambeth, 1 January 1845, CG, 18 February 1845.

12. Peter Jones quoted in "The Indian Chief and Missionary," *Greenock Advertizer*, 28 October 1845; a clipping in the McCord Museum, Montreal.

13. Douglas Firth, *The Case of Augustus d'Este* (Cambridge: University Press, 1948), p. 23.

14. Peter Jones, Lambeth, 1 January 1845, CG, 18 February 1845.

15. Maungwudaus, *Account of the Chippewa Indians*, p. 6.

16. A copy of the handbill is held by the Thomas Gilcrease Institute of American History and Art, Tulsa, Oklahoma. They also have some of Catlin's sketches of the troupe.

17. The letter appears in English in Jones, *History*, p. 219. Incorrectly, the year given in the date of the letter is 1854; George Henry and his troupe were at King Louis Philippe's palace at St. Cloud in late 1845. See "The Ojibbeway Indians," London *Times*, 8 November 1845.

18. Peter Jones to Eliza Jones, Boulogne, France, 4 March 1846, Letter Book, PJC, VUL.

19. Eliza Jones to Colonel Clench, Lambeth, 2 March 1846, RG 10, 438:697–98, PAC; Maungwudaus, *Account of the Chippewa Indians*, pp. 7–9.

20. Peter Jones to Eliza Jones, Paris, 7 March 1846, Letter Book, PJC, VUL;

William H. Truettner, *The Natural Man Observed: A Study of Catlin's Indian Gallery* (Washington, D.C.: Smithsonian Institution Press, 1979), pp. 49, 52.

21. Peter Jones to Eliza Jones, Paris, 7 March 1846, Letter Book, PJC, VUL. For information on Dr. Achille-Louis Foville see C. Sachaile, *Les médecins de Paris* (Paris: Chez l'auteur, 1845), pp. 307–8; and St. Le Tourneur, "Achille-Louis de Foville," in *Dictionnaire de biographie française* (Paris: Librairie Letouzey, 1979), 14:892.

22. Peter Jones to Eliza Jones, Paris, 6 March 1846, and 7 March 1846, Letter Book, PJC, VUL.

23. The three surviving circulars for Peter Jones's English lectures are all remarkably similar, see that for the lectures at Norwood, 28 and 29 January 1845 (New Credit Research Office, Hagersville, Ontario); for the lecture at Hastings, 1 December 1845 (Thomas Gilcrease Institute, Tulsa, Oklahoma); and for his lectures at Bristol, 12 and 14 January 1846 (New Credit Research Office, Hagersville, Ontario). The information given below on the Swan Inn is taken from J. Manwaring Baines, *Historic Hastings. A Tapestry of Life* (St. Leonards-on-Sea, England: Cinque Ports Press, 1986), pp. 266–67. My thanks to Colin Taylor of Hastings for this reference.

24. Peter Jones to Eliza Jones, Glasgow, 29 October 1845, Letter Book, PJC, VUL.

25. Peter Jones to Eliza Jones, Glasgow, 8 November 1845, Letter Book, PJC, VUL.

26. John Jones, Port Credit, 16 August 1845, CG, 27 August 1845.

27. Peter Jones cited by Eliza Jones to Colonel Clench, Lambeth, 2 March 1846, RG 10, 438:697–98, PAC.

28. Joseph Sawyer to T. G. Anderson, Port Credit, 26 January 1846, RG 10, 410:58, mfm C-9615, PAC.

29. V. B. Blake, "The Settling of a New Purchase," in *Credit Valley Conservation Report*, ed. A. M. Richardson and A. S. L. Barnes (1956), pp. 55–83; quoted in Rankin, "Claim," p. 19; Toronto township surrounded the reserve.

30. Minutes of the Council, 25 January 1837, Council Minutes, 1835–48, p. 39, RG 10, 1011, PAC; Joseph Sawyer cited in *Minutes of the General Council of Indian Chiefs and Principal Men, Held at Orillia, Lake Simcoe Narrows* (Montreal: Canada Gazette Office, 1846), pp. 16–17.

31. *Smith's Canadian Gazetteer*, p. 40. On the disappearance of the salmon, see James H. Richardson, "Salmo Salar in Ontario," *University Magazine* 8, no. 3 (January 1908): 97–103.

32. David Wright cited in *Miss. Soc. Report*, 1841–42, p. 3; Jones, *History*, p. 236; Slight, *Researches*, p. 152.

33. T. G. Anderson, First Visit to Tribes under his Superintendence 1845, RG 10, 268:163856, mfm C-12653, PAC. Anderson visited the Credit on 29 October 1845.

34. Richard Henry Bonnycastle, *Canada and the Canadians in 1846*, 2 vols. (London: Henry Colburn, 1846), 2:9; Peter Jones to T. G. Anderson, Brantford, 28 November 1850, RG 10, 405:830, mfm C-9613, PAC.

35. Affidavit of James McLean, Council House, Mississauga Reserve, 16 May 1888, RG 10, vol. 2238, file 45, 742, p. 4 (see also Charles Herkimer's testimony, p. 2). For a reference to Captain McLean and the band's joint ownership of the schooner, see the reference to the Council of 2 January 1844 in Letters, Minutes, New Credit Registry, 1847–74, p. 120; Woodland Indian Cultural Educational Centre, Brantford, Ontario. The reference to the ship's cargo appears in *CG*, 5 June 1844.

36. Jones, *History*, p. 238.

37. Peter Jones, Muncey Mission, 22 December 1847, *CG*, 12 January 1848.

38. George H. Cornish, *Cyclopaedia of Methodism in Canada*, 2 vols. (Toronto: Methodist Book and Publishing House, 1881 and 1903), 1:99, 106 (entries for "William Herkimer" and "Peter Jacobs"); David Sawyer to T. G. Anderson, dated Newash, 21 May 1846, RG 10, 410:40, mfm C-9615, PAC.

39. Jones, *History*, p. 219.

40. Council held at the River Credit, 12 September 1844, Council Minutes, 1835–48, p. 206, RG 10, 1011, PAC. For evidence of white prejudice against blacks in Upper Canada in the 1840s, see John K. A. Farwell, "Schemes for the Transplanting of Refugee American Negroes from Upper Canada in the 1840s," *Ontario History* 52(1960): 246.

41. "William Sutton," *Illustrated Atlas of the County of Grey* (Toronto: H. Beldon, 1880), p. 17.

42. "Family Registry—1840," CMCR, UCA; "Rev. Mattihas Holtby (Walsingham)," *CG*, 19 May 1880, p. 159, col. 5. My thanks to Margaret Ann Pattison, Toronto, for genealogical information on the Holtby family.

43. Petition prepared by John Mike in 1882, RG 10, 2145, file 36857, PAC.

44. For background on T. G. Anderson see Mrs. S. Rowe, "Anderson Record, from 1699 to 1896," *OHSPR* 6(1905): 109–35.

45. George Hallen, Diary, 1 January–1 August 1835, typescript in the possession of Eric Hoare, Sechelt, British Columbia, entry for 1 August 1835. My thanks to Eric Hoare for this reference.

46. A. C. Osborne, "Old Penetanguishene," *Simcoe County Pioneer and Historical Society*, no. 6 (1917): 133.

47. A full transcript of the two-day meeting appears in *Minutes of the General Council of Indian Chiefs and Principal Men Held at Orillia, Lake Simcoe Narrows, on Thursday, the 30th, and Friday, the 31st July, 1846, on*

324 Notes to Pages 208–12

the *Proposed Removal of the Smaller Communities, and the Establishment of Manual Labour Schools. From Notes Taken in Shorthand and Otherwise* by Henry Baldwin, of Peterborough, Barrister at Law. Secretary to the Chiefs in Council (Montreal: Canada Gazette Office, 1846), pp. 5–6, 9. Ironically, Anderson made his speech on the site of what had once been a large Indian settlement. In 1836, however, Francis Bond Head had disbanded the Narrows/Coldwater reserve, and three tiny reserves replaced it.

48. *Council . . . at Orillia*, pp. 23–24.

49. George Vardon quoted in *Council . . . at Orillia*, p. 28.

50. Peter Jones to Eliza Jones, Ayr, Scotland, 19 November 1845, Letter Book, PJC, VUL.

51. Claim made by Seth Crawford, Clay, New York, 3 November 1845, RG 10, 831:272, mfm C-15110, PAC. John Jones to Colonel J. B. Clench, London, 26 November 1846, RG 10, 438:765–66, PAC; Seth Crawford, Petition to the Superintendent of Indian Affairs, Grand River, Clay Township, New York, 11 January 1847, RG 10, 831:275, mfm C-15110.

52. *Miss. Soc. Report*, 1840–41, p. 8; Richard B. Lee and Irven DeVore, eds., *Man the Hunter* (Chicago: Aldine, 1968), p. 10; Strickland, *Canada West*, 2:68; Slight, *Researches*, p. 156.

53. Joseph Jones's and his wife's full names appear under the baptismal record of the birth of their daughter, Catherine Uhwuskeezkezgooqua Jones, born 10 January 1841, baptized 9 May 1841 by Peter Jones; E. C. [Elizabeth Jones Carey] Brantford, Obituary of Sarah Jones, CG, 13 March 1861. Information on Francis Wilson (sometimes referred to as Francis Wilson Jones), appears in CMCR, UCA; Peter Jones to George Vardon, Port Credit, 8 February 1847, Entry Book, 1831–48, RG 10:1011, PAC; Kahkewaquonaby [Dr. P. E. Jones], "A Mississauga in Japan," *Indian*, 21 July 1886.

54. Charles Lavell, "Mr. John Jones, alias Tyendenegan," CG, 19 May 1847.

55. Peter Jones to George Vardon, Port Credit, 21 January 1847, Entry Book, 1831–48, p. 144, RG 10, 1011, PAC.

56. Council held at the Credit River, Council Minutes 1835–48, pp. 305–8, RG 10, 1011, PAC.

57. Ibid., pp. 306–7.

58. George Vardon to Thos. G. Anderson, 19 February 1847, RG 10, 512:107, mfm C-13345, PAC.

59. Ibid.

60. "James Young," entry in CMCR, UCA; Jones, *History*, pp. 161, 267.

61. James Young cited in council held at the Credit Village, 9 February 1847, Council Minutes, 1835–48, p. 312, RG 10:1011, PAC.

62. Peter Jones, Kahkewaquonaby to the Head Chief and people of the River Credit Tribe, Credit Village, 12 and 13 February 1847, pp. 34–37,

Letters, Minutes, New Credit Registry, 1847–74, Woodland Indian Cultural Educational Centre, Brantford, Ontario. It is difficult to say how many men refused to support the petition. A band census of 11 April 1845 listed three chiefs and sixty-six warriors; "Return of Indians for Presents," enclosed in letter from Joseph Sawyer, John Jones, to S. P. Jarvis, Port Credit, 11 April 1845, RG 10, 138, file "S(1938–2240)." Allowing for the absence of several warriors at Owen Sound and Rice Lake, it appears that roughly half the men signed the petition. About three-quarters of those participating in the council meetings supported it (thirty-three had voted on the question of the removal to the Saugeen).

63. Council held at the Credit Village, 12 April 1847, Council Minutes, 1835–48, p. 316, RG 10, 1011, PAC.

64. Minutes of a Council held at the Credit Village, 26 April 1847, Council Minutes, 1835–48, pp. 318–19, RG 10, 1011, PAC.

65. Charles Lavell, "Mr. John Jones, alias Tyendenegan," CG, 19 May 1847.

66. Jones, *Life*, p. 163, entry for 12 August 1828; John Assance quoted in *Council . . . at Orillia*, p. 21; Jones, *Life*, p. 153.

67. William Wallace Crawford to David Thorburn, Brantford, 26 August 1848, RG 10, 831:278, mfm C-15110, PAC.

68. Carroll, *Case*, 5:2–3.

69. Entry in the Jones Family Bible, in the possession of Arvilla Louise Thorp, Aldergrove, B.C.

70. Entry in the Jones Family Bible, in the possession of Arvilla Louise Thorp, Aldergrove, B.C. Peter Jones to Eliza, Liverpool, 30 January 1846, Letter Book, PJC, VUL. Peter mentions the "sailor boy" on his way back from a voyage to India.

71. Schedule B, Improvements on Mill Block, Credit Mission, J. S. Dennis, P.L.S., Toronto, 12 May 1846, RG 10, 405:414, PAC.

72. Peter Jones, Muncey Mission, 27 November 1848, in *Colonial Intelligencer; or, Aborigines' Friend*, n.s., vol. 2, nos. 9/10 (January/February 1849): 148.

73. Peter Jones to T. G. Anderson, Muncey Mission, 15 May 1848, RG 10, 409:416, mfm C-9615, PAC; *Miss. Soc. Report*, 1849–50, p. x.

74. Jones, *History*, pp. 13–14.

75. Jones, *Life*, p. 412.

76. "Mount Elgin Indian Residential School," *Missionary Bulletin*, April–June 1920, pp. 174–75; Carroll, *Past and Present*, p. 246.

77. Samuel Rose to John Rose, Yellowhead Mission, 24 August 1831, Samuel Rose Papers, Ontario Archives.

78. Samuel Rose, Regulations of the Mount Elgin Industrial School, in *Miss. Soc. Report*, 1850–51, p. xii.

79. Province of Canada, *Journals of the Legislative Assembly*, Sessional Papers, Appendix 21, "Report of the Special Commissioners to investigate Indian Affairs in Canada," Toronto, 1858. The pages of this report are not numbered; the comments appear in the section "Industrial Schools at Alderville and Mount Elgin."

13. The Final Years

1. Ida Hildred Broomfield, "The History of Echo Place," manuscript, available through the Tweedsmuir Society of the Women's Institute, Brantford; Kewley, "Three Monuments," pp. 200–201.
2. Carroll, *Case*, 5:147.
3. Marion Macrae and Anthony Adamson, *The Ancestral Roof* (Toronto: Clarke, Irwin, 1963), pp. 119–20; Mary Byers and Margaret McBurney, "Missionaries Home Has Classical Look," *Globe and Mail*, 12 May 1983; John Wyatt, "Echo Villa," manuscript prepared in 1968, p. 1; Jean Waldie, "Long, Colorful Story of 'Echo Villa,'" Brantford *Expositor*, 16 November 1956.
4. Jones, *History*, p. 13; Jones Family Bible, in the possession of Arvilla Louise Thorp, Aldergrove, B.C.
5. "Great Provincial Exhibition. Conclusion of the Prize List, Class W. Foreign Stock and Implements, EXTRA PRIZES," *Globe*, 28 September 1852, p. 3, col. 3. My thanks to Don Whiteside of Ottawa for this reference. Eliza Field Jones Carey, Will, 1 January 1889, Brant County, Will/Estate File 1433, Ontario Archives.
6. Eliza Jones to Catherine Sutton, Brantford, 25 June 1856, Owen Sound and Grey County Museum, Owen Sound; Jones, *History*, p. 52.
7. Eliza Jones in Jones, *Life*, p. 422.
8. Peter Jones quoted in Jones, *Life*, p. 422.
9. Jones, *History*, pp. 58, 70, 80. The fur trader Alexander Henry's volume first appeared in 1809; Jonathan Carver's travels were published in 1778 and John Heckewelder's history in 1818. James Adair's history was one of the numerous books on Indians in Peter's library, now in the possession of the United Church Archives in Toronto. In the minutes of the "Eleventh Annual Meeting of the Aborigines Protection Society," reprinted in *Colonial Intelligencer; or, Aborigines' Friend* 2 (May/June 1848): 12, Peter Jones is mentioned as "your society's correspondent in Canada." Peter Jones's library, now in the possession of the United Church Archives in Toronto, contains a number of the Annual Reports of the Aborigines Protection Society.
10. Peter Jones to Joseph Clench, Brantford, 26 November 1850, RG 10, 438:845; Kelsay, *Brant*, p. 658.
11. Jones, *History*, p. 210.

12. M. Cuoq, "Notes pour servir à l'histoire de la Mission du Lac des Deux Montagnes," M.G. A 7-2-6, vol. 18, PAC. The best short overview of the mission's history appears in Olivier Maurault's "Les vicissitudes d'une mission sauvage," *Revue Trimestrielle Canadienne* 16(1930): 121–49.

13. Jones, *History,* pp. 171–72.

14. "For Two Nights Only; Maungwudaus," *Globe,* Tuesday, 22 April 1851. My thanks to Don Whiteside of Ottawa for this reference.

15. "One Night Only—Another Company of Chippewe Indians," Cleveland *Daily True Democrat,* 10 July 1851. My thanks to James L. Murphy of Columbus, Ohio, for this reference.

16. Affidavits of John Henry, 7 February 1888; and of George Henry, 16 May 1888, RG 10, vol. 2238, file 45, 742, PAC.

17. Oakville *Star* cited in Mathews, *Oakville,* p. 407.

18. Maungwudaus, *Remarks concerning the Ojibway Indians* (1847) and *Account of the North American Indians* (1848).

19. Maungwudaus, *Account of the Chippewa Indians* (1848), p. 8.

20. Jones, *History,* p. 14.

21. Peter Jones to David Thorburn, Brantford, 20 April 1855, RG 10, 830:507, mfm C-15103, PAC; Eliza Jones to David Thorburn, Brantford, 26 September 1856, RG 10, 833:311, mfm C-15111, PAC; Eliza Jones to David Thorburn, Brantford, 31 October 1856, RG 10, 833:433–36, mfm C-15111, PAC.

22. Peter Jones to T. G. Anderson, Port Credit, 14 October 1847, RG 10, vol. 405, PAC; Peter Jones to Colonel Clench, Munceytown, 4 March 1848, 438:796, PAC; R. Heyland in *Miss. Soc. Report,* 1851–52, p. xiv.

23. R. Heyland in *Miss. Soc. Report,* 1851–52, p. xiv.

24. Peter Jones to David Thorburn, Brantford, 21 October 1851, RG 10, 822:306–7, mfm C-15107, PAC. Fortunately Peter Jones had previously taken out partial insurance on the mill for six hundred dollars.

25. Peter Jones in *Miss. Soc. Report,* 1847–48, p. x; R. Heyland in *Miss. Soc. Report,* 1851–52, p. xiv; David Wright in *Miss. Soc. Report,* 1853–54, p. xviii.

26. *Globe,* 5 May 1850, p. 2, col. 7. My thanks to Don Whiteside of Ottawa for this reference.

27. CMCR, UCA; baptismal entry for Samuel Finger; Jones, *History,* pp. 162, 267; "Death by Intemperance," *Globe,* 5 November 1850. My thanks to Don Whiteside of Ottawa for this reference.

28. R. Heyland in *Miss. Soc. Report,* 1851–52, p. xiv; Peter Jones, Brantford, 30 June 1852; *Buffalo Christian Advocate* in *CG,* 11 August 1852.

29. James McLean to David Thorburn, Oneida, 23 February 1858, RG 10, 836:187, PAC. The new sawmill had been built by 1853; David Wright in *Miss. Soc. Report,* 1852–53, p. xii.

30. Peter Jones to David Thorburn, Brantford, 20 April 1855, RG 10, 830:506, mfm C-15109, PAC.

31. Torry, *Autobiography*, p. 305.

32. Kohl, *Kitchi-Gami*, p. 1; Jones, *History*, pp. 32, 40.

33. Eliza Jones to David Thorburn, Brantford, 26 September 1856, RG 10, 833:311, mfm C-15111.

34. Peter Jones, 9 July 1852, in *CG*, 25 August 1852.

35. Jones, *Life*, p. 385, entry for 31 July 1837.

36. Jones, *History*, p. 43.

37. J. C. Phipps, Manitowaning to the Minister of the Interior, 25 April 1875, RG 10, 1951, file 4430, "Indians in the War of 1812–14."

38. Sir Francis Bond Head to Lord Glenelg, Toronto, 20 August 1836, in Aborigines Protection Society, *Report on the Indians of Upper Canada, 1839*, p. 18.

39. Assiginack quoted in Peter Jones, 11 July 1852, *CG*, 25 August 1852. The church records of the Holy Cross Mission, at Wikwemikong, Manitoulin Island, state that Jean-Baptiste Assiginack was born in 1768 and died on 3 November 1866 at Manitowaning. My thanks to Douglas Leighton of the University of Western Ontario for this reference.

40. Peter Jones, 10 July 1852, *CG*, 25 August 1852.

41. Peter Jones, 11 July 1852, *CG*, 25 August 1852.

42. Copway, *History*, p. 197.

43. Samuel P. Jarvis's sister, Ann Elizabeth, married W. B. Robinson; see Mrs. Simcoe, *Diary*, ed. Robertson, p. 312.

44. Peter Jones quoted in the *Banner* (Aberdeen, Scotland), 15 August 1845; copy of the clipping in UCA.

45. Cited from the judgment of Chief Justice Robinson, "Totten v. Watson, Queen's Bench, Trinity Term, 21 Vic.," *Upper Canada, Queen's Bench Reports*, 15:396.

46. Peter Jones, 19 July 1852, *CG* 1 September 1852; John H. Pitezel, *Life of Rev. Peter Marksman* (Cincinnati: Western Methodist Book Concern, 1901), p. 139.

47. "Nuhguhmowin 3. Jesus Lord, We Look To Thee," in Peter Jones, *Additional Hymns Translated by the Rev. Peter Jones, Kahkewaquonaby, a Short Time before His Death for the Spiritual Benefit of His Indian Brethren, 1856* (Brantford: Printed at the Expositor Office, 1861), p. 7.

48. Pitezel, *Marksman*, p. 143.

49. Peter Jones, 11 July 1852, *CG*, 25 August 1852.

50. Jones, *Life*, pp. 416–18; RG 22, Probate Will, Peter Jones, box 14, Ontario Archives. Eliza was the other executor.

51. Buckingham, *Canada*, p. 46.

52. Peter Jones, 26 and 27 July 1852, CG, 1 September 1852. My thanks to Basil Johnston of the Royal Ontario Museum for the translation of "Uhyahbans," 27 May 1985.

53. Iris Allan, "The McDougalls, Pioneers of the Plains," *Beaver*, 304, no. 1 (Summer 1973), p. 15; see James Ernest Nix, *Mission among the Buffalo: The Labours of the Reverends George M. and John C. McDougall in the Canadian Northwest, 1860–1876* (Toronto: Ryerson, 1960).

54. J. G. Kohl, *Travels in Canada, and through the States of New York and Pennsylvania*, trans. Mrs. Percy Sinnett, 2 vols. (London: George Manwaring, 1861), 2:14.

55. About 11,900 Indians apparently lived permanently in Upper Canada in 1842 and 3,300 in Lower Canada; see "Report on the Affairs of the Indians in Canada," Appendix T, nos. 52, 53, 54, and 55, *Journals of the Legislative Assembly of Canada, 1847*. I arrived at the figure of 11,900 for Upper Canada by deducting the visiting American Indians at Manitoulin Island (2,800) from the total number of Indians given presents in Upper Canada (14,700). Anthony Hall confirms the figure of 11,000 Indians in Upper Canada in the mid-nineteenth century in his "The Red Man's Burden: Land, Law and the Lord in the Indian Affairs of Upper Canada, 1791–1858" (Ph.D. thesis, University of Toronto, 1984), p. 208. For the population of the Canadas in 1850 see Jacques Monet, "The 1840's," in *Colonists and Canadians 1760–1867* (Toronto: Macmillan, 1971), p. 206.

56. Frederic Boase, ed., *Modern English Biography* (Truro: Netherton and Worth, 1892), vol. 1 (A–H), p. 451. Jim Morrison supplied this reference.

57. Peter Jones to Joseph Clench, Brantford, 25 October 1852, RG 10, 438:879–80.

58. Jones, *History*, p. 217.

59. Peter S. Schmalz, *The History of the Saugeen Indians* (Ottawa: Ontario Historical Society, 1977), pp. 85–86, 95–96.

60. Solomon Yeomans Chesley, Diary, 1851–54, MU 839, Ontario Archives, entry for 9 November 1854. Chesley was the accountant for the Indian Department.

61. J. B. Clench Defalcation, Dismissal and Inquiry, 1854–55, Related Papers, ca. 1828–1905, RG 10, 802:10, mfm C-13625. I also benefited from reading Daniel Brock's biography of Joseph Brant Clench (1790–1857), before publication in the *Dictionary of Canadian Biography*. My thanks to the author for allowing me to see his manuscript.

62. Jones, *Life*, p. 424; Peter Jones to David Thorburn, Brantford, 4 January 1855, RG 10, 830:18–21, mfm C-15109, PAC.

63. Peter Jones to David Thorburn, 23 April 1856, RG 10, 832:399, PAC.

64. Alfred A. Digby to David Thorburn, Brantford, 4 December 1854, RG 10, 829:527–28, mfm C-15109, PAC.

65. Peter Jones to David Thorburn, Brantford, 4 January 1855, RG 10, 830:20, mfm C-15109, PAC.

66. Copy of a letter from Egerton Ryerson to Chief Superintendent Indian Affairs, 21 November 1854, RG 2, c 1, Ontario Archives. My thanks to Bob Gidney of the University of Western Ontario for this reference. A draft of the letter (no. 2358) is in the Ryerson Papers, UCA.

67. Sydney Jackman, *Galloping Head* (London: Phoenix, 1958), p. 67.

68. John Maclean, *Vanguards of the Cross* (Toronto: Missionary Society of the Methodist Church, 1918), p. 69.

69. According to the Register of Burials, Greenwood Cemetery (Parks and Cemetery Commission Office, 1 Sherwood Drive, Brantford), cited in Kewley, "Three Monuments," p. 204.

70. Jones, *Life*, p. iii.

71. See the correspondence relating to this tract in RG 10, vol. 1983, file 6253, PAC.

72. Frank N. Walker, "Birth of the Buffalo and Brantford Railway," *Ontario History* 47, no. 2 (1955): 83. My thanks to Tony Hall, Native Studies Department, Laurentian University, Sudbury, for this reference.

73. Jones, *Life*, p. 411.

74. Eliza Jones Carey, Memoir of Charles A. Jones, in the notebook marked "Exercises," PJC, VUL; Eliza Carey to the Captain of C. A. Jones's Company, n.d., PJC, VUL.

75. Peter Jones to Joseph Clench, Brantford, 7 March 1850, RG 10, 438:821, PAC; Mrs. E. Dowling to Eliza, Bristol, 1 September 1856, PJC, VUL; William Cochrane, ed., *The Canadian Album: Men of Canada; or, Success by Example* (Brantford: Bradley, Garretson, 1893), 2:262, entry for Peter Edmund Jones, M.D.

76. Eliza Jones in Jones, *Life*, p. 421.

77. Eliza Field Jones, Diary, 26 March 1854–16 August 1854, entry for 1 May 1854, PJC, VUL. Peter Edmund was born 30 October 1843.

78. "Kokomis" means grandmother in Ojibwa. Eliza used the term in a letter to Joseph Sawyer, apparently written in early March 1857, RG 10, 834:341–42, mfm C-15111, PAC. See the entry for Sarah Henry in "A list of the sick and infirm Indians belonging to the Mississauga of New Credit, Grand River for 1855," RG 10, 831:542, mfm C-15110, PAC.

79. Frederick J. Jobson, *America and American Methodism* (New York: Virtue, Emmins, 1857), p. 354. My thanks to Ernest Nix, of Mississauga, Ontario, for this reference.

80. Grand General Council, *The Grand General Council of the Chip-*

pewas, Munsees, Six Nations, etc., etc., *Held on the Sarnia Reserve, June 25th to July 3, 1874* (Sarnia: "Canadian" Steam Publishing Establishment, 1874), p. 14.

81. Susannah Moodie, *Roughing It in the Bush* (Toronto: Bell and Cockburn, 1913; facsimile edition published by Coles, Toronto 1974), pp. 300–301. In her book Mrs. Moodie also reports that her husband, on at least one occasion, gave whiskey to an Indian (p. 309), an act that would enrage Peter.

82. Keller, *Pauline*, p. 16.

83. William Perkins Bull, *From Strachan to Owen: How the Church of England Was Planted and Tended in British North America* (Toronto: Perkins Bull Foundation, 1937), p. 276.

84. He spoke on Ps. 72:9 at the John Street Chapel, 6 April, on "Spiritual Weapons," 2 Cor. 10:4–5, at the Allen Street Church, 3 April; on the "Work of God," Acts 13:41, at the Washington Street Church in Brooklyn, 10 April 1853. See the outlines of his sermons, PJC, VUL, and also the article from the New York *Spectator*, reprinted in CG, 13 April 1853.

85. Peter Jones to David Thorburn, 23 April 1856, RG 10, 832:399. The trip can be dated as taking place in late April 1854, since Peter Jones delivered a sermon, "Times of Ignorance," Acts 17:30, in Albany on 23 April 1854; see his sermon outlines, PJC, VUL.

86. D. Greene to S. Hall, dated Missionary House, Boston, 8 December 1846, ABCFM Indians, vol. 10, p. 14, LBPC, in Nute, "Missions," Minnesota Historical Society, St. Paul; "The Ojebwas. *Life, etc. of Kah-ge-ga-gah-bowh (George Copway) a Young Chief of the Ojebwa Nation* etc. Albany, 1847," Albany *Argus*, 5 March 1847; George Copway, *The Life, History, and Travels of Kah-ge-ga-gah-bowh* (Albany: Weed and Parsons, 1847); the book was registered 9 December 1846. Copway mentions being in Albany in late December 1846 in the British edition of his *Life*, entitled *Recollections of a Forest Life; or, The Life and Travels of Kah-ge-ga-gah-bowh, or George Copway*, 2nd ed. (London: C. Gilpin, 1851), p. 51.

87. He acknowledges her assistance in his *Life* (1847), p. vii. His wife also wrote; see "Mrs. George Copway's Death," from a Port Dover, Ontario, newspaper, 29 January 1904. The late D. H. Hamly, greatnephew of Elizabeth Howell Copway, kindly sent me a copy of the clipping. My thanks to Brian Carey of the Public Archives of Canada for putting me in touch with Dr. Hamly.

88. For all the editions of his autobiography see American Library Association, *The National Union Catalog Pre-1956 Imprints* (London: Mansell, 1970), 122:349–50.

89. Copway, *Recollections of a Forest Life*, pp. 211–38. Kah-ge-ga-gah-bowh (George Copway) contributed to the *Saturday Evening Post* on 30

March 1850. The magazine reprinted the piece in its bicentennial issue, 1976 (July/August), *Best of the Post, 1728 to 1976*, p. 25. My thanks to Francis Prucha for this reference.

90. George Copway, *The Traditional History and Characteristic Sketches of the Ojibway Nation* (London: Charles Gilpin, 1850); an American edition published in Boston by B. F. Mussey appeared the following year.

91. The Newspaper Collection of the British Museum in London, England, has the complete run of *Copway's American Indian*, published in New York from 10 July 1851 to 4 October 1851.

92. Jones, *History*, p. 14. Peter refers to Phoebe Palmer (1807–74).

93. William Case quoted in the *Minutes of the General Council of Indian Chiefs and Principal Men, Held at Orillia, Lake Simcoe Narrows, on Thursday, the 30th, and Friday, the 31st July, 1846* (Montreal: Canada Gazette Office, 1846), p. 10.

94. Jones, *Life*, p. 3 (on the bear hunt); Peter Jones, "Christian Union Convention of Indians," *CG*, 19 July 1854.

95. Peter Jones, "Christian Union Convention of Indians," *CG*, 19 July 1854.

96. Thomas Woolsey to Eliza Jones, Wesleyan Mission, Edmonton House, 30 April 1857, PJC, VUL. I am assuming that Peter Jones also gave his benediction to the Reverend Henry B. Steinhauer. For a sketch of Woolsey's life see MacLean, "Thomas Woolsey," in *Vanguards of the Cross*, pp. 84–100; and for information on Steinhauer consult Isaac Kholisile Mabindisa, "The Praying Man: The Life and Times of Henry Bird Steinhauer" (Ph.D. thesis, University of Alberta, 1984).

97. Benjamin Slight, Diary, entry for 8 December 1836, 1:123–24, UCA.

98. John Laurie, "First Permanent Settlement of Indians in the West," *Farm and Ranch Review*, August 1955, p. 11.

99. *Miss. Soc. Report*, 1874, p. xx.

100. John Sunday quoted in Jones, *Life*, p. 174, entry for 6 September 1828.

101. John Sunday quoted in Joseph Stinson letter, Kingston, 14 March 1836," *CG*, 23 March 1836.

102. Jones, *History*, p. 15.

14. Peter Jones's Legacy

1. Peter Jones to Miss Vance, Brantford, 16 February 1856, PJC, VUL.

2. Kennedy Creighton to Peter Jones, St. Catharines, 21 March 1856, PJC, VUL.

3. Obituary of Kennedy Creighton (1814–90) in the *Minutes of the Toronto Methodist Conference, 1892*. The late Canadian historian Donald

Creighton was the great-grandson of the Reverend Kennedy Creighton. By a strange coincidence, Stanley Ryerson, another well-known Canadian historian, is the great-grandson of Peter Jones's best white friend, Egerton Ryerson.

4. Eliza Jones, Diary for 1856, entry for Tuesday, 29 April 1856, PJC, VUL.

5. G. W. Spragge, "The Trinity Medical College," *Ontario History* 56 (1966): 98.

6. Eliza Jones to Catherine Sutton, Brantford, 25 June 1856, Owen Sound and Grey County Museum, Owen Sound.

7. Ibid.

8. The Reverend John Hannah quoted in Frederick J. Jobson, *America and American Methodism* (New York: Virtue, Emmins, 1857), p. 354. My thanks to the Reverend Ernest Nix for this reference.

9. Eliza Jones to Catherine Sutton, Brantford, 25 June 1856, County of Grey-Owen Sound Museum, Owen Sound; Jones, *History*, p. 16; Jones, *Life*, p. 415. Eliza completed these entries.

10. Jones, *History*, p. 17; Jones, *Life*, p. 416.

11. Jones, *Life*, pp. 416–18.

12. Ibid., p. 420.

13. "Death of an Indian Chief and Missionary," Toronto *Globe*, 4 July 1856.

14. "Civilization of the Indians," Legislative Assembly, 15 May 1857, Toronto *Globe*, 16 May 1857.

15. John S. Milloy, "The Early Indian Acts: Developmental Strategy and Constitutional Change," in *As Long as the Sun Shines and Water Flows*, ed. Ian A. L. Getty and Antoine S. Lussier (Vancouver: University of British Columbia Press, 1983), pp. 58–59.

16. Jones, *History*, p. 218.

17. Kathleen Jamieson, *Indian Women and the Law in Canada: Citizens Minus* (Ottawa: Minister of Supply and Services Canada, 1978), pp. 29–30.

18. S. R. McVitty, "Mount Elgin Indian Residential School. The Story of Seventy Years of Progress," *Missionary Bulletin* 16, no. 2 (April–June 1920): 176.

19. The Reverend Enos Montour, a Delaware Indian (1899–1984), attended the school immediately before World War I. Enos T. Montour, "Brown Tom's Schooldays," mimeographed, May 1985, p. 12. Available from Elizabeth Graham, Department of Anthropology, Wilfrid Laurier University, Waterloo, Ontario N2L3C5.

20. John Grant, *Moon of Wintertime: Missionaries and the Indians of Canada in Encounter since 1534* (Toronto: University of Toronto Press, 1984), p. 92.

21. Kohl, *Travels*, 2:77.

22. William Case in *Miss. Soc. Report*, 1850–51, p. xvii; David Wright, New Credit, 28 February 1858, CG, 12 May 1858; Thomas Williams, *Miss. Soc. Report*, 1861–62, p. xviii. Lloyd King, a member of the New Credit band, recalls that when he grew up on the reserve after World War I those born after the 1860s or so used English as their first language; personal communication, 19 July 1974.

23. Alexander Sutherland, editorial note in T. Ferrier's "The Indian Problem," *The Missionary Outlook*, June 1904, p. 126; cited in James Ernest Nix, "John Maclean's Mission to the Blood Indians, 1880–1889" (M.A. thesis, McGill University, Faculty of Religious Studies, 1977), p. 229.

See Gossett, *Race*, pp. 244, 429–30, 447, and elsewhere, for a general discussion of the rise and later discreditation in the mid-twentieth century of "race theory."

24. Edward F. Wilson, *Missionary Work among the Ojebway Indians* (London: Society for Promoting Christian Knowledge, 1886), p. 19. David Sawyer did remain in the Methodist church; see T. S. Howard, "David Sawyer," CG, 19 March 1890. For the reference to Dr. Peter E. Jones see *Churchman*, cited in "Hagersville—A Laudable Enterprise," *Indian* (Hagersville), 17 February 1886. Of all the Canadian churches the Anglicans made the greatest attempt (in the late nineteenth and early twentieth centuries) to use native missionaries; see Grant, *Moon of Wintertime*, p. 174.

25. Jones, *History*, p. 223.

26. Ibid., p. 230.

27. Diamond Jenness, *The Ojibwa Indians of Parry Island, Their Social and Religious Life* (Ottawa: King's Printer, 1935), p. 18.

28. Eliza Jones in Jones, *History*, p. 16.

29. W. J. McGee, "Ojibwa Feather Symbolism," *American Anthropologist* 11 (1898): 178.

30. McGee, "Feather," p. 178. The thunderbird symbol appears on Peter Jones's shotbag, shown in the Hill and Adamson calotypes.

31. Jones, *Life*, p. 356, entry for 23 November 1832.

32. Peter Jones to David Thorburn, Brantford, 20 April 1855, RG 10, 830:507, mfm C-15103; Eliza Jones to David Thorburn, Brantford, 26 September 1856, RG 10, 833:311 mfm C-15103; Eliza Jones to David Thorburn, Brantford, 31 October 1856, RG 10, 833:433–36, mfm C-15111; Eliza Jones to David Thorburn, Brantford, 7 March 1857, RG 10, 834:349–51, mfm C-15111.

33. Jones, *History*, p. 421.

34. Peter Jones's Journal, 3 May 1830, in CG, 7 August 1830.

35. Eliza Jones, Diary, 1834–35, entry for 5 February 1835, PJC, VUL.

36. Anonymous commentator in Jones, *History*, p. 12.

37. Kahkewaquonaby, M.D. to Sir John A. Macdonald, dated Hagersville, 30 May 1885, in Canada, Parliament, House of Commons, Debates, 48–49 Victoria, 1885, 19:2371. See also Malcolm Montgomery, "The Six Nations Indians and the Macdonald Franchise," *Ontario History* 57 (1965): 25.

38. *Rep. Ind. Affairs*, 1883, p. 1; *Miss. Soc. Report*, 1890–91, p. xlviii; *Rep. Ind. Affairs*, 1892, pp. 18–19.

39. P. E. Jones, Hagersville, 15 August 1888, *Rep. Ind. Affairs*, 1888, p. 17.

40. *The Indian* (Hagersville, Ontario), 1885–86.

41. George T. Shields to A. S. McGee, New Credit, 17 May 1911, Allan C. Farrell Papers, Indian Missions: Ontario, General Correspondence, 1910–11, UCA. Alfred had first taught at the day school at New Credit in 1860, *Miss. Soc. Report*, 1860–61, p. xvii.

42. [David Boyle], "Tuscarora and Oneida," *Fourth Annual Archaeological Report*, 1890–91, 54 Vic., A. 1891, Sess. Papers, no. 21, p. 12; Gerald Killan, *David Boyle: From Artisan to Archaeologist* (Toronto: University of Toronto Press, 1983), p. 124.

43. Canada, *Handbook*, p. 305.

44. See the annual reports of the Department of Indian Affairs for New Credit, 1880–1917. For the reference to the Indians' hunting see the affidavit of Dr. Peter E. Jones, 22 February 1888, RG 10, vol. 2238, file 45, 742.

45. Memoir of Charles Jones, in Eliza Jones's notebook marked Exercises, PJC, VUL; Reville, *Brant County* (1920), pp. 194–95; Eliza Jones Carey to the Captain of C. A. Jones's Company, n.d., PJC, VUL; note in Charles Augustus Jones's handwriting, by Henry George, Editor Reporter, Editorial Rooms, Sacramento Reporter, Sacramento, 1 May 1870, PJC, VUL (the Henry George who later became renowned in the 1880s for his idea of the "single tax"); Jones Family Bible, in the possession of Arvilla Louise Thorp, Aldergrove, B.C., entry for Charles Augustus Jones's marriage to Hannah Eleda Ellis, 1 June 1871; circular for the Brant Memorial, July 1876, Draper Papers, Wisconsin Historical Society, Madison, Wisconsin; Walter Burrage, *A Pioneer History of South Brant and the Adjacent Townships* (n.p., n.d.), p. 118. My thanks to Harold Senn of Victoria for this reference. Eliza Jones Carey, Diary for 1882, entry for 19 June 1882, PJC, VUL.

46. P. E. Jones, Indian Agent, to Deputy Superintendent General of Indian Affairs, dated Hagersville, 18 June 1896, RG 10, 1974, file 5620/2, PAC.

47. Eliza Jones Carey, Diary for 1882, entry for 30 April 1882, PJC, VUL; P. E. Jones, Obituary of George D. Jones; name of the newspaper is not recorded—clipping in The Elvin Dixon scrapbook, Arvilla Louise Thorp, Aldergrove, B.C.; P. E. Jones, Hagersville, 17 September 1894, *Rep. Ind. Affairs 1894*, p. 19.

48. Eliza Jones to David Thorburn, Brantford, 26 September 1856, RG 10, 833:312, PAC.

49. Eliza Jones to Catherine Sutton, 5 July 1856, Sutton Papers, County of Grey-Owen Sound Museum, Owen Sound.

50. Eliza Jones to David Thorburn, Brantford, 31 October 1856, RG 10, 833:435, mfm C-15111, PAC.

51. Eliza Jones, Diary, with miscellaneous entries for 1845, 1850, 1856–57, entry for 1 January 1857. The first reference to "Mrs. Carey" appears in a letter from James McLean to David Thorburn, dated Oneida, 14 December 1857, RG 10:835, pp. 531–33, mfm C-15111, PAC.

52. Eliza Jones Carey, comment in the notebook marked Exercises, p. 21, PJC, VUL.

53. Jones, *History*, pp. 167–68.

54. Jones, *History*, pp. 19–21; invoice to Mrs. Peter Jones, Brantford, 4 August 1857, RG 10, 836:290, PAC.

55. Death notice of Eliza Carey, in Eliza's Album, in the possession of Arvilla Louise Thorp, Aldergrove, B.C.

56. Eliza Jones Carey, Diary for 1869, entries for 13 February and 19 November 1869, PJC, VUL.

57. [Eliza Jones], *Sketch of the life of Captain Joseph Brant;* "Mrs. Eliza Carey," *CG*, 5 November 1890.

58. Eliza Jones Carey, Diary for 1882, entry for 15 September 1882. PJC, VUL.

59. Eliza Jones Carey, Diary for 1882, entries for Christmas Day and 27 December 1882; PJC, VUL.

60. Boston *Daily Journal*, 15 October 1858, p. 4, transcript in Nute, "Missions," Minnesota Historical Society, St. Paul, Minnesota; Chauncey Hobart, *History of Methodism in Minnesota* (Red Wing: Red Wing Printing Company, 1887), p. 28; M. Cuoq, "Notes pour servir à l'histoire de la Mission du Lac des Deux Montagnes," MG 17, A 7-2-6, vol. 16, PAC.

61. "Mrs. Eliza Carey," *CG*, 5 November 1890; obituary of Dr. P. E. Jones, unidentified clipping, 30 June [1909] in the possession of Arvilla Louise Thorp, Aldergrove, B.C.

62. A major dispute occurred in 1888 between what I have identified as the Jones and Herkimer parties. See the file "New Credit Agency-Correspondence," RG 10, vol. 2238, file 45, 742, PAC. For background on the involvement of Charles Herkimer (1831–1901) in the church choir, see Quarterly Meeting held 16 February 1889, New Credit Mission Book, in the possession of Lloyd King, Hagersville. Charles Herkimer was known for his deep bass voice. Interview with Lloyd King, Hagersville, 12 July 1979. A list of chiefs and councilors appears in *Mississaugas of the Credit: Past and Present,*

mimeographed, n.d., pp. 2–3. Apparently Dr. Peter E. Jones retired as Indian agent in the mid-1890s. The last Department of Indians Affairs Annual Report to carry his name as the New Credit Indian Agent is that for 1896 (p. 13).

63. *Rep. Ind. Affairs,* 1916, p. 10.

64. List of those who served from New Credit in World War II, supplied by Margaret Sault, Research Office, New Credit Reserve.

65. Dr. P. E. Jones, Hagersville, to Dr. Lyman C. Draper, Madison, 12 November 1882; Draper Papers, Wisconsin Historical Society, Madison, Wisconsin, Draper/Brant 13F14; interview with Mrs. Effie Brant Montour, Oakville, Ontario, 10 June 1978 (Mrs. Montour was Cameron Brant's sister).

66. Enos T. Montour, *The Feathered U.E.L.'s* (Toronto: Division of Communication, United Church of Canada, 1973), pp. 110–15.

Selected Bibliography

Fortunately the biographer of Peter Jones can write his life from literary materials. The native missionary has left behind a large collection of letters, diaries, and manuscripts, many of which are now in the Reverend Peter Jones Collection, held by the Victoria University Library, and in the United Church Archives, both in Toronto. The Department of Indian Affairs records in the Public Archives of Canada in Ottawa also contain valuable material. The Victoria collection includes his personal notebook, his "Anecdote Book," his incoming and outgoing correspondence; a volume of his letters to his wife, written between 1833 and 1848 and copied out in her own hand; three of his diaries for 1827–28; and hundreds of his outlines for sermons. Victoria also has the Eliza Field Jones Carey Papers, containing many of her diaries and notebooks. The United Church Archives has a short manuscript autobiography entitled "Brief Account of Kahkawaquonaby, Written by Himself," one of his diaries for 1829, and the original church registry for the old Credit Mission. Fortunately this material can be supplemented by his published diaries and his *History of the Ojebway Indians*. We also have the band's council minutes and entry and letter books, which are included in the Paudash Papers, RG 10, volume 1011, Public Archives of Canada. Peter Jones's will is in the Ontario Archives, RG 22, Probate Records, box 14.

Helpful sources for the background to the Mississauga Indians in the eighteenth century are the following published collections of manuscripts: *Documents Relative to the Colonial History of the State of New York*, for the late seventeenth and the eighteenth centuries; the Johnson Papers for the mid-eighteenth century; and the Simcoe and Russell Papers for the 1790s. The Colonial Office Records (CO 42), consulted on microfilm at the Ontario Archives, and the collection on Indian Affairs at the Public Archives of Canada (RG 10) provided essential information for the years 1800 to 1860. In the RG 10 holdings the Paudash Papers are a rich source (volume 1011) for the

1820s to mid-1840s. Peter Jones's letters in the late 1840s and early 1850s to Joseph Clench (volume 438), the western Indian superintendent, are revealing, as is his correspondence in the 1850s with David Thorburn of the Grand River Superintendency (volumes 811 to 840).

A delightful study of Indian life south of the Great Lakes in the late eighteenth and early nineteenth centuries, one full of anecdotes, is the Moravian missionary John Heckewelder's *History, Manners, and Customs of the Indian Nations Who Once Inhabited Pennsylvania and the Neighbouring States.* Johann Georg Kohl provides an engaging account of the mid-nineteenth century Ojibwas in his *Kitchi-Gami: Wanderings Round Lake Superior.* The book chronicles the German traveler's journey to Lake Superior in the summer of 1855. Very useful is the anthology edited by Penny Petrone, *First People, First Voices* (Toronto: University of Toronto Press, 1983), which contains excerpts from the writings of Peter Jones and other Methodist Indian leaders: John Sunday, George Henry, Peter Jacobs, George Copway, Henry Steinhauer, and Allan Salt.

The American Methodist Episcopal church's newspaper, the *Chri:tian Advocate and Journal,* contains a great deal of information on the early Mississauga work, as does Alvin Torry's *Autobiography.* When the *Christian Guardian,* the organ of the Methodist Episcopal church of Upper Canada, appears in 1829, it replaces the *Christian Advocate* as the most important source of data on Peter Jones and the Methodist missions of Upper Canada. For the late 1830s Benjamin Slight's *Indian Researches* and his manuscript diary in the United Church Archives provide useful information. The Reverend John Carroll's five-volume *Case and His Cotemporaries* and his *Past and Present* are essential for an understanding of Canadian Methodism. The annual reports of the Methodist missionary society, especially helpful in the 1820s, 1830s, and 1840s, decline in value as the century progresses.

MANUSCRIPT MATERIAL

John Rylands University Library, Manchester, England

Wesleyan Methodist Church Correspondence

Minnesota Historical Society, St. Paul Minnesota

Grace Lee Nute Papers

Ontario Archives, Toronto

The Archives, Archdiocese of Toronto. Documents and letters relating to the history of the Catholic church in the western part of the diocese of

Upper Canada before the establishment of the diocese of Toronto, 17 December 1841. On microfilm.

Eliza Field Jones Carey, Brant County, Will/Estate File, 1433.

Solomon Yeomans Chesley, Diary, 1851–54.

Great Britain, Colonial Office. Canada, 1760–1800; Upper Canada, 1791–1841 (CO 42). On microfilm.

Peter Jones, Probate Will, RG 22, box 14.

William Jones, Indian Agent Baldoon, Upper Canada, 1831–39. Letter Book, 1831–39.

William Hamilton Merritt, Papers. Package 6, Indian Affairs [T. G. Anderson]; Package 7, Indian Affairs.

Percy J. Robinson, Papers. Section V

John Graves Simcoe, Papers.

John Strachan, Papers.

Ontario, Ministry of Natural Resources, Survey Records Section, Toronto

Surveyor's Letters. Augustus Jones, vol. 28.

Public Archives of Canada, Ottawa

Governor-Generals' Correspondence. RG 7 G 14, vols. 3–4.

Haldimand Papers.

Indian Affairs, RG 10, Upper Canada, Civil Control, 1796–1816, 1829–30, 1841–43, vols. 1–7.

General Administration Records, 1787–1836, vols. 789–92.

Deputy Superintendent General's Office, 1789–1830, vols. 26–46, 568, 586.

Jarvis Correspondence, 1837–45, vols. 124–39, those volumes containing "J" correspondence.

Records of Chief Superintendent's Office, Upper Canada, 1829–45, Letter Books, vols. 498–505.

Indian Councils, 1819, 1826–40, vols. 663, 716.

General Administration Records, Six Nations and Niagara, 1763–1810, vols. 1834, 1835.

Paudash Papers, vol. 1011, containing the Credit Mission: Letter Book, 1825–42; Entry Book, 1831–48; Council Minutes, 1835–48.

Minutes of Indian Councils, New Credit, 1883–1910, vols. 1733, 1734.

J. B. Clench, 1854, vol. 802.

Central (Toronto) Superintendency, Correspondence, 1845–56, vols. 405–12, 419, 739–46.

Western (Sarnia) Superintendency, Correspondence, 1825–64, vol. 438.

Six Nations (Grand River) Superintendency, Correspondence, 1847–59, vols. 811–40.

New Credit Agency, Correspondence, 1883, vol. 2238, file 45, 742.

Rev. Allan Salt, Papers, 1865–1906, MG 29 H 11.

Upper Canada Land Petitions, "J" Bundles.

Metropolitan Toronto Library, Toronto

Thomas G. Anderson, Papers.

James Givins, Papers.

Samuel P. Jarvis, Papers.

Oakville Museum, Oakville, Ontario

"Notes on Reminiscences of John Aikman Williams," by Hazel C. Mathews.

United Church Archives, Toronto

Credit Mission Church Registry, 1826–85.

Rev. Peter Jones, Private Journal, 13 September 1829–1 November 1829, and "Brief Account of Kahkewaquonaby written by Himself."

Ryerson Papers.

Rev. Benjamin Slight, Journal, 2 vols., 1834–57.

Wesleyan Methodist Church (Great Britain), Missions, America, The British Dominions in North America, Upper Canada (Indian Missions) and Sundry Places (photostated copies of correspondence).

Vernon Museum and Archives, Vernon, British Columbia

Peter Jones Collection. Volumes from his personal library (now in the United Church Archives, Toronto).

Victoria University Library, Toronto

The Peter Jones Collection, comprising:

1. Eliza Field Jones Carey

   Diaries and notebooks, 1823, 1828, 1829, 1832, 1833, 1834–35, 1845, 1854, 1856, 1863–64, 1869, 1869–70, 1871, 1872, 1873–74, 1880–81, 1882, 1883.

2. Rev. Peter Jones
   Anecdote Book

   Copy of "Letter Book"; letters are to his wife, Eliza Jones; the letter book is in her hand and was copied from original letters.

   Diaries, 6 December 1827–14 February 1828; 15 February 1828–8 April 1828; 23 August 1828–17 September 1828.
   History of the Ojebway Notebook.

   Letters to and from the Reverend Peter Jones.

   Sermons.

Wisconsin State Historical Society, Madison, Wisconsin
Lyman Draper Papers

Woodland Indian Cultural Educational Centre, Brantford
Letters, Minutes, New Credit Registry, 1847–74. On microfilm.

In Private Possession, Lloyd King, New Credit Reserve, Hagersville
Mission Book, New Credit, 16 June 1852–8 May 1896.

PUBLISHED DOCUMENT COLLECTIONS

British Parliamentary Papers. *Report from the Select Committee on Aborigines (British Settlements) Together with Minutes of Evidence, Appendix and Indexes.* Anthropology, Aborigines (Shannon: Irish University Press, 1968), vol. 7 (1836).
Cruikshank, E. A., ed. *The Correspondence of Lieut. Governor John Graves Simcoe.* 5 vols. Toronto: Ontario Historical Society, 1923–1931.
———. *The Correspondence of the Honourable Peter Russell.* 3 vols. Toronto: Ontario Historical Society, 1932–36.

Johnson, Sir William. *The Papers of Sir William Johnson.* 14 vols. Albany: University of the State of New York, 1921–65.

O'Callaghan, E. B., ed. *The Documentary History of the State of New York.* 4 vols. Albany: Weed, Parsons, 1849–51.

———. *Documents Relative to the Colonial History of the State of New York.* 15 vols. New York: New York State Legislature, 1853–87.

Petrone, Penny, ed. *First People, First Voices.* Toronto: University of Toronto Press, 1983.

Sanderson, Charles R., ed. *The Arthur Papers.* 3 vols. Toronto: University of Toronto Press, 1957–59.

Spragge, George W., ed. *The John Strachan Letter Book.* Toronto: Ontario Historical Society, 1946.

BOOKS AND PAMPHLETS

Alexander, J. E. *Transatlantic Sketches.* 2 vols. London: Richard Bentley, 1833.

Buckingham, James S. *Canada, Nova Scotia, New Brunswick, and the Other British Provinces in North America with a Plan of National Colonization.* London: Fisher, 1843.

Campbell, Patrick. *Travels in the Interior Inhabited Parts of North America in the Years 1791 and 1792.* Edited by H. H. Langton. Toronto: Champlain Society, 1937.

Carroll, John. *Case and His Cotemporaries.* 5 vols. Toronto: Methodist Conference Office, 1867–77.

———. *Past and Present.* Toronto: Alfred Dredge, 1860.

Copway, George [Kahgegagahbowh]. *The Traditional History and Characteristic Sketches of the Ojibway Nation.* London: Charles Gilpin, 1850.

———. *Recollections of a Forest Life; or, The Life and Travels of Kah-ge-ga-gah-bowh, or George Copway.* 2d ed. London: Charles Gilpin, 1851.

———. *Running Sketches of Men and Places, in England, France, Germany, Belgium and Scotland.* New York: J. C. Riker, 1851.

General Council, Orillia. 1846. *Minutes of the General Council of Indian Chiefs and Principal Men, Held at Orillia, Lake Simcoe Narrows, on Thursday, the 30th, and Friday, the 31st July, 1846.* Montreal: Printed at the Canada Gazette Office, 1846.

General Council, Six Nations and Delegates from Different Bands in Western and Eastern Canada. *Minutes, June 10, 1870.* Hamilton, Ontario: Printed at the Spectator Office, n.d.

General Council, New Credit, 1882. *Minutes of the Seventh Grand General Indian Council Held upon the New Credit Indian Reserve, from Septem-*

ber 13th to September 18th, 1882. Hagersville, Ontario: Hagersville Book and Job Rooms, 1883.

General Council. *Minutes of the Eighth Grand General Indian Council Held upon the Cape Crocker* [sic] *Indian Reserve, County of Bruce from Sept. 10th to Sept. 15th, 1884.* Hagersville, Ontario: Indian Publishing Company, n.d.

Grand General Council. *The Grand General Council of the Chippewas, Munsees, Six Nations etc., etc., Held on the Sarnia Reserve, June 25th to July 3, 1874.* Sarnia: "Canadian" Steam Publishing Establishment, 1874.

Green, Anson. *The Life and Times of the Rev. Anson Green, D.D.* Toronto: Methodist Book Room, 1877.

Hale, Horatio, ed. *The Iroquois Book of Rites.* Toronto: University of Toronto Press, 1963. First published in 1883.

Hall, Basil. *Travels in North America in the Years 1827 and 1828.* 3 vols. Edinburgh: Printed for Cadell, 1829.

Heckewelder, John. *History, Manners, and Customs of the Indian Nations Who Once Inhabited Pennsylvania and the Neighbouring States.* Philadelphia: Historical Society of Pennsylvania, 1876.

Henry, George [Maungwudaus]. *Remarks concerning the Ojibway Indians, by One of Themselves Called Maungwudaus, Who Has Been Travelling in England, France, Belgium, Ireland, and Scotland.* Leeds, England: C. A. Wilson, 1847.

———. *An Account of the Chippewa Indians, Who Have Been Travelling in the United States, England, Ireland, Scotland, France and Belgium; with Very Interesting Incidents in Relation to the General Characteristics of the English, Irish, Scotch, French, and Americans, with Regard to Their Hospitality, Peculiarities, etc.* Boston: Published by the author, 1848.

———. *An Account of the North American Indians, Written for Maungwudaus, a Chief of the Ojibway Indians Who Has Been Travelling in England, France, Belgium, Ireland, and Scotland.* Leicester, England: T. Cook, 1848.

Holdrich, Joseph. *The Wesleyan Student; or, Memoirs of Aaron Haynes Hurd, Late a Member of the Wesleyan University, Middletown, Conn.* Middletown: E. Hunt, 1839.

Jacobs, Peter. *Journal of the Reverend Peter Jacobs, Indian Wesleyan Missionary, from Rice Lake to the Hudson's Bay Territory, and Returning, Commencing May, 1852.* New York: Published by the author, 1858.

[Jones, Eliza]. *Memoir of Elizabeth Jones, a Little Indian Girl, Who Lived at River Credit Mission, Upper Canada.* London: John Mason, 1838.

———. *Ke-che-ah-gah-me-qua. Sketch of the Life of Captain Joseph Brant, Thayendanagea.* Montreal: Dougall, 1872.

Jones, Peter [Kahkewaquonaby]. *Life and Journals of Kah-ke-wa-quo-na-by*

(Rev. Peter Jones), Wesleyan Missionary. Published under the direction of the Missionary Committee, Canada Conference. Toronto: Published by Anson Green, at the Wesleyan Printing Establishment, 1860.

——. *History of the Ojebway Indians: With Especial Reference to Their Conversion to Christianity.* London: A. W. Bennett, 1861. Reprinted Freeport, N.Y.: Books for Libraries, 1970.

Kohl, J. G. *Kitchi-Gami: Wanderings Round Lake Superior.* London: Chapman and Hall, 1860; Minneapolis, Minnesota: Ross and Haines, 1956.

Magrath, T. W. *Authentic Letters from Upper Canada,* ed. T. Radcliff. Dublin: William Curry, 1833.

Moodie, Susanna. *Roughing It in the Bush.* Toronto: Bell and Cockburn, 1913. Facsimile edition, Coles Canadiana Collection, Toronto, 1974. Originally published in 1852.

Playter, George F. *A History of Methodism in Canada.* Toronto: Wesleyan Printing Establishment, 1862.

Ryerson, Egerton. *"The Story of My Life" (Being Reminiscences of Sixty Years' Public Service in Canada).* Edited by J. G. Hodgins. Toronto: William Briggs, 1883.

Slight, Benjamin. *Indian Researches; or, Facts concerning the North American Indians; Including Notices of Their Present State of Improvement, in Their Social, Civil and Religious Condition; with Hints for Their Future Advancement.* Montreal: Printed for the Author by J. E. L. Miller, 1844.

Strickland, Samuel. *Twenty-seven Years in Canada West.* Edited by Agnes Strickland. 2 vols. London: Richard Bentley, 1853.

Torry, Alvin. *Autobiography of Rev. Alvin Torry: First Missionary to the Six Nations and the Northwestern Tribes of British North America.* Edited by Rev. William Hosmer. Auburn: W. J. Moses, 1864.

Traill, Catharine Parr. *The Backwoods of Canada: Being Letters from the Wife of an Emigrant Officer.* London: Charles Knight, 1836. Facsimile edition, Coles Canadiana Collection, Toronto, 1971.

Van Dusen, Conrad [Enemikeese]. *The Indian Chief: An Account of the Labours, Losses, Sufferings, and Oppression of Ke-zig-ko-e-ne-ne (David Sawyer): A Chief of the Ojibbeway Indians in Canada West.* London: William Nichols, 1867.

Waddilove, W. J. D., ed. *The Stewart Missions: A Series of Letters and Journals.* London: J. Hatchard, 1838.

Weld, Isaac. *Travels through the States of North America and the Provinces of Upper and Lower Canada during the years 1795, 1796, and 1797.* London: John Stockdale, 1799.

West, John. *The Substance of a Journal during a Residence at the Red River Colony, British North America: And Frequent Excursions among the North West American Indians.* 2d ed. London: L. B. Seeley, 1827.

ARTICLES, SERMONS, SPEECHES

Case, William. *Jubilee Sermon Delivered at the Request of and before the Wesleyan Canada Conference, Assembled at London, C.W., June 6th 1855*. Toronto: G. R. Sanderson, 1855.

Chamberlain, A. F. "Notes on the History, Customs and Beliefs of the Mississagua [*sic*] Indians." *Journal of American Folk-lore* 1 (1888): 150–60.

Collection of Hymns for the Use of Native Christians of the Iroquois. To Which Are Added a Few Hymns in the Chippeway Tongue: Translated by Peter Jones. New York: Printed at the Conference Office by A. Hoyt, 1827.

Johnson, John [Enmegahbowh]. "The Story of Enmegahbowh's Life." In *Lights and Shadows of a Long Episcopate*, ed. Henry Benjamin Whipple, 497–510. New York: Macmillan, 1902.

Jones, [Eliza]. Ke-che-ah-gah-me-qua. "Sketch of the Life of Captain Joseph Brant, Thayendanagea." *New Dominion Monthly*, October 1872, pp. 198–205; November 1872, pp. 276–82; December 1872, pp. 349–51.

Jones, Peter [Kahkewaquonaby]. *Report of a Speech Delivered by Kahkewaquonaby, the Indian Chief, in the Wesleyan Chapel, Stockton-on-Tees, September 20th, 1831*. Stockton, England: J. Beach, 1831.

———. *The Sermons and Speeches of the Rev. Peter Jones, Alias Kah-ke-waquon-a-by, the Converted Indian Chief Delivered on the Occasion of the Eighteenth Anniversary of the Wesleyan Missionary Society for the Leeds District, Held in Brunswick and Albion Street Chapels, Leeds, September the 25th, 26th and 27th 1831*. Leeds: H. Spinks, n.d.

———. *The Substance of a Sermon Preached at Ebenezer Chapel, Chatham November 20, 1831, in Aid of the Home Missionary Society*. Maidstone, J. V. Hall, 1831.

———. "A Sermon Delivered by Kahkewaquonaby, or Peter Jones, a Converted Indian Chief, at the Welch Methodist Chapel, Aldersgate Street, on Sunday Afternoon, January 22, 1832." *Wesleyan Preacher* 1 (1832): 265–72.

———. "A Sermon Delivered by Kahkewaquonaby, or Peter Jones, the Converted Indian Chief, at Ebenezer Chapel, King Street, Bristol, on Sunday Evening, February 5, 1832." *Wesleyan Preacher* 1 (1832): 422–27.

———. "Farewell Sermon Delivered by Kahkewaquonaby, or Peter Jones, the Converted Indian Chief, at City Road Chapel, on Sunday Evening, April 7, 1832, in Aid of the Funds of Methodist Sunday Schools." *Wesleyan Preacher* 2 (1832): 108–15.

———. "Report of Removal of Indians from Credit to Grand River." *Christian Guardian*, 14 January 1848.

———. *Additional Hymns Translated by the Rev. Peter Jones, Kah-ke-wa-*

qu-on-a-by, a Short Time before His Death, for the Spiritual Benefit of his Indian Brethren 1856. Brantford: Printed at the Expositor Office, 1861.

Paudash, Chief Robert. "The Coming of the Mississagas." *Ontario Historical Society, Papers and Records* 6 (1905): 7–11.

"A Visit to the Mohawk and Missisaqui Indians," *Children's Friend* 14, no. 157 (January 1837): 3–14.

PERIODICALS

Canadian Freeman (York, Upper Canada), 1831–34.
The Christian Advocate and Journal (New York), 17 August 1826–38.
The Christian Guardian (Toronto), 1829–67.
The Colonial Intelligencer; or, Aborigines' Friend, 1847–54.
Copway's American Indian (New York), 1851.
The Courier (York, Upper Canada), 1832.
The Indian (Hagersville), 1885–86.
The Methodist Magazine (New York), 1818–34.
Upper Canada Gazette (Niagara and York), 1793–1828.
The Wesleyan (Montreal), 1840–43.
Wesleyan-Methodist Magazine (London), 1823–50.

PRINTED REPORTS

Aborigines Protection Society. *Report on the Indians of Upper Canada. By a Sub-Committee of Aborigines Protection Society* (1839). Reprinted by Canadiana House, Toronto, 1968.
———. Annual Reports, 1839, 1840, 1844–47.
Canada. Legislative Assembly. "Report on the Affairs of the Indians of Canada." *Journals,* 1844–45, Appendix E.E.E.; *Journals,* 1847, appendix T.
———. Legislative Assembly. "Report of the Special Commissioners to Investigate Indian Affairs in Canada." *Sessional Papers,* 1858, appendix 21.
———. Parliament. Sessional Papers. Annual Report of the Department of Indian Affairs, 1880–1917.
Corporation for the Promoting and Propagating of the Gospel of Jesus Christ in New England, London, England. Annual Reports for 1828–29, 1832–40, 1840–45, 1868, 1869–71, 1871–72, 1873–78.
Methodist Episcopal Church in Canada. Missionary Society Reports, 1825–27, 1829–33.
Wesleyan-Methodist Church in Canada. Missionary Society Reports, 1833–73.

Methodist Church of Canada. Missionary Society Reports, 1874–83.
Methodist Church of Canada, Newfoundland, Bermuda. Missionary Society Reports, 1884–1914.
Wesleyan Methodist Church (Great Britain), Wesleyan Missionary Notices, 1825–56.
Upper Canada. "Report of the Select Committee, to Which Was Referred the Petition of Bulkley Waters and Others." *House of Assembly Journal,* 4th sess., 9th Parl., 8th and 9th Geo. IV, 15 January–25 March 1828.

SECONDARY SOURCES

The "Mississaugas" or Ojibwas, or to use their own term, the "Anishinabeg," on the north shore of Lake Ontario are among the least-studied North American Indian groups. The only anthropologist ever to have undertaken fieldwork among them was A. F. Chamberlain, who visited the Scugog band nearly a century ago. His Ph.D. thesis, a linguistic study of the Ojibwa spoken at Scugog entitled "The Language of the Mississagas of Skugog," appeared in 1892. Several years earlier he had compiled an undocumented historical sketch, "Notes on the History, Customs, and Beliefs of the Mississagua Indians," *Journal of American Folk-lore* 1 (1888): 150–60.

For historical information on the "Mississaugas" in the eighteenth century one should consult the two regional studies: Frank H. Severance, *An Old Frontier of France: The Niagara Region and Adjacent Lakes under French Control,* 2 vols. (New York: Dodd, Mead, 1917), and Percy J. Robinson, *Toronto during the French Regime,* 2d ed. (Toronto: University of Toronto Press, 1965). References to their role during the Pontiac Rebellion can be obtained from Howard H. Peckham, *Pontiac and the Indian Uprising* (Chicago: University of Chicago Press, 1961). Donald B. Smith, "Who Are the Mississauga?" *Ontario History* 67(1975): 211–22, and idem, "The Dispossession of the Mississauga Indians," *Ontario History* 73 (1981): 67–87 review the group's history in the eighteenth and early nineteenth centuries.

To obtain the background necessary to understand the developments of the eighteenth century one should also examine Bruce Trigger, *Natives and Newcomers: Canada's "Heroic Age" Reconsidered* (Montreal: McGill-Queen's University Press, 1985); his more detailed *The Children of Aataentsic: A History of the Huron People to 1660,* 2 vols. (Montreal: McGill-Queen's University Press, 1976); and A. G. Bailey, *The Conflict of European and Eastern Algonkian Cultures, 1504–1700,* 2d ed. (Toronto: University of Toronto Press, 1969). The sections on the "Ottawa" and "Chippewa" in W. Vernon Kinietz, *The Indians of the Western Great Lakes, 1615–1760* (Ann Arbor: University of Michigan Press, 1940), are also useful. Victor Konrad discusses the Iroquois occupancy of the north shore of Lake Ontario in "An Iroquois Frontier: The North Shore of Lake Ontario during the Late Seventeenth Century," *Journal of Historical Geography* 7, no. 2 (1981): 129–44. Many helpful articles appear in Bruce G. Trigger, ed., *Northeast*, vol. 15 of *Handbook of North American Indians*, gen. ed. William C. Sturtevant (Washington, D.C.: Smithsonian Institution, 1978–   ).

The Mississaugas' parent group, the Ojibwas (or Chippewas as the Americans still prefer to call them), have been the subject of several excellent monographs. Two useful bibliographical guides to the available literature have been published: *Chippewa and Dakota Indians: A Subject Catalog of Books, Pamphlets, Periodical Articles, and Manuscripts in the Minnesota Historical Society* (St. Paul: Minnesota Historical Society, 1969); and Helen Hornbeck Tanner, *The Ojibwas: A Critical Bibliography* (Bloomington: Indiana University Press, 1976). Unfortunately, though, little secondary material has yet appeared on the Ojibwas living in the lower Michigan peninsula and parts of southern Ontario. Edward S. Rogers's article "Southeastern Ojibwa," in Trigger, *Northeast*, vol. 15 of *Handbook of North American Indians*, introduces the subject. Diamond Jenness's monograph on the Parry Island Anishinabeg, *The Ojibwa Indians of Parry Island, Their Social and Religious Life* (Ottawa: King's Printer, 1935), is a valuable study. It can be supplemented by Edward S. Rogers and Flora Tobobondung, "Parry Island Farmers: A Period of Change in the Way of Life of the Algonkians of Southern Ontario," in *Contributions to Canadian Ethnology*, ed. David Brez Carlisle, pp. 247–359 (Ottawa: National Museums of Canada, 1975).

Many well-written accounts are available on the Mississaugas' neighbors, the Iroquois. A. F. C. Wallace, for example, expertly combines the talents of the anthropologist and the historian in his *The Death and Rebirth of the Seneca: The History and Culture of the Great Iroquois Nation, Their Destruction and Demoralization, and Their Cultural Revival at the Hands of the Indian Visionary, Handsome Lake* (New York: Alfred A. Knopf, 1970). For an overview of the confederacy's history see William H. Fenton, "The Iroquois in History" in *North American Indians in Historical Perspective*, ed. Eleanor Leacock and Nancy Lurie, pp. 129–68 (New York: Random House, 1971). An interesting study of the important Mohawk war chief and friend of Augustus Jones is Isabel Thompson Kelsey, *Joseph Brant, 1743– 1807: A Man of Two Worlds* (Syracuse: Syracuse University Press, 1984). For a review of the Six Nations' history in Upper Canada, see C. M. Johnston, ed., *The Valley of the Six Nations: A Collection of Documents on the Indian Lands of the Grand River* (Toronto: Champlain Society, 1964). An entertaining and useful account of the Six Nations during the nineteenth and twentieth centuries is Enos T. Montour's *The Feathered U.E.L.'s* (Toronto: Division of Communication, United Church of Canada, 1973). The essential bibliography for the Six Nations Confederacy appears in Paul L. Weinman's *Bibliography of the Iroquoian Literature*, Bulletin 411, New York State Museum and Science Service (Albany: State Education Department, 1969). An abundant literature on Canadian Indians exists. For an overview of the subject Diamond Jenness's classic *The Indians of Canada*, 6th ed. (Ottawa: Queen's Printer, 1967), first published in 1932, remains the best (though now very outdated) starting point. For more contemporary information and historical background consult E. Palmer Patterson's *The Canadian Indian: A History since 1500* (Don Mills: Collier-Macmillan, 1972); Alice B. Kehoe's *North American Indians: A Comprehensive Account* (Englewood Cliffs, N.J.: Prentice-Hall, 1981); and R. Bruce Morrison and C. Roderick Wilson, eds., *Native Peoples: The Canadian Experience* (Toronto: McClelland and Stewart, 1986). *The Handbook of Indians of Canada* (Ottawa: King's Printer, 1913), reprinted in 1971 by a Toronto publisher, is still useful. The same firm has also made available again the three-volume *Indian Treaties and Surrenders* (Ottawa: Queen's Printer, 1891–1912).

Studies of the Indian Department in the nineteenth century until the mid-1970s were relatively rare, but now a number exist. The best account published on the early period is Robert S. Allen, *The British Indian Department and the Frontier in North America: 1755–1830* (Ottawa: Parks Canada, National Historic Parks and Sites Branch, Indian and Northern Affairs, 1975).

Recently a number of articles have appeared on the Indian Department in the early nineteenth century: R. J. Surtees's essay "The Development of an Indian Reserve Policy in Canada," *Ontario History* 61 (1969): 87–98 is based on his M.A. thesis, "Indian Reserve Policy in Upper Canada, 1830–1845" (Carleton University, 1966). L. F. S. Upton's study "The Origins of Canadian Indian Policy," *Journal of Canadian Studies* 8 (1973): 51–61 is more critical of the department in these same years. John Leslie has studied the Bagot Commission of the early 1840s in "The Bagot Commission: Developing a Corporate Memory for the Indian Department," Canadian Historical Association *Historical Papers, 1982*, pp. 31–52. He provides a review of the later Pennefather Commission in an unpublished paper, "The Report of the Pennefather Commission: Indian Conditions and Administration in the Canadas in the 1850s" (1983). A good summary of developments in Indian policy in the mid-nineteenth century is that by J. E. Hodgetts in *Pioneer Public Service: An Administrative History of the United Canadas, 1841–1867* (Toronto: University of Toronto Press, 1955), pp. 205–25. Douglas Leighton treats the career of S. P. Jarvis, chief superintendent of the Indian Department in Upper Canada, in "The Compact Tory as Bureaucrat: Samuel

Peters Jarvis and the Indian Department, 1837–1845," *Ontario History* 73 (1981): 40–53. In his *Canadian Indian Policy: A Critical Bibliography* (Bloomington: Indiana University Press, 1982), Robert Surtees reviews the literature to 1980. A recent anthology, prepared by Ian A. L. Getty and Antoine S. Lussier, *As Long as the Sun Shines and Water Flows: A Reader in Canadian Native Studies* (Vancouver: University of British Columbia Press, 1983), has made a number of important texts available. Of particular interest are the two invaluable overviews of Canadian Indian policy, George F. G. Stanley's "As Long as the Sun Shines and Water Flows: An Historical Comment," pp. 1–28, and John L. Tobias, "Protection, Civilization, Assimilation: An Outline History of Canada's Indian Policy," pp. 29–38. Also useful are the four more specialized studies: John S. Milloy, "The Early Indian Acts: Developmental Strategy and Constitutional Change," pp. 39–55; Robert J. Surtees, "Indian Land Cessions in Upper Canada, 1815–1830," pp. 56–64; David T. McNab, "Herman Merivale and Colonial Office Policy in the Mid-Nineteenth Century," pp. 85–103; and F. Laurie Barron, "Alcoholism, Indians and the Anti-Drink Cause in the Protestant Indian Missions of Upper Canada, 1822–1850," pp. 191–202.

Much of the best commentary on early Canadian Indian policy can be found in recent M.A. and Ph.D. theses. Three theses, for example, set out the basic framework: Robert J. Surtees, "Indian Land Cessions in Ontario, 1763–1862: The Evolution of a System" (Ph.D. thesis, Carleton University, 1983); Anthony J. Hall, "The Red Man's Burden: Land, Law, and the Lord in the Indian Affairs of Upper Canada, 1791–1858" (Ph.D. thesis, University of Toronto, 1984); John Sheridan Milloy, "The Era of Civilization—British Policy for the Indians of Canada, 1830–1860" (Ph.D. thesis, Oxford, 1978); and Douglas Leighton, "The Development of Federal Indian Policy in Canada, 1840–1890" (Ph.D. thesis, University of Western Ontario, 1975). Perhaps the most important innovator in Indian policy in Upper Canada was Sir Peregrine Maitland, whose alterations in existing policy are reviewed in one chapter in Francis Michael Quealey, "The Administration of Sir Peregrine Maitland, Lieutenant-Governor of Upper Canada, 1818–1828" (Ph.D. thesis, University of Toronto, 1968).

A number of books have recently appeared on the contact of the North American Indians with Christian missionaries. James P. Ronda and James Axtell have provided a commentary on the literature in their *Indian Missions: A Critical Bibliography* (Bloomington: Indiana University Press, 1978). For the United States the best synthesis is that provided by Henry Warner Bowden in *American Indians and Christian Missions* (Chicago: University of Chicago Press, 1981); and for the Canadian experience one should consult John Webster Grant's *Moon of Wintertime: Missionaries and the Indians of Canada in Encounter since 1534* (Toronto: University of Toronto Press, 1984). A specific study of American missionary work is Robert F. Berkhofer, Jr., *Salvation and the Savage: An Analysis of Protestant Missions and American Indian Response, 1787–1862* (Lexington: University of Kentucky Press, 1965). The Methodists' first missions are reviewed in Wade Crawford Barclay, *Early American Methodism, 1769–1844*, 2 vols. (New York: Board of Missions and Church Extension of the Methodist Church, 1950). Elizabeth Graham surveys the activities of all the Christian missions in Upper Canada in her *Medicine Man to Missionary* (Toronto: Peter Martin, 1975). In *Traditional Ojibwa Religion and Its Historical Changes* (Philadelphia: American Philosophical Society, 1983), Christopher Vecsey attempts to explain first the old Ojibwa religion and then the impact of Christianity upon it. Mary Black-Rogers describes the Ojibwa concept of power in her article "Ojibwa Power Belief System," in *The Anthropology of Power*, ed. R. D. Fogelson and R. N. Adams, pp. 141–51 (New York: Academic Press, 1977). Edward Benton-Banai, an Ojibwa from Wisconsin, has provided a popular account of Ojibwa religion in *The Mishomis Book: The Voice of the Ojibway* (St. Paul, Minn.: Indian Country Press, 1979).

Surprisingly little has been written about individual Methodist missions and Indian missionaries. Hope MacLean has completed an M.A. thesis entitled "The Hidden Agenda: Methodist Attitudes to the Ojibwa and the Development of Indian Schooling in Upper Canada, 1821–1860" (Educational Theory, University of Toronto, 1978). A former student at the Methodist-run Mount Elgin School, Enos Montour, has written "Brown Tom's Schooldays," a collection of stories about the school in the early twentieth century. A survey, "Grape Island: Methodist Missionary Station, 1827–1837," has been compiled by Terence T. Whyte (B.D. thesis, Emmanuel College, University of Toronto, 1965). Two studies of individual Indian missionaries have been done, Isaac Kholisile Mabindisa, "The Praying Man: The Life and Times of Henry Bird Steinhauer" (Ph.D. thesis, University of Alberta, 1984); and Franz Koennecke's unpublished "Life of the Reverend Allen Salt, Wesleyan Missionary to the Anishnabek" (1983). A good review of the clash between Peter Jones and the Reverend John Strachan is Arthur E. Kewley, "John Strachan versus Peter Jones," *Bulletin: Records and Proceedings of the Committee on Archives of the United Church of Canada*, no. 16 (1963): 16–28. Another article by Kewley on Peter Jones is his "Three Monuments to the Reverend Peter Jones (Kah-ke-wa-quo-na-by, 1802–1856)," *Canadian Journal of Theology* 11 (1965): 196–206.

Studies of several individual Upper Canadian Indian bands have recently been completed. Peter Schmalz, *The History of the Saugeen Indians* (Ot-

tawa: Love Printing Service, 1977), treats the Indians of the Saugeen peninsula, as does Susan De Mille, "Ethnohistory of Farming, Cape Croker: 1820–
1930" (Ph.M. thesis, University of Toronto, 1971). G. A. MacDonald reviews
the history of the Ojibwas at the Sault in "The Saulteur-Ojibwa Fishery at
Sault Ste. Marie, 1640–1920" (M.A. thesis, Waterloo University, 1978). A
short history of the Coldwater/Narrows experiment appears in J. R. Handy,
"The Ojibwa, 1640–1840: Two Centuries of Change from Sault Ste Marie to
Coldwater/Narrows" (M.A. thesis, University of Waterloo, 1978). Mae
Whetung-Derrick's mimeographed three-volume "History of the Ojibwa of
the Curve Lake Reserve and Surrounding Area" (Curve Lake, Ont.: Curve
Lake Indian Band #35, 1976) reviews that Mississauga band's past and
present. The history of the Grape Island/Alderville Mississaugas receives
treatment in Gordon Garfield Taylor, "The Mississauga Indians of Eastern
Ontario, 1634–1881" (M.A. thesis, Queen's University, 1981). I dealt with all
the Mississauga bands in my Ph.D. thesis, "The Mississauga, Peter Jones and
the White Man: The Algonkians' Adjustment to the Europeans on the North
Shore of Lake Ontario to 1860" (University of Toronto, 1975). Laird Christie's
"Reserve Colonialism and Sociocultural Change" (Ph.D. thesis, University
of Toronto, 1976) treats the Ojibwas of the Thames, but mainly in the
modern period. A useful study of the Potawatomis who arrived in Ojibwa
communities in the 1830s and 1840s is provided by James A. Clifton in *A
Place of Refuge for All Time: Migration of the American Potawatomi into
Upper Canada, 1830 to 1850* (Ottawa: National Museums of Canada, 1975).
Roberta Miskokomon has done the first study of the origins of the Munsees
at Munceytown, Ontario, in her unpublished "Migration Route of the
Munsees to Ontario" (1983). For a general history of the Lenni Lenape, see
C. A. Weslager, *The Delaware Indians: A History* (New Brunswick, N.J.:
Rutgers University Press, 1972). Important land claim issues are raised in
Diana Rankin's unpublished research report, "The Mississaugas of the New
Credit Indian Band Claim to Two Hundred Acres Adjacent to the Credit
River" (1985).

Three volumes are helpful for the history of white community in general
in Upper Canada in the early nineteenth century: Goldwin French's *Parsons
and Politics: The Role of the Wesleyan Methodists in Upper Canada and the
Maritimes from 1780 to 1855* (Toronto: Ryerson Press, 1962); G. M. Craig's
Upper Canada: The Formative Years, 1784–1841 (Toronto: McClelland and
Stewart, 1963); and J. M. S. Careless's *The Union of the Canadas: The
Growth of Canadian Institutions, 1841–1857* (Toronto: McClelland and
Stewart, 1963). All three serve as excellent guides for the settlers' history.
Although the fur trade had declined greatly in the Lake Ontario and Lake Erie
areas by the early nineteenth century, Carolyn Gilman's *Where Two Worlds*

Meet: The Great Lakes Fur Trade (St. Paul: Minnesota Historical Society, 1982) is helpful for the activity on the Upper Great Lakes. An excellent guide to white perceptions of Indians (in the Toronto *Globe*) is Don Whiteside and S. D. Whiteside, "Articles Pertaining to Indians in the *Globe*, 1844 to 1867—Annotated" (typescript, Aboriginal Institute of Canada, Ottawa, April 1981).

BOOKS

Allen, Robert S. *The British Indian Department and the Frontier in North America: 1755–1830.* Ottawa: Parks Canada, National Historic Parks and Sites Branch, Indian and Northern Affairs, 1975. The monograph also appears as "Canadian Historic Sites." Occasional Papers in Archaeology and History, no. 14 (1975): 5–125.

Bailey, A. G. *The Conflict of European and Eastern Algonkian Cultures, 1504–1700.* 2d ed. Toronto: University of Toronto Press, 1969.

Barclay, Wade Crawford. *Early American Methodism, 1769–1844,* 2 vols. New York: Board of Missions and Church Extension of the Methodist Church, 1950.

Benton-Banai, Edward. *The Mishomis Book: The Voice of the Ojibway.* St. Paul, Minn.: Indian Country Press, 1979.

Berkhofer, Robert F., Jr. *Salvation and the Savage: An Analysis of Protestant Missions and American Indian Response, 1787–1862.* Lexington: University of Kentucky Press, 1965.

Bowden, Henry Warner. *American Indians and Christian Missions.* Chicago: University of Chicago Press, 1981.

Canada. *The Handbook of Indians of Canada.* Ottawa: King's Printer, 1913. Facsimile edition, Toronto: Coles Canadiana Collection, 1971.

———. *Indian Treaties and Surrenders.* 3 vols. Ottawa: Queen's (later King's) Printer, 1891–1912.

Careless, J. M. S. *The Union of the Canadas: The Growth of Canadian Institutions, 1841–1857.* Toronto: McClelland and Stewart, 1967.

Chippewa and Dakota Indians: A Subject Catalog of Books, Pamphlets, Periodical Articles, and Manuscripts in the Minnesota Historical Society. St. Paul: Minnesota Historical Society, 1969.

Clifton, James A. *A Place of Refuge for All Time: Migration of the American Potawatomi into Upper Canada, 1830 to 1850.* Ottawa: National Museums of Canada, 1975.

Craig, G. M. *Upper Canada: The Formative Years, 1784–1841.* Toronto: McClelland and Stewart, 1963.

French, Goldwin. *Parsons and Politics: The Role of the Wesleyan Methodists in Upper Canada and the Maritimes from 1780 to 1855.* Toronto: Ryerson, 1962.

Getty, Ian A. L., and Antoine S. Lussier, eds. *As Long as the Sun Shines and Water Flows: A Reader in Canadian Native Studies.* Vancouver: University of British Columbia Press, 1983.

Gilman, Carolyn. *Where Two Worlds Meet: The Great Lakes Fur Trade.* St. Paul: Minnesota Historical Society, 1982.

Graham, Elizabeth. *Medicine Man to Missionary.* Toronto: Peter Martin, 1975.

Grant, John Webster. *Moon of Wintertime: Missionaries and the Indians of Canada in Encounter since 1534.* Toronto: University of Toronto Press, 1984.

Hodgetts, J. E. *Pioneer Public Service: An Administrative History of the United Canadas, 1841–1867.* Toronto: University of Toronto Press, 1955.

Jenness, Diamond. *The Ojibwa Indians of Parry Island, Their Social and Religious Life.* Ottawa: King's Printer, 1935.

———. *The Indians of Canada.* 6th ed. Ottawa: Queen's Printer, 1967.

Johnston, C. M., ed. *The Valley of the Six Nations: A Collection of Documents on the Indian Lands of the Grand River.* Toronto: Champlain Society, 1964.

Kehoe, Alice B. *North American Indians: A Comprehensive Account.* Englewood Cliffs, N.J.: Prentice-Hall, 1981.

Kelsey, Isabel Thompson. *Joseph Brant, 1743–1807: A Man of Two Worlds.* Syracuse: Syracuse University Press, 1984.

Kinietz, W. Vernon. *The Indians of the Western Great Lakes, 1615–1760.* Ann Arbor: University of Michigan Press, 1940.

Montour, Enos T. *The Feathered U.E.L.s.* Toronto: Division of Communication, United Church of Canada, 1973.

Morrison, R. Bruce, and C. Roderick Wilson, eds. *Native Peoples: The Canadian Experience.* Toronto: McClelland and Stewart, 1986.

Ontario. Department of Planning and Development. *Credit Valley Conservation Report, 1956.* Toronto: Department of Planning and Development, 1956.

Patterson, E. Palmer. *The Canadian Indian: A History since 1500.* Don Mills: Collier-Macmillan, 1972.

Robinson, Percy J. *Toronto during the French Regime.* 2d ed. Toronto: University of Toronto Press, 1965.

Schmalz, Peter. *The History of the Saugeen Indians.* Ottawa: Love Printing Service, 1977.

Severance, Frank H. *An Old Frontier of France: The Niagara Region and Adjacent Lakes under French Control.* 2 vols. New York: Dodd, Mead, 1917.

Surtees, Robert J. *Canadian Indian Policy: A Critical Bibliography.* Bloomington: Indiana University Press, 1982.

Tanner, Helen Hornbeck. *The Ojibwas: A Critical Bibliography.* Bloomington: Indiana University Press, 1976.

Trigger, Bruce G. *The Children of Aataentsic: A History of the Huron People to 1660.* 2 vols. Montreal: McGill-Queen's University Press, 1976.

———. *Natives and Newcomers: Canada's "Heroic Age" Reconsidered.* Montreal: McGill-Queen's University Press, 1985.

———. ed. *The Northeast.* Vol. 15 of *Handbook of North American Indians,* gen. ed. William C. Sturtevant. Washington, D.C.: Smithsonian Institution, 1978.

Vecsey, Christopher. *Traditional Ojibwa Religion and Its Historical Changes.* Philadelphia: American Philosophical Society, 1983.

Wallace, A. F. C. *The Death and Rebirth of the Seneca: The History and Culture of the Great Iroquois Nation, Their Destruction and Demoralization, and Their Cultural Revival at the Hands of the Indian Visionary, Handsome Lake.* New York: Alfred A. Knopf, 1970.

Weinman, Paul L. *Bibliography of the Iroquoian Literature,* Bulletin 411, New York State Museum and Science Service. Albany: State Education Department, 1969.

Weslager, C. A. *The Delaware Indians: A History.* New Brunswick, N.J.: Rutgers University Press, 1972.

ARTICLES

Black-Rogers, Mary B. "Ojibwa Power Belief System." In *The Anthropology of Power,* ed. R. D. Fogelson and R. N. Adams, pp. 141–51 (New York: Academic Press, 1977).

Fenton, William H. "The Iroquois in History." In *North American Indians in Historical Perspective,* ed. Eleanor Leacock and Nancy Lurie, pp. 129–68 (New York: Random House, 1971).

Grant, John Webster. "The Hunters Hunted: Methodists of Three Countries in Pursuit of the Indians of Canada." *Papers of the Canadian Methodist Historical Society* 4 (1984): 1–13.

Kewley, Arthur E. "John Strachan versus Peter Jones." *Bulletin: Records and Proceedings of the Committee on Archives of the United Church of Canada,* no. 16 (1963): 16–28.

————. "Three Monuments to the Reverend Peter Jones (Kah-ke-wa-quo-na-by, 1802–1856)." *Canadian Journal of Theology* 11 (1965): 196–206.

Konrad, V. "An Iroquois Frontier: The North Shore of Lake Ontario during the Late Seventeenth Century." *Journal of Historical Geography* 7, no. 2 (1981): 129–44.

Leighton, Douglas. "The Compact Tory as Bureaucrat: Samuel Peter Jarvis and the Indian Department, 1837–1845." *Ontario History* 73 (1981): 40–53.

Leslie, John. "The Bagot Commission: Developing a Corporate Memory for the Indian Department." Canadian Historical Association, *Historical Papers*, 1982, pp. 31–52.

Rogers, E. S., and Flora Tobobondung. "Parry Island Farmers: A Period of Change in the Way of Life of the Algonkians of Southern Ontario." In *Contributions to Canadian Ethnology*, ed. David Brez Carlisle, pp. 247–359. (Ottawa: National Museums of Canada, 1975).

Smith, Donald B. "Who Are the Mississauga?" *Ontario History* 67 (1975): 211–22.

————. "The Dispossession of the Mississauga Indians." *Ontario History* 73 (1981): 67–87.

Upton, L. F. S. "The Origins of Canadian Indian Policy." *Journal of Canadian Studies* 8 (1973): 51–61.

THESES

Christie, Laird. "Reserve Colonialism and Sociocultural Change." Ph.D. thesis, University of Toronto, 1976.

De Mille, Susan. "Ethnohistory of Farming: Cape Croker, 1820–1930." Ph.M. thesis, University of Toronto, 1971.

Hall, Anthony J. "The Red Man's Burden: Land, Law, and the Lord in the Indian Affairs of Upper Canada, 1791–1858." Ph.D. thesis, University of Toronto, 1984.

Handy, J. R. "The Ojibwa, 1640–1840: Two centuries of change from Sault Ste Marie to Coldwater/Narrows." M.A. thesis, University of Waterloo, 1979.

Leighton, Douglas. "The Development of Federal Indian Policy in Canada, 1840–1890." Ph.D. thesis, University of Western Ontario, 1975.

Mabindisa, Isaac Kholisile. "The Praying Man: The Life and Times of Henry Bird Steinhauer." Ph.D. thesis, University of Alberta, 1984.

MacDonald, G. A. "The Saulteur-Ojibwa Fishery at Sault Ste. Marie, 1640–1920." M.A. thesis, Waterloo University, 1979.

MacLean, Hope. "The Hidden Agenda: Methodist Attitudes to the Ojibwa and the Development of Indian Schooling in Upper Canada, 1821–1860," M.A. thesis (Educational Theory), University of Toronto, 1978.

Milloy, John Sheridan. "The Era of Civilization—British Policy for the Indians of Canada, 1830–1860," Ph.D. thesis, Oxford, 1978.

Quealey, Francis Michael. "The Administration of Sir Peregrine Maitland, Lieutenant-Governor of Upper Canada, 1818–1828," Ph.D. thesis, University of Toronto, 1968.

Smith, Donald B. "The Mississauga, Peter Jones and the White Man: The Algonkians' Adjustment to the Europeans on the North Shore of Lake Ontario to 1860." Ph.D. thesis, University of Toronto, 1975.

Surtees, Robert J. "Indian Reserve Policy in Upper Canada, 1830–1845." M.A. thesis, Carleton University, 1966.

———. "Indian Land Cessions in Ontario, 1763–1862: The Evolution of a System" Ph.D. thesis, Carleton University, 1983.

Taylor, Gordon Garfield. "The Mississauga Indians of Eastern Ontario, 1634–1881." M.A. thesis, Queen's University, 1981.

Whyte, Terence T. "Grape Island: Methodist Missionary Station, 1827–1837." B.D. thesis, Emmauel College, University of Toronto, 1965.

MANUSCRIPTS

Kewley, Arthur E. "The Location of Peter Jones' Conversion." Typescript, n.d. Available at the United Church Archives, Toronto.

Koennecke, Franz. "The Life of the Reverend Allen Salt, Wesleyan Missionary to the Anishnabek." 1983. Available from the author, P.O. box 93, Morriston, Ontario NOB 2CO.

Leslie, John. "The Report of the Pennefather Commission: Indian Conditions and Administration in the Canadas in the 1850s." Paper presented at the annual meeting, Canadian Sociology and Anthropology Association, University of British Columbia, June 1983.

Miskokomon, Roberta. "Migration Route of the Munsees to Ontario." Mimeographed, 1983. Available from the author, R.R. #1, Muncey, Ontario NOL 1YO.

Montour, Enos T. "Brown Tom's Schooldays." Mimeographed, May 1985. Available from Elizabeth Graham, Department of Anthropology, Wilfrid Laurier University, Waterloo, Ontario N2L 3C5.

Rankin, Diana L. Indian Land Claims Research, Office of Indian Resource Policy, Ontario Ministry of Natural Resources. "The Mississaugas of the

New Credit Indian Band Land Claim to two hundred Acres Adjacent to the Credit River." Research report, 20 February 1985.

Tyler, Kenneth J., and Roger T. Ryan. "The Government's Management of Indian Trust Funds: A Case Study of the Chippewas and Pottawatomies of Walpole Island." Report prepared for the National Indian Brotherhood, August 1981.

Whetung-Derrick, Mae. "History of the Ojibwa of the Curve Lake Reserve and Surrounding Area." 3 vols. 1. History of the Mississaga Band, Curve Lake; 2. Social and Cultural History; 3. Recreation and Arts. Curve Lake, Ontario: Curve Lake Indian Band #35, 1976. Mimeographed.

Whiteside, Don, and S. D. Whiteside. "Articles Pertaining to Indians in the *Globe*, 1844 to 1867—Annotated." Typescript. Aboriginal Institute of Canada, Ottawa. April 1981.

SEVERAL RECENTLY COMPLETED THESES ON THE ONTARIO OJIBWAS

Peter S. Schmaltz has completed a survey of Ojibwa history: "The Ojibwa of Southern Ontario" (Ph.D. thesis, University of Waterloo, 1985). His article "The Role of the Ojibwa in the Conquest of Southern Ontario, 1650–1701" appeared in *Ontario History* 76 (1984): 326–52. Other recent theses on the Ontario Ojibwas include: Michael R. Angel, "The Ojibwa-Missionary Encounter at Rainy Lake Mission, 1839–1857" (M.A. thesis, University of Manitoba, 1986); Janet Elizabeth Chute, "A Century of Shingwaukönse and His Heirs" (Ph.D. thesis, McMaster University, 1986); I.V.B. Johnson, "The Early Missisauga Treaty Process (1781–1819) in Historical Perspective" (Ph.D. thesis, University of Toronto, 1986); and Franz M. Koennecke, "The Wasoksiwunini: A History of the Anishnawbeg of Parry Island from 1850–1920" (M.A thesis, University of Waterloo, 1984).

INDEX

Aborigines Protection Society, 164,
177, 183, 216–17
Act of Union of 1841, 178, 182
Adamson, Robert, 198
Adelaide (queen), 138–39
Agriculture, 48–49, 65, 78; at
Credit Mission, 157, 206; at
New Credit, 220, 244–45; Bond
Head's view of, 162; knowledge
of, 80
Ajetance, Chief James (Capt. Jim),
73, 76, 82, 104; adopted Jones,
67–68; council on land rights,
98, 100
Alcohol, 10–11, 30; at New Credit,
219–20; converts abstained, 72–
73, 76; Jones's view of, 38, 53,
68; Rice Lake traders, 95
Alder, Rev. Robert, xxxiii, xxxv, 140,
167
Alderville, 162
Alexander, Capt. J.E., 144
Algonkins. See Algonquins
Algonquians. See Ojibwas
Algonquins, 17, 19–20, 23, 69
Alley, Gerald, 105
American Methodists. See Method-
ist Episcopal Church
American Revolutionary War, 2,
22–25, 56, 101
Ancaster, 55, 58
Anderson, Capt. Charles, 185

Anderson, Thomas G., 105, 107,
207–8
Andowish, 107
Anglican Church. See Church of
England
Anishinabeg, 1, 17, 242. See also
Ojibwas
Arthur, Lieut. Gov. George, 175,
176–77, 178
Assance, Chief John, 108, 111, 175,
208, 212–13
Assignack, Jean-Baptiste. See
Blackbird, Chief

Bagot, Sir Charles, 183, 192
Bagot Commission, 183–84, 192–
93, 194
Bangs, Rev. Nathan, 114, 115, 118
Barnes, Eliza. See Case, Eliza
Barnes
Battle of Fallen Timbers, 30
Bay of Quinte: Jones's visit to, 90–
94; mission on Grape Island, 99,
119–22, 162
Beasley, Richard, 3, 34
Beaver, Peter, 89, 110, 115
Beaver, William, 93, 95
Bell, Patrick, 143
Big Jacob, 95
Blackbird, Chief, 106–8, 221,
223
Blackstock, Moses, 84, 85, 90, 96

Economic development: after conversion, 78; at Credit Mission, 157, 206; effects of War of 1812, 38–39; European farming at Davisville, 65; Iroquois, 48–49
Edinburgh, 199, 218–19
Edinburgh Ladies' Own Journal, 199
Edinburgh Witness, 199
Education: Credit Mission schoolhouse, 145–46, 159, 206; manual labor schools, 193–95, 208, 213; school at Mount Elgin, 214, 240
Elgin, Gov. Gen., 224, 225
Ellis, Hannah, 245
Erie Canal, 113, 231
Eries, 18–19
Eshtonquot, Francis. *See* Maconse
Esquesing Township, 33
Evans, James, 153, 163, 164, 179, 185, 187, 240
Exhorter, 64

Faber, George Stanley, 128
Falmouth Packet, 166
Field, Charles, 131–32, 135, 136, 137, 138–39, 167, 200, 215, 228
Field, Edmund, 191, 192
Field, Eliza. *See* Jones, Eliza Field
Field, Elizabeth, 135
Field, Frederick, 191, 192
Field, John, 136
Field, Mary, 135
Finger, Samuel (Nowiqueyasika), 220
Five Nations. *See* Iroquois
Fothergill, Charles, 95
Foville, Dr. Achille-Louis, 202
French traders, 22, 24

George III (king), 170
Givins, Col. James, 29, 66, 71, 72, 73, 79, 99, 101, 102, 104
Glenelg, Lord, xxxiii, xxxiv, 165, 167, 175

Gnadenhütten massacre, 88
Golden Eagle, Chief, 27, 32, 36–37, 38, 160
Gordon, Duchess of, 198–99
Gore, Lieut. Gov. Francis, 39
Gradual Civilization Act, 238–39
Grand River, 44, 45, 49, 61
Grape Island, 99, 119–22, 162
Great Lakes Indians, 23, 106, 109, 172, 174
Great Spirit, 10–11, 13, 16, 59, 173, 174
Green, Rev. Anson, 180, 189

Haldimand, Gov. Frederick, 25
Halifax Express, 134
Hall, Basil, 82, 138
Hall, Francis, 113, 118, 119, 141, 151
Hall, Sherman, 185
Hamilton. *See* Head of the Lake
Handbook of Indians of Canada, 244
Handsome Lake, 49, 51, 61
Hannah, Rev. John, 235
Head, Sir Edmund, 227
Head of the Lake (Hamilton), 1, 5, 16, 32, 35, 37, 44, 49
Heckewelder, Rev. John, 109, 216
Hedding, Bishop Elijah, 114
Henry, Alexander, 216
Henry, George (half-brother), 185, 187–88, 200–202, 217–19, 229, 317
Henry, George, Jr., 218, 317
Henry, Hannah, 202
Henry, Isaac, 210
Henry, John Tecumseh, 218
Henry, Sarah. *See* Tuhbenahneequay (mother)
Herkimer, Charles, 247
Herkimer, Jacob, 80
Herkimer, Lawrence, 77, 80, 155, 156, 157, 158, 165, 184, 247
Herkimer, William, 80, 155, 156, 157, 158, 165, 184, 207, 247